Julia Pardoe

The Court and Reign of Francis the First, King of France

Vol. 3

Julia Pardoe

The Court and Reign of Francis the First, King of France
Vol. 3

ISBN/EAN: 9783743407329

Manufactured in Europe, USA, Canada, Australia, Japa

Cover: Foto ©ninafisch / pixelio.de

Manufactured and distributed by brebook publishing software (www.brebook.com)

Julia Pardoe

The Court and Reign of Francis the First, King of France

THE COURT AND REIGN

OF

FRANCIS THE FIRST

KING OF FRANCE

THE
COURT AND REIGN
OF
FRANCIS THE FIRST
King of France

BY

JULIA PARDOE

AUTHOR OF 'LOUIS XIV.' 'THE CITY OF THE SULTAN,' ETC.

IN THREE VOLUMES

VOL. III.

NEW YORK

SCRIBNER AND WELFORD

1887

Printed by R. & R. CLARK, *Edinburgh*

CONTENTS

OF

THE THIRD VOLUME

CHAPTER I

1534

The female Court of Francis I.—The Queen of Navarre—Madame de Châteaubriand—Queen Eleanora—The Duchesse d'Etampes—Fleeting favouritism—Catherine de' Medici—The king's household—Lax morality of the royal circle—The rival *rouĕs*—Resignation of Queen Eleanora—Montmorency conceives a passion for the queen—He declares it, and is haughtily repulsed—An eccentric compact—Mirth of the courtiers—Marriage of Henry VIII. and Anne Boleyn—He is excommunicated by the Pope—Death of Katherine of Aragon—Henry VIII. persecutes the Romanists—Death of Clement VII.—Accession of Paul III.—Francis reorganizes his army—Charles V. takes Tunis—Francis is accused of maintaining an agreement with Solyman—Barbarity of Francis towards the reformers—The silver image—Frightful executions . . . . Page 1

CHAPTER II

1535-36

The persecution of the Protestants is continued—Francis abolishes printing throughout his kingdom—The league of Smalkalden declare against the French king—Francis invites Melancthon to France—Francis declares war against the Duke of Savoy—Chabot overruns the duchy—The duke urges the emperor to assist him—Death of Sforza—Charles V. restores Alessandro de' Medici to the sovereignty of Florence—Death of the Chancellor Duprat—The Queen of Navarre at Amboise—Ostentation and

profligacy of Madame d'Etampes—The tournament—A street brawl—
Narrow escape of the Duc d'Angoulême—Removal of the Court to Chambord—The king and Diane de Poitiers—A moral mission—Diane resolves
to attempt the conquest of the Duc d'Orleans—Her personal attractions—
Her ambition—A poem of the sixteenth century—Jealousy of the
Duchesse d'Etampes—She demands the exile of Diane from the Court—
Charles V. offers to concede the duchy of Milan to the Duc d'Angoulême
—Francis demands it for the Duc d'Orleans—Tergiversation of the emperor—Charles V. renews his alliance with the Venetians—The negotiation concerning the Milanese is renewed—The emperor proceeds to
Rome—The French ambassador urges him to perform his promises—
Charles V. harangues the conclave, and insults Francis—He temporizes
with the French ambassadors—The Pope endeavours to pacify them—
The address to the conclave is garbled and forwarded to France—
Moderation of Francis—The Cardinal de Lorraine is despatched to the
emperor to terminate the affair of the Milanese, and fails—Imperial
superstition—Treason of the Marquis de Saluzzo—The Pope declares his
neutrality—Charles V. excites the German Protestants against Francis—
The army in Savoy is disarmed—Montmorency ensures the safety of the
frontier—Francis proceeds to Lyons—Charles V. declares himself suzerain of Provence—Francis prepares for an invasion . . Page 21

CHAPTER III

1536

The emperor besieges Turin—The fortress of Fossano is entrusted by Francis
I. to the Marquis de Saluzzo—He impedes the progress of the works—
The French officers suspect his good faith—He retires to Raval—He
betrays his trust—Antonio da Leyva invests Fossano—The Marquis de
Saluzzo is appointed the emperor's lieutenant beyond the Alps—Charles
V. invades Provence—M. de Montejan is surprised, and made prisoner
by the imperialists—Empty boasting of the emperor—Death of the
dauphin by poison—Trial and execution of Montecuculli—Francis accuses
the imperialists of instigating the murder—Indignation of Charles V. and
his generals—Catherine de' Medici is in her turn accused by Da Leyva—
Progress of the imperial army—The emperor enters Aix—Prince Henry
joins the French camp—Marseilles successfully resists the imperialists—
Francis determines to head the army in person—He is dissuaded by his
generals—Doria supplies the emperor's camp—Retreat of Charles V.
—The tower of Muy—The imperial forces establish themselves in Savoy
—The emperor proceeds to Spain, and is overtaken by a storm—The victor
and the vanquished 53

CONTENTS vii

CHAPTER IV

1536-38

Consternation of the Italian princes—The siege of Turin is raised—The imperial troops enter Picardy—Heroism of the women of St. Regnier—Capitulation of Guise—The imperialists besiege Peronne—They are repulsed by Fleuranges—Death of Fleuranges—Alarm in Paris—Annebaut and Burie defend Turin—Burie is made captive at Casal—Francis strengthens the frontiers of Provence—James V. of Scotland meets the king at Lyons—James V. is married to the Princesse Marguerite—Jealousy of Henry VIII.—Knight-errantry of James V.—Death of the Princesse Marguerite—James demands the hand of Marie de Guise—Feud between the royal favourites—Virulence of the Duchesse d'Etampes—Disunion in the royal family—Infatuation of Francis I.—Apprehensions of Madame d'Etampes—Her passion for Montmorency—Francis lays claim to Flanders, Artois, and Charlerois—Convocation of the parliament—Charles V. is cited to appear before the French tribunals—The emperor disregards the summons—The French enter Artois—They take Hesdin—The imperialists invest St. Pol—The city is taken by De Buren—De Buren marches upon Térouenne—Annebaut relieves the city—A fatal skirmish—A truce is effected between France, Picardy, and the Low Countries—Francis openly avows his alliance with the Sultan—Solyman enters Albania—Del Guasto successfully pursues the war in Piedmont—M. d'Humieres is appointed to the chief command of the French army in Italy—The Marquis de Saluzzo assists Del Guasto in the siege of Carmagnole—He is killed by a musket ball—Carmagnole surrenders—Cruelty of the imperialist general—The dauphin and Montmorency march to Lyons, and are followed by the king—Del Guasto fortifies the Pas-de-Suze, which is forced by the French—The imperialists raise the siege of Pignerol, and encamp at Montcalier—The dauphin compels them to retreat, and takes the city—Francis resolves to take the field in person—The truce is extended to Piedmont—The Duke of Savoy retires to Nice—Charles V. endeavours to effect a European peace, and offers the hand of his niece to the Duc d'Orleans—Francis objects to the proposed conditions—Montmorency is created connétable—Death of the Chancellor du Bourg . . . . Page 74

CHAPTER V

1538

Paul III. endeavours to effect a reconciliation between the emperor and the French king—A meeting of the three potentates is proposed at Nice—Alarm of the Duke of Savoy—He appeals to the emperor—His envoy is coldly received—The populace of Nice close their gates against the Pope—Peril of Queen Eleanora—The Pope mediates between the two sovereigns—The truce is renewed for a period of ten years—The three potentates separate—Declaration of the Duke of Savoy—The emperor despatches an ambassador to Francis—The two sovereigns meet at Aigues-Mortes—La Belle Feronnière—Illness of the French king—Increasing power of Montmorency—Revolt of Ghent—Charles V. obtains permission to traverse the French territories—Madame d'Etampes and the connétable—A Court intrigue—A Court buffoon—The enamelled chain—Montmorency loses the favour of the king . . . . . Page 106

CHAPTER VI

1539-40

The emperor arrives at Bayonne—He refuses to receive hostages—The two sovereigns meet at Chatellerault—Triumphant reception of Charles V.—Distrust of the emperor—Unfortunate coincidences—The imperial retinue—A Court ball—The diamond ring—The emperor enters Paris—The French princes and Montmorency accompany him to Valenciennes—Charles refuses to ratify the cession of the Milanese—Francis becomes suspicious of his counsellors—Arrest of the Maréchal de Brion Chabot—Chabot is tried and condemned to death—Cruel policy of Poyet—Chabot is pardoned by the king—Arrest of Poyet—Female influence at Court—Death of Chabot—The emperor proposes an alliance between his son Philip of Spain and the Princess of Navarre, between his own daughter and the Duc d'Orleans—Refusal of Francis to comply with the required conditions—Disappointment of the King and Queen of Navarre—The negotiation is pursued—Marriage of the Duc de Cleves and the Princess of Navarre—Madame d'Etampes and the captain of the king's guard—Exile of Montmorency from the Court—The marriage festivities—The Duc de Cleves leaves France—Benvenuto Cellini arrives at the French Court—Exile of the Cardinal de Lorraine . . . 130

CHAPTER VII

1541-42

Changed aspect of the French Court—Favour of the Maréchal d'Annebaut—The emperor invests his own son with the duchy of Milan—The Venetians threaten to form an alliance with Solyman—Charles V. and Francis despatch ambassadors to Venice—They are coldly received—Murder of

Fregosa and Rincon—Du Bellay-Langei accuses the imperialists of the crime—The assassins are put to death by the states of Venice—Francis summons the emperor to make reparation — Contemptuous reply of Charles V.—Francis arrests the Archbishop of Valence—Charles enters into a truce with the Protestant princes—Benda taken by the Turks—Charles V. conducts an expedition against the Algerines—His fleet is dispersed by a tempest—The imperialists return to Spain—Francis resolves to declare war against the emperor — The French armies open their campaign—The Maréchal de Gueldres attacks the Flemish frontiers —Alarm of the Dowager-Queen of Hungary—Treachery of the Duchesse d'Etampes—D'Annebaut seconds her views—Suspicion of the king—The Duc d'Orleans takes Luxembourg—D'Annebaut supersedes Langei in his command in Piedmont—Death of Langei—D'Annebaut is appointed Admiral of France—Exile of Montpezat—Growing enmity of the two princes—Female policy—The Court of Catherine de' Medici—The "light-brigade"—Revolt of La Rochelle—Francis proceeds thither, suppresses the insurrection, and pardons the citizens . . Page 172

CHAPTER VIII

1542-43

Francis persecutes the Lutherans—He despatches an ambassador to the Sultan — The French army marches northward — D'Annebaut takes Landrecies—The French besiege Binche—The dauphin is compelled to raise the siege—Francis fortifies Landrecies—The French Court arrives at Rheims—Charles V. effects a rupture between England and France—The emperor organizes a new army—He attacks Dueren—The citizens refuse to surrender—The city is taken by assault—The Duc de Cleves throws himself en the mercy of the emperor—He is restored to the imperial favour—The marriage of the Duc de Cleves and Jeanne de Navarre is annulled—The emperor besieges Luxembourg—He raises the siege, and establishes a blockade—The imperialists take Cambray, and establish their winter quarters at Guise—Solyman despatches a fleet under Barbarossa to the assistance of Francis—The Comte d'Enghien takes the command of the war-galleys at Marseilles—The combined fleets attack Nice, and are repulsed—D'Enghien returns to Landrecies—The European powers are indignant at the alliance formed by Francis with the Turks—Enormities perpetrated by Barbarossa—Termination of the campaign of 1543 199

CHAPTER IX

1544

Renewal of hostilities—Financial embarrassments of Francis—Sale of judicial offices—The French king raises a new army—D'Enghien blockades Carignano—Blaise de Montluc proceeds to Court to demand supplies, and permission to engage the enemy—Successful eloquence of Montluc—Victory of Carignano—The citizens of Ast close their gates against the imperialists—Mortifications of Del Guasto at Milan—The jewelled watch—The emperor and Henry VIII. invade France—Siege of St. Dizier—Renewed treachery of the Duchesse d'Etampes—St. Dizier surrenders—Mutual distrust of Charles V. and Henry VIII.—The English king besieges Boulogne and Montreuil—The two potentates cease to act in concert—Charles V. advances to Châlons . . . . Page 222

CHAPTER X

1544-45

Effects of the resistance of St. Dizier—Charles V. endeavours to effect a peace—The queen and Madame d'Etampes induce the king to enter into a negotiation with the emperor—The dauphin demands the recall of Montmorency—The Comte de Furstemberg is made prisoner by the French—Charles V. determines on a retreat to the Low Countries—Madame d'Etampes enables him to possess himself of Epernay and Château-Thierry—Alarm of the Parisians—Prudent measures of the dauphin—Henry VIII. takes Boulogne—Francis concludes a treaty with the emperor—The negotiation of marriage between the Duc d'Orleans and the daughter of the emperor is renewed—Discontent of the dauphin—He protests against the treaty—The French army marches into Picardy—The dauphin makes a night-attack upon Boulogne—The French are repulsed—Gallantry of Montluc—Termination of the campaign of 1544—The emperor resolves to suppress the league of Smalkalden—Charles V. determines to bestow the hand of his daughter upon the Duc d'Orleans—The emperor endeavours to conciliate the Pope—Persecution of the Flemish reformers—Massacre of the Vaudois—Imprudence of the dauphin—A Court banquet—Disgrace of the dauphin—Francis raises a naval armament against England—He sends succour to the dowager-queen of Scotland—An army is despatched to Picardy—The banquet on board the Carragnon—D'Annebaut sails with the French fleet—Operations on the English coast—The French land in Sussex—Destroy Brighton and Newhaven—And take possession of the Isle of Wight—The French fleet returns to Havre 249

CHAPTER XI

1545-46

Military operations before Boulogne—The Comte d'Aumale is seriously wounded—The German levies of Henry VIII. arrive at Liege—Francis I. opposes their passage—Death of the Duc d'Orleans—Invasion of the Terre d'Oye—A treaty of peace is concluded between England and France—The emperor refuses to cede the duchy of Milan to the French Crown — Francis strengthens his frontiers — Death of Luther—The emperor makes war upon the Protestant princes—Horrible persecution of the Lutherans in France—Francis I. as a monarch and a man—Death of Henry VIII.—Last illness of Francis I.—Death of Francis I.—The chamber of the dauphiness—Accession of Henry II. .   . Page 284

BIOGRAPHICAL NOTES

TO

THE THIRD VOLUME

	PAGE		PAGE
Cardinal de Lorraine . .	8	The Duc de Cleves . . .	151
Paul III.	15	Claude, Duc de Guise . .	184
Alessandro de' Medici . .	26	Martin von Rossem . .· .	184
Antoine de la Rochefoucauld .	51	M. de Boutières . . .	189
The Maréchal de Montejan .	56	François de Tournon . .	195
Ferdinand de Gonzaga . .	61	Paulin Iscalin, Baron de la	
The Comte de Tende . .	71	Garde	200
Garcilasso de la Vega . .	72	Pietro-Luigi Farnese . .	207
The Maréchal d'Annebaut .	79	The Prince of Melfi . .	211
M. de Burie	79	M. de Lalande . . .	212
M. de la Pommeraye . .	82	The Sieur d'Esse . . .	212
Maximilian d'Egmont, Comte		The Comte d'Enghien . .	215
de Buren	90	M. de Montluc . . .	226
Jean d'Estouteville, Seigneur de		M. de Dampierre . . .	233
Villebon	91	Marguerite de Bourbon, Duch-	
The Seigneur de Piennes . .	93	esse de Cleves . . .	238
The Comte d'O, Seigneur de		Martin de Gusman . . .	250
Gresner	93	Jacques de Lorges, Earl of	
Louis Revot, Baron de Sansac .	93	Montgomery . . .	276
The Marquis de Villars . .	94	François Olivier de Lieuville .	290

ENGRAVED PORTRAITS

VOL. III

1. DIANA OF POICTIERS . . . . *Frontispiece*
   From the Picture by Primaticcio in the Collection of the Right Hon. the Earl Spencer, at Althorp, and engraved by Joseph Brown.

2. FRANCIS THE FIRST . . . . *To face page* 98
   Engraved by Dean from a Painting by Titian.

3. CATHERINE DE' MEDICI . . . . . . ,, 194
   Engraved by E. Radclyffe from Wageman's miniature, after the Portrait by Janet.

4. THE DUCHESSE D'ETAMPES . . . . . ,, 246
   From the Original in the Musée Royal, engraved by S. Freeman, after Belbard.

5. THE EMPEROR, CHARLES V. . . ,, 292
   Engraved by C. Cook from a Painting by Titian.

THE COURT AND REIGN

OF

FRANCIS THE FIRST

CHAPTER I

1534

The female Court of Francis I.—The Queen of Navarre—Madame de Châteaubriand—Queen Eleonora—The Duchesse d'Etampes—Fleeting favouritism—Catherine de' Medici—The king's household—Lax morality of the royal circle—The rival *roués*—Resignation of Queen Eleonora—Montmorency conceives a passion for the queen—He declares it, and is haughtily repulsed—An eccentric compact—Mirth of the courtiers—Marriage of Henry VIII. and Anne Boleyn—He is excommunicated by the Pope—Death of Katherine of Aragon—Henry VIII. persecutes the Romanists—Death of Clement VII.—Accession of Paul III.—Francis reorganizes his army—Charles V. takes Tunis—Francis is accused of maintaining an agreement with Solyman—Barbarity of Francis towards the reformers. —The silver image—Frightful executions.

Two years only had elapsed since Francis had been emancipated by death from the domination of Louise de Savoie, and already in the person of Catherine de' Medici a new power had arisen, by which he was to be equally enthralled. Of all the female members of his family his wives alone had failed to influence either his affections or his actions. Alike gentle and unambitious, they shrank before his coldness and trembled at his frown; while women of meaner rank and of less than questionable virtue braved his displeasure, and moulded him to their will. In the Queen of Navarre he had recognized at once a companion and a friend; he was conscious of her superiority of intellect, and grateful for her tenderness; and had Marguerite exerted the power which she really possessed over his mind to wean him from those habits of profligacy by which his memory is disgraced, instead of treating the most sacred duties with disregard when by such a concession she felt that she was ministering to his temporary gratification, it is probable that he would have become more estimable both as a monarch and a man. But the daughter of Louise de Savoie had been reared in a school little likely to render her a moral monitress; and the author of the *Heptameron*, or "all the naughty tricks played by women on the poor men," as she describes it in her preface, could scarcely be expected to afford any efficient aid in the reformation of his character. Of the Duchesse d'Angoulême, both as a mother and as a guide, we have already said enough. Of the influence of Madame de Châteaubriand, during her period of favour, many baneful effects remained; although, when the opportunities of evil which she had once possessed are taken into consideration, even her career may be deemed comparatively harmless. But at the period of Catherine's advent to France the full-blown vices of Madame d'Etampes were the marvel and the anathema of the nation.

The queen, conscious that she possessed no power

sufficiently great to counteract that of the favourite, had ceased even to strive against it; and thus the only pure-hearted woman who would have loved him for his own sake, and who might eventually have restored him to a more fitting sense of the duties which he owed alike to himself and to society, was reduced to weep over the errors that she was unable to eradicate.

We pass over, for obvious reasons, the minor influences, each perhaps insignificant in itself, but in the aggregate fearfully mischievous, which were exercised by the fair and frail maids-of-honour, each, or nearly each, being in her turn the "Cynthia of the minute," and more than one of whom owed her temporary favour to the Duchesse d'Etampes herself, whose secret intrigues and undisguised ambition absorbed more of her time than could have been left at her disposal, had she not provided the inconstant but exacting monarch with some new object of interest; and the tact with which she selected these facile beauties was not one of the least of her talents. Never, upon any occasion, did she direct the attention of the king to a woman whose intellect might have secured, after the spell of her beauty had ceased to attract him. The young and the lovely were her victims, only when their youth and their loveliness were their sole attractions. She was ever ready to supply her royal lover with a new mistress, but never with a friend, a companion, or a counsellor; and thus, as she had rightly foreseen, the French Sardanapalus soon became sated by the mere prettiness of his female satellites, and returned to his allegiance to herself, wearied, and more her slave than ever.

Such was the state of the Court in which the Duchesse d'Orleans was called to assume her station as a princess of the blood; and, mere girl as she was, she at once appreciated alike the difficulties and advantages of her position. A king whose leading passions were dissipation and magnificence; a queen who shrank from publicity of all kinds, and who had neither inclination to upbraid nor energy to resist injustice; a dauphin staid and serious beyond his years; a powerful and insolent favourite; a licentious nobility; a morose and careless husband—such were the elements out of which she had to construct a future for herself; and Catherine de' Medici did not fail to prove herself worthy of the name she bore.

Nature had admirably fitted her for the part which she was about to enact. De Thou describes her as a woman of "immense mind and superb magnificence;" while Brantôme expatiates upon her personal attractions and her feminine accomplishments; to which, however, were added the masculine attainments of riding, playing at tennis, shooting with a crossbow, and boar-hunting.

No less ambitious and intriguing than Louise de Savoie, Catherine, even from the very period of her marriage, possessed a power of dissimulation which enabled her to veil her vices under a mask of fascination that few were able to resist; and thus she became at once not only the idol of the whole Court, but also that of Francis himself; and it soon required the most finished art on the part even of Madame d'Etampes to counteract her daily increasing influence.

Although a girl in years, Catherine was already old in heart; and her unexpected elevation, instead of satisfying, had merely served to excite the love of power and domination which her after-career so fatally developed. Haughty and imperious in spirit, she possessed sufficient command over not only her words and actions, but even her very looks, to render the real sentiments of her heart subservient to her ambition, and to conceal her most serious designs under a playful carelessness of manner by which those who surrounded her were duped into a belief that she was occupied only by the pleasure of the hour.

Thus constituted, the young princess could not but prove a dangerous rival even to the astute and experienced Madame d'Etampes; but this was not the only peril to which her favour was at that moment exposed. On the decease of Louis de Brézé, Grand Sénéchal of Normandy, his young and lovely widow, Diane de Poitiers, had taken up her residence at the Court, where she was warmly welcomed by the king, who treated her upon all occasions with a marked distinction well calculated to arouse the apprehensions of the jealous duchess. The impression produced upon the heart, or perhaps more properly speaking upon the fancy of Francis, by the extraordinary personal attractions of la Grande

Sénéchale on her first appearance before him had long been matter of notoriety; and, as the twelve years which had since elapsed had only tended to change the lovely and graceful girl into a dignified and dazzling woman, not a few among the courtiers began to indulge themselves in a spirit of prophecy little calculated to flatter the vanity of the reigning favourite. Meanwhile Catherine de' Medici became ere long the fast friend of the beautiful young widow; and thus the position of Madame d'Etampes was apparently rendered tenfold more precarious.

Such was the circle in which Francis I. passed his leisure moments; and they, as we have shown, comprized no small portion of his entire existence; while the manner in which his household was constituted tended rather to increase than to diminish the pernicious effects of such an association. The principal officers of whom the royal household had formerly been composed were at the same time officers of the Crown—great nobles, representing the highest and most ancient families in the kingdom, and who held this dignity as an hereditary and unalienable right. They possessed authority not only over the subordinates in their several departments, but also over all the private citizens who were in the employment of the Court; and were, in short, while fulfilling their duties to the sovereign, in the position of feudal barons, their service being more honourable to the throne than agreeable to the monarch; the tenacity with which they insisted upon the observance of their privileges, and the punctilious parade with which they performed the ceremonials of their several offices, rendering them more frequently the opponents than the instruments of their royal master's will. Francis, as it may be readily imagined, could ill brook the partial subserviency to which he was reduced by such a system; and accordingly he confined the grand officers of the Crown to the Crown itself, and formed a personal household totally distinct from these dignities, selecting for that purpose such of the nobles and courtiers as he considered the most calculated to contribute to the magnificence and brilliance of his own circle.

This arrangement revolutionized the whole Court; neither birth nor extent of territory any longer ensured to its possessor the right of attendance upon the person of the sovereign. Wealth failed where wit triumphed; the uncle of the favourite became Great-Almoner of France; and the minor appointments were made upon the same principle. Younger brothers, who under a different reign would have despaired of figuring in the immediate circle of royalty, saw their elders compelled to yield to their better fortune; and obscure abbés, celebrated for their gallantry, or patronized by a frail beauty, found themselves on a level with mitred bishops and lordly abbots. In a Court so constituted, it is not wonderful that every species of amusement, splendour, and profligacy soon abounded; the haughtiest of the nobility devoured their mortification, and laid aside their *morgue*, in order to obtain an entrance within the magic circle; while even the Church dignitaries did not disdain to follow their example. Ambition as well as inclination led to this result; for it soon became apparent that Court favour was the only avenue to personal advancement; and thus prelates of the highest rank soon taught themselves to participate in frivolous and degrading pursuits ill suited alike to their sacred calling or to the example which they were bound to offer to the laity.

And in the midst of this vain and eager and voluptuous throng of sycophantic courtiers, who acknowledged no law save the will of the monarch, and no religion save his pleasure, were congregated the most noble and the most beautiful women of whom France could boast. The circle of the queen had been formed from that of Louise de Savoie; the Court of Marguerite de Navarre, during her frequent visits to her royal brother, was comprized of wit, fascination, and gallantry; Catherine de' Medici had been followed to France by a train of ladies equally attractive and equally facile; and thus it will cease to be subject of surprise that ere long purity and virtue were not only disregarded but even made the common theme of sarcasm and contempt.

We dare not comment upon this frightful feature of the reign of Francis I.; but as faithful chroniclers we are compelled to record, that while the highest honours of profligacy were unanimously awarded to the king himself, the second were conceded to the Cardinal de Lorraine,[1] one of the first prelates of the kingdom.

[1] Charles, Cardinal de Lorraine, was the younger brother of

Turn we rather to the one fair oasis in this desert of corruption—to the pure if not peaceful solitude of the forsaken queen. On one at least of the giddy throng by whom Francis was surrounded the meek but dignified resignation of Eleonora had made a profound impression, and that one was the Maréchal de Montmorency. High in the favour of the king, and as upright as he was brave, the godson of Anne de Bretagne could not, nevertheless, contemplate the unhappy position of the queen without experiencing a deep interest in her fate, which soon grew into a warmer feeling. He knew the pride of her Spanish spirit, and he was, consequently, well aware of the daily and hourly struggle to which she was condemned; and although he had hitherto remained insensible to the blandishments of beauty and the fascinations of coquetry, he suffered himself to be betrayed into a passion for the wife of his sovereign. Conscious of the enormity of his error, he strove for many months to conceal from Eleonora the state of his affections; while she, utterly unsuspicious of the feeling which she had elicited in the breast of the stern soldier, continued to welcome him to her presence with a warmth and kindness which only tended to increase the evil. It was under his protection that she had entered France; he had known

François, Duc de Guise, who was shot at the siege of Orleans, in 1563, by Poltrot de Méré, after having obtained the reputation of being the ablest soldier of his time, and the appointment of Lieutenant-General of the kingdom. Charles de Guise, Cardinal de Lorraine, more celebrated for his dissipation than his sanctity, and accounted one of the handsomest nobles in France, became Finance Minister under Francis II.

her in her own sunny Spain, where she was honoured and happy; she could converse with him upon the past, and, for a time at least, forget the present. He alone cared to remember that she was neglected and desolate; no wonder, therefore, that even in her most melancholy moments she had ever a smile and a gentle greeting for the gallant marshal.

The moment came at last, however, in which Montmorency could no longer maintain his self-command. The Court were hunting in the woods of Chambord. The Queen of Navarre and Catherine de' Medici had followed in the train of the king; the blue litter of Madame d'Etampes had passed the gates, and proceeded apparently in the same direction; and the palace of Amboise was deserted by all save Eleonora and the maréchal, who, on a pretext of indisposition, had been permitted to absent himself from the royal sport.

The wife of Francis I. was seated at an open casement overlooking the bright current of the Loire. Her head rested upon her hand, and an expression of acute suffering was visible on her fine features; but her eyes were tearless as they followed unconsciously the course of the sparkling ripples upon which they lingered. She started, however, from her reverie when Montmorency was announced, and extended towards him her hand, which he raised respectfully to his lips.

"You here, M. le Maréchal!" she exclaimed with undisguised astonishment; "I heard that the whole Court were at Chambord."

"Your majesty is at Amboise," was the abrupt reply.

"True," said the poor queen, forcing a smile. "I, as you are aware, am unequal to such an exertion either of strength or skill as that of a royal hunt. But you, monsieur? Can it be that you have lost taste for this courtly diversion? or, what I should much more deplore, that the king——"

"No, Madame, no," interposed Montmorency; "his majesty did not decline my attendance; and I am as keen a sportsman as even your august husband himself; but, nevertheless, I have not followed the hunt."

"And wherefore?" demanded Eleonora absently, as she passed her hand across her brow, and endeavoured to arouse herself more thoroughly from her reverie.

"I will tell you, Madame," said the maréchal with an unsteady voice, as he fixed his eyes earnestly upon her, "because your unhappiness is destroying my existence. Because you are at once the most admirable and the most ill-used of your sex—because —ay, wither me if you will, Madame, with your frown, but I have already suffered for months, and I must now speak or die—because I love you, and would rather expire here, at your feet, than live on longer in the same torment."

"Do you know to whom you speak, sir?" asked the queen, rising from her seat as the maréchal sank on his knee before her. "Can you, too—*you*—have forgotten that I am the Queen of France; the wife of your sovereign?"

"That you are Queen of France may the saints be praised!" murmured Montmorency; "that you are the wife of Francis I live only to deplore."

"Sir!" said Eleonora haughtily, as she seized the small rattle of polished steel which was at that period the substitute for a bell, and which lay on a table at her side, "will you compel me to summon my attendants, and to dishonour you? Do you seek to dishonour *me?*"

"Heaven forbid, Madame," said the maréchal, rising from the floor; "I have already sinned more than enough. That I love you is my misfortune; do not make it my crime. I will deserve your forbearance. Neither commands nor threats can compel me to do otherwise than regard you as the most perfect of your sex. Say or do what you will, that fact must remain unaltered; but I will never again intrude it upon you. Grant me only one favour, and I am yours in life and death."

"And that favour, sir?"

"Is simple enough, your majesty. Only allow me, whenever I have the honour to approach your person, to pronounce the words 'Good morrow, Madame,' that when they meet your ear they may remind you of the humble and obedient lover whom even your contempt could not alienate."

"So be it, M. le Maréchal," said the queen, striving to suppress the smile elicited by so extraordinary a request; "thus much I may in honour concede, but I rely on your good faith."

"Nor shall you repent the trust, Madame," was

the reply of the supplicant, as he made his parting salutation; "but should you ever want a hand to support, or an arm to avenge you, remember Montmorency."

In another instant the maréchal had disappeared; and while the brilliant train which followed Francis through the woods of Chambord filled the echoes of the forest-paths with the clamours of their joyous revelry, his deserted wife flung herself back upon her seat; and, with her face buried in her hands, wept the hot tears of mortification, wounded pride, and that unutterable anguish which not even tears can solace.

Montmorency religiously adhered to the compact into which he had voluntarily entered; and from thenceforward never omitted, while respectfully performing his obeisance to the queen, to say in a slow and melancholy tone, "Good morrow, Madame," without on any occasion adding a single word of homage or of compliment. This peculiarity soon attracted the attention of the Court, to whom the "audiences" of M. de Montmorency became a perpetual source of curiosity and amusement; but neither the sneers of some nor the smiles of all disturbed for a moment the gravity of the maréchal; although at times even the lip of Eleonora herself quivered with a transient expression of mirth.

It is certain, moreover, that the self-command and good faith of her eccentric admirer made a gradual impression upon the feelings of the queen; her womanly vanity was flattered, and her gratitude excited by a constancy of devotion to which she had long been unaccustomed; and whereas she originally replied to his address only by a grave bow, she ere long relented so far as to repay his perseverance by a more gracious gesture, although she still received his greeting with dignified reserve.

The marriage of Henry VIII. with Anne Boleyn had meanwhile taken place, despite the refusal of the Pope to recognize the divorce of Katherine; and although it had been solemnized in the presence of not more than half a dozen witnesses, the fact soon transpired, and excited the indignation of both the pontiff and the emperor to so high a degree that, despite the entreaties of Francis, who earnestly endeavoured to avert such a calamity, sentence of excommunication was fulminated against the English monarch. This extreme step had only been taken a couple of days when a courier arrived in Rome, empowered by Henry to declare his willingness to abide the judgment of the Holy See for his disobedience, provided that certain of the cardinals, who were inimical to him, should not be included in the council. It was, however, too late. The Pope had suffered his passion to betray him into a precipitation as unwise as it was irremediable; and the English king was no sooner informed that the walls of the Eternal City were placarded with the bull which had been fulminated against him, than he openly avowed himself as the head of the Reformed Church, and declared both himself and his kingdom independent of all papal interference or control.

The unfortunate Katherine of Aragon expired in the January of 1534—an event which rendered the impolitic haste of Clement still more conspicuous, and there is little doubt that the annoyance and regret to which he was subjected by a consciousness of the serious error into which he had been betrayed, and the perpetual remorse induced by the reports that reached him of the virulence with which Henry, in order to avenge the insult offered to his own dignity, was persecuting the Romanists in England, accelerated his own end. He died on the 24th of September in the same year, and was succeeded by Alessandro Farnese, who assumed the title of Paul III.[1]

A short time subsequently the Count of Nassau, with his son the Prince of Orange, visited the French Court on their way from Spain into Flanders, and were entrusted by Charles V. with proposals of friendship and alliance, in which he represented to Francis the importance of a perfect understanding between the two most powerful monarchs of Christendom, who, were they to combine their strength and their resources with mutual faith and goodwill, might defy and control the whole of Europe. In order, as he moreover asserted, to prove his own sincerity in this belief, he offered the hand of one of his nieces to the dauphin, and that of his son to a

[1] Pope Paul III. (Alessandro Farnese) was a native of Rome, Bishop of Ostia, and Dean of the Holy College. When unanimously elected by the Conclave, he had already attained his sixty-eighth year. He had, previously to entering into holy orders, become the father of two children—a daughter, who married Bosio Sforza, and a son, Pietro Luigi Farnese, whom he made Duke of Parma.

princess of France; and, in return for his thus taking the initiative, he requested that the French king, should he decline this double alliance, would at least abstain from invading his territories during his absence on a campaign against the Infidels which he was about to undertake; but the moment was an unpropitious one for the success of such a negotiation.

The death of Clement VII. was a severe blow to the previsions of Francis, who had depended upon the exertions of the Medici to ensure to the Duc d'Orleans a powerful sovereignty in Lombardy. The late peace, brief as it was, had nevertheless sufficed to weary him of inaction. The treaty of Cambray was an undying source of irritation; the nation was relieved from civil discord, and had ceased to oppose the system of taxation which he had introduced; the bequest of his mother and the public revenues had once more replenished his treasury; he was surrounded by a young and impetuous nobility, eager for adventure and distinction, and looking back restlessly upon their past successes; he believed himself secure of the alliance of Henry VIII., in whose cause he had so strenuously exerted his influence with the late Pope, and who had, by his repudiation of Katherine of Aragon, so exasperated the emperor, that he was anticipating a descent of the imperialists upon England; and he calculated, moreover, that he could rely not only upon the assistance of the Protestant princes, in the event of his engaging in a new war, but also upon that of the Sultan.

No wonder then, that, eager at once for excitement and revenge, Francis soon found a pretext for the renewal of hostilities against his old rival. He accordingly busied himself in the reorganisation of his army, and formed a militia upon the model of the ancient Roman legions, which was composed entirely of his own subjects, and in which no individual of either the German or Swiss troops who were in his pay was permitted to serve. This force amounted to forty-two thousand men; and in May 1534 he made a progress through the seven provinces, each of which had supplied its quota of six thousand troops, accompanied by his whole Court, and passed the several legions successively in review.

Charles V. was meanwhile actively engaged against the pirates of Africa. His success was signal, and in little more than two months he had landed in that country, defeated Barbarossa before Tunis, reinstated Muley Hassan, taken possession of all the seaports of Barbary, and released upwards of twenty thousand Christian slaves, whom he conveyed to their several countries to bless and extol the name of their deliverer.

All Christendom rang with the praises of the emperor. To every nation in Europe he had restored some of its lost subjects, and the voice of gratitude was loud on every side, while, on the other hand, the agreement which the French king was known to maintain with the Infidels had excited universal indignation and distrust. In vain did

Francis deny the accusation, and denounce the emperor as his enemy for having suffered it to gain credence. It was known that Solyman had secret agents at his Court, he felt that his reputation was shaken throughout the whole Christian world, and he was conscious that he dare not attempt to attack the power of Charles while he was engaged in protecting religion and humanity from the barbarity of the Moslem.

But the year 1534 was, nevertheless, not fated to terminate without its own peculiar tragedy. Alarmed by the evil feeling which existed against him, Francis pursued with redoubled animosity the professors of Protestantism within his own kingdom. The tenets of Calvin were already beginning to rival those of Luther, and were promulgated throughout France and the Low Countries by his disciples; placards, denying the truth of the doctrine of transubstantiation, were scattered in the streets, and even pasted upon the walls of the Louvre; and the king eagerly availed himself of this circumstance to regain the influence which he had lost over papal Europe.

He first instituted a rigid search for the authors of these obnoxious documents, and his agents succeeded in discovering six individuals who were declared to be implicated in the crime. He then instructed Jean du Bellay, the Bishop of Paris, to order a solemn procession, in public reparation of the insult which had been offered to the most holy sacrament of the Church; and not only travelled from Blois to Paris to assist at it in person, but was also accompanied by the queen and his three sons. The procession proceeded from the church of St. Germain l'Auxerrois to the cathedral of Notre Dame; and the Eucharist was borne by the bishop attired in full pontificals, attended by a number of priests laden with relics. The king followed with a lighted taper in his hand; the three princes and the Duc de Vendôme supported the canopy; and all the foreign ambassadors, cardinals, prelates, and nobility then resident in the capital closed the *cortège*. Nor did the king satisfy himself with this tacit demonstration of devotion; for, before the ceremonial was at an end, he publicly declared that, if his right arm were infected with the cancer of the new heresy, he would with his left hand lop it from his body, and that, in like case, he would not spare his own children.

Our next paragraph we must transcribe *verbatim et literatim* from Le Père Daniel, for we should be unable to find words of our own in which to record so horrible a butchery.

"The evening of the same day, the six culprits were conveyed to the public square, where fires had been prepared to burn them. There was, in the centre of each pile, a sort of tall pulley, to which they were attached; the flames were then lighted beneath them, and the executioners, gently loosening the cord, allowed these wretches to descend sufficiently near to the fire for them to feel all its agony; then they were once more hoisted up, and after having made them suffer this cruel torment several times, they were flung into the midst of the flames, where they expired."

Sismondi (quoting from Jo. Sleidani) gives a somewhat different, although equally terrible, description of the instrument of torture. He says, speaking of the victims, " Had the people torn them to pieces, they would have shown them mercy; their ferocity would not have equalled that of the king. He had commanded that these unfortunates should be attached to a lofty machine, which was a beam so nicely balanced that, as it descended, it plunged them into the blaze of the pile, but rose again almost instantly, in order to prolong their sufferings, until the flame seizing upon the cords by which they were bound, they fell into the middle of the fire."

"Six," says Mezeray, "were burnt at Paris, and more than twice as many in several other places; but for two who were put to death, a hundred others rose from their ashes."

God be praised that it was so! For such enormities, perpetrated by such agents—a profligate king, a licentious prelacy, a venal and corrupted Court—were assuredly more than enough to turn the hearts of the right-minded and the prayerful from a faith for which as there was no mercy, so also there could be no hope.

CHAPTER II

1535-36

The persecution of the Protestants is continued—Francis abolishes printing throughout his kingdom—The league of Smalkalden declare against the French king—Francis invites Melancthon to France—Francis declares war against the Duke of Savoy—Chabot overruns the duchy—The duke urges the emperor to assist him—Death of Sforza—Charles V. restores Alessandro de' Medici to the sovereignty of Florence—Death of the Chancellor Duprat—The Queen of Navarre at Amboise—Ostentation and profligacy of Madame d'Etampes—The tournament—A street brawl—Narrow escape of the Duc d'Angoulême—Removal of the Court to Chambord—The king and Diane de Poitiers—A moral mission—Diane resolves to attempt the conquest of the Duc d'Orleans—Her personal attractions—Her ambition—A poem of the sixteenth century—Jealousy of the Duchesse d'Etampes—She demands the exile of Diane from the Court—Charles V. offers to concede the duchy of Milan to the Duc d'Angoulême—Francis demands it for the Duc d'Orleans—Tergiversation of the emperor—Charles V. renews his alliance with the Venetians—The negotiation concerning the Milanese is renewed—The emperor proceeds to Rome—The French ambassador urges him to perform his promises—Charles V. harangues the conclave, and insults Francis—He temporizes with the French ambassadors—The Pope endeavours to pacify them—The address to the conclave is garbled and forwarded to France—Moderation of Francis—The Cardinal de Lorraine is despatched to the emperor to terminate the affair of the Milanese, and fails—Imperial superstition—Treason of the Marquis de Saluzzo—The Pope declares his neutrality—Charles V. excites the German Protestants against Francis—The army in Savoy is disarmed—Montmorency ensures the safety of the frontier—Francis proceeds to Lyons—Charles V. declares himself suzerain of Provence—Francis prepares for an invasion.

THE year 1535 commenced by a new persecution of the reformers. By order of the king, all those who had been arrested were put upon their trial, and many of them perished by the swinging beam described in the last chapter.

Francis was desirous to make his peace with the Church; and notwithstanding the ambition which he still retained to be considered as the protector of letters, he was no sooner accused by Béda of favouring the new faith in compliance with the entreaties of his sister than, after having, in the first burst of his indignation, caused him to be arrested and imprisoned in the ecclesiastical dungeons, he condemned him to make the *amende honorable* before the church of Notre Dame, and to avow that he had spoken against the truth and the king. He, however, subsequently became alarmed lest this act of severity might fail to remove the impression produced upon the minds of those before whom Béda had asserted his heresy; and availing himself of the circumstance of the placards, to which we have alluded above, he — the proposed founder of the royal college, the correspondent of Erasmus, and the successor of Louis XII.—issued letters-patent abolishing the use of the press, and forbidding the printing of any book, be it what it might, within the confines of the kingdom of France, upon pain of death! This retrogressive measure paralyzed, as a natural consequence, the energies of all the learned men who had sought his Court as an assured asylum; and it also produced another and very fatal result, for while Francis, by the blow which he thus struck at the very root of civilization, pacified the priesthood, the Court of Rome, and the more fanatical of his subjects, he most imprudently and recklessly overlooked the probable effect of such proceedings upon the minds of the Protestant princes, whose continued alliance had become doubly valuable to him since he had resolved upon renewing the war against the emperor.

The conviction of his error was soon forced upon him. The enormous cruelties which he had perpetrated upon their co-religionists excited the horror and indignation of the members of the league of Smalkalden, who openly declared that the interests of their faith would be less endangered by their adherence to the house of Austria than to those of a monarch whose barbarity had already sacrificed so many valuable lives.

In vain did Francis, anxious to regain the confidence of the German princes, address each separately, asserting that the culprits had suffered rather as political than as religious delinquents; in vain did he write to Melancthon with his own hand, entreating him to repair to France and to discuss the subject of his faith with the doctors of the Sorbonne, assuring him that he did not consider it impossible to unite the French and German Churches; the league were not to be deluded by a subterfuge; and consequently, although, when urged to the step by Luther, Melancthon consented to undertake the journey to France, in order, if possible, to prevent a recurrence of the butchery of the past months, the Elector of Saxony positively refused to permit him to take a step of such importance without the sanction of the emperor.

While thus occupied at home, Francis still maintained his resolution of once more invading the Milanese; and having authorized the Comte Guillaume de Furstemberg to levy troops in Germany, he despatched the President Poyet to Savoy to request from the duke a free passage for the French army through his territories. Charles of Savoy, however, at the instigation of his wife, refused to hearken to such a proposition, and his refusal so exasperated the king that he immediately declared war against him; upon which Admiral de Brion Chabot, who, having entered Brescia, had taken possession of all the towns, none of which were garrisoned, thence proceeded to Savoy, where he made himself master of Chambery and Montmelian, with all the territory on that side of Mont Cenis.

The Duke of Savoy, alarmed by a promptitude of hostilities for which he was thoroughly unprepared, urged the emperor to lose no time in coming to his succour; and his ambassadors encountered Charles V. at Naples, where he had just disembarked amid the acclamations of the people, with the laurels recently gained at Tunis fresh upon his brow. The envoys of the duke were instructed to propose to the conqueror, with a view of inducing him to espouse at once the interests of their master, the exchange of Nice, and other territories then in the possession of the duke on the French side of the Alps, against such as might be afterwards agreed upon between them; an offer which augmented at once the anger and the alarm of Francis, as the cession of these particular portions of the duchy of

Savoy opened up a way into his own kingdom, of which the emperor could avail himself at his pleasure by invading Dauphiny and Provence, and thus securing an entrance into the very heart of France.

This negotiation was, however, abandoned, the death of Francisco Sforza, which occurred just at this period, having arrested the proceedings of Chabot, who, as well as the king his master, anticipated that the duke having died without issue, the claim of the French princes would no longer be disputed by the emperor, and that, consequently, it would be mere wanton cruelty to take cities by force which must ere long recognize their legitimate sovereign in the person of Francis. Both the one and the other had, however, forgotten that ambition was no less the ruling passion of Charles than of his rival, and that he was little likely, at the very proudest moment of his life, to detach one gem from the coronal which he wore with so much jealousy.

Nor did the feeling evinced by the Neapolitans when, by the death of Sforza, they saw the duchy of Milan about to fall once more into his hands, and ascertained that the same distrust and dissatisfaction had manifested itself throughout the whole of the Italian states, tend to render the emperor more compliant. He had entered Naples as the protector of Christendom against the Infidels; his train had been swelled by the ambassadors of all the princes of Italy, who had submitted to him, as to a supreme arbitrator, their several subjects of dispute and misunderstanding; the Florentine patriots had appealed to him to re-establish them as a republic, and they had yielded passively to his will when he insisted upon confirming Alessandro de' Medici[1] in his sovereignty, stained as he was with crime; and, moreover, as an earnest of his favour, guaranteed to him, in accordance with a pledge already given, the hand of his natural daughter Margaret, to whom the duke was subsequently married on the 28th of February 1536.

On the 8th of July of the year which we are now recording (1535) France was delivered from an unjust minister in the person of the Chancellor Duprat, who expired of phthyriasis, at his château at Nantouillet, in intense suffering, not less of mind than of body; the agony of the hideous disease to which he fell a victim being even exceeded by the torments of a guilty and remorseful conscience, which vented itself in tears and groans, but to which he had listened too late. He was succeeded in the chancellorship by Antoine du Bourg, the president of the parliament of Paris.

The Court was at this period sojourning at

[1] Alessandro de' Medici was the son of Lorenzo II., Duke of Urbino, or, as some historians assert, the natural son of Clement VII. He was forced upon the Florentines by Charles V. in 1532 as their duke, and the succession secured to his children. His tyranny and extortion caused him to be universally detested, while his cruelty made him the scourge of the duchy and the terror of all by whom he was surrounded. He caused the death, by poison, of the Cardinal Hyppolito de' Medici, the son of Julio II. and grandson of Lorenzo I., surnamed the Great. He married Margaret of Austria, the natural daughter of Charles V., in 1536, and was assassinated in the following year by Lorenzino de' Medici, the son of Lorenzo III. and grandson of Pietro Francisco.

Amboise, where the Queen of Navarre was on a visit, and her arrival had been hailed as the occasion for a succession of festivities, at which the Duchesse d'Etampes openly presided. The favour of Anne de Pisseleu had now reached its extreme point. She had enriched and ennobled her family; she had seen herself powerful enough to assume the place and almost to usurp the dignity of the wife of the sovereign; she had secured the friendship of Catherine de' Medici; and she had become the dispenser of all the royal bounties. Many a noble courtier assumed her colours in the lists, and many a titled abbot was content to stand beside her at her toilette. None cared to remember that her life was one of the most unblushing licentiousness; and while the rabble of the Pré-aux-Clercs bandied her name among them like that of the vilest of her sex, and made her profligate adventures the theme of their ribald gossip, there was neither prince nor prelate at the Court who did not obey her behest as though it had been that of an oracle.

Among other entertainments ostensibly provided for the amusement of the king's sister, a tournament was held in the great court of the castle, at which all the nobles and gentlemen then resident at Amboise were invited to assist. Not only the princes, but even the king himself, had in turn taken their place in the lists, and the Duc d'Angoulême had particularly distinguished himself by his prowess. Of all his children, Charles d'Angoulême, his younger son, was the especial favourite of Francis, whom he greatly resembled both in person and temperament. Impulsive, reckless, and daring, he despised alike danger and difficulty; while, although yet a boy in years, he had already seriously attached himself to one of the most beautiful women of the Court. Unlike the dauphin, he was fair, with a profusion of light hair, and dark blue eyes, one of which he had, however, lost at an early age from the effects of smallpox. His ardent love of all warlike amusements and field sports, his frankness, courage, and gallant bearing had greatly endeared him to the king, who was repelled by the cold stateliness of the dauphin and irritated by the heavy and unsocial manners of the Duc d'Orleans. Nevertheless, Francis occasionally endeavoured to restrain the impetuosity of the young prince, but with little effect; and on the occasion to which we are now referring, his exultation was so unbounded when he found himself the hero of the day that it betrayed him into an imprudence which nearly cost him his life.

The fatigue that he had undergone in the lists, and his consequent exhaustion, induced the young prince to swallow a large goblet of spiced wine a few moments before the king arose from the supper-table; and this insidious draught acted the more potently upon him from the fact that he had previously pledged the flatterers by whom he was surrounded with more than sufficient vigour. In this state of excitement he no sooner ascertained from one of the chamberlains that the monarch had retired to his apartment, than he rose abruptly from his seat, exclaiming to a group of wild young courtiers who were in attendance upon him—" Now then, gentlemen, his majesty is safe for the night, and we are the lords of Amboise. Let us go and take the air upon the bridge, and see if we cannot thrash some of the rascally lacqueys who amuse themselves by stopping up the thoroughfare, and striking those who thrust them aside."

This proposal met with unanimous applause, and the hot-headed young prince, and his equally wild companions, at once sallied from the palace, and rushed upon the lounging group on the bridge, who, being in the service of the Court, and many among them even in that of the king himself, all carried arms. The darkness of the night rendered it impossible for them to recognize their assailants ; and, consequently, when the Duc d'Angoulême, at the head of his little party, fell upon them sword in hand, they defended themselves vigorously ; while, as he persisted in retaining his position, he soon became the principal object of their attack, until at length a stroke was aimed at him with so sure a hand that M. de Castelnau, a Gascon noble, and one of his favourite companions, had only time to throw himself between the duke and his antagonist, and to receive the blow intended for his master, at whose feet he fell dead upon the instant. At once sobered and heart-stricken at the result of his imprudence, the young prince shouted imperiously—" Put up your swords, gentlemen ; I am the Duc d'Angoulême."

At this startling announcement every weapon was withdrawn, and in a few seconds the bleeding body of the faithful and devoted Castelnau, the victim of this ignoble broil, was surrounded only by the prince and his followers. Charles d'Angoulême, as he bent over him, shed tears of unaffected sorrow, as sincere as they were unavailing; he did not even seek to ascertain by whose hand his friend had fallen, for he was self-convicted, and he could not disguise from himself that he had been more guilty than the actual murderer.

In order to dissipate the annoyance which he felt at this disgraceful adventure, and if possible to overcome the gloom which the fate of a friend to whom he had been greatly attached had shed over the spirits of the young prince, the king, after having severely reprimanded his son, removed with the Court to Chambord; and it was, probably, the dread which he felt lest the hitherto lively youth should belie the promise of his boyhood, that led him to observe, more closely than ever, the demeanour of his other sons. On one occasion, as he was leaning over the balcony of the great hall, watching the three princes who were engaged at tennis in the court below, he turned suddenly towards the Grande Sénéchale, who was standing near him, and motioning to her to advance, he directed her attention to the listlessness with which the Duc d'Angouléme was pursuing the game.

"I scarcely recognize him," he said with a sigh; "his natural enthusiasm is quenched. Even the dauphin exhibits more excitement."

"Give him time, Sire," replied Diane de Poitiers soothingly; "he is young, and he has lost a friend. His royal highness loved M. de Castelnau."

"Doubtless you are right, madame," acquiesced the king. "At least you are an admirable consoler, and I dare not doubt your words. He *is* young, and we know that time cures all evils."

"Not all, Sire."

Francis looked at her steadfastly. "You are right again, madame; not all. There are certain evils which time and memory can only canker; and others for which it affords no hope. You see the dauphin. Time fails to make a Frenchman of the Spaniard."

"Monseigneur is grave beyond his years, assuredly, Sire," said Madame de Brézé; "but his mind is all nobleness."

"And Henry, madame? What will you say of Henry?" asked the king almost peevishly. "For my own part, I despair of him. Since his marriage he has become more unsocial and impracticable than ever."

"Surely your majesty did not anticipate that a wife would render him more frank and joyous?" said Diane with a slight accent of sarcasm. "For the Duc d'Orleans there was no cure but love."

"Aha! is it so, fair Diane?" asked Francis, suddenly roused into excitement; "then we have committed a fatal error, for I fear that love and marriage are almost incompatible."

The beautiful widow was silent.

"Catherine is, however, handsome enough to animate a statue," pursued the king; "it can scarcely be difficult to love her."

"True," said Madame de Brézé, with an arch look, "but love cannot be compelled; make it a duty, and it turns to loathing."

"He is, then, irreclaimable?"

"By no means. A sincere and ardent passion would arouse him from his present apathy; for none love more deeply than those who resist moral coercion."

"On the faith of a gentleman, you possess more wisdom, madame, handsome as you are," exclaimed Francis energetically, "than all the doctors of the Sorbonne. I only wish that some one as fair and as fascinating as yourself would undertake his conversion. I should be her debtor beyond all requital."

"The experiment might at least be tried," murmured Diane, twisting her pearl *châtelaine* about her taper fingers.

"But by whom?" asked the king. "For such an undertaking it would require a miracle to ensure success. If, indeed, *you* could be prevailed upon to sacrifice yourself——"

"Your majesty does not possess a more devoted servant than Diane de Poitiers."

"I know it, madame, I know it;" said Francis, as a strange expression passed over his face; "and I am equally aware that you at least could not fail; but perhaps, the past——"

"Do you fear, Sire," asked the Grande Sénéchale with an ironical smile, "that the memory of M. de Brézé——"

The king forced an uneasy laugh, as he hastily replied, without awaiting the conclusion of her inquiry, "I have no such apprehension, fair lady; therefore let the old Sénéchal rest in peace. We will revert no more to bygone years; nothing is so idle as retrospection; while as regards the future I do not for a moment doubt your power, and only wish that it could be successfully exerted."

"Your wishes are my law, Sire," was the rejoinder of the fair widow, as her rich lips parted in affected merriment; "but Madame d'Etampes is approaching, and I will no longer intrude upon your majesty."

"The duchess is jealous," said the royal libertine, as he acknowledged her parting curtsey, "and we must not violate the proprieties at Chambord. I will not detain you, Madame la Grande Sénéchale," and as Diane moved away the favourite advanced to the balcony—a liberty upon which the neglected queen would have feared to venture.

At this period the widow of Louis de Brézé had already attained her thirty-first year, while the prince Henry was only in his seventeenth; and at the first glance it would appear as though so formidable a disparity of age must have rendered any attempt on her part to engage the affections of so mere a youth alike abortive and ridiculous; but so perfectly had she preserved even the youthful bloom which had added so much to her attractions on her first appear-

VOL. III   53

ance at Court, that she appeared ten years younger than she actually was. Her features were regular and classical; her complexion faultless; her hair of a rich purple black, which took a golden tint in the sunshine; while her teeth, her ankle, her hands and arms, and her bust, were each in their turn the theme of the Court poets. That the extraordinary and almost fabulous duration of her beauty was in a great degree due to the precautions which she adopted, there can be little doubt, for she spared no effort to secure it; she was jealously careful of her health, and in the most severe weather bathed in cold water; she suffered no cosmetic to approach her, denouncing every compound of the kind as worthy only of those to whom nature had been so niggardly as to compel them to complete her imperfect work; she rose every morning at six o'clock, and had no sooner left her chamber than she sprang into the saddle, and after having galloped a league or two returned to her bed, where she remained until mid-day engaged in reading. The system appears a singular one, but in her case it undoubtedly proved successful, as after having enslaved the Duc d'Orleans in her thirty-first year, she still reigned in absolute sovereignty over the heart of the King of France when she had nearly reached the age of sixty! It is certain, however, that the magnificent Diane owed no small portion of this extraordinary and unprecedented constancy to the charms of her mind and the brilliancy of her intellect.

The short dialogue between Francis and herself

which we have given above, inspired the ambitious widow with new ideas and aspirations. Hitherto she had been content to await a reaction in the heart of Francis himself. She did not believe that Madame d'Etampes could long conceal from him the extent of her profligacy, and, well aware that should the favourite be disgraced her successor would soon be determined, she contented herself by exerting all her fascinations against the facile heart of the monarch, and watching for the hour of her own triumph.

The few sentences which had passed in the balcony, however, had sufficed to open up a new career before her. That the king had spoken rather in bitter mirth than in sober seriousness she was well aware; but this conviction failed to shake her purpose. The saturnine and forbidding nature of the Duc d'Orleans, moreover, rendered the task which she was about to undertake one of no common difficulty, but this very consciousness piqued her vanity and determined her to persevere.

The prince was at first annoyed, and even abashed, at the undisguised preference exhibited towards him by the most beautiful woman at Court; but Diane soon succeeded in subjugating his heart through his vanity. Conscious that he possessed neither the dignity of the dauphin nor the frank gracefulness of his younger brother, Henri d'Orleans had hitherto carefully avoided the society of the opposite sex, and had even received the hand of his wife with a marked repugnance which had drawn down upon him the displeasure of the king; but he soon found that there was no resisting the seductions of a syren who, while she looked into his face with the brightest smile and the most brilliant eyes in the world, discovered in himself a thousand estimable qualities and personal attractions to which he had never dreamt he could advance any claim.

That he did not long combat his growing passion is evident from a poem addressed to him by his fair and frail conquest only a few weeks subsequently; and this production, extracted from the MSS. of the Bibliothèque Royale, is so characteristic alike of the taste and the morals of the time that we offer no apology for its insertion.

> " Voicy vraisment qu'Amour un beau matin
> S'en vint m'offrir flourette très gentille,
> ——Là, se prit-il, a ournez vostre teint
> Et vistement violiers et jonquille
> Me rejetoit, à tant, que ma mantille
> En estoit pleine, et mon cœur se pasmoit ;
> (Car, voyez-vous, flourette si gentille
> Estois garçon frais, dispos, et jeunnet).
>
> Ains tremblottante et destournant les yeux . . .
> Nenni . . . disois-je . . . Ah, ne screz déçue,
> Reprit Amour, et soudain à ma vue
> Va présentant un laurier merveilleux.
> ——Mieux vault, lui dis-je, estre sasge que Royne
> Ains me sentis et fraimir et trembler,
> Diane faillist, et comprendrez sans peine
> Duquel matin je praitends reparler."

What effect the triumph of Madame de Brézé over the heart of the prince produced upon the mind of the king, the old chronicler who dilates complaisantly upon all the preceding details does not inform us ; but the impression which it made upon Madame d'Etampes soon became apparent, and was destined to exert a most unhappy influence over the fortunes of the nation. The first weapon which the haughty favourite wielded against the mature mistress of the young duke was that of ridicule. She affected to discredit the report that M. d'Orleans could be enthralled by the antiquated charms of a "wrinkled old woman ;" and in support of her argument amused herself by asserting that she was born in the same year in which the daughter of St. Vallier had espoused the Grand Sénéchal of Normandy. Of course she found many and attentive auditors, not one of whom attempted to disprove her words, although all were aware that Madame de Brézé was the senior of the duchess only by seven years. She next attacked the person of her victim, forewarning those who were bold enough to uphold her claims to admiration that the beauty of which she was so vain was known to be the result of sorcery, and that they would ere long see it vanish as mysteriously as it had been bestowed. Diane, however, was not to be conquered by means so puerile as these ; and, secure of the affections and support of the prince, she treated the calumnies of her persecutor with proud and silent disdain.

The nature of Madame d'Etampes was ill calculated to brook this tacit assumption of superiority, and, foiled in her efforts to rid herself of the intrusive beauty by her own agency, she carried her vindictiveness so far as to demand of the king that he should exile Madame de Brézé from the Court ; but Francis, who had already begun to congratulate himself upon the altered deportment of the duke, which he attributed entirely to the influence exerted over him by Diane, refused to accede to her wishes; reminding her that while the Duchesse d'Orleans uttered no complaint, and continued to exhibit towards the Grande Sénéchale the same consideration and regard as ever, it was impossible that he could interfere to prevent the progress of the *liaison*. Not even this declaration could, however, discourage the pertinacious favourite, who thenceforward studiously avoided all reference to Diane herself, but strenuously endeavoured to disparage the duke in the eyes of his royal father; drawing invidious comparisons between that prince and the dauphin, and seeking by every means in her power to crush his rapidly increasing favour.

It must not, nevertheless, be supposed that although Madame de Brézé possessed sufficient self-command to exhibit nothing save contempt towards the vindictive duchess, she did not acutely feel and bitterly resent the sarcasms of which she had been made the subject. Jealous of the superior power of the royal mistress, and exasperated by her insults, even while she displayed worldly wisdom enough patiently to abide her time of vengeance, her heart was to the full as much agitated by hatred as that of Anne de Pisseleu herself; and a conviction that such must in reality be the case once more divided the Court into two separate factions, which the doubtful aspect of public affairs alone tended to render for a time innoxious.

Anxious if possible to avoid a war with Francis, while still apprehensive of a Turkish invasion, and awaiting a favourable opportunity to subjugate the princes of the Protestant league, whom he regarded as rebels alike against his own authority and that of the Church,—and, moreover, alarmed by the rapid spread of Lutheranism in the Low Countries,—Charles determined rather to temporize with his rival on the subject of the duchy of Milan, than by an abrupt rejection of his claim to excite him to hostilities; and accordingly he informed the Sire de Velly, who was awaiting him at Naples with the congratulations of the French king upon his victories in Africa, that he was willing to cede the Milanese to one of the sons of Francis, on condition that the duchy should remain a distinct sovereignty, and that Germany and France should become so closely allied by marriage as to prevent the possibility of future aggression on either side.

He declared, moreover, that he was so sincere in this declaration that he should take no steps towards the disposal of the province until he received the reply of the king upon three points on which he was anxious to ascertain his intentions. Namely, whether he were prepared to lend his assistance against the Turks, to compel the Protestant princes to revert to the Romanist religion, and to co-operate with him in the pacification of all Christendom. Should Francis accede to these terms, he asserted that he was ready to bestow the duchy upon Charles, the youngest of the three princes, on condition that the

Duc d'Orleans should accompany him to the siege of Algiers.

As he had anticipated, however, Francis, while he consented to the three points upon which he had first insisted, refused to comply with those which regarded his sons; and he instructed M. de Velly to explain to the emperor that he desired the Milanese for the Duc d'Orleans, and that he was ready to offer four hundred thousand crowns of gold for the investiture, directing him at the same time to press for a reply. When this decision was made known to him, Charles contented himself by vague declarations of his good faith, and evaded a direct answer, while the measures which he meanwhile adopted augured ill for the success of the negotiation. He had not only purchased the fealty of Alessandro de' Medici by a marriage which at once flattered his vanity and secured his sovereignty, but he also entered into a new league with the Venetians, who, dazzled by his triumphs in Africa, and induced by the persuasions of the Duc d'Urbino, once more declared themselves his allies; and he directed the Dowager-Queen of Hungary, who had succeeded to the government of the Low Countries on the death of Margaret of Austria, as well as his lieutenants in Spain, to make levies both of men and money, while he was himself occupied in raising supplies throughout Naples and Sicily, and in the reinforcement of his African army.

Francis, nevertheless, deluded himself with the belief that as the emperor had spontaneously offered the duchy of Milan to his third son (a concession which he could only attribute to his reluctance to renew the war), he would, when he became convinced that he had no other alternative, ultimately consent to transfer it to the Duc d'Orleans, or even, should he insist upon such an arrangement, to himself. He was at this period suffering from severe illness at Dijon, and was totally unprepared for the communication which he received from De Velly, to the effect that the emperor had declared that had he been aware of the rigorous treatment which the Duke of Savoy had experienced at the hands of the French king, he should never have condescended to the proposition which he had made, but that having mooted the subject he would not retract his offer; while he trusted that his forbearance would induce Francis to arrange matters in Savoy, and to act with similar consistency.

The negotiation was consequently continued, but the position of the two potentates was no longer the same. Charles had by this clever policy gained a supremacy far greater than it at first appeared to be; and he continued to make strenuous exertions to protect himself in the event of any aggressive measures on the part of his rival. He revealed to the Pope the correspondence into which he had entered with the French king, and made the same overtures to him which he had made to Francis; while he, moreover, volunteered to renew his old friendship with Henry VIII., alleging that the death of his aunt had removed the cause of dissatisfaction which had induced him to abandon the interests of

England for those of France; and that he, consequently, felt himself at liberty to recur to his former and more genial associations.

These important steps once taken, he proceeded to Rome with great pomp, where he remained for thirteen days, holding constant conferences with the pontiff; and finally requested him to summon the cardinals and foreign ministers, before whom, bareheaded, and with his plumed hat in his hand, he indulged in the most unmeasured invectives and menaces against Francis; recapitulating all the grievances of which he had to complain; accusing him of constantly infringing the peace upon frivolous pretexts, of falsifying his word, of troubling the tranquillity of both Italy and Germany, and of persecuting the Duke of Savoy; and ultimately concluding his harangue by declaring that the French king must either consent to accept the Duchy of Milan for his younger son upon the conditions which he had stipulated, or meet him in single combat with sword and dagger, on the recognized and solemn pledge that the successful combatant should, with all the resources he could command, and under the orders of the sovereign-pontiff, undertake a crusade against the Infidels, or engage in a war which could end only in the total ruin of one of the two powers.

At this period of his speech he also suffered his irritation to betray him into an insult to the French army as unjust as it was offensive; for, in alluding to the result of the late hostilities, he exclaimed, "If I had no better soldiers than those of Francis, I would forthwith go with my hands tied, and a halter about my neck, and implore the mercy of my enemy."

This address having been delivered in the Spanish language was very imperfectly understood by either M. de Velly, or the Bishop of Maçon, the French ambassador at the papal Court; but the extraordinary and unaccustomed vehemence of Charles, and the few sentences which they were enabled to connect, rendered them suspicious that a public affront had been offered to their sovereign; whereupon they demanded an audience of the emperor on the following morning, and required to be informed if they had rightly interpreted his words, and if they were empowered to inform their master that his imperial majesty had defied him to single combat. Charles, in reply, assured them that he had in no way assailed the honour of their sovereign, although he had justified himself; and declared that he should be deeply hurt were his words misconstrued, as he had a great esteem for the king his brother, and had never had cause of complaint against him.

De Velly had, a day or two previously, urged him afresh upon the subject of the negotiation, when he became irritated, and demanded impetuously, "And you who are so importunate, have you authority to conclude the treaty?"

The royal envoy admitted that he was invested with no such powers; but added that the Admiral

Brion de Chabot and the Cardinal de Lorraine were already on their way, and fully accredited.

"Such being the case," broke in Charles, "as you have no power to act, by what right do you tell me that I give you nothing but words, when in point of fact it is your own case towards me? But of those I have already given you so many, that I shall waste no more until you are authorized to complete the negotiation."

On ascertaining the result of their audience, the pontiff frankly declared to the French ambassadors that he saw no prospect whatever of a successful issue to so intricate an affair; and that he was satisfied the emperor was merely amusing them by words in order to gain time, for that he never would be induced to cede Milan to the Duc d'Orleans, who, in the event of his surviving the dauphin, would thus merge the duchy in the Crown of France.

Moreover, there could be no doubt that the sudden violence betrayed by Charles in the assembly, when his previous policy had been to temporize, was occasioned by the intelligence which had just reached him, that Francis, wearied by his procrastination, had authorized his generals to pursue their operations in Piedmont, which they had done so successfully as to compel his brother-in-law, the Duke of Savoy, to fly.

That he instantly repented is sufficiently evident, however, from his conduct on the morrow, when he endeavoured once more to cajole the French ambassadors as he had previously done; but the time for forbearance, as was evident to all the foreign ministers who had been present at the meeting, was now past; and they accordingly did not lose a moment in writing to their several Courts to prepare them for the war which appeared inevitable; and that the impression produced upon the mind of the sovereign-pontiff was precisely similar, was made apparent by the fact that he summoned M. de Velly and the Bishop of Maçon to his presence the same evening, and endeavoured by every argument he could advance to dissuade them from any act of impetuosity which might tend to augment the animosity of their sovereign against the emperor, and thus disturb a peace of which Europe had only just begun to reap the benefit. He did not conceal his own displeasure at the intemperate language uttered by Charles, but he entreated them to palliate it in their report, and, if possible, to avert the peril by which the whole of Christendom was threatened.

In reply, the French envoys respectfully but firmly represented to his holiness that they had no alternative save to render a faithful account to their sovereign of all that had occurred, the insult having been too public to afford a chance of its concealment; but they, nevertheless, willingly consented to use the greatest circumspection, and to abstain from all comment which might aggravate the evil; reminding the Pope, moreover, that his own neutrality would tend more powerfully to secure the maintenance of peace than any other measure. This Clement at once promised to observe; and the ambassadors so far complied with his request as to modify certain expressions uttered by the emperor, while they omitted no portion of his after-explanation; and as, upon their application for a copy of the address which he had delivered in the assembly, they were informed by the imperial ministers that it had been already forwarded to Leidekerke, the ambassador of Charles V. at the French Court, by whom it was to be presented to the king, they felt assured that the more temperate language they had adopted would not be gainsaid by the official document.

Such indeed proved to be the case, for the ameliorations which had been made by all parties had so much weakened the offensive character of the emperor's address, that the reply of Francis was extremely temperate. He declared the treaty of Madrid to be invalid, inasmuch as he had acted under constraint; while as regarded the renewed proposal of the duel, he asserted that he did not consider himself to have received a challenge, the emperor having stated that his words had been misconstrued, and that he had no such intention; although, had he not been dissuaded by his ministers, he would have accepted it with pleasure if it could have tended to spare the blood of his subjects.

This answer, which astonished as much as it disappointed those who believed that he was too high-hearted to brook a second affront of so marked and unmeasured a nature, Francis communicated to all the foreign Courts whose ministers had been present at the harangue of the emperor; and at the same time he despatched the Cardinal de Lorraine to Piedmont in order to stay the progress of his army, that Charles might have no plausible pretext for entering upon hostilities. Thence the prelate proceeded to Sienna, where the emperor was at that period sojourning; and having obtained an audience, he respectfully reminded him of his promise to cede the duchy of Milan to the French prince.

The demeanour of Charles V. was cold and calm. He said that he had only made the concession under certain conditions, which had been infringed by the invasion of the territories of his vassal the Duke of Savoy; but that he was, nevertheless, willing to perform his promise in favour of Charles d'Angoulême, and to give him, moreover, one of his nieces in marriage.

The cardinal in reply stated that his instructions were to demand the investiture of the Duc d'Orleans; and that should his imperial majesty withhold his assent to that arrangement, he was commanded to proceed to Rome to acquaint the sovereign-pontiff with the failure of the negotiation.

Charles, with a faint smile which conveyed more of contempt than courtesy, merely retorted by bidding him farewell, and assuring him that he should see him with pleasure on his return; and thus civilly dismissed, M. de Lorraine at once proceeded on his journey to Rome. Late events had rendered the emperor more impracticable than ever; and since he had seen the armies of the Sultan and Barbarossa flee before him, he had begun to entertain the idea that he was destined to be invincible; a delusion in which he was strengthened by the predictions of the astrologers, who early in the present year (1536) had put forth the most extraordinary statements concerning him. What some had merely advanced from a desire of flattering his vanity, others soon affected to confirm in order to further their personal interests; and these extravagant fallacies were industriously circulated throughout Europe, where they produced an impression difficult to understand in the present day.

Among others who were infected with the weakness of believing that it was useless to contend against one whose destiny had been declared by the stars, was the Marquis de Saluzzo, who, not content with the mere treachery which he meditated, remained for some time with the French troops, in order to ascertain their proposed plan of operations, and thus to render himself more welcome to the new master to whom he had resolved to transfer his services.

The mission of the Cardinal de Lorraine to the Pope meanwhile produced no effect upon the timid nature of Paul III., who admitted the justice of his representations and the bad faith of the emperor, but persisted in declaring that he should content himself by remaining neuter, and would not engage either himself or the Roman states in a war which he deprecated. With this unsatisfactory reply the French cardinal was accordingly compelled to quit Rome; nor did he fare better upon his parting interview with Charles V., who affected great moderation and an earnest desire for peace, but who had, in fact, matured his plans, and was about to put them into operation.

In addition to the astrological predictions to which we have already alluded, the emperor had been careful to circulate throughout Germany exaggerated accounts of the cruelties which Francis had committed against the Protestants within his kingdom, already sufficiently atrocious without the aid of fiction; and the detail was rendered the more revolting to his German subjects by the assertion that all the victims were of their own nation; that all Germans were banished from France, and that the French king had entered into a league with the Infidels, by whom he was to be assisted in the invasion of their empire. As the necessity of disabusing the German people soon became fearfully apparent, Francis deputed Guillaume du Bellay Langei to explain to them the fallacy of these mischievous misrepresentations; and that wise and upright minister ultimately succeeded, although not without great difficulty, in convincing them that their credulity had been abused.

Meanwhile, the Cardinal de Lorraine, on his return to France, had an interview with the king on the 17th of May, in which he assured him that there could no longer exist a doubt, from the preparations made by the emperor, that he meditated the invasion not only of Piedmont but even of France itself.

By a singular and unaccountable fatality, Francis, only a short time previously, when he should have become more than ever suspicious of an enemy by whom he had been so frequently deceived,—who had wantonly insulted him in the face of all Europe, and had spent the last few months in the most active preparations for war,—had persisted, in defiance of his counsellors, in disarming his troops in Savoy, as though by such means he could compel a peace; but Montmorency, justly alarmed by an imprudence which he foresaw might involve the safety of the kingdom of France, having earnestly represented the peril of such a measure, the king was at length reluctantly induced to authorize him to direct Brion Chabot, if he desired really to serve his sovereign, to fortify some of the strongest places which he then held, in order that his troops might be secure of a refuge in the event of the emperor's descent upon Piedmont.

Thus forewarned, Chabot lost no time in fortifying Turin, garrisoning Ivrée with a force of two thousand men, and planning a camp on the Po; after which he wrote to entreat Francis not to terminate his negotiation with the emperor for the space of another month, as he should require that time to complete his defensive operations; and the king being anxious to render Charles the aggressor, convinced as he now was that he could no longer avoid a renewal of hostilities, at once acceded to this arrangement; instructing Chabot at the same time to abandon all idea of forming an encampment, and to confine himself to the completion of his fortifications, which were to be further strengthened by an immediate reinforcement of fifteen thousand infantry, and certain squadrons of horse, and brigades of artillery, each under the command of its particular chief, and in readiness to march against the imperialists at an hour's notice.

He also despatched instructions to the governors of Picardy and Champagne to garrison their frontier-fortresses with a force of fourteen thousand men, who were to await within the walls such orders as he might find it expedient hereafter to issue. The defence of Guienne was entrusted to the King of Navarre; that of Dauphiny to M. d'Humieres, a tried and brave general; Barbesieux[1] was sent to Marseilles to protect that city against the anticipated attack of the Genoese admiral, Doria; and Francis himself, once more awakened from his dreams of pleasure and intrigue, repaired in person to Lyons with the main body of his army, to resist the attempt of the emperor to invade Provence, of which he had declared himself the sovereign by virtue of a cession that he affirmed to have been made to him of that province by the Connétable de Bourbon, as well as by other rights which he did not condescend to explain.

[1] Antoine de la Rochefoucauld, Seigneur de Barbesieux, General of the Galleys in 1528, was a descendant of the Langeac branch of that distinguished family. He died in 1537.

Unaware that his descent upon this particular point had been anticipated, Charles V. was prepared for an easy conquest. He had, or feigned to have, emissaries in all the principal cities; and confidently asserted that the consternation of the inhabitants, the weakness of the several garrisons, and the dilapidated condition of the fortifications, rendered his success certain. The precautions which had been hastily but efficiently taken were, however, destined to convince him of his error. The French king, warned by past experience, had left nothing to chance which could be secured by prudence. Marseilles, Arles, Tarascon, and Beaucaire were all strongly defended. The minor cities, which were unprovided with the means of resistance, were swept of their inhabitants; the adjacent country was laid waste; the mills, the grain, and all agrarian edibles which could not be conveyed away were burnt, and all supplies cut off against the arrival of the enemy. An encampment was then formed near Cavaillon, between the Rhone and the Durance, of which the Maréchal de Montmorency took the command, while with the other moiety of his army Francis established his own quarters at Valence; and thus prepared, he awaited the advent of the imperial forces.

CHAPTER III

1536

The emperor besieges Turin—The fortress of Fossano is entrusted by Francis I. to the Marquis de Saluzzo—He impedes the progress of the works—The French officers suspect his good faith—He retires to Raval—He betrays his trust—Antonio da Leyva invests Fossano—The Marquis de Saluzzo is appointed the emperor's lieutenant beyond the Alps—Charles V. invades Provence—M. de Montejan is surprised, and made prisoner by the imperialists—Empty boasting of the emperor—Death of the dauphin by poison—Trial and execution of Montecuculli—Francis accuses the imperialists of instigating the murder—Indignation of Charles V. and his generals—Catherine de' Medici is in her turn accused by Da Leyva—Progress of the imperial army—The emperor enters Aix—Prince Henry joins the French camp—Marseilles successfully resists the imperialists—Francis determines to head the army in person—He is dissuaded by his generals—Doria supplies the emperor's camp—Retreat of Charles V.—The tower of Muy—The imperial forces establish themselves in Savoy—The emperor proceeds to Spain, and is overtaken by a storm—The victor and the vanquished.

THESE measures were by no means premature, as Charles, having engaged to re-establish the Duke of Savoy in his dominions, had already despatched an army under the command of Antonio da Leyva to besiege Turin, while Francis had instructed his generals to abandon all their other conquests in Piedmont, and to confine their operations to ensuring the security of that city and the fortresses of Coni and Fossano, the latter of which places he confided to the keeping of the Marquis de Saluzzo, with strict directions to increase its strength and means of resistance to the utmost extent of his ability.

We have already recorded the meditated treachery of the marquis, who accordingly no sooner found himself in a position to serve his new sovereign than he commenced his operations by impeding the exertions of the engineers, preventing the entrance of provisions and ammunition into the town, and delaying by every subterfuge which he could invent the efforts of the French officers to complete the defence of the place. Suspicions of his good faith, however, were soon entertained; and, alarmed by the hostile demonstrations of those about him, he abruptly withdrew to his estate at Raval, declaring, that as his authority was not recognized, he would not be responsible for the result.

Baffled at Turin, he no sooner found himself beyond the vengeance of the French officers than he wrote to apprize the imperialist general of the unprotected state of Fossano, and to urge him to take possession of the fortress before the enemy had time to strengthen it. Antonio da Leyva did not hesitate for an instant, but availing himself of this unexpected and welcome intelligence, he left a force of ten thousand horse and a few squadrons of cavalry before Turin, under the command of his lieutenant, and marched upon the betrayed city, before which he sat down, in the full conviction that it would become an easy prey.

Ill-supplied and unprepared as they were, however, the garrison defended themselves with great courage and pertinacity; and even when they were compelled to capitulate, from the utter hopelessness of overcoming a force which quadrupled their own, and which was, moreover, well provided both with provisions and artillery, they stipulated that they should hold the fortress for the space of a month longer, at the termination of which time they were to vacate it if they failed to receive succour from without. As he believed all external aid to be impossible at the moment, Da Leyva consented to these terms, and meanwhile attempted the conquest of two other towns in the neighbourhood, but without success; and a few days before that which had been named for the surrender of Fossano, the emperor arrived in person at Savillano, where he accepted the fealty of the Marquis de Saluzzo, and appointed him his lieutenant beyond the Alps.

Then and there it was that Charles V., intoxicated by his late successes, imparted to his generals the design which he had formed of invading Provence; nor would he be turned from his purpose either by their sober arguments or their vehement expostulations. In vain did Antonio da Leyva even kneel at his feet, imploring him not to endanger his military reputation by so dangerous a measure; he remained deaf to every persuasion, and made immediate preparations for carrying his intention into effect. His army consisted of ten thousand horse, and between forty and fifty thousand infantry; a force with which, as we have already stated, he anticipated that he should be enabled without difficulty to possess himself of the whole province, and thus secure ingress to the very heart of the French dominions. He accordingly passed the Var on the 25th of July, and at the head of his troops marched to Saint Laurent, the first town on the French frontier, where he planted his standards and took up his residence for a short time, in order to await the arrival of the fleet under Andrea Doria, which was freighted with ample supplies for the invading army.

After his temporary halt at Saint Laurent, the emperor pursued his march to Provence, and advanced without encountering the slightest opposition until he reached the village of Tourbes, situated between Brignolles and St. Maximin, where he surprised a small force under M. de Montejan[1] and Boisy, the son of the late Admiral Bonnivet, who, being unprepared for his immediate approach, and unable to contend against an enemy so formidable, were, after a bold but ineffectual struggle, during which the whole of their little band, amounting to no more than five hundred men, were cut to pieces, themselves made prisoners by the imperialists. This mischance was rendered the more mortifying from

---

[1] The Maréchal de Montejan was an officer of great courage, but vain and impetuous, and was, in consequence, frequently compared to M. de Lautrec. Having occasion, while acting as the king's lieutenant in Piedmont, to carry on a negotiation with the Marquis del Guasto, he pushed his arrogance so far as to propose that they should treat through the medium of ambassadors, an arrangement which was carried into effect, to the great indignation of Francis I., who reprimanded him severely for assuming the state and privilege of a crowned head; nor, although he availed himself of his courage and experience as a general, did he ever again restore him to favour.

the fact that these two imprudent young nobles, wearied of inaction, had obtained the reluctant consent of Montmorency to indulge that taste for adventure so prevalent at the time, and so destructive of good discipline, and to sally forth in search of adventures, their object being to harass the skirmishing parties of the enemy, and, if possible, to gain the first laurels won during the campaign; and thus, through their own idle folly, they forfeited all future hope of assisting in the war.

The intelligence of their capture was a source of great annoyance to the king, who immediately foresaw that his vainglorious adversary would profit by the circumstance to assert that he had beaten the French on their first encounter; but the event even exceeded his previsions, as Charles, anxious to maintain the *prestige* which had attached to him since his recent triumphs, caused it to be reported throughout Europe that he had slaughtered or driven back the whole vanguard of the French army.

This comparatively unimportant incident was, however, fated to be soon obliterated from the mind of Francis by the deepest calamity which had yet befallen him. The dauphin, after an illness of only four days, had ceased to exist. This prince, then only in his nineteenth year, had already, by the urbanity of his disposition, his literary attainments, and his calm and lofty courage, greatly endeared himself to all by whom he was approached. The only defect which he had inherited from his royal father was an inordinate love of dissipation; and besides his accredited mistress, the beautiful Mademoiselle de Lestrange, he indulged in other intrigues less public. This error was, however, counterbalanced by so many amiable qualities that it did not avail to weaken his popularity, and even Francis himself had begun to express his satisfaction that the Spaniard had at length been converted into a Frenchman. The dauphin had recently joined the army at Lyons, where he had been welcomed with enthusiasm, and the rejoicings consequently on his arrival were not yet over when he was attacked by the illness which terminated his existence.

His death was at first attributed to his imprudence in having, when heated at tennis, drunk a copious draught of water; but he had no sooner expired than symptoms of poison became apparent which awoke the most sinister suspicions. He was, moreover, in the constant habit of drinking water almost to excess, under circumstances which would have rendered such an indulgence fatal to most constitutions; and this propensity was so well known that Donna Anna Beatrix de Pacheco, one of the maids of honour to Queen Eleonora, had presented to him an earthern vase of a peculiar clay, which induced an effervescence in the water without divesting it of its coolness, and which she had brought with her from Portugal.

The unhappy dauphin had, as we have mentioned above, been engaged at tennis; and the weather being sultry, he suffered so severely from the heat that the moment the game was concluded he desired one of his pages to bring him a draught of water. The youth hastened to obey his commands; and as there chanced to be a well in the meadow which had been selected for the sport, he at once lowered the bucket, placing the vase from which the prince constantly drank upon the margin of the well while he drew up the water. The weight causing him to be somewhat tardy in this operation, it was soon remembered that the Comte Sebastian de Montecuculli, a nobleman of Ferrara, who had been appointed sewer in the household of the dauphin, had approached the spot as if with the intention of hastening his movements, but without interfering to assist him; and as no other individual was near the spring at the time, the fatal event which afterwards took place was attributed to his agency by all who were aware of this circumstance.

Having drawn the water, the page without waiting to rinse the vase plunged it into the bucket, and carried it to the prince, who in accordance with his usual habit emptied it at a draught. In a few seconds he complained of giddiness and intense pain; frightful convulsions supervened; nor could all the science of his physicians afford him the slightest relief. It had been previously arranged that he should leave Lyons early on the following morning for Tournon, in order to join the king, who had halted in that city on his way to Valence; nor could the entreaties of his friends dissuade him from persisting in his purpose. The only concession which they could obtain was that he would abandon the idea of pursuing his journey on horseback, and proceed by water; but this exertion, mitigated as it was, probably hastened his death, for he had scarcely reached the presence of his father when he sank exhausted into the arms of his attendants, and in a few hours expired.

During the first paroxysm of his anguish none dared to inform the king of the peculiar symptoms exhibited by the disorder of the prince; but ere long the existence of arsenic, which was discovered in his body, rendered all further prospect of concealment hopeless; still, even when the fact was ascertained beyond all doubt, each of the attendants shrank from revealing the fatal truth. It was soon evident, however, that Francis had himself become suspicious that his son was the victim of an assassin; and the hesitation of the Court physicians was terminated by his vehement questionings; for as during their passage up the Rhone they had strictly watched every phase of the disease, and conferred together upon its nature, they deemed it expedient at length to request the Cardinal de Lorraine to communicate to the king their solemn conviction that the dauphin had died by poison.

At this confirmation of his own misgivings the anguish of the parent yielded to the indignation of the sovereign; and averting his face from the death-bed, Francis sternly commanded all who were present, as they valued their heads, to point out to him the suspected author of the crime. Thus adjured, more than one of the dauphin's attendants were prepared to accuse Montecuculli; and the king had no sooner heard the grounds upon which the accusation was based than he made instant preparations for his return to Lyons.

Montecuculli was immediately arrested, and, under the agony of the question, the wretched man admitted his guilt; but whether from compunction or in order to escape the torments to which he was subjected, it would be now impossible to decide. Thus much is certain, however, that he not only confessed to the murder of the prince, and declared that while the page was drawing up the water he had flung arsenic into the vase, but even added that it was his intention to destroy the king himself and his two remaining sons by the same means.

When questioned as to his motive for committing such deadly crimes, he replied that he had been instigated to them by Antonio da Leyva and Ferdinand de Gonzaga;[1] asserting, moreover, that they had, like himself, acted under superior authority. Although the miserable culprit (if such indeed he were) never once directly accused the emperor by name as the authority to which he alluded, he nevertheless

[1] Ferdinand de Gonzaga was the representative of a noble family of Parma, whose ancestor, Louis I., became, on the death of Passerino Buonacolsi (in the 14th century), Count of Mantua; Jean-François, the great-grandson of Louis, was created Marquis of Mantua in 1503; and finally the marquisate was erected into a duchy for Ferdinand in 1530. This prince commanded the Spanish troops at the siege of Florence; was Colonel-General of the light-horse under the Duc de Bourbon; became Viceroy of Sicily; accompanied the emperor on his invasion of France as his lieutenant-general; and was finally appointed prime-minister to the son of his sovereign in Flanders, whom he served as faithfully as he had previously served his father. He died full of years and honours, with the proud boast of having gained many battles, and never lost a fortress.

left no doubt of his meaning by entering into details which tended to implicate him in the crime. Among other circumstances, he stated that on one occasion, when he had an audience of Charles V., that monarch had expressed considerable curiosity as to the diet of the French king and his habits at table; an assertion which acquired additional importance from the fact that, only a short time previous to the death of the dauphin, Don Lopez de Soria, the imperial ambassador at Venice, had inquired who would become king of France in the event of the demise of the reigning sovereign and his sons.

Francis convened a council, before whom the confession of the culprit was read, and by whom his condemnation was instantly pronounced. He was sentenced to be first scourged, and then torn to pieces by horses.

Thus far, even barbarous as such a sentence undoubtedly was after the fearful tortures which the wretched culprit had already undergone, some excuse may be found for the king in the fact that he had not only been deprived of his first-born son by the most cruel means, but that his own life, and those of the two younger princes, had likewise been menaced —and this, moreover, by an agent of his most hated enemy; but surely nothing can extenuate the fact that, not content with a description of the dying agonies of the victim of his vengeance, he resolved to become a spectator of the hideous scene, and even commanded the attendance of the princes of the blood, the prelates, the foreign ambassadors, and all the men of rank then resident in Lyons. Nay more, if the evidence of Rœderer is to be credited, the Court ladies themselves were not exempted from this revolting spectacle; nor was the vengeance of the king appeased until he had seen the mangled remains of the culprit torn into fragments by the infuriated populace.

At the close of the execution Francis addressed circulars to the· Protestant princes, informing them of all the details of the murder and the fate of the murderer; and in these letters he openly accused the two imperialist generals of having instigated Montecuculli to the commission of the crime for which he had suffered. Charles V. resented, with the deepest indignation, an accusation which he could not but feel was directed against himself, and declared that he would rather have forfeited his empire than have had his name implicated in so heinous and revolting a crime; while Gonzaga and Da Leyva, with still more vehemence, protested that were Montecuculli still alive, they would prove their innocence by meeting him in arms, as they were now willing and anxious to do all those who should dare to affix so foul a stain upon their honour. Nor were they satisfied with mere self-exculpation; for, after demanding to know what benefit could have accrued either to their imperial master or themselves by the extirpation of the royal family of France, they retorted by throwing the guilt of the assassination upon Catherine de' Medici, who, by the death of the elder prince, became dauphiness, and stood upon the very step of the throne.

In ordinary cases such an accusation would have been as incredible as it was monstrous; but her early education, her known subtlety, and her undisguised ambition, rendered the niece of the pontiff, young as she was, so obnoxious to suspicion, that there were not wanting many, even in France, who believed her to be guilty.

Throughout the whole commencement of its march the imperial army had been enabled to subsist upon the hoards made by the inhabitants of the several villages devastated by order of the French marshal, in order to arrest its progress by famine; the unhappy peasantry having hidden away their stores of grain and wine in the caves and forests, in the vain hope of securing them until the contending armies should have vacated their immediate neighbourhood. But these secret depositories, which had escaped the hurried researches of the French troops, owing to their eagerness to lay all waste before the advent of the enemy, did not succeed in eluding the more anxious eyes of the imperialists, who, having once discovered that the agrarian wealth of the province had been rather displaced than destroyed, instituted a perpetual survey, which, as we have stated, rendered them independent of the precautions of Montmorency.

Doria had, moreover, taken possession of the port of Toulon, and had even announced to the emperor the practicability of navigating the Rhone with his galleys, and of assuring to the invading army all the supplies of which it might stand in need. In this endeavour he, however, found himself frustrated; and as the French troops persisted in remaining within their entrenchments, and the *cachettes* of the peasantry became exhausted, Charles no sooner found himself in the plain, surrounded by dismantled cities, abandoned villages, and a devastated country, with the enemy entrenched at Avignon and no chance of supplies save from Toulon (which he was aware must be cut off before they could reach him), than he resolved to avert the famine which stared him in the face by compelling an engagement.

He consequently encamped in the middle of August before Aix, where the increasing necessities of his troops induced him to enter the city, which he did, asserting that, as the suzerain of Arles and Provence, he took possession of the capital by that right. He, however, found only a desert where he had looked to possess himself of a flourishing and wealthy population. Not only the archbishop and his clergy had abandoned the place, but also the judicial officers and the principal inhabitants; and although by virtue of the claim he had advanced he summoned them to return, as they made no response to his citation, he delivered over the town to pillage; and before its final abandonment on the 13th of September issued an order for the destruction by fire of the Palace of Justice, at the request of the Duke of Savoy, who accompanied his army, and who was anxious to revenge the excesses of which the French troops had been guilty in Piedmont.

Baffled in his hopes of establishing his permanent

headquarters at Aix, and of securing by such means the revictualling of his army, Charles discovered that he had no alternative save to possess himself of Arles or Marseilles. The camp of Montmorency was too well defended to encourage an attack; and although the position of Arles was favourable to his enterprise, should the siege prove tardy he was aware that the famine which had already commenced in his ranks must inevitably militate against his success, while, even should he make himself master of the city, he might find it as utterly devastated as Aix; whereas in the event of his taking Marseilles the fleet of Andrea Doria could in a few hours arrive to his relief.

Henri, Duc d'Orléans, now Dauphin of France, had meanwhile joined the French army at Valence, and was no sooner apprized that the emperor had caused his light-horsemen to reconnoitre the camp at Avignon than he earnestly entreated the king to allow him to join the Maréchal de Montmorency, and to share in the honours of the engagement which appeared inevitable. But Francis, who had been so lately bereft of one son, trembled at the prospect of losing a second; and for a considerable time he firmly refused to allow the prince to separate himself from his own person. His importunities were, however, so vehement and so unceasing, that the king at length yielded, only enjoining him with great earnestness to obey under all circumstances the dictates of Montmorency, who would, as he declared, while he guarded the honour of the dauphin as jealously as his own, be even more careful of his safety. Moreover, with a prudence which, in so haughty and despotic a monarch as Francis I., sufficiently revealed his anxiety, he bade the enthusiastic young prince remember that he held no official rank in the army which he was about to join; but that he would be a mere volunteer, who could assume no authority whatever, and who must be contented to obey, in order that he might hereafter be competent to command.

Satisfied with his success, the dauphin promised all that his royal father required; and, attended by several of his personal friends, he at once took leave of the king and proceeded to the camp, where he was received with the same enthusiasm which had only a few weeks previously greeted the appearance of his murdered brother.

As we have shown, however, the emperor abandoned all idea of attacking Montmorency; and the total pillage of a supply which had been landed at Toulon by Doria, and which became the prey of the impoverished peasantry, convinced him that he must at once compel an engagement or abandon his hitherto abortive enterprise.

He first, therefore, proceeded to Marseilles; but after two or three hostile demonstrations, he discovered that all attempts to take the city would prove utterly vain. In addition to a garrison of seven thousand men there were thirteen galleys in the port; while his own troops, famished for want of proper and wholesome nourishment, threw themselves eagerly upon the grapes, and even the immature fruits by which they were surrounded, and soon added to the horrors of famine the sufferings of dysentery. Within one month a third of his army perished, and among the rest his brave and faithful general, Antonio da Leyva; while the forces of the French king were augmented by a reinforcement of twenty thousand Swiss and six thousand Germans.

He was next compelled to abandon the siege of Arles; for although its position, in the midst of heights by which it was commanded, appeared at the first glance to afford great facilities to a besieging army, the emperor soon ascertained that it was not only strongly and efficiently fortified, but that it contained within its walls some of the first chivalry of France.

Nothing was consequently left for Charles save an open battle or a precipitate retreat; while, as no one for a moment suspected that he would adopt the latter alternative, the enthusiasm in all ranks of the French army was excited to the highest pitch; and the king himself, who had hitherto remained at Valence, in compliance with the advice and entreaties of his generals, summoned a council, at which he expressed his determination to join the main body at Avignon, in order to be present at the forthcoming engagement.

In vain did Montmorency, so soon as he was apprized of this resolution, entreat Francis not to expose his person unnecessarily, and implore him not to incur the risk of involving the kingdom in inevitable confusion in the event of his death or capture, while, by remaining at Valence, the result of a victory must be equally honourable to him, without involving the same contingencies. In vain did he represent that the present opportunity was unusually favourable for the first essay in arms of the dauphin, and express his conviction that the young prince, with the assistance of his own experience and that of the principal generals, would win honour to himself and to the French name by convincing the emperor that the subjects of his majesty were invincible upon their own soil,—the resolution of the king remained unshaken.

Equally unavailing were the assurances of the maréchal that the emperor was no longer in a position to maintain his ground, and that, decimated as his camp had become by disease and famine, he must of necessity retreat should their own troops refuse to give him immediate battle. The hour of forbearance was past, and Francis refused to defer to his arguments. Du Bellay added his entreaties to those of Montmorency, but with no better success. Still, however, the maréchal ventured to insist; and he was prompted to this pertinacity by the fact that a superstitious feeling had grown up in the French army that the presence of the king upon any field of battle would inevitably entail defeat — an unfortunate and mortifying belief, which the monarch was naturally anxious to eradicate.

"Enough, my lords, enough," exclaimed Francis impatiently. "On the faith of a gentleman, it shall never be said that while my arch-enemy is at the head of his armies, sword in hand, I am content to remain cooped up within the walls of Valence, as though I feared to beard him on my own territories. No, sirs; harangue as you may, I will go forth to meet him; and perchance the duel of which he hath made such loud bruits throughout all Christendom may chance to be fought when he least expects it. I am well aware that many among you who are endeavouring to dissuade me from what I hold to be a right royal duty are infected by a frivolous superstition, to which, as a Christian king, I cannot yield my faith. My confidence is in GOD: He alone rules the destinies alike of individuals and of armies."

On the following morning Francis, after having attended the early mass, accordingly embarked upon the Rhone, and proceeded to Avignon, having left a strong garrison for the protection of Valence; and despite the disparaging apprehensions of his army he was received with joyous acclamations, and entered the camp with a brilliant staff, escorted by the whole of the gendarmerie, who had hastened to meet him.

At this period Doria had succeeded in landing and forwarding supplies to the emperor, which enabled him to silence the murmurs of his troops, and to inspire them in some degree with renovated hope; but the evil had taken too deep a root; and while the French were hourly expecting the engagement for which they had long panted, Martin du Bellay Langei, who had been sent to reconnoitre the movements of the enemy, returned with the astounding intelligence that the imperialists were in full retreat; and that, in order to facilitate their march, they had abandoned all their sick and wounded.

The accuracy of this statement was soon proved; for, on the entrance of Francis and his troops into the deserted camp, a most frightful spectacle presented itself. Nevertheless, Montmorency refused to pursue the retreating enemy; he dreaded lest the hunted lion should turn to bay, and in the extremity of his despair he should sacrifice himself rather than not wreak his fury upon his enemy. Peronne was, moreover, menaced, and he was compelled to detach a strong force to its assistance. He consequently contented himself, so soon as he had ascertained that the emperor was on his march towards Flanders, by despatching the light-horse under the command of the Comte de Tende,[1] Du Bellay Langei, and Bonnivet, to harass his rear-guard, by which means a great slaughter of the imperialists took place, as the flank squadrons cut off all the foraging parties

---

[1] The Comte de Tende was a gallant soldier, who was Colonel of the Swiss troops in Naples, and subsequently Governor of Provence, where he rendered good service to the king, until he became suspected of Lutheranism, which faith his wife openly professed. The Provençals then rebelled against his authority, and caused him to be replaced by his son, the Comte de Sommerive; declaring that Provence was destroyed by three equal plagues — the winds, the Durance, and the Comtesse de Tende; the first overthrowing everything, the second flooding everything, and the third perverting everything.

that were detached from the main body, sparing neither men nor horses, until the road between Aix and Frejus was strewn with arms and baggage, the wounded and the dead.

This was not the only impediment, however, which the emperor experienced to his retreat; for, as his troops were defiling beneath a tower of the village of Muy, which he had supposed to be abandoned, some peasants who had taken refuge there, upon seeing the splendid train of the Spanish leader Garcilasso de la Vega,[1] the first poet of his day and nation, whom, from the magnificence of his appearance, they mistook for Charles himself, simultaneously fired a volley, by which they mortally wounded De la Vega and killed several of his immediate suite. Enraged by this irreparable loss, the emperor, careless of the danger to which he might be exposed by such a delay, instantly halted his army, stormed the tower, which was unable to withstand so formidable an attack, and having secured the miserable men within, hung them from the portal of the tower, and then pursued his march, leaving this ghastly memorial of his passage as his last legacy of vengeance.

Mortified and disappointed, with a diminished and discontented army and an exhausted exchequer,

[1] Garcilasso de la Vega, otherwise Garcias Lasso, the celebrated Spanish poet, was born at Toledo in 1503. He served in the army of Charles V. as a volunteer, in Germany, Italy, and France, and died of the wound received in the retreat of Frejus, at Nice, in 1536. He was the head of a new school of poetry, and enriched his native language by the introduction of the most elegant of the foreign idioms. He was principally famous, however, for his odes, his eclogues (among which the most popular were *Nemoroso* and *Salicio*), his elegies, his sonnets, and his ballads.

Charles despatched his troops, under the command of the Marquis del Guasto, into the Milanese, where he quartered them in the cities of the Duke of Savoy (who thus, invaded alike by his friends and his enemies, found himself dispossessed of all his territories save the city and fortress of Nice, into which he had retired); and this arrangement effected, he himself proceeded to Genoa, where his galleys were awaiting him, and where he remained for a fortnight before he embarked for Spain. His whole expedition was, however, fated to be unfortunate; for he was no sooner in mid-sea than he was overtaken by so terrific a storm that not only were six of his galleys sunk, but also two larger vessels, one of which was freighted with his plate and the other with his stud.

Never was failure more complete or more disastrous. The loud boastings with which Charles had undertaken his campaign were yet ringing in the ears of all Europe, for only two months had elapsed from the period of his embarkation for France and of his retreat thence as a fugitive who had not even met the enemy whom he went forth to defeat. To Francis his triumph was bloodless, while to the emperor his failure was a blot which could never be effaced. The *prestige* of his military glory was gone; the conqueror of Solyman and Barbarossa was shorn of his laurels; and his keenest pang arose from the consciousness that he had been compelled to fly before the very troops whom he had affected to despise.

CHAPTER IV

1536-38

Consternation of the Italian princes—The siege of Turin is raised—The imperial troops enter Picardy—Heroism of the women of St. Regnier—Capitulation of Guise—The imperialists besiege Peronne—They are repulsed by Fleuranges—Death of Fleuranges—Alarm in Paris—Annebaut and Burie defend Turin—Burie is made captive at Casal—Francis strengthens the frontiers of Provence—James V. of Scotland meets the king at Lyons—James V. is married to the Princesse Marguerite—Jealousy of Henry VIII.—Knight-errantry of James V.—Death of the Princesse Marguerite—James demands the hand of Marie de Guise—Feud between the royal favourites—Virulence of the Duchesse d'Etampes—Disunion in the royal family—Infatuation of Francis I.—Apprehensions of Madame d'Etampes—Her passion for Montmorency—Francis lays claim to Flanders, Artois, and Charlerois—Convocation of the parliament—Charles V. is cited to appear before the French tribunals—The emperor disregards the summons—The French enter Artois—They take Hesdin—The imperialists invest St. Pol—The city is taken by De Buren—De Buren marches upon Térouenne—Annebaut relieves the city—A fatal skirmish—A truce is effected between France, Picardy, and the Low Countries—Francis openly avows his alliance with the Sultan—Solyman enters Albania—Del Guasto successfully pursues the war in Piedmont—M. d'Humieres is appointed to the chief command of the French army in Italy—The Marquis de Saluzzo assists Del Guasto in the siege of Carmagnole—He is killed by a musket ball—Carmagnole surrenders—Cruelty of the imperialist general—The dauphin and Montmorency march to Lyons, and are followed by the king—Del Guasto fortifies the Pas-de-Suze, which is forced by the French—The imperialists raise the siege of Pignerol, and encamp at Montcalier—The dauphin compels them to retreat, and takes the city—Francis resolves to take the field in person—The truce is extended to Piedmont—The Duke of Savoy retires to Nice—Charles V. endeavours to effect a European peace, and offers the hand of his niece to the Duc d'Orleans—Francis objects to the proposed conditions—Montmorency is created connétable—Death of the Chancellor du Bourg.

THE sensation created throughout Italy by the proposed invasion of France had meanwhile been intense. The petty princes of that country, aware that should the emperor be successful the preservation of their independence could only be secured by an universal coalition, made instant preparations for a league; and not daring to declare their purpose openly, entered into secret negotiations to that effect with the more powerful states. The French king, anxious to second their efforts, had appointed as their general the Comte Guy de Rangon, under whose command they placed a force of ten thousand men, with which they attempted to possess themselves of Genoa, but a reinforcement of imperialists which had just reached that city rendered their attack abortive. They next marched upon Ast, when the Spaniards raised the siege of Turin, and allowed them to take Carignano, Raconis, Carmagnoles, and, with slight exceptions, the whole marquisate of Saluzzo.

During the invasion of Provence by the emperor, the Count of Nassau, and Adrian de Croy, Comte de Rœux, had entered Picardy at the head of twenty thousand foot and seven thousand horse; and after laying waste the open country and pillaging all the villages upon their route, had made themselves masters of Bray-sur-Somme and several other places of less importance. Encouraged by this success, they next endeavoured to reduce St. Regnier; but the town being well garrisoned and the walls furnished with artillery, they received a check for which, from the apparent insignificance of the place, they were totally unprepared. They had, moreover, in this attempt, to combat not only the troops but also the citizens, and even the women, who in many instances ascended the ramparts and assisted in repelling the besiegers by pouring hot water and boiling tar upon their heads; while others, with a courage which should have immortalized their memory as heroines, however incompatible it might be with their nature as women, assumed the garb of their husbands, and fought bravely with sword and spear, until they succeeded in wresting two standards from the enemy.

Thence the imperialists had directed their march towards the city of Guise, where the Duc de Vendôme, who despaired of making an effectual resistance, had issued orders to the garrison to shut themselves up in the citadel; they had not time, however, to effect this arrangement before the enemy was upon them, and they were accordingly compelled to capitulate. Nassau then proceeded to attack Peronne, which was even less capable than Guise of sustaining an assault; and so great was the alarm of the inhabitants when they became apprized of the approach of the imperialist army that they resolved to save themselves by flight—a determination which was only abandoned when they were recalled to a more prudent line of conduct by the courageous example of a wealthy landholder in the neighbourhood, M. d'Estourmel, who, instead of flying from the city, caused all his grain and other edibles to be transported within the walls, and himself took up his abode there with his family. The example so boldly given was immediately followed;

and the unexpected appearance of Fleuranges, at the head of a small force, restored them in some degree to confidence. Their means of defence were, however, so scanty, and the operations of the enemy so vigorous, that hope soon began to fail; their ammunition became exhausted, their fortifications were dilapidated, and their provisions were inadequate for the supply of the inhabitants.

The emperor's artillery had told fearfully within the first four and twenty hours, and several large breaches were made in the walls. Nassau, moreover, opened a mine under the old tower of Peronne (an historical pile, famous as the prison of Charles the Simple and Louis XI.), which overthrew it to half its height, and buried in its ruins the Comte de Dammartin, who shared the command of Fleuranges. Notwithstanding this misfortune, however, the gallant little band still held out; and just as they were about to become the prey of the enemy, the Duc de Guise, who had been apprized by Fleuranges of the extremity to which they were reduced, no longer possessing either food or powder, succeeded in supplying them with both, as well as in reinforcing them by four hundred crossbow-men, whom he introduced into the town across the marshes, which, being considered impassable, were less carefully guarded than the other avenues to the city. Although this fact was ascertained too late by the imperialists, they nevertheless continued the siege, and made two or three more assaults upon the outworks; but they were soon compelled to abandon the enterprise, leaving their ladders and a number of their bravest troops in the ditches. On the 10th of September, finding all their efforts to take the place unavailing, while the loss of life became daily greater, they raised the siege, and thus abandoned their enterprize the very day before that on which the emperor had commenced his own retreat from Provence.

The enemy had no sooner withdrawn his forces than Fleuranges hastened to meet the king, who was on his march homeward, and to report the result of his courageous defence. He was not long destined, however, to enjoy the triumph which he had so nobly earned, for only a short time subsequently he received intelligence of the death of his equally brave father at Sedan; and while on his way to pay the last tribute of respect to his remains he fell a victim to a malignant fever, and France was thus deprived of one of her best and noblest soldiers.

When it became known in Paris that Peronne was in a state of siege the alarm was universal, little hope being entertained that the enemy would be arrested in their march towards the capital by a city so ill prepared against aggression; and it was entirely owing to the zealous and judicious exertions of the Cardinal du Bellay, the metropolitan bishop, that confidence was ultimately restored. The king on his departure for the south had, in addition to his ecclesiastical rank, appointed Du Bellay lieutenant-general of the capital; and he had lost no time in conveying all the wheat and wine which could be obtained within a round of six leagues into the storehouses of the city, both of which proved to be so abundant in quantity as to suffice not only for the supply of the whole population during the space of an entire year, but also for that of a garrison of thirty thousand men. The energy of the Parisians on this occasion equalled his own; for they no sooner became convinced of his power as well as of his will to protect them than they volunteered to give him a brigade of artillery and ten thousand troops, to be maintained at their own cost so long as the enemy should occupy the frontier. The gallantry of Fleuranges and his little garrison soon relieved them, however, from their apprehensions, and the fortifications which they were hastily constructing were accordingly abandoned.

Meanwhile the Admiral d'Annebaut[1] and M. de Burie,[2] who commanded at Turin, not only defended

---

[1] M. d'Annebaut was a celebrated general, who made his first campaign under the Maréchal de Montmorency at Mezières, where he acquired a reputation which he never subsequently forfeited. He was Colonel of the Light-Horse under the Comte de Saint-Pol in Italy, and narrowly escaped sharing his captivity when that prince was made prisoner by Antonio da Leyva at Milan. He was afterwards appointed Governor of Turin, and was rewarded for his bravery and judgment while holding that dignity by the vacant *bâton* of the Maréchal de Montejan.

[2] M. de Burie commenced his career as a simple bowman, but soon distinguished himself so much as to attain to high military rank. He was a man of good family, but so poor that the first horse which he was compelled to provide while serving under the Grand-Master of Savoy was presented to him by the Comte de Bordeille, who was aware that he was unable to purchase one. His personal prowess, however, soon enabled him to attain the grade of a colonel of infantry, and he was so accomplished an engineer that he was the rival in that science of Pietro da Navarro, previously considered the first engineer of the age. He next obtained the government of Guienne, where he

that place with the greatest zeal, but harassed the enemy by frequent and daring sallies beyond the walls, continually making prisoners and securing booty. On one of these occasions, however, Burie, whom his previous successes had rendered less cautious than heretofore, was surrounded by the troops of the Marquis del Guasto in Casal, which town he had just taken, and was made prisoner after a vigorous resistance, together with the remnant of his men who survived. M. d'Humieres was forthwith despatched to replace him with a reinforcement of ten thousand lansquenets; and the French king, having thus provided for the safety of Turin, proceeded to Marseilles, where he confirmed the municipal privileges both of that city and of Aix, although he refused to remit the taxes until the devastations to which they had been subjected could be repaired; declaring that however deeply he felt the hardships to which they had been subjected, the outlay necessary for the defence of the kingdom at that period would not permit him to accede to their request. He then strengthened all the frontier fortresses of Provence and Languedoc; and having thus secured the safety of his southern territories, and the season being adverse to all further operations, he once more set forth for the capital.

acquitted himself with so much honour that the king conferred upon him the order of St. Michael. During the intestine commotions which succeeded he was suspected of Lutheranism, from the reluctance which he evinced to put to death such of the reformers as fell into his hands. He died poor, never having enriched himself by the spoils of the provinces over which he had been called to rule, as was too much the fashion of that day.

At Lyons he was met by James V. of Scotland, who, eager to prove his sense of the alliance which had so long existed between his own ancestors and the French sovereigns, and doubtless also anxious to secure the support of Francis against England, had voluntarily embarked with a force of sixteen thousand men to assist him in his campaign. Nor had the Scottish king persisted in his purpose without considerable difficulty, as the fleet which conveyed his little army was three times driven back by adverse winds; but so soon as he was enabled to land at Dieppe with a portion of his troops he had hastened to make his way to the theatre of war, when, as we have already stated, he encountered the king on his return.

Francis was not slow to express his gratitude for so signal an act of friendship and goodwill; and upon his expressing his desire to requite it, James replied by reminding him that he had already led him to hope for the hand of Madame Marguerite, his eldest daughter, and warmly urging him now to fulfil his promise. At such a moment, and under such circumstances, the French monarch did not hesitate, although James was already affianced to a daughter of the Duc de Vendôme; and accordingly the Scottish king accompanied the royal train to the capital as the future son-in-law of the sovereign.

On the 1st of January 1537 the marriage was solemnized with great magnificence at the episcopal palace; and it sufficed to alienate the friendship and confidence of Henry VIII., who looked with extreme jealousy upon this alliance. His own position was at the moment so embarrassing, however, that he contented himself by turning his back upon M. de la Pommeraye,[1] the ambassador who had been sent by Francis to announce it to him; the unfortunate Anne Boleyn having just fallen a victim to his ruthless caprice, while he had already become the husband of Jane Seymour. In obedience to his passions he had alternately persecuted both the Protestants and the Romanists, and was consequently distrusted by both parties; the alliance of James V. with a French princess destroyed, as he was well aware, the balance of the two kingdoms, and rendered his position more onerous than before; nor could he overcome his mortification when he remembered that the hand of his own daughter Mary, whom he had recently bastardized, had been twice offered to the Scottish king— once by the emperor, who had pledged himself that, although thus legally disinherited by her father, she should nevertheless succeed to the throne of England; and on another occasion by himself, as a pledge of alliance between the two countries, on the sole condition that James should, like himself, become the avowed protector of the reformed religion.

The Scottish king, whose Romanist principles were averse to this concession, but who was nevertheless desirous to form an alliance which would enable him to counteract the devices of the enemies by whom he was beset in his own nation, went

---

[1] M. de la Pommeraye was steward of the king's household.

incognito, in the first instance, as some historians assert, to Vendôme, in order to obtain a sight of his affianced bride; and being dissatisfied upon finding that she was less attractive than he had been led to suppose, departed as secretly as he had gone, and at once resolved to demand the hand of the Princesse Marguerite, then in her seventeenth year.

The fair and delicate character of her beauty at once fascinated James, and the languor which incipient consumption had already cast over her person added, in his romantic eyes, to the charms of her appearance. It would seem, moreover, according to Buchanan, that the attraction was mutual, and that Marguerite bestowed not only her hand but also her heart upon her enamoured suitor—a most uncommon case in royal marriages.

Whether James in reality played the knight-errant as thus represented must for ever remain doubtful. Thus much, however, is certain, that, after passing three or four months of constant festivity at the French Court, he finally departed with his bride for Scotland, where they landed on the 28th of May; and that on the 7th of the July ensuing, the young queen, unable to withstand the fluctuations of a climate to which she was unaccustomed, fell a victim to the insidious disease under which she had long laboured. Her amiability had already, however, endeared her alike to the Court and to the people, who mourned her loss as that of one who would not easily be replaced; although her excessive attachment to her aunt, the Queen of

Navarre, had alarmed the priesthood, who dreaded her influence over the mind of the king, and who consequently urged James to take another wife at the termination of his mourning.

To the surprise of all who had witnessed his excessive affection for his young bride, the widowed monarch at once consented to comply with their advice; and, at the expiration of that period, despatched ambassadors to France to solicit the hand of Marie de Guise, the widow of the Duc de Longueville, with whom he had made acquaintance at the French Court.

It is probable that Francis, the father of the deceased queen, regarded the demand as somewhat premature; for although from considerations of policy it was conceded, Marie de Guise did not reach Scotland until the 14th of June in the ensuing year, when her nuptials with the Scottish king were immediately solemnized.

During the festivities consequent upon the marriage of the Princesse Marguerite, the Court of France was, to all appearance, entirely occupied by gaiety and splendour; but such was far from being in reality the case. The death of the elder prince, and the consequent succession of Henry his brother to the rank of Dauphin of France, had effected so great a change in the position of the two royal favourites, that the schism to which we have already made allusion became every day more apparent and more alarming. The separate factions had, in fact, virtually declared themselves, and they were so nicely balanced that none could decide upon the ultimate triumph of either. At the head of one of these parties were the Duchesse d'Etampes, Charles, now Duc d'Orleans, and Brion de Chabot; at that of the other Diane de Poitiers, the Dauphin, and the Connétable de Montmorency; while Catherine de' Medici, with a dissimulation as profound as it was politic, remained resolutely neutral, affecting the greatest regard for both the ambitious rivals, and even honouring Madame de Brézé, who had for ever alienated from her the affection of her husband, injured her interests and wounded her vanity, with a display of confidence and attachment wholly incompatible with their relative position. Although perpetually urged by both parties to declare her real sentiments, the wily Italian resolutely refused to side with either. Like Louise de Savoie, she was content to "bide her time;" and for twenty long and weary years she so far controlled herself as never to remove the mask which she had assumed towards the mistress of her husband.

The rivalry of the favourites was productive, meanwhile, of the most disastrous results to the kingdom; and its first fruits were to promote disunion in the family of the king, who, influenced by the representations and prejudices of the unscrupulous Duchesse d'Etampes, soon began to treat the dauphin with a marked coldness, which contrasted painfully with the favour and indulgence which he evinced towards the younger prince; and a feeling of jealousy and distrust consequently sprang up between the two brothers, which threatened to overwhelm France with anarchy and confusion. The birth of a daughter had rendered Diane more than ever dear to the dauphin; and, secure of his affection, she ceased to conceal the hatred which she had long harboured against Madame d'Etampes, and repaid in kind every affront to which she was subjected by the arrogant favourite.

In the magnificence of her establishment the Grande Sénéchale was already enabled to vie with the duchess, and she did so with an ostentation as insolent as it was reckless; but meanwhile her rival, aware that the health of the king was rapidly failing, exerted all her energies to undermine the interests of the dauphin, through whose disgrace alone she could hope to ruin the prospects of Diane,—prospects which were, moreover, based upon her own overthrow,—and at the same time to enrich herself.

How completely she succeeded in the latter attempt the public treasury bore only too ample testimony. Splendid residences in the capital and estates and châteaux in the country passed rapidly into her possession, and even while Francis was engaged in new intrigues she had become so necessary to his home-happiness that all her wishes remained, as before, a law to the infatuated monarch. So jealous, indeed, did he prove himself of securing her society by every possible method that, on discovering the preference she evinced for a stately hôtel which he had presented to her in the Rue de l'Hirondelle, he caused a small palace to be built at the angle of that street, where it is connected with the Rue Gît-le-Cœur, which, communicating with her residence, he fitted up in the most costly manner. The frescoed walls, the pictures, the groups of statuary, the tapestried hangings, and all the embellishments of the apartments, were made subservient to the display of a passion which was dishonourable alike to both parties; the gilded cornices were ornamented with carvings, in which a heart, whence flame was issuing, was placed between the words *alpha* and *omega;* while the salamander, the device of the king, surmounted the large mirrors and held back the draperies that veiled the windows.

And amid all this magnificence, guilty and heart-sick, she saw the health of the king gradually declining, and was aware that on his demise Madame de Brézé would dispossess her of all her ill-acquired influence. For Francis, as an individual, it was evident that she felt no affection, while even her gratitude for the benefits which he had so profusely showered upon her was extremely questionable. To the most inordinate personal vanity she had ever been so notoriously a victim that she considered him as still her debtor; nor did the slavish adulations of the courtiers, who saw in her only the favourite of the monarch, tend to weaken her self-appreciation. Powerful by her attractions, her riches, and her position, she found herself perpetually surrounded by homage; and the terror with which she contemplated the probable loss of these advantages deprived her of all peace. Nor did she escape other and keener feelings of mortification and disappointment. The only noble of high rank at Court who had remained totally insensible to her fascinations was Montmorency, who, between his chivalric adoration of the queen and a violent passion for Madame de Brézé, had coldly withstood all her blandishments, and at length so piqued her vanity that even her callous heart had yielded itself, although unsought, while the constant terror which she felt lest her more ignoble intrigues might become known to the king, kept her in a perpetual state of unrest.

Fortunately, however, for the frail favourite, the recent successes of Francis, and his desire to increase their effect by still further humiliating the pride of the emperor, sufficed to distract his attention from her disgraceful irregularities. After having secured the safety of Picardy, he determined to reclaim the counties of Flanders, Artois, and Charlerois, which, although they formed a portion of the patrimonial estates of Charles, had been held alike by himself and his ancestors as fiefs of the French Crown. This proceeding, which was in point of fact utterly futile, was rather intended by Francis to mark his contempt for the power of the emperor than to aggrandize his own; but having once resolved upon the measure, it was not long ere his counsellors furnished him with a sufficient pretext for its enforcement, which was supplied by the assertion that, from his having declared war against France without any provocation, Charles had violated the treaty of Cambray, and thereby annulled the cessions made by France in that negotiation ; among the rest, the homage and cognizance of the counties of Artois and Flanders, by which he was, as his predecessors had previously been, the vassal of the Crown.

In order to issue an official edict to this effect Francis assembled the parliament, and proceeded to hold a bed of justice, surrounded by the princes of the blood, the King of Navarre, the peers, and between forty and fifty bishops; and at which Jacques Cappel, the king's advocate, read upon his knees a long statement previously prepared by the chancellor, wherein the emperor was merely styled Charles of Austria. In this document, with a sophistry as shallow as it was high-sounding, he attempted to prove that the emperor was a feudatory of the French king for the three counties in question, while he had, nevertheless, frequently taken up arms against his suzerain—an act of rebellion which, as it set forth, justified the reclamation of these fiefs, and their consequent confiscation to the Crown. No allusion was made to the treaty of Madrid, by which Francis had relinquished his title to the sovereignty he now asserted, and no discussion was permitted by the chambers ; but so soon as the speech was terminated the chancellor collected the votes of the assembly, commencing with those of the dauphin and the other princes of the blood, and concluding with those of the parliament themselves, after which it was decreed that heralds should be sent to the frontiers of the Low Countries to summon the emperor to appear in person, or by deputy, to answer within a given time to the charges brought against him.

To this citation. Charles V., as a natural consequence, vouchsafed no attention; and the parliament accordingly decreed the forfeiture of the three counties to the French Crown—an empty act of bombast, which only tended to degrade the judicial authority of the country without affecting the tenure of the emperor, who continued to hold the reclaimed counties as though no such edict had ever been promulgated. Exasperated by the silent contempt of his adversary, Francis resolved to enforce his self-constituted claim; and towards the end of March he entered Artois with a force of twenty-six thousand infantry and a few squadrons of cavalry, and took the city of Hesdin by siege, after which he attacked the castle, a post of considerable importance as a frontier-fortress. This success, however, was dearly bought, as it cost him the lives of Antoine de Mailli and Charles de Beuil, the young Comte de Sancerre, as well as those of many other brave men. Saint-Pol, Saint-Venant, Lillers, and several other towns of less strength fell successively into his hands; after which he placed a portion of his troops in cantonment upon the frontier, establishing his headquarters at Pernes, and then marched the remainder into Piedmont, where the enemy were collecting a large force.

The latter division was, however, soon recalled, intelligence having reached the French lines that d'Egmont, Comte de Buren,[1] the lieutenant-general

[1] Maximilian d'Egmont, Comte de Buren, was a descendant of

of the emperor, had already invested Saint-Pol. As this city was of the greatest importance to Francis, he had no sooner entered the gates than he issued stringent orders for its immediate and efficient defence, but before his commands could be obeyed the imperialists appeared before the walls. The engineer to whom the king on his departure for Saint-Venant had entrusted the reparation of the fortifications had assured him that they should be completed within the space of three weeks; but before the expiration of that time, and while they were still in an unfinished state, they were, as we have said, assaulted by the enemy. The garrison was, however, strong; and many able officers were assembled within the walls, under the command of Jean d'Estouteville, Seigneur de Villebon,[1] who had been appointed governor of the city; and thus, while the pioneers continued their labours under the very fire of the imperialists, the attack was met by the troops with such tenacious courage that they were enabled to hold out until the 15th of the month, when Buren took the place by assault, and slaughtered the whole of the inhabitants, as well as the greater portion of the garrison. Many of the bravest of the French officers shared the fate of their followers; and Martin

the Ducs de Gueldre, Knight of the Golden Fleece, and General of the armies of Charles V. At the head of 30,000 infantry and 8000 horse he retook the city of Saint-Pol from the French, and subsequently burnt it. He died at Brussels in 1548.

[1] Jean d'Estouteville, Seigneur de Villebon, was descended from an ancient and illustrious family of Normandy, and counted among his other distinguished ancestors the celebrated Guillaume d'Estouteville, Archbishop of Rouen, famous for his diplomatic services under Charles VII. and Louis XI. The family became extinct in 1566.

du Bellay was only saved by being dragged from under a heap of dead by a German officer, whose prisoner he became, together with M. de Villebon. The two nobles were forthwith conveyed to Gravelines, where the ransom of the former was fixed at three thousand crowns, and that of the latter at ten thousand, which, having been immediately paid, they were permitted to return to France.

This intelligence reached the dauphin and Montmorency as they were on their march to relieve the city; and although their assistance came too late to save Saint-Pol, they continued to advance rapidly, in order to reinforce the other frontier towns in the event of their being attacked; while the Comte de Buren, finding his position untenable from the near neighbourhood of so large an army as that which was approaching, set fire to the city and razed the citadel; he then abandoned his fruitless conquest, and marched upon Térouenne, where his appearance would have excited no alarm had not a scarcity of powder rendered the garrison unable to protect their ramparts.

The great importance of this place determined the dauphin and the Maréchal de Montmorency, who were assembling their army at Amiens, to attempt its relief; and d'Annebaut was entrusted with the perilous duty of introducing the necessary ammunition within the walls. He accordingly placed himself at the head of a corps of gendarmerie, a regiment of light-horse, and four hundred harquebusiers, each of whom bore at his saddle-bow a bag of powder;

and his arrangements were so skilfully carried out that, under cover of the darkness, the whole supply reached the beleaguered garrison in safety; but just as he had commenced his retreat with the same caution as he had evinced on his approach, he was startled by the sound of musketry, and discovered that a party of the young nobles who were serving with the army as volunteers had, without his knowledge, joined the expedition, and thus imprudently given the alarm to the enemy's camp.

He immediately sent an order that they should retire on the instant, and waited for some time to enable them to rejoin him; but as the morning was just breaking, and Buren had kept his cavalry on the alert throughout the night, that wary general was not only enabled to charge those who had lingered behind, but also to take possession of a bridge across which the whole of the French force must necessarily pass in their retreat. Annebaut thus found himself opposed to a strong body of cavalry, which he was enabled for a time to repulse; but the imperialists having scattered themselves on all sides, he was ultimately surrounded, his horse was shot under him, and he was taken prisoner together with Piennes,[1] d'O,[2] Sansac,[3] the

---

[1] The Seigneur de Piennes was the representative of a noble and ancient family, and was one of the favourites of Francis I. He was present at Fornoue and at the Battle of the Spurs, and was ultimately appointed Governor of Picardy.

[2] The Comte d'O, Seigneur de Gresner, was descended from an illustrious Norman family, which became extinct in 1734.

[3] Louis Revot, Baron de Sansac, was of a noble house of Angoumois; he was page to the Maréchal de Montmorency, and com-

Marquis de Villars,[1] and several other men of high rank.

Nevertheless, the city had received the necessary supplies, and although by an act of the most reckless imprudence the French had sustained an irreparable loss, the temporary safety of the place was secured. But the dauphin, who had lost several of his personal friends in the skirmish, at once resolved, with the sanction of Montmorency, to compel Buren, who was still besieging Térouenne with a pertinacity which threatened its ultimate destruction, to a general engagement. On the very eve of his contemplated attack, however, a herald despatched by Mary, the Dowager-Queen of Hungary and Gouvernante of the Low Countries, reached his camp, with the intelligence that the emperor had proposed a truce to which the French king had acceded, and that the negotiation was entrusted to herself. All hostilities were consequently to terminate on the frontier,

menced his career in arms under Bonnivet. After the battle of Pavia, where he was made prisoner, he succeeded in effecting his escape and in returning to France, whence he was several times despatched by Louise de Savoie to Madrid with confidential messages to her son during his captivity. He acquired great renown by his conduct at Mirandola in 1554, where he compelled the enemy to raise the siege. He was the first equestrian of his time, and instructed Francis in the noble science of equitation. He subsequently became governor of the sons of Henry II., and died in 1570.

[1] The Marquis de Villars was the son of Réné, the Bastard of Savoy, and Grand-Master of France, and brother of the Comte de Tende. He was a brave and experienced soldier, but was unfortunate enough to be made prisoner, not only at Térouenne, but subsequently also at the battle of St. Quentin, where he was, moreover, severely wounded. Having been appointed to the government of Guienne, he established at Bordeaux a society for the suppression of the Protestants.

and M. de Buren had already received orders to discontinue the siege of Térouenne. Commissioners were appointed on both sides, who met at the village of Bommy; and on the 30th of July a suspension of the war in Picardy and the Low Countries was concluded for the space of ten months.

Francis had at this period entered into an open alliance with Solyman, by which he had excited the indignation of all the Christian princes; and when, according to the conditions of the truce, he withdrew his army from the Low Countries while Buren raised the siege of Térouenne, it was suspected that he contemplated entering Italy, in accordance with the treaty that he had signed with the Turks, who were at the same time to make a descent upon Naples. The Sultan had, in fact, already marched a hundred thousand men into Albania upon the faith of this treaty, and was daily awaiting there the appearance of his ally, when he ascertained that he was engaged in a war with Flanders, upon which he withdrew his own army and abandoned the enterprise.

In Piedmont the affairs of France were progressing even less satisfactorily, the Italian officers having quarrelled among themselves, the lansquenets mutinied, and the French troops deserted in great numbers; while the Marquis del Guasto, profiting by the anarchy of the enemy, was strengthening the cause of the emperor by overrunning the marquisate of Saluzzo.

In this extremity Francis appointed M. d'Humieres to the chief command of his Italian army, and directed Du Bellay Langei, upon whose zeal and discretion he was aware that he could rely with safety, to effect a reconciliation between the contending parties. This, however, proved to be impossible, as the virulence of Italian hate was proof against the cool and dispassionate arguments of the royal envoy, who consequently urged the king to lose no time in despatching a strong force to Piedmont if he wished to retain his possessions in that country. With this advice, judicious as it was, Francis could not at the moment comply; and the French troops, unable to cope with the superior force of their adversaries, were gradually driven from their fortresses until they retained only that of Carmagnole, which was in its turn besieged by the imperialist general.

The Marquis de Saluzzo, whose treason towards Francis we have already recorded, and who was conversant with the weak points of the citadel, undertook the command of the artillery, and, in his eagerness to drive the French from his territories, even worked one of the guns with his own hands. Having blown up a couple of houses in order to cover his position, he fired two successive volleys against the city, and was in the act of directing a third when he was shot dead by a musket-ball. The Marquis del Guasto, who feared that the fall of the marquis might discourage his troops, hastily threw a cloak over the body, and once more summoned the besieged to surrender, promising not only to spare their lives, but to allow them to depart unmolested. The garrison, which consisted only of two hundred men, who had resisted while a hope remained of their ultimate success, were compelled to accede to the offered terms; upon which the gates were thrown open, and the marquis entered the town, warmly expressing his admiration of the courage with which it had been defended, and desiring that the individual might be pointed out to him who had been on duty at a particular window of the fortress. The soldier who had occupied the post indicated, unsuspicious of the motive of this inquiry, and moreover unconscious that he had shot Saluzzo, immediately stepped forward, when del Guasto caused him to be seized and hanged from the same spot.

On the 8th of June M. d'Humieres reached Pignerol, where he established his headquarters, and reiterated the demand of Du Bellay for a reinforcement of troops, when, in reply to his requisition, the king sent him an assurance that he would himself join him during the month of October with a large force; and meanwhile the dauphin and Montmorency proceeded to Lyons, at the head of a small body of men, to join a levy of fifteen thousand Swiss, who were appointed to meet them in that city for the purpose of continuing the operations in Italy.

In order to secure the safety of the kingdom during his absence, Francis appointed Charles, Duc d'Orleans, his second son, lieutenant-general in

Picardy, Normandy, the Isle of France, and Paris, and attached Martin du Bellay to his person as his chief councillor. Burgundy and Champagne were entrusted to the Duc de Guise; the King of Navarre was declared Governor of Guienne, Languedoc, and Châteaubriand in Brittany; and these arrangements completed, on the 6th of October Francis, in accordance with his promise, arrived in his turn at Lyons, with a strong and efficient army, well prepared to resume the campaign.

His approach was no sooner communicated to the Marquis del Guasto than that general proceeded to lay waste the whole of the country through which the French troops must pass, and transported all the provisions and forage which could be accumulated into the different fortresses of which he had possessed himself; while at the same time he detached Cesare da Napoli with a force of ten thousand men to guard the Pas-de-Suze, by which pass he anticipated that the enemy would attempt to enter Italy. Upon the entrenchments which were hastily thrown up at this point (already a formidable obstacle in itself to the passage of a strong army), the devastation of the lower lands, and the near approach of the winter season, Del Guasto confidently trusted for the defence of Piedmont; but as this design could not be concealed from the French scouts, Francis no sooner ascertained his intention than he hastened to provide for the victualling of his troops, and impressed a large number of horses, which he laded with the produce

FRANCIS THE FIRST

of the adjacent provinces, for the supply of the camp.

As, however, the greatest difficulty against which the army had to contend was the passage of the Suze, he at once issued orders for the march of his vanguard under the dauphin and Montmorency, who, on arriving at the entrance of the pass, found the imperialists already awaiting them behind their entrenchments. As the maréchal instantly perceived that it would be vain to attack them in front, it was decided that a portion of the troops should endeavour to ascend the two precipitous heights, hitherto considered to be inaccessible, which shut in and commanded the defile.

Notwithstanding the extreme difficulty and danger of such an enterprise, it was successfully accomplished during the night, and with so much caution that Cesare da Napoli never once had cause to suspect that his position was hopelessly forced, nor was it until dawn that he became aware of the perilous emergency in which he was placed. But when, as morning broke, the imperialists found themselves exposed to a heavy fire of musketry from the rocks, against which they could neither shelter nor defend themselves, while their entrenchments were vigorously assailed in front by the main body of the troops under the dauphin and the maréchal, they were not long ere they discovered that the post which they had hitherto believed to be impregnable was not even tenable; and, accordingly, they fled in such haste and confusion that they abandoned not only their baggage but also the store of provisions which they had housed in the town of Suze. Montmorency at once hastened to possess himself of the important pass thus abruptly deserted; and having strongly garrisoned both the town and the fortress, descended into the valley to await the arrival of the king and the main body of the army.

Del Guasto was no sooner apprized that the French had made themselves masters of the pass than he raised the siege of Pignerol, which, but for this fortunate occurrence, would have been shortly compelled to surrender from famine; and immediately marched his army towards Turin, with the intention of taking that city while the enemy were engaged in securing their new conquest. Montmorency had, however, foreseen this contingency, and willingly yielded to the solicitations of the dauphin, who pursued the imperialist general so vigorously that he compelled him to pass the Po, and to encamp at Montcalier. As the prince subsequently, however, relaxed in his march in order to possess himself of some small fortresses in the neighbourhood, as well as to relieve Turin, where the garrison were exposed to such severe privation that they had been reduced to subsist on horses, rats, and even food of a still more revolting description, the marquis resolved to recross the river and entrench himself at the entrance of the bridge; but the dauphin no sooner became aware of this movement than he pressed forward, in the hope of forcing him to an engagement. In this expectation he was, however, disappointed, as Del Guasto immediately returned to his camp, and finally took shelter under the guns of Ast; while, on his reaching Montcalier, the prince found himself in possession not only of the town but also of an enormous mass of grain, which sufficed for the support of the garrison of Turin throughout the entire year.

The French troops having strengthened the town, where they found the inhabitants zealous in seconding their measures, next encamped at Villedestellon, near Guiers, which was strongly garrisoned by the enemy. Constant skirmishes consequently took place, and Montmorency had determined at once to commence the siege, when his operations were suddenly arrested by a courier from the king, who conveyed to the maréchal his express commands that he should not enter into any further hostilities until he was himself at the head of his army.

The mortification alike of the dauphin and his general exceeded all bounds when this order reached them, but they were compelled to obey. Francis, still untaught by experience, was jealous of the successes of his own son; and he was, moreover, apprehensive that his enemies might attribute his diligence in overrunning Piedmont to his desire of forming a coalition with Solyman, which would have ensured the destruction of Italy and rendered his name odious to all Christendom, it being matter of notoriety that the Sultan was at that moment engaged in the formation of a more formidable army than any with which he had previously menaced Europe, and that his fleet was already prepared for their conveyance to the Italian shores. Under these circumstances, therefore, the French king preferred the alternative of terminating the war by a negotiation; and alleging the pledge which he had given to the Queen of Hungary, he not only renewed the truce already accorded to the Low Countries for three additional months, but, at the solicitation of the Pope and the Venetians, extended it to Piedmont.

The document authorizing this prolonged cessation of hostilities was signed on the 16th of November, in the presence of the king himself, with orders that it should be published on the 27th of the same month, and that immediately after its promulgation the two armies should be simultaneously disbanded. The arrangement was favourable to the interests of both monarchs, as it was decreed that each should retain the territory of which he had possessed himself during the campaign, with liberty to garrison the fortresses and strengthen the cities; its only victim was the unfortunate Duke of Savoy, whose interests were thus sacrificed by both monarchs, and who saw himself despoiled of all his ducal inheritance save the city and citadel of Nice.

The truce was no sooner officially concluded than Francis, having disbanded the costly army which he had experienced so much difficulty in raising, repassed the Alps, and established himself at Montpellier, having appointed M. de Montejan his lieutenant-general in Piedmont, and bestowed upon Guillaume du Bellay the governorship of Turin. He then despatched the Cardinal de Lorraine and the Maréchal de Montmorency to Leucate, to meet the imperial envoys who were authorized on the part of the emperor to enter into negotiations for effecting a permanent peace between the two hostile sovereigns.

The proposals that were transmitted by Charles were no longer couched in the arrogant terms which he had formerly adopted. He offered to bestow the hand of his niece, the elder daughter of the King of the Romans, with the duchy of Milan as her dowry, upon Charles, Duc d'Orleans, on condition that the French king would confirm the treaties of Cambray and Madrid, restore Hesdin and the territories of the Duke of Savoy, co-operate with himself in effecting the entire pacification of Europe, and consent that the Duc d'Orleans should reside at the imperial Court for three years after his marriage ; or, failing this concession, that he should retain the fortresses of Milan in his own possession during the same period.

Although, in order to second the emperor in the re-establishment of a general peace, Francis was required not only to join in a league against the Turks, but also to abandon the German Protestants, he raised no objection to this clause of the treaty. He had already proved that, in order to ensure his own interests, he could desert those of his allies with out compunction; and at this particular period nothing could be more desirable to him than a cessation of hostilities; but the demand respecting the sojourn of his son in Spain, or his cession of the Milanese cities, appeared to imply some covert design on the part of Charles to which he at once demurred. On the 10th of January 1538 he accordingly replied to the effect that he held his claim to the duchy to be indefeasible, although he was willing to receive it as the dowry of the emperor's niece, and to effect a marriage between her and his son; but that he considered it only just that he should either retain his fortresses, or receive those of Milan simultaneously with their evacuation.

As neither power appeared disposed to yield this point, the ministers on both sides agreed to prolong the truce until the 1st of June; and at the close of the congress the French ambassadors hastened to rejoin Francis at Moulins, where he was awaiting the result of the negotiation, in order to acquaint him with the obstacles which opposed themselves to the project of peace that had been mooted by the emperor.

At this period the favour of Montmorency had reached its culminating point. He was, as we have shown, already a marshal and grand-master of France; but there was still a higher dignity to be attained, and it was precisely at Moulins, the capital of Bourbon's appanage,—at Moulins, where the king had once condescended to visit the rebel duke, on what was affirmed to be a bed of sickness,—that he conferred the sword of connétable (which had remained unappropriated since the defection of that prince) upon Montmorency as a reward for the valuable services which he had rendered to France during the war in Italy, while at the same time he confided to him the absolute disposal of his finances. The ceremony took place on the 10th of February, with extreme magnificence, in the presence of the princes and all the great nobles of the state; and when the new connétable had been duly invested with the insignia of his exalted office, the *bâton* of maréchal, vacant by his promotion, was bestowed upon the Admiral d'Annebaut; and that of Fleuranges, who had fallen at Peronne, upon M. de Montejan.

In the spring of this year the Chancellor Antoine du Bourg, who was following in the train of the king on his return to Lyons, was thrown from his mule, and, owing to the density of the crowd, was so severely trampled upon by the horses of the royal retinue that he expired before he could be removed from the spot. He was succeeded in his office by Guillaume Poyet, the president of the parliament, who had rendered himself conspicuous from the part which he had taken in the process sustained by Louise de Savoie against the Duc de Bourbon.

CHAPTER V

1538

Paul III. endeavours to effect a reconciliation between the emperor and the French king—A meeting of the three potentates is proposed at Nice—Alarm of the Duke of Savoy—He appeals to the emperor—His envoy is coldly received—The populace of Nice close their gates against the Pope—Peril of Queen Eleonora—The Pope mediates between the two sovereigns—The truce is renewed for a period of ten years—The three potentates separate—Declaration of the Duke of Savoy—The emperor despatches an ambassador to Francis—The two sovereigns meet at Aigues-Mortes—La Belle Feronnière—Illness of the French king—Increasing power of Montmorency—Revolt of Ghent—Charles V. obtains permission to traverse the French territories—Madame d'Etampes and the connétable—A Court intrigue—A Court buffoon—The enamelled chain—Montmorency loses the favour of the king.

THE menacing position assumed by the Sultan, and the consequent jeopardy of the Italian states, had excited the apprehensions of Paul III., who, aware that he could effect nothing so long as the emperor and the French king remained at enmity, took advantage of the momentary pause afforded by the truce to attempt their reconciliation. In order to accomplish this object he despatched a legate to each sovereign, through whom he entreated them to meet at some convenient spot on the frontiers of Provence; volunteering, should they accede to his request, despite his great age (for he had already attained his seventy-fifth year), to join them there, and to act as a mediator between them. In conclusion, he proposed Nice as an eligible place for the conference—a suggestion which filled the Duke of Savoy with consternation, that city being the sole portion of his duchy which still remained to him.

Such a proposal, coming as it did not only from the head of the Church, but also from an aged man whose infirmities rendered so long a journey a fatiguing and even dangerous undertaking, admitted of no hesitation on the part of either monarch; although the French king, after he had declared his readiness to meet his holiness whensoever and wheresoever he should see fit to appoint, hesitated to fulfil his promise when he was apprized that the pontiff hoped, during his interview with the emperor, to obtain the imperial consent to a marriage between his nephew, Ottavio Farnese, the elder son of the Duke of Parma, and Margaret of Austria, the natural daughter of Charles, whose husband, Alessandro de' Medici, had been assassinated during the previous year. The French ambassador at the papal Court and the Cardinal de Macon having ventured to hint to his holiness that this project was displeasing to their sovereign, Paul III. answered with considerable asperity; and then, after a moment's reflection, he inquired, with a slight shade of sarcasm, if it were forbidden for a pope to ally his family with that of a sovereign prince, adding that the King of France might, should he so will it, confer the same honour upon the house of Farnese as the emperor by admitting one of its members into his own.

Meanwhile the Duke of Savoy, who, as we have

already shown, began to apprehend that he should lose the last remnant of his territories if he permitted the conference of the three potentates to be held at Nice, despatched an envoy to Charles V. to entreat that he would not compel him to resign his citadel to the Pope; and while awaiting his reply, he declared to a chamberlain whom the pontiff had sent to make the request that he could not take so important a step without the consent of the emperor. The messenger met Charles at Villa Franca, where he communicated the request of his master; but in answer to the entreaties of the duke the emperor coldly remarked that he would advise M. de Savoie to comply with the request of his holiness without further delay.

Before this mortifying intelligence was made known to him, the duke received a visit from the Viscount de Martigues and the Bishop of Lausanne, who strongly urged him to refuse the use of the citadel to the Pope, and assured him on the part of the Connétable de Montmorency that in the event of his desiring to form a closer alliance with France, either in his own person or that of his son, the Prince of Piedmont, the king would readily consent to his wishes. The duke, however, had long learnt to mistrust the promises of his selfish allies, and he accordingly answered without hesitation that he was grateful for the honour which was proposed to him, but that having so recently lost his wife, he had no intention of contracting a second marriage, while his son was too young to avail himself of the proffered privilege; but that if, instead of so high an alliance, his majesty would graciously reinstate him in his possessions, he should consider himself his debtor to the last hour of his life.

Finding from the reply of the emperor that he had no other resource, the duke, who was still as unwilling as before to admit the two belligerent sovereigns within his last stronghold, and who was, at the same time, too timid openly to oppose his imperial master, determined to have recourse to the citizens, to whom he represented the inevitable consequences of introducing a foreign garrison into the citadel; and, as he had anticipated, his arguments were so ably seconded by their own fears, that when the officers of the Pope's household arrived to prepare the apartments allotted to him for his reception, all the population rose *en masse*, declaring that the entrance of foreign troops into their city was an infringement upon their privileges to which they would never consent; and having announced this determination, they proceeded without further delay to close their gates. The Pope, who soon after reached Nice, was accordingly compelled to take up his residence at the monastery of San Francisco in the suburbs; while the emperor cast anchor at Villa Franca, a little port in the states of Monaco, where he remained on board his galley; and Francis, accompanied by Queen Eleonora, the Queen of Navarre, the dauphiness, and his two sons, established himself at Villa Nuova, about two miles distant.

Before the conference was opened the French queen proceeded to Villa Franca by sea to visit her brother, who had caused a wooden pier to be constructed for her accommodation from the point at which she must cast anchor to the port; and as she left her galley he advanced along this pier to receive and conduct her on shore, when the frail fabric gave way beneath their weight, and they were both precipitated into the sea, with several of their attendants. Fortunately, prompt assistance being at hand, the whole party were quickly rescued from their perilous situation.

Although the two sovereigns had thus become close neighbours, the Pope could not prevail upon them to consent to a personal interview, and he consequently expressed his willingness to negotiate between them. A marquee was accordingly pitched in the court of the convent, in which he twice received the emperor, and subsequently the French king and his sons; while the royal ladies by whom Francis was accompanied in their turn made visits both to Charles and the pontiff.

During these interviews Paul III. endeavoured by every argument in his power to reconcile the jarring interests of the two jealous potentates, and proposed sundry conditions and concessions by which the peace which he so earnestly desired might be concluded; but while he was enabled to overrule every other objection on both sides, he found himself powerless on the subject of the Milanese, and he was finally compelled to content himself with effecting a renewal of the truce for ten years, during which time he hoped to carry into execution the offensive league into which he had entered with the emperor and the Venetian states against the Infidels.

The truce was no sooner signed than Francis left Villa Nuova for Avignon, while the Pope returned to Rome, and the emperor proceeded by sea to Barcelona; and meanwhile the ill-fated Duke of Savoy, who had incurred the displeasure of both potentates, by each of whom he was openly charged with having excited the revolt of the citizens of Nice, found himself even more powerless than ever, the whole remaining portion of his territories being possessed by the two belligerent sovereigns, who were severally fortifying their strongholds within his dominions with a deliberate caution which rendered him hopeless of their ultimate recovery. He was, moreover, fated to undergo another and a crowning mortification a few months subsequently, when the connétable, on the part of Francis, proposed to him to exchange the county of Nice for lands in France to the value of twenty thousand annual crowns. The despoiled duke could ill brook this last degradation, and declined the offer with an asperity and vehemence unusual to him, declaring that he had already been victimised sufficiently both by his friends and by his enemies, and that although he now held little of his duchy save the empty title which it had conferred upon him, he would, nevertheless, at least live and die Count of Nice. He, moreover, as if to give additional weight to this declaration, immediately adopted a new device, which consisted of a naked arm grasping a sword, with the motto *Spoliatis arma supersunt;* but, as he had never been remarkable for his prowess in the field, this empty vaunt only excited the contempt of his oppressors.

Contrary winds having compelled the emperor, while on his return to Spain, to cast anchor at the island of St. Marguerite, he despatched from thence a nobleman to Avignon to greet the French monarch, and to express his desire to have an interview with him, for which purpose he offered, should his proposal be accepted, to land at Aigues-Mortes.

Francis, equally surprised and gratified, eagerly acceded to the proposition; and, in order to show his confidence in the good faith and friendly intentions of his imperial visitor, he proceeded without further delay to Marseilles, where he rowed off in his barge to the galley of Charles to bid him welcome. As he reached the vessel the emperor extended his hand to assist him in gaining the deck, and responded by an affectionate salutation to his smiling address of—" Brother, here I am once more your prisoner." This proof of confidence, as it subsequently appeared, was fully appreciated by the emperor; for when, at the close of a long and friendly conference, during which he had requested the French king to admit Doria to his presence, and the Genoese admiral had been courteously received, the latter requested permission to set sail with Francis on board, and thus terminate the war, his proposition was indignantly rejected.

On the following day the emperor landed at Aigues-Mortes, where he was received with great magnificence, and the two Courts vied with each other in courtesy and friendliness. Every appearance of jealousy or hostility was at an end, and the most complete confidence was exhibited on both sides. But perhaps the most happy individual of that courtly circle was the queen, who, after having long despaired of a reconciliation between her brother and her husband, now saw them seated side by side in the most familiar conversation. The principal officers of both sovereigns were admitted to the presence, and every allusion to former meetings. of a less amicable nature was mutually avoided. The dauphin and dauphiness, the Queen of Navarre and the Duchesse d'Etampes, were severally presented to the emperor, who expressed his admiration of the galaxy of beauty by which his brother-monarch was surrounded. None would have supposed, while gazing on the brilliant group assembled in that obscure seaport, that it included the two enemies who had so long troubled the peace of Europe, and made all the interests of Christendom subservient to their ambition.

The festivals continued for four days; and while the nobles and ladies of the two Courts were occupied by pleasure and gallantry, several long and secret interviews took place between the sovereigns, to which none were admitted save the queen, the Cardinal de Lorraine, and the connétable on the part of France; and Granvelle, the keeper of the seals, and the grand commander Gouvea, on that of the emperor. The subject of their discussions was not made public, but they nevertheless tended to increase the alarm of the Duke of Savoy, who hastened to ratify the truce by which he was despoiled of his territories, and which he had hitherto refused to do, lest he should draw down upon himself the further hostility of the two sovereigns thus suddenly and inexplicably reconciled.

On his return to his capital Francis plunged once more into an abyss of dissipation, and, regardless alike of his failing health and his regal dignity, vied in profligacy with his arrogant mistress. Satiated with the affectations of the Court beauties and the ceremonious restraints of his own circle, he at this period sought his conquests in a more humble sphere of society; and, in order the more readily to pursue his intrigues, adopted the habit of disguising himself as an archer of the royal guard, in which guise he was accustomed at twilight to perambulate the streets of the city. On one of these excursions he was attracted by the extreme loveliness of a fair citizen, the wife of an armourer, who chanced as he passed to be standing at the door of her dwelling, conversing with a neighbour; and after having remained for a moment steadfastly gazing upon her animated face and graceful figure, he beckoned as he moved on to a chamberlain by whom he was accompanied, and with a significant gesture drew his attention to the unconscious beauty.

"You will recognize the house?" he said in a low voice.

"Readily, Sire."

"Enough. The day after to-morrow I shall be at the château of Madrid."

His attendant bowed in silence; and ere long the king returned to the palace of the Tournelles.

The royal confidant had no sooner been dismissed than he mounted his horse and retraced his steps to the Rue de Fer; where, pretending business, he entered the shop of the armourer, during whose absence from home his beautiful partner was accustomed to superintend the commercial interests of the house. The appearance of such a customer, even at that somewhat untimely hour, failed to excite any suspicion of his motive in *La belle Feronnière;* nor was it until he changed the discourse from the casques and corselets amid which they stood to a more tender subject that she discovered the imprudence of which she had been guilty. After having exhausted himself in the most hyperbolical admiration of her attractions, he proceeded to appease her indignation at his impertinence by declaring that she totally misapprehended the purpose of his visit, which was, as he asserted, to inform her that the queen, who was desirous to retain about her person the most beautiful women of the kingdom, having chanced to see her during one of her progresses through the city, had been struck by her appearance, and desired to establish her in her household.

For a time the young and timid woman stood abashed, assuring the messenger that he must be mistaken, as neither her birth nor her position entitled her to so much honour; but the reiterated assurances and dazzling promises of the royal emissary at length produced their effect, and she consented to accompany him to the palace of the Tournelles, where he declared that she would be instantly admitted to the presence of the queen.

Having closely enveloped herself in her hood and mantle, the fair citizen finally permitted herself to be lifted upon the pillion with which her treacherous companion had come provided; but it was not long ere she discovered that, instead of proceeding towards the palace, they were travelling in a totally different direction; and they had consequently no sooner reached the gate by which they were about to leave the city than she called loudly for help, when a party of the night-watch, alarmed by her cries, hastily seized their arms and attempted to arrest the progress of her captor. We have, however, already shown that the civic guard of Paris was composed of men who cared little to expose themselves to danger; and, accordingly, they no sooner saw two of their number cut down by the undaunted horseman than they fell back, and abandoned the terrified victim to her fate.

Whatever might have been the original scruples of *La belle Feronnière*, it is certain that she soon became reconciled to her fate, and that the splendour of a royal palace and the *prestige* of a royal lover sufficed to blind her to her moral degradation. But this *liaison*, which soon became the talk of all Paris, was not destined to be of long endurance, the increasing infirmities of the king compelling him to restore her to her family at the expiration of three months, at once enriched and disgraced.

The extreme beauty of this woman, whose real station in life has never been thoroughly ascertained, and of whose rank and position we have consequently been compelled to adopt the most popular version, was so remarkable that, although an intrigue of such brief duration might well have been passed over in silence, her name has become matter of history; and the life of Francis I. would consequently be incomplete were the episode of *La belle Feronnière* omitted. Her portrait, which adorns the Musée at Paris, is one of surpassing loveliness; the forehead is high and smooth, the eyes are large, dovelike, and expressive, the nose is finely shaped, the mouth faultless, and the whole outline of the face full of feminine grace and dignity.

About this period Francis was attacked by so severe an indisposition that he was for a considerable time unable to attend to the business of the state, the whole of which devolved upon Montmorency, who assumed an authority to which no former connétable had ever aspired. His avowed admiration of the emperor, and his equally undisguised aversion to Henry VIII., awoke the misgivings of many of the higher nobility, especially those of the ambassadors at the several European Courts, who still felt the same mistrust of the motives of Charles V. as they had previously entertained, and who were loud in their regrets that France should for his sake deprive herself of the allies which it had cost her so much blood and gold to secure. Montmorency, however, haughtily disregarded their representations, and thus unconsciously laid the foundation of his own overthrow.

The policy of the emperor in thus suddenly and with such apparent inconsistency seeking the friendship of the French monarch soon revealed itself. The expenses of the war having compelled him to levy new imposts upon his subjects, he had, in 1536, directed Queen Marie, the Gouvernante of the Low Countries, to raise a sum of money in Flanders, by taxation or otherwise, which might enable him to pursue his operations. In compliance with this command she proceeded to levy a subsidy of one million two hundred thousand florins on the Flemish provinces, of which the city of Ghent was to furnish the sum of four hundred thousand. To this imposition the citizens resolutely refused to submit, alleging that by the ancient privileges conceded to their city they were exempted from the payment of all taxes; and as they persisted in their refusal, the queen, in order to terrify them into submission, caused several of the principal inhabitants to be arrested, and declared her determination to retain them as prisoners until her orders were obeyed. Firm in their resistance, the Ghentese disregarded her menaces, and for nearly a year, during which their relatives and townsmen remained her captives, they contested the point; and, finally, in August 1537, they presented a petition to the Gouvernante, in which they set forth in detail the privileges which had been accorded to them by former sovereigns, and by virtue of which they were, as they had stated, exempted from taxation.

In reply to this document the queen-dowager informed them that she would cause their claims to exemption to be duly investigated, either by her own council or by the parliament of Malines, but that meanwhile they must furnish their quota to the general subsidy,—a decision by which they were so much exasperated that they immediately determined to revolt against her authority. The citizens, accordingly, flew to arms, compelled the imperial officers to leave the city, and took possession of several fortified places in the environs, declaring that they recognized no sovereign save the King of France, to whom they at the same time appealed for protection, pledging themselves, should he afford them his support, to render him master of the whole of the Low Countries.

The opportunity was tempting, and there can be little doubt that had the emperor received such a proposition from a revolted province of France he would have evinced no hesitation in acceding to the request; but Francis, with a more generous policy (in which he was strengthened by the advice of Montmorency and the entreaties of the queen), not only refused to accept an allegiance extorted by fear, but even hastened to apprise his brother-monarch of the menacing attitude assumed by his Flemish subjects.

Charles V. was no sooner made aware of the extent of the emergency than he resolved to proceed to the Low Countries, and to effect the immediate suppression of the rebellious faction, which was becoming daily more formidable; but however judicious such a project could not fail to prove, there were serious obstacles to its accomplishment. In order to reach this portion of his dominions it was necessary that the emperor should either make his way through Italy into Germany, where the animosity of the Protestant princes would render it necessary for him to be accompanied by a strong army, in which case he might be subjected by casualties to a delay that would enable the Ghentese to strengthen their position, and thus frustrate the object of his journey; or by sea, where, in the event of contrary winds, he might be cast upon the English coast, and so fall into the hands of Henry VIII., with whom he was at that moment at open enmity; or, finally, through France, which was at once the shortest and the surest route. Had Charles V. possessed less discernment of character than he displayed upon this occasion it is probable that this would, nevertheless, have been his last alternative; but he was so well acquainted with the peculiar disposition of the French king that he unhesitatingly determined to confide in his generosity. He had, moreover, as he was aware, a warm partizan in the then all-powerful connétable; nor did he fail to calculate upon the influence of his sister, although he had long known that her position at the Court was at once onerous and unhappy.

Having made this resolution, he directed the Bishop of Tarbes, who was at that period the French ambassador at his Court, to write to Montmorency, requesting him to obtain the consent of Francis to his traversing the French territories, in order to reach the Low Countries with greater expedition; and pledging himself that, should this be accorded, he would, in requital of so signal a favour, at once meet the wishes of the French king by investing either himself or one of his sons with the sovereignty of the duchy of Milan, on condition that no further concessions should be demanded of him.

Francis, having convened his council, decided upon acceding to the request; but while every other member of the assembly insisted that, before he was permitted to pass the frontier, Charles should be compelled to give good sureties of his peaceable intentions, and declare in writing that he traversed the French soil only upon sufferance, Montmorency alone protested against such an exhibition of distrust, which he declared to be unworthy of so great a monarch as Francis, and calculated to lessen his dignity in the eyes of the very sovereign upon whom he was about to confer a signal and important benefit.

A warm discussion took place, but it was finally decided by the king that the advice of the connétable should be adopted, and that the emperor should be invited to enter France not only unconditionally, but also that hostages should be offered in the persons of the two princes for his safety during his sojourn in the country.

This was fated to be the last occasion upon which Montmorency was enabled to prove to the other nobles of the Court the extent of his influence over the mind of the monarch. We have already alluded to his romantic passion for the queen; and Francis had no sooner passed from the council chamber to the apartments of the Duchesse d'Etampes to announce to her the approaching advent of the emperor than the mine was sprung which was to accomplish his overthrow.

As the king entered the beautiful favourite was seated before her toilet table, wrapped in a robe of silver brocade, and almost buried in the cloud of luxuriant hair which one of her women was preparing to bind up. On his appearance the whole of the attendants withdrew, and the monarch hastened to impart his tidings.

"And this, Sire, if I understand aright," said the duchess with a supercilious smile, "was the advice of the connétable?"

"Even so, *ma mie*," replied Francis, as he passed his fingers fondly through the dark tresses which fell from the tapestried coffer upon which Anne de Pisseleu was seated to the ground. "And it appeared to me to be so chivalrous and so high-hearted that I resolved at once to follow it. You will be glad to see our brother Charles again, shall you not? On the faith of a gentleman! he esteemed your beauty at its just value."

"Her majesty must be enraptured at such a prospect," said the insolent mistress, with the same equivocal expression, and totally regardless of the question put by the king. " Montmorency is an able courtier."

" Doubtless it will afford her pleasure," replied the monarch, with a languid yawn. " I will desire him to acquaint her that she owes this gratification in some degree to his agency."

" He has, in all probability, already accomplished so agreeable an errand," spitefully retorted the duchess.

" Our good connétable is assuredly enamoured of Charles of Austria," replied Francis, as he listlessly unlocked a costly casket of inlaid sandal-wood which stood upon the table, and began to examine the jewels it contained.

" His imperial majesty is the queen's brother," said Madame d'Etampes, still maintaining the tone of bitter sarcasm in which she had hitherto indulged. " But remember, Sire," she added more emphatically, "that although he be the brother of your queen, he has ever proved himself your own enemy ; nor do I anticipate that you will henceforward find him other than he has been to this day. It is not yet too late ; recall your dangerous resolution, and do not risk the safety alike of your person and your kingdom in order to afford to M. de Montmorency the privilege of extending the 'good morrows' for which he is so famous."

A cloud rose to the brow of the king, which was rapidly succeeded by a smile. " You are truly, at this moment, refuting those calumniators, Anne," he said tenderly, "who accuse you of too great a sensibility for the connétable."

A gesture of proud disdain was the only reply vouchsafed by the haughty favourite.

"We must afford our imperial guest a splendid welcome," pursued Francis after a pause; "we must give him good reason to remember his visit to our dominions."

"And you will do well, Sire," said the duchess eagerly. "Remember Pavia; remember Madrid. Let him come, since such is your will; but once in France, suffer him not to repass the frontier until you are revenged. You have dungeons as secure as those of the Escurial, and jailors as sure and as zealous as M. de Lannoy."

Francis started. "You cannot be serious, madame?" he said incredulously.

"At least, Sire," persisted Madame d'Etampes, "I shall not be unsupported in my advice, like the connétable; you will find that all the best and noblest spirits in France will counsel you as I do."

As she uttered this assurance Triboulet, the king's jester, a misshapen dwarf who was permitted to intrude upon his privacy at all hours, quietly entered the apartment, and approaching a buffet poured out a goblet of Malvoisie, which he carried to his royal master.

"Nevertheless, I am resolved," said Francis, in reply to his fair companion; "Charles has asked for a safe passage through our dominions, and he shall depart as freely as he comes."

These words had scarcely passed the lips of the king when Triboulet, replacing the yet untasted wine upon the buffet, drew an ivory tablet from the pocket of his pourpoint, and deliberately inscribed some characters upon it.

"What have you there, *maître-fou?*" asked the monarch, amused by the assumed solemnity of his manner.

"I am making a fresh entry in my journal, which is filling rapidly," was the calm reply. "Men have called me 'fool,' but I have my revenge daily; I am busied upon a catalogue of madmen, and I shall ere long be short of space."

"Let me see this famous list," said the king, extending his hand for the tablets. "Why, how now, sir!" he exclaimed angrily; "when did you venture to add the name of my imperial brother to such a record as this?"

"Only a moment back," answered the dwarf, perfectly unmoved; "when I heard you tell fair Madame Anne that he was about to visit France."

The duchess laughed triumphantly, and threw a golden coin into the hand of the jester.

"And when he has returned to his own dominions, sirrah, what will you next do?" inquired Francis.

"Then," said Triboulet, "if, indeed, Charles should ever live to see the day you mention, I shall efface his name and insert yours."

"The fool speaks wisdom," said Madame d'Etampes.

"It may be so," was the reply of the monarch;

"but it is mere worldly wisdom, and unworthy of a great sovereign. I will not recall my pledge."

During this interview another had taken place between the queen and the connétable, which was destined to involve important consequences. Montmorency had related in detail to his royal mistress the proceedings that had taken place in the council, and she had warmly expressed her gratitude for the eminent service which he had so boldly rendered to the emperor. With true feminine tact she at once discovered the motive of his conduct; but she, nevertheless, carefully abstained from betraying any symptom of such a conviction, and as the manner of Montmorency became more impassioned she gradually assumed a coldness of demeanour which was foreign to her feelings.

At the close of the interview, however, conscious that she had ill responded to the zeal and devotion he had displayed, and relieved by his absence from the terror of misapprehension which his presence never failed to inspire, she became anxious to convince him that she was less insensible to his good offices than she had striven to appear; and after revolving many projects in her mind, unable to overcome her reluctance to address him in writing, she resolved to send to him, by one of her pages, a rich chain of amber set in enamelled gold which had been wrought for her in Florence, and was of great value.

It chanced upon this particular occasion that a slight indisposition caused the queen to receive her evening circle in her own apartments; and as she had hesitated for a long time ere she could decide on the propriety of conferring upon the connétable so marked a token of her favour, the company were already assembling when she confided the chain to her messenger. It happened also that, by a singular coincidence, Francis, who had never hitherto visited the queen save by the state gallery, was induced, by some sudden caprice, to avail himself of a private staircase, in ascending which he encountered the page, who, from boyish vanity, had flung the costly chain about his neck, and thus decorated was proceeding to perform his errand.

The quick eye of the king enabled him at a glance to recognize the ornament; and as the startled youth drew back to allow him to pass, he laid his hand upon the chain, and inquired how he became possessed of so costly a jewel. The page, who was totally unconscious of the necessity of concealment, and who only apprehended a reprimand for his presumption in having availed himself of such an opportunity to gratify his ostentatious tastes, unhesitatingly replied that he had been entrusted by the queen to convey it to the connétable; at the same time accounting for the fact of its being suspended from his own neck by declaring that in his dread of losing it by the way he had adopted that method as the most secure, and imploring the king to pardon a liberty which had been suggested by caution.

"Fear nothing," said Francis composedly; "you are both prudent and trustworthy, but such a responsibility is too great for your age. Give me the chain. I will myself deliver it to M. le Connétable."

The page obeyed, and the amber chain was placed in the hands of the king, who at once threw it about his own neck, and then pursued his way to the queen's apartments.

The amazement and alarm of Eleonora may be conceived when, as she rose to receive her royal husband, the first object upon which her eye rested was the amber chain, rendered unusually conspicuous by the fact that Francis wore a plain pourpoint of maroon-coloured velvet, without embroidery of any description. He, however, approached her in his usual courteous but cold manner; and after having made a few civil inquiries regarding her health, without any allusion to the obnoxious decoration, turned away to converse with Madame de Brézé.

The anticipated arrival of the emperor furnished ample subject for conversation throughout the evening; but the spirits of the poor queen, who had been greatly elated at the prospect of again seeing her imperial brother, were painfully subdued by her apprehensions of the misconstruction which the king could not fail to put upon the motive of her present to the connétable; and when Montmorency, a short time subsequently, drew near to her with his unvarying "good-morrow," she replied by a bow so chilling as to excite still further the suspicions of Francis, who had jealously watched the meeting. The inferences of the Duchesse d'Etampes were now explained; and although the monarch was too proud to betray that he was conscious of a rival in one of his own subjects, and too indifferent to his royal consort to feel wounded in his affections, he, nevertheless, conceived a hatred towards the connétable which was ere long fated to produce its effect.

CHAPTER VI

1539-40

The emperor arrives at Bayonne—He refuses to receive hostages—The two sovereigns meet at Chatellerault—Triumphant reception of Charles V.—Distrust of the emperor—Unfortunate coincidences—The imperial retinue—A Court ball—The diamond ring—The emperor enters Paris—The French princes and Montmorency accompany him to Valenciennes—Charles refuses to ratify the cession of the Milanese—Francis becomes suspicious of his counsellors—Arrest of the Maréchal de Brion Chabot—Chabot is tried and condemned to death—Cruel policy of Poyet—Chabot is pardoned by the king—Arrest of Poyet—Female influence at Court—Death of Chabot—The emperor proposes an alliance between his son Philip of Spain and the Princess of Navarre, between his own daughter and the Duc d'Orleans—Refusal of Francis to comply with the required conditions—Disappointment of the King and Queen of Navarre—The negotiation is pursued—Marriage of the Duc de Cleves and the Princess of Navarre—Madame d'Etampes and the captain of the king's guard—Exile of Montmorency from the Court—The marriage festivities—The Duc de Cleves leaves France—Benvenuto Cellini arrives at the French Court—Exile of the Cardinal de Lorraine.

THE emperor commenced his journey without further delay, and the French king no sooner learned that he was on his way to the frontier than, being unable from illness to undertake so long a journey, he commanded the two princes and the connétable to proceed to Bayonne, giving them express injunctions to receive the imperial visitor with every demonstration of respect and affection, and to escort him in like manner to the capital.

In accordance with these instructions the dauphin, the Duc d'Orleans, and Montmorency, accompanied by a great number of the Court nobles sumptuously mounted and apparelled, set forth in time to reach the city before the arrival of Charles; and the dauphin had no sooner greeted him in the name of the king than he hastened, according to the directions he had received, to offer himself and his brother as hostages to the emperor until he should have reached the Low Countries. Of this proposition, however, Charles, under the circumstances, found it inexpedient to avail himself; and he consequently replied that, after the important service which had just been conferred upon him by the king his brother, he should be inexcusable did he entertain the slightest suspicion of his good faith. The august party accordingly proceeded in company to Bourdeaux, where they were welcomed with acclamation, and entertained with a magnificence worthy of their illustrious rank. During a long sojourn in that city the favour of the connétable daily increased with the emperor, who also lavished upon the young princes the most marked tokens of regard and affection; nor was it without apparent reluctance that he at length resumed his progress through Xaintonge and Poitiers to Chatellerault, where Francis was in person awaiting his imperial guest, and whence, after a few days passed in splendid festivity and reciprocal assurances of friendship and confidence, the two sovereigns and their brilliant train finally set forward to the capital.

Throughout the whole of their journey (which occupied a considerable time in consequence of the preparations that had been made in the several cities by which they approached Paris to render due honours to the emperor) all the local nobility and militia accompanied the royal travellers to the limits of their respective communes; and although Charles had reached Bayonne in the month of October, he halted for so long a time at Bourdeaux, at Lusignan, and at several other places upon his route, for the purpose of enjoying the sports of the field, that he did not arrive at Poitiers until the 9th of December. His reception in that city exceeded in splendour and ceremonial all that he had hitherto experienced. As he arrived at the gates he was met by the whole nobility of the province, and was conducted into the town by five hundred cavaliers superbly habited, and followed by two thousand of the citizens dressed in velvet and satin, laced with gold and silver. At Orleans, which he reached on the 20th of December, his escort was composed not only of all the local nobility and militia, but also of a guard of "ninety-two young merchants of the city, mounted upon fine horses, all attired in overcoats of black velvet, with doublets of white satin, fastened by gold buttons; velvet caps, covered with precious stones, and edged with goldsmith's work; and boots of white Spanish leather, with golden spurs. One of these caps was estimated at two thousand crowns; nor was there an individual among them who did not carry upon his person the value of more than two thousand francs in jewellery."

From this description the enormous aggregate

expenditure consequent upon the reception of the emperor in France may be inferred. At that period it was calculated at two millions of livres, which, when the relative value of money in those days and our own is remembered, presents an amount amply sufficient to have supplied the French army throughout an entire campaign. In every city upon his passage the doors of the prisons were opened in his presence, and the prisoners liberated in his name, without any regard to the nature of their offences; and no opportunity was permitted to escape which could afford the means of convincing Charles that his visit was intended to make one wide holiday throughout the country.

At Chatellerault a magnificent banquet awaited him; and the two sovereigns, after an interview in which they vied with each other in expressions of affection and regard, repaired to the stately hall where it had been served up, followed by the princes of the blood and the cardinals. On reaching the table Francis insisted that the emperor should occupy the upper seat, and after he had with extreme difficulty induced him to do so, he still further testified his respect for his imperial guest by causing a large space to intervene between them.

But still, despite the flattering nature of his reception, Charles V. was ill at ease. He was aware that he had little deserved such a display of confidence and hospitality at the hands of the French king, and, accustomed to practise deceit in his own person, he was unable, with all his efforts, entirely to conceal the alarm which he occasionally felt. This apprehension was, moreover, during his sojourn in France, heightened by several circumstances, each perhaps trivial in itself, but so ill-timed as to arouse his suspicions that they were not altogether accidental. On one occasion the Duc d'Orleans, who, as we have already stated, was of a gay and thoughtless disposition, and who was moreover extraordinarily active, sprang upon the crupper of the horse which the emperor had just mounted, and flinging his arms about his waist, exclaimed gaily, "Your imperial majesty is my prisoner." Although he recovered his self-possession in an instant, it was remarked by those near him that Charles turned pale, and that it was only by a powerful effort he was enabled to reply to the jest of the young prince.

A short time subsequently, as the Chancellor Poyet approached to pay his respects while the emperor was at table, the skirts of his robes became entangled among the wood which had been piled in a corner of the apartment for the supply of the stove; and as he sought to disengage them he so disturbed the heap that a large log upon the summit lost its balance and fell upon the head of Charles, who remained stunned for several minutes, and although he partially recovered the blow and affected to make light of the accident to the discomfited minister, he was nevertheless compelled to be bled before he could overcome its effects.

At Amboise, which he subsequently visited, he was destined to encounter two other perils, as easily explained, but equally startling at the moment. On one occasion the tapestried hangings of his bed were fired by an attendant; and on the other he was nearly suffocated by the vapours engendered by a foreign perfume, intended to fill his apartment with an agreeable and refreshing odour. When the latter occurrence took place the king, irritated by these repeated accidents, and anxious to convince his imperial guest that they were not premeditated, caused the arrest of the unlucky perfumer, and commanded that he should immediately be put to death—a fate which he would inevitably have incurred had not the emperor strenuously demanded his pardon, declaring that he had not visited France to become the cause or witness of a criminal execution.

The imperial retinue was rather elegant than either numerous or magnificent. The great-grandson of Charles the Bold was accompanied only by a hundred men-at-arms, chosen for their personal beauty and dexterity in warlike exercises; by a body of Spanish grandees, whose ambition appeared limited to a desire to excel in the splendour of their costume the nobles of the French Court; and by four and twenty pages, habited in costumes of orange, gray, and violet velvet, which were at that period his peculiar colours. He himself was clad in a complete suit of polished armour, girt about the waist by a sash of cloth of gold; and rode an Andalusian horse of extraordinary strength and symmetry. His cap was of black velvet, embroidered with gold and jewels, and his weapons were of the same costly description.

From Chatellerault the illustrious party proceeded to Amboise, where the alarm of the emperor was fated to reach its climax. Assured as he was of the devotion of the connétable, he had not sojourned so long in France without detecting certain indications of his unpopularity with the mass, not only of the nobles but also of the citizens, which rendered him anxious to pursue his journey to the Low Countries so soon as this measure could be effected without giving umbrage to his royal entertainer. Meanwhile, however, he dissembled his misgivings, and entered into all the amusements of the Court with apparent zest and enjoyment. On the occasion of a ball which he had opened with the queen his sister, and which took place by daylight, as was the common custom of the period, the *royales* and *gaillards*, which were the state dances, were executed with infinite grace and dignity by the dauphiness, the Duchesse d'Etampes, and Madame de Brézé; and at their termination the emperor, who had carefully abstained from resenting the neglect that was evinced towards his royal relative, and the supremacy of the favourite, who openly usurped her privileges, approached the haughty duchess, and expressed his admiration of the consummate elegance with which she had acquitted herself of her arduous duties. They were still engaged in conversation when the king, flattered by the deference shown to his cherished mistress, hastily approached them, and laying his hand upon the arm of Charles V., said gaily—

" Be sparing of your compliments, good brother,

for permit me to assure you that the fair lady who is now bending beneath their weight was bold enough to advise me to make you my prisoner until you had consented to the revocation of the treaty of Madrid."

A shadow gathered upon the brow of the emperor, and his features assumed a stern expression as, turning from the discomfited favourite, he said coldly, "If the advice seem good, your majesty will do well to follow it."

This reply for a moment silenced the whole group; but the king soon rallied, and the amusements resumed their course.

The warning was, however, opportune, for Charles was aware that he could not have a more dangerous enemy than the fascinating and unscrupulous duchess; but he was also conversant with her real character; and, accordingly, a few days afterwards, when he was about to seat himself at table, and Madame d'Etampes, who assumed to herself the office which should by the rules of etiquette have devolved upon a royal princess, presented a napkin, he adroitly drew a magnificent brilliant from his finger and suffered it to fall to the ground.

The duchess immediately stooped, picked up the jewel, and with a low curtsey presented it on her open palm to its imperial owner.

"Nay, madame," said Charles, with an obeisance as profound as her own, "the bauble looks so much more attractive in your hands than in mine that I dare not reclaim it."

"Your imperial majesty surely jests!" was the

reply of the favourite as she still tendered the ring ; " I am unworthy of so precious a gift."

" Of what are you not worthy, madame ? " said Charles in an accent of gallantry, as he possessed himself of her hand and passed the gem over one of her slender fingers. " You, who have won the heart of one monarch, need feel no compunction in wearing the jewel of another."

It is needless to explain that the offering was accepted, or that from that moment the avaricious favourite ceased to exhibit any hostility towards the politic donor.[1]

From Amboise the emperor was conducted to Blois, and thence to Fontainebleau, where the fêtes recommenced ; but the crowning triumph was his entry into the capital, which took place on the 1st of January 1540.

The dauphin and the Duc d'Orleans, the princes of the blood, the French cardinals, the parliament, and all the officials of the government, met him at the gates, where the two princes took their places upon his right and left hand ; while the connétable preceded him with his sword of office unsheathed, as

---

[1] " This anecdote, accepted by some French writers, is wholly rejected by Mézeray and others. It does indeed seem a singularly awkward and rather discourteous way of making a lady a present. It is doubted, too, whether a diamond would have bought her alliance. She cared less for jewels than for political influence, and since the death of the dauphin, foreseeing that when the king also died her importance at Court would cease, and she would have everything to fear from Henry and Diane, she attached herself to the king's youngest son and sought to promote his interests, to ensure herself a safe retreat and the prince's protection."—Lady Jackson's *Court of France in the Sixteenth Century*, vol. ii. p. 100.

though he were escorting his own sovereign, and so accompanied him through the city, The keys of the several prisons were delivered to him, as they had previously been in the provinces, and before he entered the palace of the Tournelles he declared the freedom of their occupants. When he reached the Hôtel de Ville he found all the sheriffs assembled before the portal of the building to compliment him; and at the close of their harangue they presented, as the offering of the city of Paris to its august visitor, a Hercules in silver the size of life, with the lion skin in which he was draped richly gilt and chased. Thence he proceeded in the same state to Notre Dame, where a solemn Te Deum was chanted; after which he was conducted to the palace, and took possession of the magnificent suite of apartments that had been newly decorated for his use; and throughout the whole of the eight days during which he remained the guest of the French king the most splendid festivals were given in his honour.

On his departure, when he had taken leave of the queen his sister, the Queen of Navarre, the dauphiness, and their respective courts, he left the city with the same pomp as he had entered it, accompanied by his royal host and the two princes, and proceeded to Chantilly, where he was entertained in the most costly manner by the connétable.

It is asserted by some historians that the dauphin, the King of Navarre, and the Duc de Vendôme had entered into a conspiracy to arrest him in the château of Montmorency, and that the latter was only enabled to dissuade them from their purpose by representing the odium which he should personally incur throughout Europe were he to permit such an outrage to be committed beneath his roof. Be this as it may, however, it is certain that after having passed the night at Chantilly, the emperor on the following day pursued his journey to St. Quentin without molestation; and having taken leave of the king in that city, proceeded to Valenciennes, still attended by the two princes and the connétable.

On their arrival at Valenciennes, Montmorency respectfully reminded the emperor of his promise relative to the duchy of Milan, and requested him to appoint a given time for its fulfilment; upon which Charles with some bitterness replied, that all the courtesy displayed towards him by his royal brother had been counterbalanced by the perpetual annoyance to which he had been subjected upon that question, and that he was at the moment so engrossed by the affairs of Ghent that he could not afford time for the consideration of any other and less pressing interest.

As the connétable, however, persisted in urging him to a decision, he at length declared that he should refer the matter to his council, as he did not feel himself justified in alienating so important a portion of his empire without previously obtaining the sanction of his brother, the King of the Romans; but that he should no sooner have done so than he would be careful to make such an arrangement as could not fail to prove agreeable to the French monarch.

With this equivocal assurance Montmorency was compelled to content himself; and having taken his final leave of the imperial dissembler, he returned to Court with the two princes. The emperor meanwhile proceeded to Ghent, where he succeeded in a few days in suppressing the revolt by an exhibition of severity which effectually terrified the rebels into submission. And this was no sooner accomplished than the Bishop of Laveur again demanded the promised investiture on the part of his sovereign, when Charles, who had secured his own safety, and who had no longer anything to fear from the enmity of his late lavish host, unblushingly asserted that he had given no pledge and had no intention of making so serious a sacrifice.

This shameless tergiversation of the emperor produced the most baneful effects upon the moral nature of Francis I. Hitherto, amid all his faults, he had been unsuspicious of those about him, and frank and open-hearted to all in whom he believed that he could confide; but the deceit practised by Charles was so monstrous, and his ingratitude so glaring, that he lost confidence even in his best and truest friends, and eagerly listened to all the whispers which were circulated against those in whom he had hitherto reposed the greatest trust.

The first victim of this morbid feeling was the Maréchal de Brion Chabot, the playmate of his boyhood, the companion of his youth, and, moreover, the near relative of Madame d'Etampes, who, incensed by the coldness of Montmorency, exerted all her influence to undermine his interests with the king, and to second those of her cousin. For a considerable time Francis had confided the direction of public affairs to the connétable, whose power had become so notorious that, with the exception of the monarch himself and the Cardinal de Lorraine, all who were in correspondence with him addressed him by the title of *Monseigneur*. Between the cardinal and Montmorency an aversion had long existed which was no secret to the Court; and it was, consequently, without any suspicion of their new alliance that they reconciled their differences in order to meet a common danger when they discovered the energy displayed by Madame d'Etampes in the cause of Chabot.

In the life of a public man it is always easy to discover some foundation for blame. Human nature is ever fallible, and where great power has been entrusted to an individual it is rare, indeed, to find that it has never been abused. Nevertheless, Chabot felt so convinced of his own general uprightness that when he became aware that through the machinations of some unexpected enemy he was accused of having mal-administered the affairs of the king in Piedmont, he merely smiled at what he considered as an abortive attempt to injure him.

Such, however, it was not destined to prove, for he had not only excited the indignation of Montmorency by his ostentatious display of the wealth and power for which he was indebted to the partiality of the monarch, but he had also aroused the jealousy of

Francis himself by the extreme interest which Madame d'Etampes undisguisedly evinced in his advancement, and wounded his vanity by presuming upon a familiarity which had commenced in their boyhood, and which no after events had diminished in the manner of the presumptuous favourite.

The train thus laid, it was easy for the king to discover an opportunity of offence ; and, accordingly, when upon some trivial occasion Chabot ventured as usual to dissent from his opinion, he turned sternly towards the astonished maréchal, declaring that he could no longer tolerate his insolence, and threatening that, should he persist in so unbecoming a course as that which he had thus arrogantly adopted, he would put him upon his trial.

Indignant at this menace, Chabot, instead of quailing before the displeasure of his royal master, which the latter had anticipated that he would do, answered in as high a tone that his majesty was quite at liberty to arrest him upon the instant, should such be his pleasure, as he felt so secure that neither his life nor his honour could be touched that he should feel no uneasiness regarding the result of the investigation.

This boldness, which appeared to Francis to be intended as an open defiance of the authority of which he was so jealous, at once decided the fate of the imprudent Chabot, who, with his usual impetuosity, had not paused to remember that the friendship of a sovereign cannot be enjoyed upon equal terms, and that it must always be received as a boon rather than claimed as a right, whatever may have been the obligations incurred by that sovereign towards his subject.

It is, however, evident from the result that the old affection of Francis for the maréchal was still too powerful to permit him to contemplate any ultimate injury to his favourite, and that all he sought was to humble his vanity and to diminish his pretentions; but he, nevertheless, gave an order to the chancellor Poyet to appoint commissaries from the several parliaments of France, and to proceed at once to the trial. Chabot was arrested, imprisoned in the castle of Melun, and several times interrogated by the chancellor himself, who presided over the proceedings contrary to all precedent, as his jurisdiction did not extend to the criminal courts. But Poyet, who was at this period the creature of the king as blindly and unscrupulously as he had formerly been that of Louise de Savoie, boldly set all legal conventionalities at defiance, and pursued his undertaking with such overweening zeal that he ere long announced to Francis that he had convicted the maréchal of no less than five and twenty crimes, any one of which merited the pain of death.

Such had not, however, been the opinion of the commissaries, who, upon acquainting themselves with the extreme puerility of the several accusations, declared that they saw nothing in the conduct of the prisoner which could subject him to any penalty beyond that of a brief imprisonment; but, believing that Francis wished to rid himself of an importunate courtier of whom he had become weary, Poyet no sooner found that the other members of the Court disregarded alike his arguments and his expostulations than he proceeded to threats, which proved more efficacious; and thus sentence of death was ultimately signed against the unfortunate noble by his venal and profligate judges.

This result was, however, no sooner communicated to the king than he expressed his indignation at the absurdity of which both the chancellor and his subordinates had been guilty, in thus condemning a man to die for errors not one of which amounted to a crime; and having so done, he desired that the maréchal might immediately be summoned to his presence. As Chabot entered the apartment, already aware of the decision of the Court, he met the eye of the king respectfully but firmly, and having made a deep obeisance, stood silently before him awaiting the event.

"You see, sir," commenced Francis sternly, "to what a pass your arrogance has brought you; and that it ill became you to challenge your sovereign to so dangerous a proof as he has now given you of his power."

"I admit my error, Sire," said the maréchal; "but at least your judges have been unable to convict me of any want of zeal or fidelity in your service."

"Do you then still consider yourself irreproachable?" asked the monarch hastily.

"By no means, Sire," was the calm and pointed reply; "I have learnt in my prison that before God and his sovereign no man can call himself innocent."

"It is well, sir, that you have been awakened to a sense of your indiscretion," said the king, but less sternly than before; "we will, however, spare your life. Whatever may have been your faults, you have ere now done us good service, which we care not to forget. Let the remembrance of the latter cheer your exile, as that of the former cannot fail to sadden it."

The maréchal attempted no remonstrance, and a sentence of perpetual banishment was recorded against him, to which was superadded a fine of a hundred and fifty thousand livres; but, believing that he had now sufficiently humbled the vanity of his old and faithful servant, whose presumption had been fostered by the extreme familiarity to which he had been admitted by himself, wearied by the remonstrances of Madame d'Etampes, and aroused once more to his old jealousy of the connétable by her representations, Francis had no sooner thus cruelly suffered his victim to experience all the bitterness of anticipated ruin and disgrace than he once more set aside the decree of the Court, and restored him unrestrictedly to his former property and honours.

The vanity of the sovereign had, however, miscalculated the character of the subject. Chabot was a man of quick and sensitive feelings, and he had been wounded to the very core. The pardon which had been granted to him as a boon failed to satisfy his self-respect, and he accordingly declined to resume his official functions until he had undergone a second trial before the regular tribunal—a favour which was at length reluctantly accorded to him. The result of this second investigation was an unqualified acquittal; and it was no sooner promulgated than he returned to Court, where he was welcomed by no one more warmly than by Marguerite de Navarre, who, aware that Montmorency had been the original instigator of his disgrace, and remembering only too keenly the insult which he had offered to herself on the subject of her religious tenets, hastened to assure him of her lively satisfaction at the triumph which he had obtained over his enemies—a triumph in which she was ere long destined to share.

To the maréchal it was, however, of small avail, for the mortification to which he had been exposed, and the anxiety that he had suffered during his imprisonment, had acted so injuriously upon his health that he never recovered from their effects; and in little more than a year Francis was deprived by death of one of the most attached and devoted of his subjects.

The next arrest which took place was that of his persecutor, Poyet, who, although his disgrace was well merited, nevertheless owed it less to his crimes than to the vengeance of Madame d'Etampes and the wounded dignity of Marguerite de Navarre.

Jean de Bary la Renaudie, a gentleman of Perigord, was engaged in a lawsuit against M. du Tillet, the registrat-civil of the parliament of Paris, which had already extended over several years, and being anxious to see it terminated he had applied for letters of evocation, which the chancellor upon sundry pretexts refused to sign, although he had been expressly urged to do so by the favourite, who at length, irritated by his opposition, obtained an order from the king by which he was compelled to immediate obedience. It chanced that when this order arrived he was closeted with the Queen of Navarre, who was soliciting his interest in favour of an individual of her family who had recently been convicted of eloping with an heiress; and he had no sooner run his eye over the missive of the king than, taking up the letters of La Renaudie, he held them towards his royal petitioner, exclaiming bitterly—

"There, madame, is a proof of the purposes to which the ladies of the Court apply their influence. Not satisfied with confining themselves to their legitimate sphere of action, they undertake even to violate the laws, and to give lessons to the most experienced magistrates."

The sister of the king, who apprehended that this taunt, which there can be little doubt simply applied to Madame d'Etampes, was intended as an insult to herself, immediately rose, refusing to resume with the minister the subject upon which she had been induced to visit him; and she had no sooner reached the palace than she hastened to communicate to the favourite the insolence of the fated Poyet.

On the 2d of August the French chancellor was a prisoner in the Bastille, where he remained until the conclusion of his trial on the 23d of April 1545, which had been constantly prolonged by the charges that poured in against him from all directions. Found guilty of malversation, peculation, and legal corruption, he was sentenced "to be deprived of the dignity of chancellor, declared incapable of holding office under the Crown, and condemned to a fine of a hundred thousand livres, as well as five years' imprisonment in whatsoever fortress the king might see fit to select." He was then removed to the town of Bourges, where he was detained until he had surrendered the whole of his property in payment of the fine; and he ultimately died in Paris in a state of the most squalid poverty, without a home or a friend.

Despite the unworthy requital which had been made by Charles V. to the impolitic hospitality of the French king, he was anxious to avoid an open rupture between the two countries; and after his return to Spain he accordingly hastened to propose to Francis a double alliance between their families, which might ensure their lasting friendship, and by such means invest them with a supremacy over the whole of Europe. For this purpose he declared his readiness to accept for his son, Dom Philippe, the hand of Jeanne d'Albret, the daughter of Henri de Navarre and Marguerite, the king's sister; pledging himself to permit Francis to redeem the principalities of Bearn and Lower Navarre, both of which were situate within the French territories, for two millions of livres; and to give his own daughter, the Princess of Spain, in marriage to Charles, Duc d'Orleans, with either the duchy of Milan, or the Low Countries and the counties of Burgundy and Charolois, as her dower, on condition that the king should increase the appanage of his son.

To this proposition Francis, however, refused to accede, although a more brilliant alliance could not have presented itself for the young prince. He declared, in reply, that he could not consent to receive the duchy of Milan as the dowry of the Princess of Spain, inasmuch as such a concession would tend to invalidate his just claims to that sovereignty, to which he considered that he had an undisputed right, either in his own person or in that of one of his sons; while he was equally indisposed to accept the Low Countries and the provinces specified on the condition assigned, that should the prince die before his wife these territories were to revert to the emperor himself, while he moreover declined to give any definite reply as to the marriage of Jeanne d'Albret with Dom Philippe.

Charles V., who had anticipated a very different result, was extremely chagrined by this unexpected obstacle. He declared that while Francis was exacting in his own demands, he avoided all personal sacrifice; but he, nevertheless, abstained from any demonstration of hostility, believing that upon mature deliberation the French king would accede to his proposals.

The policy of Francis upon this occasion, meanwhile, caused severe disappointment to the King and Queen of Navarre, who saw their wildest dreams of ambition realized in the alliance proposed for their daughter; but the idea of a union between this princess and the son of the German emperor alarmed alike the king and his ministers, who foresaw, should it be effected, the almost certain usurpation of the kingdom of Navarre by the Spaniards, as well as that of a considerable portion of territory at the base of the Pyrenees; and, consequently, not all the importunities of his much-loved sister could induce Francis to yield. Either, as he asserted, both the marriages must take place, or neither; adding, moreover, that nothing should induce him to dismember his kingdom in order to increase the territories of Charles V.

The negotiation was, however, continued, but listlessly and indifferently, until the arrival in France of the Duc de Cleves and Juliers,[1] who, having been disappointed in his hope of obtaining the duchy of Gueldres (to which both Antoine de Lorraine and himself laid claim as the near relatives of the deceased Duke William) at the hands of Charles V., who was anxious to retain its sovereignty and to merge it in that of the Low Countries, at once proceeded to the Court of Francis to solicit his assistance and protection. It happened, unfortunately for the interests of the young princess, that a short time previously the

[1] Guillaume de la Mark succeeded his father, Jean III., in the duchies of Cleves, Berg, and Juliers. On the 27th of January 1538 he was also summoned by the States of Gueldres and Zutphen, then assembled at Nimeguen, to inherit the sovereignty of their aged duke, Charles d'Egmont, who was at that period seventy-one years of age, and childless, and who died on the 30th of June following. An old and close friendship united the two families, and the Gueldrians refused to recognize a treaty into which their duke had been compelled to enter, and by virtue of which his duchy passed, upon his death, into the house of Austria.

Cardinal de Grammont, Archbishop of Bordeaux and Lieutenant-Governor of Guienne, had succeeded in intercepting a secret correspondence between the emperor and the King of Navarre on the subject of the proposed marriage of their children; and this letter having been forwarded to the king, he became so incensed by this daring opposition to his will that he forthwith offered to the Duc de Cleves, as an earnest of his friendship, the hand of his niece—an offer which was gratefully accepted. In vain did Henri de Navarre remonstrate and his sister weep; Francis remained immovable, declaring that he would not retract a pledge voluntarily given; and, despite the opposition of both parents, he accordingly made known to the duke that his marriage would be solemnized at Chatellerault on the 15th of July.

On that day the ceremony accordingly took place with a magnificence which excited much murmuring among the people, upon whom a new tax was levied in order to liquidate the outlay consequent upon this demand on the treasury; and the only consolation experienced by the disappointed mother was afforded by the fact that as the poor child, who had only just attained her eleventh year, was so overloaded with jewels, and gold and silver damask, that she had not strength to walk under their weight, the king commanded Montmorency to take her in his arms and carry her to the altar—an order which startled the whole Court, such an office being derogatory to the exalted rank of the connétable, and obviously intended as an affront.

Montmorency, however, obeyed in silence; but as he lifted the little princess, who was clinging to the side of her mother, his cheek flushed upon hearing Marguerite remark scornfully to Madame d'Etampes, "Is it not amusing? Here is the man who would fain have ruined me in the good graces of my royal brother now playing the part of lacquey to my daughter,"—a taunt which had no sooner reached his ear than he in turn exclaimed to one of his friends, "My season of favour is over, and I bid it farewell for ever."

The event proved the justice of his previsions, for at the close of the banquet it was announced to him that the king authorized his retirement to one of his estates, and would dispense with all leave-taking.

The next morning the once-powerful connétable was on his way to his château at Chantilly.

The positive cause of his disgrace was never publicly ascertained. Many ascribed it to the evil counsels by which Francis was induced to allow the emperor a free passage through his kingdom—an act of impolicy which he had since repented; and others to the jealousy felt by the king at the excessive attachment existing between him and the dauphin; but its undoubted motive was revealed by the fact that while that prince was on one occasion repeating his entreaties for the recall of his first tutor in arms, the king exclaimed bitterly, "No more of this, sir. Never again mention to me the name of that dispenser of 'Good-morrows!'"

The Duchesse d'Etampes was revenged. No one

thenceforward dared to plead the cause of the outraged connétable; and his enforced exile terminated only with the death of the ungenerous monarch who had so ill requited his brilliant services.

The departure of Montmorency was no impediment to the gaiety of the Court, which, on the occasion of the marriage of Mademoiselle de Navarre, drank deep of every species of dissipation. Superb banquets and magnificent tournaments daily took place, and at the latter a number of knights-errant presented themselves in the lists, who rigorously observed all the traditional ceremonies of the Knights of the Round Table. / The most costly gifts were showered upon the bride; and at the conclusion of the festivities the Duc de Cleves took his leave of the royal circle, and returned to Aix-la-Chapelle, whither his young wife was to follow him when she should have attained her fourteenth year. ' This arrangement, however, was never completed, as Marguerite and her husband, against whose consent the alliance had taken place, caused it to be annulled a short time afterwards; nor was the princess finally married until the year 1548, when she became the wife of Antoine de Bourbon, Duc de Vendôme, who succeeded his father-in-law as King of Navarre.

From Chatellerault Francis removed with his Court to the capital, where an incident occurred which occasioned considerable amusement to the idle and licentious circle. The monarch, soon wearied by the gloomy palace of the Tournelles, proceeded with a few chosen courtiers to the château of Madrid—an arrangement which afforded great satisfaction to the favourite, who, whatever contempt she affected to feel for the forsaken queen, evinced on all occasions the utmost anxiety to escape from her vicinity. The royal party had no sooner arrived at the villa than the king commanded a grand hunt in the Bois de Boulogne, from which, however, the duchess, being slightly indisposed, absented herself. It is true that the gallant and handsome Christian de Nançay, the captain of the body-guard, had been prevented by his duties from joining in the sport; and it was well known that Madame d'Etampes had long ceased to conceal her passion for this noble young soldier. Suffice it, that while she sat musing in her own apartment, De Nançay, leaning from the balcony of the outer gallery, was watching the shades of evening as they thickened, in as deep a reverie as her own.

At length the great clock of the château struck seven, and De Nançay, starting from his waking dream, adjusted his helmet and coat-of-mail, and hastened to his post to arrange his pikemen, after which he returned to the gallery, whence he proceeded to the private apartments; and having traversed the arched corridor by which they were approached, suddenly stopped before a hanging curtain of blue silk, richly fringed with gold, and embroidered all over with the royal salamander in the same costly bullion. A deep flush rose to his cheek, and for a moment his eyes fell before the significant device; but he was young, bold, and fully conscious of his personal advantages. It was not, consequently, from any dread of personal danger that he paused; but only one short year had elapsed since he had been a personal attendant of the sovereign, who, in requital of his services, had permitted him to exchange the plumed cap and embroidered pourpoint of the page for the helm and halberd of the soldier; and he was conscious that, by his meditated intrusion, he was about to violate the respect which he owed to his royal master.

Behind that mystic curtain was an apartment into which no one had a right to penetrate save the king —the apartment of the Duchesse d'Etampes, who, dear as she might be to the monarch, the enthusiastic youth believed could be loved by no one so devotedly as by himself. As we have said, he paused for a moment; but as he apprehended no severity on the part of the fair favourite herself, he soon forgot all save his mad and ungovernable passion. With a desperate clutch he drew back the folds of the frail barrier, and cautiously entered the forbidden chamber.

The room was of small dimensions, oval-shaped, and imperfectly lighted by the faint flame which was confined within a lamp of ground glass, placed upon a precious secretaire of ebony, inlaid with sandalwood, ivory, and coral; rich hangings of purple damask veiled the walls, and were looped back at intervals by hands wrought in polished steel; a noble Venetian mirror faced the portal; and a gorgeous sofa, upon which were scattered cushions of gold-coloured satin, tasselled with pearls, stood immediately beneath it. Two of the velvet-covered coffers, which were at that period the ungraceful and inconvenient substitutes for chairs, were placed near it; while the only window by which the daylight was admitted into the apartment was flung open, its draperies drawn aside, and its space partially occupied by the slight figure of a woman, whose head was bowed over her bosom, and whose hands rested upon the sill.

The breath of De Nançay came thick and fast as he stood with his eyes riveted upon the dimly-traced outline of the solitary muser; he could neither speak nor move a limb; he felt like one who is deprived of all power of volition. How long this trance might have continued is uncertain, had not Madame d'Etampes suddenly started, swept back her dishevelled hair, and, moving from the window, approached a table on which lay the miniature rattle destined to summon her attendants; when, as she reached the centre of the floor, the rays of the lamp, feeble though they were, glinted over the armour of the intruder, upon which she uttered a faint scream, and sank fainting on the sofa.

"It is only I—Christian—most adored of women!" murmured De Nançay, as he hastened to reassure her. "It is only I, your worshipper. Will you not pardon me?"

"You mad boy!" gasped out the terrified favourite, "do you seek your own destruction?"

"What could I do, Anne?" urged the impassioned youth. "I knew that you were here—here, and alone."

"But the king——"

"The king!" echoed De Nançay petulantly. "Can you not forget him at such a moment as this? He is still in the forest. The stag has afforded him right royal sport, and he cannot return hither for hours."

"Nevertheless, you have acted with great imprudence," said the duchess tenderly, as she wreathed her slender fingers in his clustering curls; "you may have been suspected—even seen."

"I thought only of you, sweet Anne."

"I dare not trust you. You will involve both yourself and me."

"Spare your reproaches," said Christian impatiently, "for I have exercised more discretion than you seem willing to believe. The king, I repeat, cannot be here for two happy, blissful hours."

"From whom did you ascertain that fact?"

"From the Comte de Saint-Pol, who has this moment returned from the hunt."

"Enough," said the duchess with a smile, "the boy is, I see, fast ripening into the man, and must not be idly chidden." Then, springing her small rattle, a summons which was instantly answered by the entrance of one of her women, she made a significant gesture, and the attendant departed as silently as she had appeared.

Scarcely had half an hour elapsed when a great noise was heard in the courtyard. The archers and pikemen flew to their arms, and the *suivante*, who had slumbered upon her watch, rushed into the apartment, exclaiming hurriedly, "Madame, you have not a moment to lose! His majesty has returned."

In an instant both the duchess and De Nançay sprang to their feet; the clatter of horses' hoofs and the baying of hounds became every instant more audible. There was no longer time either for concealment or for flight, and moreover the captain of the royal guard was absent from his post. Meanwhile the king had sprung from his horse; and, booted, spurred, and muddy as he was, had hurriedly entered the château and ascended by a private staircase which led immediately to the apartments of the duchess, in order to allay her uneasiness by assuring her of his safety.

Already the clanking of his spurs echoed sharply through the arched gallery. The duchess had recognized his footstep, and the young guard had resigned himself to his fate. The silken curtain of the portal was flung back, and in another instant Francis appeared upon the threshold of the apartment, preceded by two pages bearing flambeaux. On discovering De Nançay in the saloon of Madame d'Etampes the king suddenly stopped short, and his eyes flashed with rage; but he nevertheless maintained sufficient control over his feelings to suppress his indignation. Christian stood, with bowed head, in the centre of the floor, and beside him knelt a female, whose face was buried in her hands and whose whole frame quivered with emotion.

"You here, sir!" said Francis sternly.

Christian replied only by a respectful bow.

"And apparently in good company!" pursued the king bitterly. "Who is this woman? Let her stand up."

The recumbent figure slowly rose from her Magdalen-like attitude.

"You are indeed overbold, young sir," thundered the indignant monarch; "would no light-o'-love serve your turn save one of the attendants of the Duchesse d'Etampes? and no place of rendezvous suffice except her private chamber? Hola! guards! seize your prisoner."

De Nançay respectfully drew his sword from its scabbard, and in silence laid it at the feet of his irritated master; after which, with a profound obeisance, he surrendered himself to the royal archers, who awaited him at the entrance of the apartment.

About a month subsequently Francis summoned the delinquent to his presence. "M. de Nançay," he said, "I have been induced to pardon the crime of which you were lately guilty, at the powerful intercession of the noble lady to whom you offered so deep an insult that she might well have been excused had she rather solicited your lasting disgrace, but who, with a generosity for which you can never sufficiently prove your gratitude, condescends to overlook the outrage committed upon her dignity, and in consideration of your youth, freely forgives you. It is to her, and her alone, I repeat, that you owe your escape from a fate which, to a young and proud spirit like yours, would have been worse than death. Do not suffer the lesson you have now received to prove unprofitable. Return to your duty. Here is your sword, sir; and endeavour to guard it better in time to come."

Christian knelt, and having dutifully kissed the knee of the sovereign, once more took possession of his forfeited weapon; pledging himself, upon the honour of a soldier, that he would never again be guilty of the enormity of pursuing with his addresses any of the attendants of the outraged favourite.

The clever duchess was saved. She had, indeed, sacrificed the fair fame of one of her women, but she had succeeded in securing her own immunity. And, after all, what was the value of character to the daughter of a citizen, or to an inmate of the Court of Francis I.?

During the course of this year that maddest of all mad geniuses, Benvenuto Cellini, was introduced to Francis by the Cardinal de Ferrara, when he soon drew upon himself the enmity of the Duchesse d'Etampes; and although he enriched the collection of the king by several of the finest specimens of his art, he was compelled, notwithstanding the partiality evinced towards him by Francis himself, to request permission to leave the country a short time afterwards, feeling unequal to cope with so dangerous an adversary.

[We are tempted to add here a fuller account of Benvenuto Cellini's experiences at the Court of Francis, taken from the brilliant pages of Lady Jackson, which have already afforded some useful notes.

"Francis and his Court were, as of old, ever on the move—more to his own satisfaction than theirs—for it was not only Venetian ambassadors who found in these royal rambles less pleasure than fatigue and expense. Even one whose energy, daring exploits, hairbreadth escapes, and strangely turbulent adventures should have made him proof against far greater discomforts than camping out in the open air on a wet or windy night—as was sometimes the case on these jaunts when weather suddenly changed—complained bitterly of the discomforts of thus journeying from place to place under, to him, the sullen skies of France.

"This was that wild, harum-scarum, but most renowned and skilful sculptor and engraver, Benvenuto Cellini, who at this time returned to France—from which he had fled, disgusted with its climate, shortly before the emperor's visit. In Italy, as usual, owing to his impetuous temper, he soon got into trouble; and once again into prison, whence he made several desperate but ineffectual attempts to escape. The intervention of Francis and Cellini's friend, Cardinal Ferrara, procured his release; and a summons from the cardinal brought him posthaste and full of brilliant expectations to Fontainebleau.

"There he saw the king, whose knee, he tells us, he kissed, while he thanked him for the part he had taken in restoring him to liberty; assuring him that 'such meritorious actions were set down in the books of the Almighty before any other virtuous deeds whatever.' Francis seemed gratified by this assurance. But when Cellini placed before him the famous silver cup and basin he had designed and chased for the cardinal, the king declared that although he had seen all the *chefs-d'œuvre* of the artists of Italy, he had seen none that could compare, for beauty and grace of design and perfection of chiselling, with this new specimen of Cellini's skill. 'I will think,' said Francis, 'of some great and curious piece of work which you shall execute for me. Meanwhile, repose after your fatigues, and take your pleasure.'

"'The king,' says Cellini, 'was, as usual, on the eve of departure. So we' (he and his two men) 'followed the Court, and truly we were in great straits while we did so. The king in time of peace travels with upwards of twelve hundred horses, and a retinue of several hundred persons. Sometimes the halt was made in places where scarcely a house was to be met with, when we were compelled to put up with wretchedly uncomfortable tents, and to live like gipsies.' Cellini thought it derogatory to a man of his talent to be tramping the country in the king's suite—unnoticed, unemployed.

"Always dilatory, Francis thought more of his amusements than of the great work he had promised the artist; while Cellini, in his feverish impatience, thought of nothing else. What was its nature? When and where was it to be begun? How much longer must he wait for the king's commands concerning it?—were questions he put to the cardinal, and prayed him to speak to the king, reminding him of his promise. This Ferrara took the first opportunity of doing. 'It was a pity,' he said, 'to let a man of such genius lose his time, he being also so very anxious to get to work.' 'Arrange about his salary,' replied the king.

" This piece of good news, as the cardinal thought it, he communicated to the artist. 'I propose,' he said, 'that a salary of three hundred crowns be given you, which I think will be abundantly sufficient; and you may leave the management of it to me, as I am always ready to assist you.'

"Scarcely could the superb Cellini restrain his indignation until the cardinal ceased speaking. Then, with all the dignity of speech and manner he could summon to his aid, he answered: 'Your reverence sent me an express order to Ferrara to ride post to France—as though riding post was a part of my business. But if you had then said that three hundred crowns was the salary that awaited me as a suitable one for my services, I should not have moved, or have thought it worth my while to do so for double that sum. But since God has made you the instrument of my deliverance from imprisonment, with all my heart I thank you for the great blessing for which I am indebted to you. I shall always pray for your reverence, in whatever part of the world I may be—and now I take my leave of you.'

"'Go wherever you please!' exclaimed the cardinal, in a passion; 'one cannot serve a man against his will.'

"Right or wrong, and it was as frequently one as the other, when Cellini had decided on doing a thing he did it. He now called for his two workmen, Paolo and Ascanio; informed them, to their surprise, of his immediate departure; dismissed them from his service; gave them his blessing, and money for their journey home. For himself, he proposed to make a pilgrimage to the Holy Sepulchre; his object being to model while there a figure of Christ, 'approaching as nearly as possible to the divine beauty which had been displayed to him in a vision of the Saviour.'

"His horse was soon saddled, his saddle-bags soon ready. Off he rode, intending to get some thirteen or fourteen leagues on his pilgrimage that day. He had ridden about two leagues, when he entered a wood, and had fallen into a dreamy sort of contemplation of the beauty of the scenery around him, from which he was suddenly aroused by the sound of horses' hoofs. He turns to see who are his pursuers. It is a company of seven or eight horsemen; and expecting that he is about to be assailed by robbers, he draws his rapier and, facing them, waits their attack.

"As they approach he perceives that his man Ascanio is one of the party; he then recognizes others, and finally the cardinal himself. They are come to bring him back. For the king was frantic with rage when he heard that Cellini had left. 'Gone to Jerusalem,' as his workmen said—'deeply wounded in his self-love, his artist-pride, by the offer of a salary of three hundred crowns.' 'Three hundred crowns!' exclaimed the king—'I give him seven hundred; the same salary as Leonardo da Vinci had; and let messengers be instantly sent in pursuit of him. Take him five hundred crowns for the expenses of his journey from Ferrara, and tell him that he will receive extra payment for all the work he does for me.'

"This was such good news that the cardinal, who had been the cause of Cellini's flight, thought fit, as a further inducement to him to return, to be the bearer of it himself. He had known him long; therefore doubted whether Cellini—so well aware of his own great merit as an artist, and naturally of so vain and so impetuous and turbulent a spirit—would condescend to change his newly formed plans. But he was obedient to the command of the king, to whom he was escorted back in triumph. Thus did the celebrated Benvenuto Cellini enter the service of Francis I., continuing in it some four or five years from that time.

"Twelve silver candlesticks, representing six gods and six goddesses, of the height of three cubits each—which Cellini says was about the height of the king[1]—was the 'great and curious work' in which Francis first employed him: and so well pleased was he with the designs, the celerity and *con amore* with which the artist worked — for Cellini was always diligent and almost always in love with his own

---

[1] This must have been an error—if the cubit was not more than eighteen inches. Four cubits would be more likely, as Francis was nearly six feet in height.

productions—that before the work was completed he ordered a large sum of money to be sent to him.

"The cardinal, who seems to have been strangely averse to this famous workman in the precious metals being too well paid for his labours, contrived by some means to get the order revoked. Perhaps the State-coffers were empty, or the king may have repented of his hasty generosity, and the cardinal have taken on himself the blame of its nonfulfilment. At all events, his majesty compensated the disappointed artist by making him an abbot. 'If the revenue of one abbey is not enough, let him have two,' he said, 'or three.' Thus worthily did the king exercise his power of filling vacant benefices.

"Cellini was less successful in gaining the favour of Madame d'Etampes. He offended her first by turning her hairdresser out of the court of the old Palais de Nesle, and throwing his blocks, his wigs, his pomades, and all the paraphernalia of his trade into the street after him. The king had given this château as a studio and residence to the artist, who found that many persons had made their home in it and its principal courtyard, without any right to do so. They seemed disposed rather to dislodge the artist than to allow him to dislodge them.

"He complained to the king, who replied abruptly, 'Who are you, and what is your name?' Cellini was mute with astonishment. The question was repeated. 'My name,' he answered, 'is Benvenuto Cellini.' 'If, then,' said the king, 'you are that same Benvenuto who has been described to me, act like yourself. You have my full permission.' A word to the wise is sufficient. Cellini soon cleared his palace of intruders, a few angry brawls ensuing, a few broken bones, and just a little bloodletting from the artist's free use of that favourite weapon, his rapier.

"Francis was perhaps in want of a new sensation, a new pleasure, when he told the excitable artist to act like himself, so much was he amused by the details of Cellini's reckless proceedings. He visited him in his studio, accompanied by the queen, the duchess, and his courtiers, to see the designs for the bas-reliefs that were to ornament the fountain of Fontainebleau. Cellini had introduced the figure of the king as the God of War, which was generally admired both for its martial *pose* and the resemblance to Francis in feature. Nowhere, however, could the prying eyes of Madame d'Etampes discover a Venus under her own form and likeness, and the omission did not please her.

"To recover her favour Cellini determined to present her with an elegant silver-gilt vase, exquisitely engraved, and chased in fanciful and graceful designs. On arriving at her hôtel (afterwards l'Hôtel de Luynes) the duchess sent him word by one of her women to wait until she could receive him.

"Up and down the anteroom, in an irritable mood, he paced, until, his patience quite exhausted (no very long time, it may be presumed), he went off in a terribly indignant state of mind, and presented the offering intended for the duchess to the Cardinal de Lorraine.

"This incident afforded much amusement to the Court. The king laughed heartily, and rallied Madame d'Etampes on the loss of her vase. But she was highly incensed at 'the insolence of that mad fellow,' and probably would have prevailed on the king to resent the act by some heavy mark of his displeasure, but that the dauphin and Madame Marguerite, the king's daughter, interceded for him.

"Cellini was then desirous of leaving France; but the king would not hear of it, and instead of permission to leave sent him letters of naturalization, the meaning of which he did not comprehend. Besides, the king commissioned him to make the bronze gates of Fontainebleau. He would have also employed him to fortify Paris had not Madame d'Etampes urged him to send for Bellaminta, an engineer of Siena, as a fitter person to undertake such a work. This seems reasonable advice, and the duchess was then his chief adviser—the king having cleared his Court of all his old favourites. But Cellini attributed the suggestion to her enmity towards him.

"She, however, again visited his studio with the king and the Court to see the bronze gates, which received their due tribute of admiration, Francis declaring that they 'could not have been more beautiful had they been intended for the gates of Paradise.'

"This work concluded, again the artist expressed a wish to revisit Italy—on leave of absence, to see his relatives. But Francis was still unwilling to part with him, and was irritated by the request, to which he replied that 'Cellini was a blockhead for making it.' Cellini afterwards availed himself of some misunderstanding with the cardinal that the king gave him permission to leave, and at once took his departure. Francis lost in him not only an artist of great genius, but a *protégé* whose eccentricities and turbulent spirit were a source of great amusement to him. Consequently he was allowed to commit with impunity many strange acts that would have brought severe punishment on another who had not, like Cellini, the gift of investing all he did with a certain air of wild romance.

"He had many quarrels and lawsuits on hand when he left. He had fought several duels, and it was his custom after all these brawls and escapades and successful use of his rapier, devoutly to return thanks to the Almighty for his triumph and escape unharmed. Between him and Primaticcio, whom Madame d'Etampes favoured, there was open war; and indeed amongst the Italian artists generally there appears to have been great jealousy of feeling and much intrigue and treachery."]

The exile of Montmorency from the Court was speedily followed by that of the profligate Cardinal de Lorraine, who was accused of having accepted an annual revenue of six thousand crowns from the emperor, on the archbishopric of Saragossa — an equivocal meanness in which he was countenanced by several of his colleagues, but to which the king affected to attach a suspicion of treachery in his case, in order to escape from the continual importunities rendered necessary by the enormous outlay in which he indulged.

CHAPTER VII

1541-42

Changed aspect of the French Court—Favour of the Maréchal d'Annebaut—The emperor invests his own son with the duchy of Milan—The Venetians threaten to form an alliance with Solyman—Charles V. and Francis despatch ambassadors to Venice—They are coldly received—Murder of Fregosa and Rincon—Du Bellay-Langei accuses the imperialists of the crime—The assassins are put to death by the states of Venice—Francis summons the emperor to make reparation — Contemptuous reply of Charles V.—Francis arrests the Archbishop of Valence—Charles enters into a truce with the Protestant princes—Benda taken by the Turks—Charles V. conducts an expedition against the Algerines—His fleet is dispersed by a tempest—The imperialists return to Spain—Francis resolves to declare war against the emperor — The French armies open their campaign—The Maréchal de Gueldres attacks the Flemish frontiers—Alarm of the Dowager-Queen of Hungary—Treachery of the Duchesse d'Etampes—D'Annebaut seconds her views—Suspicion of the king—The Duc d'Orleans takes Luxembourg—D'Annebaut supercedes Langei in his command in Piedmont—Death of Langei—D'Annebaut is appointed Admiral of France—Exile of Montpezat—Growing enmity of the two princes—Female policy—The Court of Catherine de' Medici—The "light-brigade"—Revolt of La Rochelle—Francis proceeds thither, suppresses the insurrection, and pardons the citizens.

THE exile of Montmorency and M. de Lorraine, and the death of De Brion-Chabot, had meanwhile changed the whole aspect of the French Court. The connétable had no sooner retired to Chantilly than Francis transferred to the Maréchal d'Annebaut all the confidence which he had formerly bestowed upon his old favourite; but it was not long ere he was destined to feel his error, for the moment in which he had deprived himself of his two most zealous and devoted friends was pregnant with menace, and the nation could ill afford to sustain so serious a loss.

The emperor, after having awaited for some months a renewal of the negotiations into which he had entered with the French king, was no sooner apprized that a marriage was about to take place between the Duc de Cleves and Jeanne d'Albret, whose hand he had demanded for his own son, than, feeling the futility of anticipating any satisfactory result to his propositions, on the 11th of October 1540, he had at Brussels invested Dom Philippe with the duchy of Milan; and this important step once taken, his next care was to promote a rupture between the Courts of Paris and Constantinople, and at the same time to excite the suspicions of the Christian princes as to the good faith of Francis.

The Sultan was already prepared to view the policy of the French king with a jealous eye, first from his having failed him in Piedmont, and still more recently from the fact of his having suffered the passage of Charles V. through his dominions; while the Venetians, conscious that they had narrowly escaped destruction, and convinced by experience that they had more to fear from the enmity of the Infidels than they had to hope from the support of the emperor, had determined to affect an alliance with Solyman. This was a catastrophe which had not been foreseen by Charles V., and one so formidable that all his measures were at once arrested by the necessity of maintaining the semblance of a perfect amity with the French king. In order to accomplish so desirable an object, he therefore at once wrote to request of Francis that he would permit the Maréchal d'Annebaut to proceed to Venice in the company of the Marquis del Guasto, to assure the States that their apprehensions were unfounded, and to endeavour to include them in their league against the Infidels. His request was immediately complied with, but the Venetians had been so frequently deceived by statements of the same nature that they received the envoys very coldly, declaring that no real friendship could exist between their several sovereigns until the Milanese were ceded to France—an event which had now become more improbable than ever. Del Guasto argued and remonstrated in vain; the States civilly declined to declare themselves convinced; and it was not long ere they concluded a truce with the Ottomans, which was subsequently ratified by a treaty of peace.

This open demonstration of contempt on the part of the Venetians aroused the indignation of Francis, who, not without cause, attributed the affront to which he had thus been subjected to the double-dealing of the emperor, and he at once resolved to justify himself in the opinion both of the Sultan and the states of Venice by imparting to them without reserve details of all that had taken place between himself and Charles V. For this purpose he despatched as his ambassadors to the council of Venice a gallant officer named Cæsar Fregosa, a knight of the order of St. Michael, who had done him good service in Piedmont; and Antoine Rincon, one of the gentlemen of his bed-chamber, who was invested with the like dignity, and instructed to proceed to Constantinople by the same route, and, consequently, to accompany his colleague to his allotted post. Rincon, however, having some private business to arrange at Lyons, first visited that city, where he was detained for a short time; while Fregosa advanced as far as Suza, to inspect a troop of gensdarmes of which the command had recently been confided to him. Du Bellay-Langei, who had been appointed lieutenant-general in Piedmont after the death of Chabot, was at that period residing at Turin; and the delay of the two ambassadors afforded him an opportunity of discovering a treacherous plot which had been laid by the Marquis del Guasto for their destruction.

The extreme corpulency of Rincon rendering him unable to attempt the exertion of riding, it had been decided that the envoys and their suite should avail themselves of the barges upon the Po, which, by virtue of the then existing truce, was considered to be an equally safe and convenient method of performing the journey. Del Guasto had, however, no sooner ascertained this arrangement than, disregarding the sacredness of the pledge given by his imperial master, he hired assassins, who were stationed at different points along the river, for the purpose of intercepting their progress and possessing themselves of their despatches, with strict orders to secure them at all hazards, even should the lives of the envoys be sacrificed in the struggle, or their destruction rendered necessary to ensure the secrecy of their mission.

On the 1st of July the two ambassadors reached Rivoli, where they were met by the vigilant Langei, who strongly urged them to abandon the river, and at any sacrifice to pursue a different route; but Rincon, who, as we have stated, could ill brook the saddle, and who had, moreover, been long accustomed to travel in uncivilized countries, disregarded the advice, declaring that, whatever might be the determination of his companion, he should himself proceed by water; nor was it without extreme difficulty that Du Bellay finally induced him to entrust his despatches to his own care, pledging himself for their safe delivery in Venice. Fregosa, who had not the same reasons for exposing himself to gratuitous danger, hesitated for a time as to which measure he should adopt; but he soon permitted himself to be won over by the confident assurances of his colleague; and, despite the persevering expostulations of the more prudent Langei, the ill-fated envoys left the city at twilight, on the 2d of July, in two swift boats, each pulling eight oars.

At midday on the morrow, when they were within three miles of the mouth of the Ticino, and about the same distance from Pavia, they were suddenly attacked by a couple of barges full of armed men, who immediately cut off all communication between the two boats; and they had no sooner boarded that containing the ambassadors than a desperate encounter took place, in which both Fregosa and Rincon lost their lives ; when their rowers were immediately secured, and conveyed to the dungeons of Pavia.

Meanwhile the boat which conveyed their attendants, forgotten for the instant by the miscreants, who were intent upon their principal prey, was enabled to reach the opposite bank, where all its occupants sprang to land and escaped into the forest, whence they made their way to the quarters of Du Bellay, and gave him a detailed account of the frightful catastrophe. With his usual caution, however, that able general, until he could succeed in securing the most irrefragable proofs of the delinquency of Del Guasto, forebore all complaint ; and even compelled himself to receive with civility the affected condolences of the marquis, and to appear to give credit to his assurances that the crime had been committed by brigands ; but he had no sooner possessed himself of sufficient evidence of the guilt of the imperialist assassin, than he formally accused Del Guasto of the outrage which had been offered to his sovereign in the persons of his accredited ambassadors, and challenged him to prove his innocence.

This was, however, impossible, as Langei, resolved to leave no method unattempted to unmask the whole conspiracy, upon learning from the fugitives that the rowers of the captured boat had been made prisoners and conveyed to Pavia, soon found means to bribe a servant of the governor of that citadel, who secretly provided the boatmen with files, by which they were enabled to effect their escape, and from them he obtained all the information which he could desire.

The reply of Del Guasto to this overt accusation was the puerile expedient of challenging his accuser, the overwhelming proofs of his guilt possessed by Du Bellay depriving him of all means of self-justification; while the Republic of Venice, indignant that so base a murder should have been committed within their territories, pursued the assassins and succeeded in arresting several of their number, all of whom were recognized to be in the pay of the marquis; but, although they were publicly tried and executed, Del Guasto, in order to complete his work of treachery, suffered them to undergo their sentence without the slightest effort at interference, simply protesting that, if they were justly condemned, they had acted upon their own responsibility and without his knowledge.

This investigation was no sooner terminated than Du Bellay drew up in duplicate a detailed statement of the whole occurrence, one copy of which he forwarded to the emperor, and the other to the diet of the German States which was shortly afterwards assembled at Ratisbon; and ere long all the princes of Christendom were informed of the atrocious deed which had been perpetrated, in violation of the recognized rights which are held sacred by all civilized nations.

Great was the indignation expressed by the respective sovereigns, who thus saw the very foundations of their safety shaken; but it was still feeble beside that of Francis, who at once summoned the emperor to make reparation for the affront which had been offered to him, and reminded him that this was not the first occasion upon which he had been called upon to suffer from the treachery of his assassins. Charles, however, replied to this demand only by recriminations; alleging that if, instead of pursuing a correspondence with Solyman, Francis had, like himself, been preparing for a new crusade against the Infidels, his envoys would not have fallen victims to his crooked policy, or, as he himself believed, to the cupidity of a horde of robbers. Although he could not mistake the meaning of the French king, he abstained from any allusion to Montecuculli, or to the murder of Maraviglia, as if in disdain of accusations so vague and monstrous; and thus the outraged monarch found himself compelled to adopt more stringent measures in order to secure his vengeance.

Charles V. was at that precise moment raising a powerful fleet to operate against the African corsairs; his previous successes against the Infidels having roused his ambition to maintain the distinction which he had already won, and to be regarded as the champion of Christendom—a title of which, moreover, he was aware that Francis was more jealous than of any other he had acquired.

The opportunity of reprisals so ardently desired by the French king was not long in presenting itself. George of Austria, Archbishop of Valence, the natural son of the emperor, who was on his way from Spain to Belgium, having halted at Lyons, Francis caused him to be arrested, declaring that he would retain him as a hostage until Fregosa and Rincon, if still living, were restored to him in safety; or in the event of this being impossible, that their murderers should be consigned to an ignominious death—a mode of revenge which, puerile as it appeared, was far from being so in fact, the extreme partiality of the emperor for this prelate being matter of notoriety. A short time subsequently, moreover, Francis, having ascertained that Charles V. and the Pope were to have an interview at Lucca before the embarkation of the former for Algiers, desired his ambassador to attend the conference, and to demand once more, in his name, the restoration of his murdered envoys or the condign punishment of their assassins.

This demonstration was, however, met as coldly as the last, Charles being well aware that a considerable period must elapse ere the king could proceed, with any chance of success, to aggressive measures; and it was in consequence of this conviction that he persisted in disregarding the expostulations of the pontiff, who earnestly represented that he would better consult the safety of Christendom by remaining to guard the frontiers of Italy against Solyman (by whom his brother Ferdinand had recently been vanquished before Buda, and compelled to abandon that city) than by any distant expedition, however important.

The arguments of his holiness availed nothing, the emperor feeling convinced that he must at once set sail, or altogether abandon his darling project; as, should he afford Francis sufficient time to assemble an army, he would inevitably avail himself of the opportunity of his absence to possess himself of the Milanese. He therefore continued to hasten his preparations, having already at the diet at Ratisbon accorded to the Protestant princes, whose friendship he was anxious to secure during his foreign campaign, an *interregnum* or truce, by which they were authorized to retain the free exercise of their religion until the decision of the general council; while, in requital of this concession, the diet consented to supply him with a large body of troops to assist against the Turks; declared the Duc de Cleves the enemy of the empire; engaged to co-operate in the reinstatement of the Duke of Savoy in his sovereignty; and prohibited all subjects of the empire from serving in the armies of France.

Although the original intention of the emperor had been to proceed at once to the coast of Africa, it was anticipated that the defeat of his brother would induce him to commence his campaign by an attack upon Solyman; but, contrary to all expectations, he persisted in his original project, although, the close of autumn having arrived, the season was most unpropitious to such an enterprize. Accordingly, on the 18th of October, he set sail from Majorca with twenty thousand infantry and two thousand horse, the *élite* of his combined armies. On the following day a severe storm scattered his vessels, and exposed the troops to severe suffering from the crowded state of the ships; but on the 20th the imperial fleet was enabled with considerable difficulty, owing to the continuance of the hurricane, to cast anchor between the city of Algiers and the river of El Harach, where the disembarkation took place. The soldiery effected their landing in safety; but before the bulk of their ammunition and provisions could be secured, the tempest became once more so violent that fifteen vessels of war, a hundred and forty transports, and eight thousand seamen, were swallowed by the waves; while at the same time an immense water-spout burst over the camp, which caused a great sacrifice of life, and thus the elements within five days revenged Barbarossa for his former defeat.

Andrea Doria, with the wreck of the gallant fleet which had so recently excited such brilliant hopes, had taken refuge behind Cape Métafuz; and he was fortunate enough to be enabled within a few hours to apprize the emperor, whose situation was at that moment desperate, of his safety. The small quantity of powder which had been landed was utterly destroyed by the water, and a considerable number of the troops were drowned; while the remainder, utterly without food of any description, and harassed by the Algerine horsemen, had scarcely sufficient strength left to make their way to the ships, although the distance did not exceed four leagues; but at length, on the 31st of October, they once more found themselves on board, although no longer in a condition to molest the Infidels. Nor were they more fortunate in their exodus than in their advent, for the tempest, still unsated with its prey, pursued the fleet so relentlessly that it was once more dispersed; nor was it until the 3d of December that the emperor arrived at Carthagena, storm-tossed and alone, each of the vessels which were fortunate enough to survive the passage having made a different port.

Great was the terror which the knowledge of this calamity spread over Europe. The Turks were now masters of Hungary, and were threatening Vienna; the whole coast of the Mediterranean was defenceless; the triple army of Charles destroyed; and all Christendom exposed to the power of the conquering Solyman. In France alone was a secret *Te Deum* raised, for her most dreaded enemy was laid low; and Francis resolved no longer to postpone a war which he justified by the non-fulfilment of his demand for vengeance on the murderers of his two ambassadors.

Some of the more cautious of his councillors suggested the expediency of delay until he should have completed the fortification of his frontiers, and terminated the treaties into which he had entered; but he merely referred them to the ruined condition of the emperor's army, and refused to listen to their representations. He was next advised to make an immediate descent upon Piedmont, an act which would in itself be equivalent to a formal declaration of war; and had he acted upon this suggestion he must speedily have made himself master of the whole of that province; but his desire to avoid the immense outlay necessary to maintain an army in Italy determined him to commence his campaign by the Low Countries, to which he had been urged by several of the German princes, who pledged themselves to support him in any act of aggression against Charles which might assist their own views. He was also anxious to secure the co-operation of the Duc de Cleves, of whom Charles had vowed the destruction, and he accordingly proceeded formally to declare hostilities against the emperor.

This was no sooner done than he divided his troops into five distinct bodies, in order simultaneously to attack the enemy on as many different points. The dauphin proceeded to Perpignan, with Antoine Desprez-Montpezat as his lieutenant; the Duc d'Orleans was despatched to Luxembourg, seconded by Claude, Duc de Guise;[1] a third division marched to Brabant, under the joint command of Nicholas de Bossu, Sire de Longueval, and of Martin Von Rossem,[2] Maréchal de Gueldres; a fourth, under Charles, Duc de Vendôme, was entrusted with the protection of the Flemish frontiers; and the fifth was

[1] Claude, Duc d'Aumale and de Guise, was the seventh son of Réné II., Duc de Lorraine.

[2] Martin von Rossem (or Roscheim) was one of the bravest generals of the Duc de Cleves, and acquitted himself with great distinction on several occasions. He defeated the Prince of Orange in the campaign of 1542, and compelled him to shut himself up in Antwerp, of which city he might have possessed himself had not his love of dissipation caused him to suffer the propitious moment to escape. When too late he attempted to retrieve his error, but failed, although he destroyed half the faubourgs by fire. Dueren having been taken by assault, and the province of Gueldres reduced to submission by the emperor, the monarch restored both the duke and his valiant maréchal to his favour, and appointed the latter to a high command in his army. Von Rossem ultimately fell a victim to the plague at Antwerp in 1555.

marched into Piedmont by the Maréchal d'Annebaut. The latter, however, having been compelled to remain inactive for the space of two months, was recalled to join the army under the dauphin, which ultimately amounted to forty-five thousand men, headed by the first nobility of France.

The Maréchal de Gueldres, who was a general of consummate skill and daring, and, moreover, utterly without scruple as regarded the means by which he carried out his measures, was anxious to follow the example of Seckingen, and to make the war pay its own expenses. He consequently no sooner found himself at the head of twelve thousand lansquenets and two thousand German horse than he permitted his troops to indulge in every species of excess towards the inhabitants of the invaded provinces, while he, nevertheless, maintained the most rigorous discipline among themselves.

The Queen of Hungary, Gouvernante of the Low Countries, terrified by the enormities committed on her frontiers, appealed to the Duc de Cleves to declare the nature of his intentions; but he contented himself by assuring her that the force of which she complained was not in his pay, nor was he responsible for its proceedings, although he imagined that it was composed of volunteers about to march against the Turks. She then addressed herself to Francis, who merely replied by telling her that his own intentions were pacific; and thus left to her own resources, she had the mortification of seeing Von Rossem advance to Liege, cross the Meuse, and ultimately compel the Prince of Orange to shut himself up in Antwerp, after a loss of fourteen hundred men and six standards.

The assemblage of a strong army in the south awakened all the ambition of Marguerite de Navarre, who entreated her brother to employ it in the recovery of her husband's kingdom; but he was dissuaded from the attempt by the Maréchal de Montpezat, and it was determined that the dauphin should at once proceed against Roussillon, while the emperor was concentrating his forces upon the Milanese.

This campaign was destined to complete the moral turpitude of the unprincipled favourite, who, in her anxiety to ruin Diane de Poitiers through her lover, entered into a secret correspondence with the emperor, which tended to counteract all the endeavours of the dauphin. Her agent in this act of treachery was the Comte de Bossut, of the house of Longueval, who, at the commencement of the following reign, narrowly escaped decapitation for his share in the nefarious transaction. This noble was one of the many lovers of the duchess, and was induced to requite her condescension by betraying the interests of his sovereign.

The two young princes were equally brave and equally ambitious of renown, but the advantage was on the side of the elder, who, more prudent, more self-possessed, and less the victim of impulse than his brother, was far better calculated for the command of an army. Nevertheless, he was compelled to abandon the siege of Roussillon, the enemy having, through the agency of Madame d'Etampes, been apprized of his design upon the city in time to strengthen it by throwing ten thousand troops into the citadel; while D'Annebaut, whom tradition boldly affirms to have been united to her by closer bonds than those of mere friendship, was guilty of such extraordinary errors during the siege as to draw down upon him the suspicions of all the other generals, and even to extort from the king himself the avowal that he was aware he had been betrayed, and that he did not attribute the failure to the dauphin personally, but to those by whom he had been misled, either through ignorance, or a jealousy of others who had succeeded better than themselves.

This allusion bore reference to the Duc d'Orleans, who had in succession taken Danvilliers, Yvry, Arlon, Montmedy, and even Luxembourg, although, from some motive which has remained unrevealed, he suddenly quitted the army and rejoined the king his father at Montpellier—an imprudence of which the enemy immediately availed themselves to recover the two latter cities. The Duc de Guise, however, succeeded in once more possessing himself of Montmedy, but Luxembourg remained in the hands of the imperialists.

The war in Roussillon was languidly pursued; Perpignan, which the French had trusted to find an easy conquest, from the imperfect state of its fortifications, still held out, and had been so strongly garrisoned by the emperor as to resist every effort of the French generals to take it by assault, while the appearance of dysentery among the troops and the approach of winter compelled the dauphin to dissolve his camp and to abandon the siege of the city; upon which Francis despatched D'Annebaut to Piedmont, where Du Bellay-Langei had, with a very insufficient force, been employed in thwarting the operations of Del Guasto, not having it in his power, for want of troops, to adopt any more active measures. To the mortification of the veteran commander in thus finding himself superseded in his command by a younger and less experienced general than himself, was superadded that of discovering that D'Annebaut, inflated by Court favour, was little disposed to defer to his advice, and he consequently resolved immediately to withdraw from a position alike irksome to his feelings and perilous to his honour, and to make a personal communication to Francis of such circumstances as he believed to be of importance to the interests of the kingdom.

Injured and wounded as he had been, Langei would not permit any selfish consideration to influence his sense of duty as a loyal subject, and accordingly he had no sooner made the requisite arrangements than he commenced his homeward journey; but the exertion proved too great for his infirm and war-worn constitution, and on reaching St. Saphorin, near the mountain of Tarare, he was seized with a sudden attack of gout in the stomach, which terminated his valuable existence on the 9th of January 1543.[1]

[1] M. de Langei was accompanied in his homeward journey by the

Another pearl had fallen from the diadem of Francis I.

Du Bellay-Langei was a wise counsellor, a brave soldier, an able scholar, and an honest man ; but his very virtues had operated against his fortunes. His merit had been cheerfully and frequently admitted by the king, but his reward had been merely lip-deep. Charles V., however, did him nobler justice, by exclaiming when the intelligence of his death was communicated to him, " Is Langei dead ? Then have I nothing more to apprehend from a man who has done me more mischief in his time than all the other subjects of France combined."

He was succeeded by his brother, Martin du Bellay, who in his turn assumed the family name of Langei, and was promoted to the government of Turin on the departure of D'Annebaut, who during the winter repaired to France to confer personally with the king upon the measures necessary to be pursued in the campaign of the following spring, leaving the command of the army to M. de Boutières.[1]

celebrated Rabelais, who was at that period his physician, and to whom he bequeathed a pension of fifty annual livres "until his heirs should have provided for him, or that he should have acquired Church preferment to the amount of a hundred Tournay livres a-year." It is believed that it was to this clause in the will of the Maréchal Du Bellay that Rabelais was subsequently indebted for the cure of Meudon.

[1] M. de Boutières commenced his military career at the age of sixteen, as an archer in the company of Bayard at Padua, where he took a standard from the imperialists, and made prisoner the captain by whom it had been carried, who, on being taunted with his surrender to a mere boy, declared that he had been overpowered by numbers, and did not consider himself as the captive of the lad who

The sustained and even increased disgust which Francis exhibited towards the disgraced connétable was destined to react in a favourable manner upon the Maréchal d'Annebaut, who, a short time after his arrival at Court, was appointed to the rank of admiral, vacant by the death of Chabot; but still the king, irritated by the equivocal success of the war, which he had commenced under the conviction that, like Cæsar, he had only to come, to see, and to conquer, could not reconcile himself to the failure before Perpignan; and accordingly, having resolved not to visit upon D'Annebaut the humiliating defeat which he had suffered upon that occasion, he was persuaded into attributing the disaster to his colleague Montpezat, who was accordingly deprived of his office and sent into exile for not having implicitly obeyed the orders of his superior officer.

The health of the king, which at this period was beginning rapidly to fail, rendered him unable to pursue the course of dissipation in which he had hitherto indulged; while the moroseness and suspicion to which we have already alluded increased with his infirmities, and was, moreover, augmented by the growing enmity of the two princes.]The dauphin had now attained his twenty-third, and the Duc d'Orleans his twenty-first year. Each was

claimed his ransom; whereupon Boutières requested that the horse and arms of the prisoner might be restored to him, in order that they might decide the question single-handed—a proposal which was declined by his prisoner. He afterwards became the lieutenant of Bayard, and during the siege of Marseilles by Charles V. afforded the most valuable assistance to Barbesieux and Montpezat.

emulous of renown, and personally brave; but there the resemblance between them ceased. Henry was grave and taciturn, with a pale complexion, languid expression, and singularly heavy eyes; while Charles was high-coloured, vigorous, frank, and active. The dauphin inspired awe; but his brother won the affections of all about him.

It might have been anticipated that, under these circumstances, the king would have sought sympathy and comfort in the society of his amiable and forbearing wife, but he still continued to evince the same indifference towards her as he had done in his days of pride and strength. Catherine de' Medici, Madame d'Etampes, and Diane de Poitiers were all-powerful; and although the undying hatred of the two latter ladies convulsed the Court with broils, Francis permitted them to pursue their career of jealousy unrebuked; while the deportment of the dauphiness was so remarkable as to elicit his increased admiration and regard, although in many who looked deeper it awoke a feeling of apprehension which was afterwards fatally justified. Coldly respectful with the queen, and even obsequious towards the favourite, she apparently attached herself more warmly to her rival than to any other individual of the royal circle; soothing her wounded vanity whenever it was stung by the bitter and epigrammatic wit of the duchess, and affecting to be totally unconscious of her *liaison* with the dauphin.

Catherine was a thorough Medicis; she did not exhaust her hatred in vain complaints or passionate sarcasm, but, like the tiger, was content to watch until she could make her spring deadly. As she was now rarely called upon to hunt or play tennis with the king, whose debility compelled him to abjure all violent exercise, she at once assimilated her own habits to his, and, abandoning the pursuits in which she had hitherto appeared to take delight, she turned her whole attention to such an organization of her little court as could not fail to render it attractive to the sensual monarch. The ladies of her household were all eminent for their beauty, their accomplishments, and the splendour of their apparel; while, as regarded their moral attributes, no further detail is necessary than the mere fact that, by the gallants of the Court, they were distinguished as *the light brigade*. Nothing, in short, could be more profligate than their whole deportment; and although Catherine herself preserved the dignity of her sex, she attempted no interference with the conduct of her attendants; and thus her immediate circle became a hot-bed of vice and intrigue, rendered only the more pernicious by the specious gloss of wit, fascination, and splendour. Her saloons were bright with light and vocal with song and laughter. Every day brought its pleasures, many of them ruinous to the royal treasury, but all welcome to the querulous invalid, who yet clung to the shadow of his former vices, and was eager to encourage himself in the delusion that a few roses were still strewn among the thorns of his painful existence.

It is consequently scarcely surprising that the private apartments of his beautiful daughter-in-law became the chosen resort of the king; nor was it long ere, in the intervals of a ballet, or during the representation of a comedy, she succeeded in possessing herself of all his secrets and influencing all his actions. Indisposed by bodily suffering for public business, it was only at rare intervals that he would permit his ministers to intrude the subject upon him; but he, nevertheless, discoursed freely on the most important measures with Catherine, who, seated at her tapestry frame near the cushioned divan upon which he reclined, found means, now by one of those equivocal witticisms which never failed to awaken the mirth of the king, and now by a shrewd suggestion, calculated to determine his decision, to mould him to her purpose; and thus, unsuspected and unenvied, to exercise immense influence over state affairs.

That, notwithstanding her extraordinary self-command, she nevertheless failed in concealing at all times the real vindictiveness and hypocrisy of her character, is evident from the fact that she never addressed any individual as "My friend" without exciting their apprehensions. From her lips this apparently familiar and confidential appellation was considered to be as ominous as the "My father" of Francis himself had proved to the unfortunate Semblançay. "Ah, madame!" exclaimed upon one occasion a gentleman of her household whom she had so named, "I would far sooner that you called me your enemy, for the title which you have just bestowed upon me convinces me that you either esteem me a fool or that I have forfeited your favour, so well and so thoroughly do I understand your nature."

Catherine laughed heartily at this frank expostulation; and it is a curious fact that, with a heart as callous and as bitter as ever beat in the bosom of a woman, she was remarkable for her addiction to laughter, in which she frequently indulged to a most uncourtly excess.

Her worldly wisdom, however, met its reward; for when, on her continuing childless throughout several years, the king was urged by his advisers to induce the dauphin to divorce her, in order to secure a successor, so firm a hold had she taken on his affections that he resolutely refused to countenance such a measure; nor was the prince himself more willing to yield to the suggestion: his attachment to Madame de Brézé, who had made him a father, and his total indifference to the dauphiness, whose forbearance left him at liberty to follow his inclination without comment or reproach, being more congenial to his apathetic and easy disposition than the prospect of a wife who might consider herself aggrieved by his infidelity.

The pecuniary resources of Francis had been so much exhausted by the unprofitable campaign of his sons that before he could again undertake a renewal of the war he found himself compelled to devise some new method of raising the necessary funds;

and he accordingly embraced with eagerness the suggestion of his two closest friends, D'Annebaut and the Cardinal de Tournon,[1] that he should augment the receipts of the salt-excise by equalizing the price of that important article of consumption throughout the kingdom.

The inhabitants of La Rochelle, however, resisted this impost, and not only refused to pay the additional tax, but, pleading the privileges accorded to them by previous monarchs, and ratified by Francis himself, proceeded to eject by force the officers commissioned to collect it. When apprized of the attempt about to be made, they had assembled within their walls a garrison of three hundred volunteers; and the revolt ere long became so serious that the king found it necessary to despatch the Duc d'Orleans and the Maréchal de Tavannes with a strong body of men to the rebellious city in order to subdue it. As, however, by virtue of an ancient charter, the Rochellois had the right of defending their own walls, it was considered expedient to introduce a portion of the troops by stratagem; after which the main body applied for admittance, which

[1] François de Tournon, the representative of an ancient and illustrious family, was the son of Jacques de Tournon and Jeanne de Polignac. Having entered the Church at an early age, he first became a monk of the abbey of St. Antoine, in the diocese of Vienne; then Abbé of La Chaise-Dieu; and subsequently Archbishop of Embrun in 1517, of Bourges in 1523, of Auch in 1537, and of Lyons in 1559. In 1530 he was called to the conclave by Clement VII.; and his abilities as a diplomatist were so highly appreciated by Francis I. that he admitted him into his privy council. He was entrusted with three different embassies, to England, Italy, and Spain; founded a college in the city of Tournon, which was the property of his family, and died in 1562.

was peremptorily refused; when M. de Tavannes showed himself in the main street, at the head of a hundred cuirassiers, while a strong force marched against the gates, declaring that if free ingress were not immediately accorded to the troops of the king the whole population would be put to the sword and the city burnt to ashes. Terrified by this menace, the citizens abandoned a resistance to which they felt unequal, and laid down their arms.

Francis no sooner learnt that the town was in the possession of his son, but that the same spirit of disaffection continued to exist along the coast and in the neighbouring islands, than he at once proceeded to Rochelle in person, announcing that he would inflict condign punishment upon the instigators and abettors of the revolt. The threat produced its anticipated effect. A deputation of twenty-five of the principal citizens were sent to meet him from the town, and a similar number from the islands for the purpose of deprecating his wrath; but they were instantly seized and placed in irons. In the meanwhile he ordered a vast platform to be erected near the residence which had been prepared for him, and caused it to be made known in the city that on the 31st of December he would preside over a tribunal before which the whole of the inhabitants were summoned to appear; and on that day he accordingly made his entrance into the town, preceded by the manacled deputies; while the whole population, to whom it had been forbidden to cross his path, to ring their bells, or in any other way to recognize his arrival, crowded the churches, where, by prayers and processions, they implored the Almighty to deliver them from a destruction which appeared inevitable.

At one o'clock Francis, in his royal robes, ascended the throne which occupied the centre of the platform, surrounded by the princes and great officers of state; and there he summoned the advocates of the rebels, who declared, that far from seeking to justify their disobedience, the burghers of the city and the inhabitants of the islands were alike anxious to confess their error, and to implore the clemency of their offended monarch. This short but pithy address was barely concluded when the whole population, who were collected at the foot of the platform, throwing themselves on their knees, with bare heads and outstretched hands, joined in a shrill, wild, thrilling cry for mercy.

It was a grand moment for Francis,—one which enabled him to perform an act worthy of the crown he wore; and to his eternal honour be it recorded that he did not suffer it to escape him. Waving his hand with a quiet dignity which at once silenced the agonized crowd, he looked around him with an expression of reproachful sadness, in which there was no vestige of severity.

"Rise! men of La Rochelle and of the Isles," he said in a low but distinct tone; "rise. You are pardoned. You have recognized your crime, and I will not punish you for a treason of which you have already repented. Resume your privileges, and receive back your deputies. The royal troops shall be withdrawn from your city; your arms shall be restored to you; and all that I ask from you in return is to be loyal and faithful to a sovereign who knows how to forgive. Your persons and your property shall alike be respected; nor will I act towards you as a neighbouring monarch acted only a short while since towards the revolted citizens of Ghent; for I love mercy more than justice, and the affection of my subjects better than their confiscated wealth. Nay, more, to convince you of my willingness to forget the past, I will this evening sup with your magistrates, and be served and guarded only by your citizens."

The scene must have been an impressive one. For an instant the immense and closely-packed crowd remained motionless and silent; then another cry—the cry of relieved and grateful hearts—went up to heaven; and ere long numerous individuals detached themselves from the mass and disappeared. In a few minutes every belfry in the city gave forth its peal, a sound unheard during the last three days; the Hôtel de Ville was brilliantly illuminated in honour of the king's visit; murmurs of happiness resounded on every side; the soldiers and the citizens pledged each other in brotherly amity; and Francis was thenceforward secure of the loyalty of La Rochelle.

CHAPTER VIII

1542-43

Francis persecutes the Lutherans—He despatches an ambassador to the Sultan—The French army marches northward—D'Annebaut takes Landrecies—The French besiege Binche—The dauphin is compelled to raise the siege—Francis fortifies Landrecies—The French Court arrives at Rheims—Charles V. effects a rupture between England and France—The emperor organizes a new army—He attacks Dueren—The citizens refuse to surrender—The city is taken by assault—The Duc de Cleves throws himself on the mercy of the emperor—He is restored to the imperial favour—The marriage of the Duc de Cleves and Jeanne de Navarre is annulled—The emperor besieges Luxembourg—He raises the siege, and establishes a blockade—The imperialists take Cambray, and establish their winter quarters at Guise—Solyman despatches a fleet under Barbarossa to the assistance of Francis—The Comte d'Enghien takes the command of the war-galleys at Marseilles—The combined fleets attack Nice, and are repulsed—D'Enghien returns to Landrecies—The European powers are indignant at the alliance formed by Francis with the Turks—Enormities perpetrated by Barbarossa—Termination of the campaign of 1543.

THE bright page with which our last chapter concluded was the last which we are fated to turn in the history of Francis I., for, as his malady gained upon him, he became a prey to superstition of the grossest description; and even while he clung with a tenacity as puerile as it was unyielding to the follies and ribaldry of a Court which had become the proverb of all Europe, he believed that he could take heaven by storm through the persecution of the Lutherans. On the 30th of August 1542 he issued an edict, by which he enjoined the national parliaments, "with all diligence, and in precedence of all other business, to proceed vigorously and without delay against those who disobeyed the statutes and holy decrees of the Catholic Church, in order that justice, punishment, correction, and demonstration may be so fully and severely administered that the example may be a lasting one to others."

This public proclamation was not, however, so dangerous to the persecuted reformers as the system of *espionnage* which was at the same time organized, and by which the *curés* of the several parishes were instructed to examine with caution and subtlety all the inhabitants of their districts whom they suspected of heresy, and to endeavour to lead them to convict themselves; the parliament of Paris, moreover, fulminating the most severe threats against the vendors of obnoxious books, and especially the "Christian Institution" of Calvin.

This barbarous policy was also, undoubtedly, dictated in some degree by the fearful position in which the king found himself placed by his alliance with Solyman, which had excited against him the ire of all the Christian princes. After the murder of Rincon he had appointed as his successor, by the advice of Du Bellay, a certain captain of infantry and soldier of fortune, named Paulin Iscalin,[1] a man

[1] Paulin Iscalin was the son of a peasant of the village of La Garde, whose personal beauty when quite a boy attracted the attention of a French corporal, as he was gambolling upon the threshold of his father's cabin. The soldier, struck by his bold and manly appearance, at once offered to adopt him; but, poor as he was, the honest labourer for a long time refused to be separated from his

of extraordinary nerve and capacity, who at once proceeded to Constantinople with a caution which enabled him to reach that city unsuspected by the spies of the emperor. On his arrival, however, he found himself beset by difficulties. Charles V., who was aware of the Sultan's indignation at the failure of Francis during his meditated invasion of Italy, had profited by the circumstance to detach him still further from the French interests; and accordingly, when Iscalin presented himself as the accredited envoy of his sovereign, he refused to grant him an audience, alleging that, as he had lost faith in his master, he desired no communication with him upon any subject.

The zealous agent was not, however, to be so easily repulsed; and, while he abstained for a time from prosecuting his mission, he employed himself in securing friends about the Court, in which attempt he proved so successful that he at length ingratiated himself with an aga of the Janissaries, by whose influence he obtained the desired interview, when he so skilfully ministered alike to the vanity and the ambition of Solyman, while he plausibly explained all the motives by which Francis had been induced to turn his arms against the Low Countries instead of prosecuting his design on Piedmont, that the

child; nor was it until the boy himself, dazzled by the weapons of his new friend, joined his entreaties to those of the corporal, that the father at length consented to permit him to avail himself of the prospect which had suddenly opened upon him. His courage and discipline soon enabled him to rise to the grade of captain; and after his successful mission to Solyman, Francis I. created him Baron de la Garde.

Sultan ultimately declared himself convinced, and ready to fulfil all the pledges to which he was bound by the treaty that existed between them.

Iscalin then urged his highness to despatch a fleet to Marseilles, to co-operate with that of the French king; and Solyman, to whose warlike spirit every period of inaction was a pang, at once consented to send Cheir-Eddyn Barbarossa, the King of Algiers, his own high admiral, to the coast of Italy, with express orders to follow the counsels of his Christian colleague in every emergency. Iscalin next attempted to engage the Venetian states to include themselves in this alliance against the power of the emperor; but the gold of Charles proving more influential than any representations which he could offer, he was unable to effect his object.

Meanwhile the campaign of 1543 was commenced, as that of the previous year had already been, by Von Rossem, the maréchal of the Duc de Cleves. The duke himself, profiting by a dense fog, had in the month of November succeeded in retaking Dueren; and Von Rossem, on the 24th of March, followed up this advantage by defeating the imperialists at Sittard in the duchy of Juliers.

This event at once determined the measures of Francis, who decided upon marching his whole army northward, but at the same time instructed Antoine, Duc de Vendôme, who had recently succeeded to that title by the death of his father, to throw supplies into Térouenne; while D'Annebaut was ordered to attack Avesnes. This he did with so much vigour that the town was on the point of a surrender, when, by a counter-order, he was recalled to undertake the siege of Landrecies. The state of that city was, however, so deplorable, that, although the garrison were well provided both with ammunition and provisions, they no sooner learnt the approach of the enemy than they determined to abandon it; and had Francis been guided by the advice of Langei, he might have cut off their retreat; but, instead of making them prisoners, he allowed them time to burn down the fortifications and the spacious magazines containing their stores, and to make their escape to the forest of Mormaux, where they were beyond his reach.

D'Annebaut, consequently, only took possession of a waste of ruins, and it soon became evident that the king had arranged no fixed plan for the campaign, as the Duc de Vendôme had scarcely taken the town of Bapaume and ascertained that the citadel was on the point of capitulating than he was recalled in his turn, and compelled to abandon his conquest and join the main army at Marolles, a league beyond Landrecies, Francis having hastily resolved upon fortifying that city, and being anxious to cover the engineers with as formidable a force as he could assemble; but in order that the army should not remain altogether inactive, he authorized the dauphin to possess himself of the citadel of Emery, the towns of Barlemont and Mauberge, and ultimately to attack Binche. In the first three of these enterprizes the prince succeeded, and he encountered such slight resistance at Binche that he anticipated equal good fortune; but, although the town yielded with facility, the citadel resisted with a pertinacity by which he was soon undeceived.

Prepared for the attack, the imperialists had strengthened the garrison and victualled it for a siege—a precaution which afforded them an immense advantage over the dauphin, whose army was not only a small one, but moreover considerably harassed, and very scantily provisioned. The incessant fire of the imperialists meanwhile told fearfully upon his troops, and becoming rapidly aware of his inability to sustain a conflict so unequal, he applied to the king both for supplies and a reinforcement. To this appeal, however, Francis replied by declaring that he could not weaken the defence before Landrecies until the fortifications were completed, and that the dauphin must raise the siege of Binche if he found himself unable to prosecute it without aid. This decision, against which there was no appeal, was a bitter disappointment not only to the prince himself, but also to the officers under his command, among whom was Gaspard de Coligny, who afterwards fell a victim in the bloody massacre of St. Bartholomew.

The fortifications of Landrecies were no sooner completed and the city well garrisoned, than Francis struck his camp, abandoned the unimportant places taken by his son, disbanded a portion of his army, and took up his residence at Rheims, where, in order to recompense himself for his late exertions, he summoned the ladies of his Court to join him; and profiting by a temporary return of strength and relief from pain, once more divided his time between the chase and the society of the bright circle which he had collected about him.

Nothing in the ancient city where he had taken up his temporary abode prophesied an early and inevitable war, in which the best interests of the whole kingdom were involved. The splendid litters of the two royal favourites, with their attendant train of pages and footmen, traversed the picturesque streets, exciting the wonder and admiration of the honest burghers; groups of magnificently dressed nobles followed in their wake; the royal guards flaunted their white plumes in the cathedral square; bands of musicians disturbed the silence of midnight; and torches flitted like meteors on all sides, as they lighted the young and gay upon their errands of gallantry and debauch. During the day the horns of the royal hunt re-echoed through the forest, and many a wondering peasant concealed himself in the underwood as the gallant train swept by, almost persuaded that it was a mere vision which he beheld. Every moment was at that time precious to France, and while her monarch thus suffered them to pass unimproved, his more prudent enemy was rendering each subservient to his interests.

Previously to a contemplated progress through Italy, Germany, and the Low Countries, for the purpose of alienating their several populations from the interests of Francis, Charles earnestly endeavoured once more to detach Henry VIII. from his favourite ally, and he could scarcely have made the attempt at a more fortunate juncture. Enraged at the invasion of his territories by the troops under the Duke of Norfolk, the Scottish king resolved, in his turn, to attack the English; but he found no responsive feeling on the part of his subjects, who either openly resisted or tacitly disobeyed all his orders—an insult to his dignity which he resented by transferring the command of his army to Oliver Sinclair, whose authority the Scottish barons refused to recognize.

A second and unimportant demonstration on the part of the English, before which his own troops fled without resistance, leaving many of their principal officers in the hands of the enemy, and which, moreover, involved a great sacrifice of life, completed the discomfiture of the unhappy prince, who, yielding without any further effort to his fate, fell into a state of hypochondria, which terminated his existence on the 14th of December 1542, leaving an infant daughter, the fair and unfortunate Mary, Queen of Scots, whom Henry VIII. at once resolved to render a bond of union between the two countries, by uniting her to his own son and successor.

In this project he was, however, destined to be thwarted. The dowager-queen, Marie de Guise, was supported by all the national nobility in her desire to secure the protection of France against the pretensions of Henry—a step to which she was, moreover, strongly urged by Bethune, the Cardinal of St. Andrews; and she accordingly applied to Francis for protection, who, without hesitation, furnished her with troops and money, when a series of intrigues on both sides excited such ill feeling between the two sovereigns that the English king readily accepted the overtures of Charles, and furnished him with ten thousand men as an earnest of his future support.

Although the army of Algiers had been destroyed, the emperor had only required time to organize a second, and this the supineness of Francis enabled him to do. From Barcelona he had proceeded to Genoa, where he was met by Del Guasto, Pietro-Luigi Farnese,[1] Fernando Gonzaga, and Cosmo de' Medici, Duke of Florence — the latter of whom redeemed from him the fortresses of Florence and Livourna, at the cost of two hundred thousand golden crowns. Towards the close of June he had a conference with the Pope, which produced no political results, and ultimately he continued his route to Germany, where he immediately

[1] Pietro-Luigi Farnese was the son of Paul III., who united the states of Parma and Placenza, and erected them into a duchy in his favour, creating him Lord of Nepi, Duc de Castro, and Standard-bearer of the Church. In 1540 he was despatched by the Pope against Perugia, which had revolted, and endeavoured to throw off the papal authority; and having taken the city, he devastated all the adjacent country, and put the principal citizens to death. After his elevation to the duchy he excited the enmity of the nobility by his assumption and arrogance; and a conspiracy having been formed against him, he was assassinated in 1547.

commenced his operations by an attack upon the Duc de Cleves. On the 22d of August he presented himself before the city of Duerne with an overpowering army, consisting of thirty thousand foot soldiers and four thousand cavalry, under the banner of the Prince of Orange—a demonstration for which the citizens were ill prepared, having been assured by the agents of Francis that the emperor had perished in his retreat from Algiers.

The imperial heralds who summoned them to surrender were accordingly treated with ridicule, the garrison declaring that they did not recognize the summons of a dead enemy—a sarcasm which so irritated the troops that they immediately opened a battery and effected a breach in the walls, which enabled them to take the place by assault on the 26th. Still writhing under the taunt with which their heralds had been dismissed, the infuriated soldiery no sooner found themselves masters of the city than they indulged in the most frightful excesses. They were aware of the declaration of the emperor, that he would so revenge himself upon the Duc de Cleves as not to leave one stone upon another in any of his fortresses; and they, accordingly, threw off all restraint. Not a single citizen of the ill-fated town escaped; neither age nor sex afforded protection to the vanquished, and before the day closed no soul remained alive save those who had entered the breach.

This fatal massacre paralyzed the other cities of the duchy; and while the Duc de Cleves despatched courier upon courier to implore the aid of the French king (who, by disbanding his army while Charles was augmenting his own, had rendered himself powerless), the imperialists took in succession Juliers and Ruremonde, neither of which attempted even a show of resistance; and Venloo, which surrendered immediately that the enemy appeared before its gates. Until this moment the duke had relied upon the support of France, but now, as he saw city after city of his duchy fall into the power of the emperor, against whom he was utterly unable to contend without assistance, he resolved, in a paroxysm of despair, to throw himself at the feet of the conqueror and implore his clemency. After considerable difficulty he was enabled to make his way to the imperial presence, and to explain his errand; but the vengeance of Charles was not yet satiated, and he was suffered to kneel for a considerable time before any notice was vouchsafed by his haughty suzerain; nor was his pardon ultimately conceded until he had bound himself to renounce the reformed religion; to acknowledge himself the vassal of the emperor and the King of the Romans; to renounce the alliance of France; to release the population of the duchy of Gueldres from their oath of allegiance to his person; and, finally, to transfer Von Rossem and his band of quasi-freebooters to the imperial service. To these conditions, bitter as they were, the unfortunate prince was compelled to accede; and, in consideration of his obedience, he was reinstated by Charles in his sovereignty of the duchy of

Juliers, now almost entirely in the hands of the imperialists.

Throughout the whole of this struggle Francis, although unable to render any efficient aid to his nephew and ally, had never ceased to give him assurances of effectual support; and in order, as he declared, to prove his sincerity, he confided the hereditary Princess of Navarre, his bride, to the care of Du Bellay, with orders to convey her to her husband; after which, having at length succeeded in assembling a strong body of troops, he entered the duchy of Luxembourg, where he retook several minor cities, and ultimately possessed himself of the capital, whence he was about to despatch a force of ten thousand men under D'Annebaut to the support of the Duc de Cleves, when he was apprized that the latter had made his submission to the emperor.

This intelligence at the same time reached M. du Bellay and Jeanne de Navarre, who had already reached Soisson; and the young princess was no sooner informed of the fact than she resolutely refused to proceed beyond that city. She was well aware that her marriage had been distasteful to both her parents, and, young though she was, for she had only at this period attained her fourteenth year, she had retained memories of her enforced husband by no means agreeable to her own tastes; and thus Guillaume de Cleves, the brother of the ill-used Anne, whom the English king had repudiated, was destined to meet a similar fate at the hands of a mere girl. Du Bellay remonstrated in vain; the

princess remained firm ; and when, enraged by her
opposition, the duke despatched a herald-at-arms to
Francis to demand his wife, for whom he had received
a safe-conduct from the emperor, he had the additional
mortification of being told that, so protected, he could
require no assistance from the monarch of France,
and that he had only to apply to the King and Queen
of Navarre.

As we have already stated, Marguerite and her
husband availed themselves of this opportunity to
annul the marriage; and the hand of the princess
was, five years subsequently, bestowed upon Antoine
de Bourbon, Duc de Vendôme, while the Duc de
Cleves obtained that of a daughter of Ferdinand,
King of the Romans.

Contrary to the advice of his generals, Francis
had determined upon fortifying Luxembourg, and
having confided the command of that city to the
Prince de Melfi,[1] he retired to Coucy, five leagues
beyond Laon ; while the emperor, having augmented
his army to fifty thousand men, including the troops

[1] The Prince de Melfi was the grandson of Giovanni Caraccioli,
the secretary of Jeanne II., Queen of Naples, in whom he inspired
so violent a passion that, not contented with enriching him, she made
him Grand Connétable of the kingdom and Duc de Melfi. In 1432,
however, either wearied of her favourite or dissatisfied with the
return which he made for her munificence, she caused him to be
assassinated. The prince bravely defended the city of Melfi against
M. de Lautrec until compelled to surrender, together with his wife
and children. The whole of his cities were sacked, his property
destroyed, and himself made prisoner. The emperor having refused to pay his ransom, he had recourse to Francis I., by whom he
was pardoned and liberated at great cost. He proved worthy of the
favour thus accorded to him, and became one of the most zealous
and trustworthy of the king's generals.

furnished by Henry VIII., commenced simultaneously the sieges of Landrecies, Guise, and Luxembourg; the former in person, and those of the latter by Fernando Gonzago and Guillaume de Furstembourg, who had abandoned the cause of Francis for that of his rival. The siege of Luxembourg was continued until the winter was far advanced; Gonzago, after several attempts, renounced his attack on Guise; and the main body of the imperialists concentrated itself in the neighbourhood of Landrecies. The great strength of the citadel determined the joint governors, M. de Lalande[1] and the Sieur d'Esse,[2] to abandon the lower quarter of the town, which, from its defective means of defence, would, as they apprehended, involve considerable difficulty, while it promised no adequate advantage; and the imperialists no sooner became aware of this fact than they threw a strong body of troops into the vacated streets, by whom the garrison were so much harassed that it was resolved to dislodge them at any sacrifice.

[1] M. de Lalande was a veteran officer of great merit, but of small fortune, whose courage at Landrecies was recompensed by Francis with the appointment of steward to his household. Owing to his military rearing and warlike habits, the courtiers were wont to declare that he carried his staff of office like a pike. He was nevertheless greatly respected, although he never attained to any higher grade, from the fact of his obscure birth.

[2] The Sieur d'Esse was the descendant of a noble and ancient family, who commenced his career as page to the Sénéchal de Poitou, whom he accompanied to Naples when his master went thither in the train of Charles VIII. At the close of a few years he was permitted to join the army, where he distinguished himself so greatly as to be appointed the lieutenant of the king at Landrecies, and, for his gallant conduct during the siege, was made a gentleman of the Privy Chamber. He was also captain of a company of fifty men-at-arms, and a knight of the Order of St. Michael.

The skill and courage evinced by both officers throughout this enterprise acted so powerfully upon the men under their command that they undertook without a murmur the most threatening enterprises. Constant sallies were made from the citadel, headed by one or other of their brave and adventurous leaders; and these were uniformly so well conceived, and so courageously executed, that they succeeded in spiking the guns, killing the miners, and fatiguing the troops of the enemy almost without intermission. The winter had, however, set in with great severity, and the garrison were beginning to suffer from a scarcity of food. Their wine and beer were totally exhausted, and the troops, men and officers alike, were reduced to a half ration of bread.

Aware of this circumstance, the emperor, desisting from all further attack, contented himself with blockading the city, in the belief that he should soon be enabled to reduce it by famine; but, despite the vigilance of his spies, Du Bellay, by a clever stratagem, contrived to throw in abundant supplies, and at the same time to alarm the imperialists, by concealing the cattle and sumpter-horses in the centre of his escort, and thus giving it the appearance of a dense and formidable body of cavalry. Under this impression the emperor, fearing that he should be surrounded, hastily retired from the city—a movement which determined the fate of the siege; and although Francis had constantly assured his troops that he ardently desired an engagement, it is a curious and inexplicable fact that, while the two armies were in such close contact that constant skirmishes took place between the outlying picquets, he suffered the enemy to withdraw without molestation, and, in his turn, made a night retreat to Guise, where he took up his winter quarters.

The emperor had not, however, wholly lost his time, as four days after he raised the siege of Landrecies he took possession of Cambray, which he garrisoned, and strengthened by the erection of a citadel at the cost of the inhabitants, silencing their murmurs by assuring them that he did so solely to secure the safety of their city in the event of any molestation from the French.

Solyman meanwhile redeemed his word. He pursued his conquests in Hungary, and took Strigonia and Alba, at the same time that he despatched Barbarossa with a hundred and twelve galleys, forty vessels of war, a number of transports, and fourteen thousand fighting men, to join the fleet of the French king. At Calabria the Moslem admiral cast anchor, and having landed a considerable body of troops, he cut down the olive trees, vines, and palms, and carried off a number of the peasantry, whom he subsequently sold as slaves; he then burnt down the city of Reggio, which had been abandoned by its inhabitants, the whole of whom had fled to the mountains. His appearance at the mouth of the Tiber next spread consternation throughout Rome; but this was allayed by Iscalin, who assured the Cardinal de Carpi, its governor, that the Turkish allies of his master would respect the neutrality of the Pope; and on the 5th of July this formidable armament reached the shores of Provence without committing any further ravages along the coast.

It would appear that Francis, even although he had invited the co-operation of the Infidels, had placed but little faith in their advent; for it is certain that instead of preparing a fleet whose magnitude might have inspired them with respect, and placing it under a commander whose age and experience must have secured his authority, he merely despatched to Marseilles François de Bourbon, Comte d'Enghien,[1] then in his twenty-third year, at the head of twenty-two galleys, with a few hundred men-at-arms, and with a sum barely adequate to their immediate subsistence. Undismayed, however, by this circumstance, discouraging as it was, the young prince, who was eager to distinguish himself, eagerly acceded to a proposition which was made to him that he should attempt the reduction of the citadel of Nice, accompanied by an assurance that he would receive support from within the walls. Inexperienced as he was, however, the Comte d'Enghien had too much prudence to endanger the whole of his force; and, apprehending treachery, he resolved to send four of his galleys to reconnoitre, while he lay to with the remainder within gunshot of the shore. The result proved the sagacity of his previsions, for the

[1] The Comte d'Enghien, the son of Antoine de Bourbon, King of Navarre, and brother to the Duc de Vendôme, was born at La Fère, in 1519. In 1543 he took the city of Nice, advanced into Piedmont, and won the celebrated victory of Cerisola. In the following year he became governor of Hainault, Piedmont, and Languedoc, and was killed in action in 1545.

four galleys had no sooner rounded a small headland behind which Doria was lying in ambush than they were attacked by an overpowering force, and he was compelled to set sail with the remainder of his fleet.

When Barbarossa arrived at Marseilles and saw the insignificant preparations which had been made for the campaign in which he was called upon to assist, his rage knew no bounds. Bitterly did he vituperate the dogs of Christians who had invited a great fleet from a distant country only to endanger the lives of the men and the honour of their leader, by requiring them to act in conjunction with a handful of troops and a beardless boy; and so great was his irritation that Iscalin found it necessary to travel post to Guise, in order to urge upon the king the expediency of forwarding an immediate reinforcement and a supply of money and ammunition, as well as instructions for the commencement of the campaign, the Algerine monarch having threatened that should the summer pass by without affording him an opportunity of signalizing himself, he would induce the Sultan to avenge him upon those by whom he had been deceived.

Eager to pacify his dangerous ally, Francis accordingly despatched a few troops with Iscalin to strengthen the fleet, together with an assurance that more should follow without delay, and instructed the Comte d'Enghien to make an immediate attack on Nice. This was accordingly done; and on the 10th of August seven thousand French and fifteen thousand Turks appeared before the city. After some difficulty the town itself fell into the hands of the besiegers, not being sufficiently strong to resist the powerful artillery which was brought against it; but the victors gained little by their conquest, as the inhabitants had removed every article of value beyond the walls; while the citadel resisted all their attempts, its natural position, together with its artificial defences, rendering it almost impregnable. Moreover, the Comte d'Enghien had nearly exhausted both his provisions and his ammunition; while the citizens of Marseilles, to whom he appealed in his extremity, refused to render him any assistance, declaring that they would not, even inferentially, act in conjunction with the enemies of Christendom.

In this emergency the prince had no other alternative than to apply to Barbarossa himself, humiliating as he could not but feel such a necessity to be; nor did the Infidel ally of Francis spare him one drop of the bitter draught which he was compelled to drain, for, already indignant at a defeat which he had not anticipated, the exasperation of the Turkish admiral increased to such a degree that he openly ridiculed the pretensions of a Christian monarch who undertook a war when he was unable to provide his troops with powder and ball. A final attempt was made, however, with the assistance of the ammunition thus procured, but it proved as abortive as those by which it had been preceded; and the siege was accordingly raised on the 8th of September.

Francis had the less cause to regret this result, as Barbarossa had, immediately upon the surrender of the town, claimed a right to garrison it with his own troops, upon the plea that they were its real captors—a claim which was imperatively denied by M. d'Enghien, who was well aware that although the city was comparatively of little value to France, there was not another port on the northern coast of the Mediterranean so valuable to the Algerine pirates, from the facility which it afforded of extending and protecting their depredations. Moreover, the count was informed that the Duc de Savoie and the Marquis del Guasto were advancing with a strong force to aid the town at the very moment when he became convinced that he could not calculate upon the good faith of his discontented colleague, and the unfortunate city was consequently sacked and then fired; after which the prince, who was led to believe that a general engagement was about to take place between the emperor and his own sovereign at Landrecies, marched his troops towards that citadel.

This ill-omened and unnatural coalition with the Infidels was destined to prove fatal to the French king in many ways. In the first place, nothing had been accomplished. A mighty array had been brought before a single stronghold, and had signally failed. All Christendom had been thrown into a state of panic, when a handful of native troops might have achieved the same result. The last possession of a petty and unoffending sovereign (that sovereign being moreover his own uncle, and perfectly independent of any rupture between himself and the emperor) had been recklessly and unjustly attacked;

and, as a climax, Francis had been so much alarmed by the indignant menaces of the Turkish admiral, and so much wounded by his expressed contempt for the inefficiency of his allies, which he persisted in attributing to their poverty, that he could not venture to allow him to return to Constantinople until he had appeased his discontent.

Presents were consequently despatched to Barbarossa and his officers in such profusion that these and the maintenance of his fleet, to which the French king was pledged, are stated to have cost the nation the immense sum of eight hundred thousand crowns. The port of Toulon was, moreover, abandoned to the Turkish fleet for the winter ; and all the inhabitants of the city were compelled to retire beyond the walls, in order to leave the town free for the occupancy of the Infidels. Barbarossa repaid this generosity and confidence in the manner which might justly have been anticipated. When he at length withdrew in his turn, he celebrated his departure by attacking several cities on the coast of Naples and Tuscany, and by sacking and depopulating the island of Lipari, whose inhabitants he carried into slavery.

The relief of Nice was no sooner effected than Del Guasto returned to Piedmont, where the strength of his army enabled him ere long to render himself master of the whole of the open country; while M. de Boutières, from want of troops, was compelled to remain inactive. The city of Montdovi was besieged, and, being unable to withstand the forces brought against it, was constrained to capitulate, on the understanding that the garrison should march out with all the honours of war, carrying with them their property and ammunition. The treaty was, however, shamefully violated, for the unfortunate men had no sooner opened their gates than they were put to the sword. After this act of perfidious cruelty, the insatiable marquis next marched against Carignano, where he was again destined to prove successful; and De Boutières, having received a reinforcement of nine thousand men, advanced into the north of Piedmont, in the hope of retrieving his reverses, and laid siege to Ypres, which he had nearly succeeded in taking when he was apprized that he was superseded in his command by the Comte d'Enghien, whom the king had recently appointed his lieutenant in that province, and who, having already reached Chiras, had sent to him to demand an escort.

This was an affront which the zealous veteran, who had failed rather from want of resources than from any deficiency of courage or ability, could not calmly brook; and he accordingly raised the siege, and marched his whole army to Chiras, where he transferred his authority to the prince, declaring that he wished him better fortune than he had himself experienced; nor could all the expostulations of the count induce him to remain at his post.

"It has been considered expedient to supersede me in my command," he said bitterly, "and to place the troops who have fought and suffered with me in the hands of a younger general than myself. My path, therefore, is plain."

On the following morning he left the city, and, having retired to one of his estates, he appeared to have forsworn altogether his military career. But Boutières was as generous as he was brave, and it was not long ere, at the battle of Cerisola, he avenged himself in a manner worthy of his high character.

The indignation of all the Christian princes was at once profound and legitimate. An indelible disgrace had fallen upon the French banners—they had been unfurled side by side with those of the enemies of the Church; nor had Francis even hesitated to direct his own cousin to tread the deck of a Turkish corsair. Cities had been burned, villages ravaged, countries laid waste, free men captured, helpless women outraged, and the progress of civilization retarded by his selfish and narrow-hearted policy; he had weakly and unprofitably justified the enmity of the emperor, and had alienated the confidence and regard of all who had trusted in him. The blood that had been spilt, the desolation that had been created, and the enormous outlay which had been made, had availed him nothing; and with an exhausted treasury, diminished popularity, and general distrust, Francis I. terminated the campaign of 1543, so bright in prospect and so disastrous in its results.

CHAPTER IX

1544

Renewal of hostilities—Financial embarrassments of Francis—Sale of judicial offices—The French king raises a new army—D'Enghien blockades Carignano—Blaise de Montluc proceeds to Court to demand supplies, and permission to engage the enemy—Successful eloquence of Montluc—Victory of Carignano—The citizens of Ast close their gates against the imperialists—Mortifications of Del Guasto at Milan—The jewelled watch—The emperor and Henry VIII. invade France—Siege of St. Dizier—Renewed treachery of the Duchesse d'Etampes—St. Dizier surrenders—Mutual distrust of Charles V. and Henry VIII.—The English king besieges Boulogne and Montreuil—The two potentates cease to act in concert—Charles V. advances to Châlons.

THE campaign which had just terminated, despite the blood that had been spilt, the treasure that had been lavished, and the panic which it had caused to the whole of Europe, ended, as we have shown, most unprofitably for both parties, and had, nevertheless, left each in a position which necessitated a renewed struggle. Personal animosity was so interwoven with national policy on either side that a reconciliation upon equal terms had long been hopeless, and it was evident that the peace of Christendom hinged upon that unequivocal supremacy of one or the other sovereign which was yet to be decided. The attitude of Charles V. was threatening. He had surrounded himself by allies all more or less powerful, and he had organized an immense army;

while Francis had made enemies even of those who were previously devoted to his cause, and although the legions which he had formed provided a strong body of infantry, his treasury was exhausted; and the undue favour he evinced to his gendarmerie, which was composed entirely of men of good family, gave umbrage to his foot soldiers, who, whatever might be their merit, were treated with comparative neglect. Aware of the discontent which had been thus engendered, but still influenced too entirely by the *prestige* of birth to renounce so fatal an error, the king placed no reliance upon these latter troops, while from want of funds he was unable to make such levies of Swiss and German soldiers as might have supplied their place. He could no longer raise a loan, as the merchants who had formerly advanced money to the government, having been unable to recover it, declined to furnish further supplies; and he was equally unable to impose new taxes, the country being crushed beneath the weight of those which had been already inflicted. In this extremity Francis resolved to create a number of new judicial offices, which were sold at an exorbitant rate without regard to the rank of the purchasers, and were eagerly bought up by the citizens, who by such means acquired augmented importance, and were protected from many abuses to which their want of birth had hitherto exposed them.

Aware that the failure of De Boutières in Piedmont had arisen entirely from his want of supplies, although unwilling to admit such a conviction,

Francis had no sooner completed his financial arrangements than he raised a force of four thousand Gascons and five thousand Italians and Swiss, levied in the cantons of Berne and Fribourg, of which he formed an army for the Comte d'Enghien. Nevertheless, the position of the prince was an onerous one; his youth excited the jealousy and distrust of the veteran officers, his near relationship to the king discouraged the higher nobility engaged in the war, whose ambition was thus checked; and the extreme severity of the season rendered every manœuvre at once hazardous and difficult. The intensity of the frost was so great that the wine became frozen in the barrels, and was obliged to be broken up in lumps and sold to the troops by weight. Everything, in short, appeared to conspire against the new general, for although the military talents of De Boutières were not of that brilliant description which could inspire an army with entire confidence, he had nevertheless so endeared himself to the soldiery that they did not attempt to conceal their discontent at his departure.

Soon, however, the young prince, by his affability, his firmness, and his watchful care of their interests, succeeded in allaying this regret; and he had no sooner taken the necessary measures to ensure the safety of the few fortresses which still remained in the hands of the French than he proceeded to blockade Carignano, in the hope of reducing it by famine. Since its capture Del Guasto had repaired the fortifications of the city, furnished it with a garrison of four thousand men, and provided it with ammunition and stores; while his own army was moreover greatly superior to that of his adversary. He, therefore, no sooner perceived the intention of the prince than he endeavoured by manœuvring in the vicinity of Carignano to throw in additional supplies; after which he designed to pass the Po, and thus cut off the communication of the enemy with the marquisate of Saluzzo, whence they derived all their subsistence.

Had he succeeded in this attempt the French troops must have perished from famine, as they would have been driven back upon a stretch of country entirely devastated; and he was induced to believe that he should ultimately compel them to this measure on perceiving that D'Enghien carefully avoided the risk of a general engagement.

Such, indeed, was the fact. The parting command of the king having been that the prince should avoid an open battle, and confine himself to the capture of such fortresses as he might be able to reduce. But ere long the ardent spirit of the young commander revolted against this enforced supineness; a long arrear of pay was due to his troops, who complained that while they suffered all the privations of poverty they were not permitted to revenge themselves upon the enemy; and the taunts of the imperialists, who believed, or affected to believe, that he was afraid to meet them, rendered him equally dissatisfied. Early in March, therefore, he resolved to despatch a messenger to the monarch to represent the difficult and humiliating nature of his position, and to entreat the royal permission to give battle to the opposing army.

The prince was fortunate in his selection of an envoy, his choice having fallen upon Blaise de Montluc,[1] a veteran Gascon, no less remarkable for his fearless frankness than for his daring courage and the exuberance of his animal spirits.

On the arrival of M. de Montluc at Court, Francis, after having read his despatches, summoned a council, at which he desired him to attend. All the princes and great officers of State were present, including the dauphin, who stood behind the seat of the king; the Comte de Saint-Pol being placed on his right hand and D'Annebaut on his left. The circle was no sooner formed than the monarch opened the proceedings by addressing the anxious envoy.

"Montluc," he said, "you will return without delay to Piedmont, in order to inform M. d'Enghien

[1] Blaise de Lasseran-Masencomme, Seigneur de Montluc, was descended from a branch of the house of Montesquieu, and was born about the year 1500. He entered the army at the age of seventeen, and was knighted in 1544. He distinguished himself on several important occasions—at Bicocca, Pavia, and the sieges of Perpignano and Casal; and was appointed Governor of Montcalquier and Alba. While lieutenant of the king at Sienna he defended that city for a considerable time against the imperialists, and only surrendered after a long and hopeless siege. For this act of gallantry he was rewarded by the Order of St. Michael. In 1558 he became colonel-general of the French infantry; in 1564 lieutenant-general of the Government of Guienne; and throughout twenty years was an active and remorseless persecutor of the Calvinists. In 1574 he was created Maréchal of France; and three years subsequently he expired at his estate of Estillac in the Agénois. He was the author of a work entitled *Commentaires à l'exemple de César*, which Henry IV. called "the Soldier's Bible"; and of some curious and gossiping chronicles, highly illustrative of the times.

of the decision at which I and my council have arrived; and I wish you to hear the reasons by which we are compelled to refuse his request."

The Comte de Saint-Pol then entered into a detail of these reasons, urging the meditated invasion of Picardy and Champagne by the emperor and Henry VIII., and declaring that the success of the prince, even could it be ensured, would be comparatively unimportant, while his defeat would involve the most serious consequences, and might even tend to endanger the safety of the kingdom. "Rather," he concluded, "let us abandon Piedmont altogether than incur so useless a hazard; or, if we deem it expedient to retain our present possessions in that province, let us simply act on the defensive, and avoid all gratuitous contact with the enemy."

These sentiments were echoed by D'Annebaut; and finally all the members of the council expressed the same opinion.

Meanwhile the excitable and eager Montluc had been standing first upon one leg and then upon the other, quivering with impatience, and making the most hideous grimaces in his attempt to control himself. At length, however, his forbearance was exhausted; he had forgotten even the presence of the sovereign, and was about to speak unbidden when his intention was detected by the Comte de Saint-Pol, who with an imperative gesture whispered, "Gently, gently." This attracted the attention of Francis, who, upon witnessing the contortions of the rebuked envoy, could not restrain a smile. In an instant, however, he recovered his gravity, and once more addressing the discomfited soldier, he asked: "Have you perfectly comprehended, Montluc, the reasons which restrain me from complying with the wishes of M. d'Enghien?"

"Perfectly, Sire," was the ready reply; "but if your majesty could be induced to allow me to give my opinion upon the subject, I should be glad to do so, although it may have no effect either upon yourself or your council."

"Speak then," said the king good-humouredly; "speak freely, and we will hear you."

"Then, Sire," said Montluc, throwing himself into a military attitude, which, however, he did not long retain, and increasing in gesticulation as he proceeded with his harangue, "I will not trouble your majesty with a lengthy speech: there are between five and six thousand of my countrymen beyond the Alps, all good and tried soldiers, who are eager for glory; besides these, there are as many Swiss, who will fight for you to the death, as we are ready to do. There, then, Sire, are nine thousand men upon whom you can depend. We will lead the van; and it will be hard if we are not followed by the Italians and Gryérians, who cannot fail us for very shame. With one arm tied up we should beat the enemy; fancy, therefore, what we shall do with both arms free, and a good blade in our right hand."

"Surely, Sire," interposed M. de Saint-Pol, "you will not suffer yourself to be influenced by the rhapsodies of this madman, who is intent only upon fighting, and careless of the consequences which such an imprudence may involve ? Considerations of so serious a nature as this are too important for the heated brain of a Gascon."

The enthusiasm of Montluc had, however, produced its effect; and while the king remained for a moment silent, the dauphin continued to make the most encouraging gestures to the envoy.

D'Annebaut, who, with the quick apprehension of a courtier, at once detected the hesitation of Francis and the anxiety of the dauphin, now interposed in his turn. "Confess, Sire," he said, "that the energy and good faith of this brave captain have almost induced you to waver in your resolve. God alone knows what may be the result should you decide upon allowing this battle. Take my advice, therefore, appeal to Him; and then declare your final resolution."

Thus adjured, Francis removed his plumed cap, and with clasped hands and upraised eyes remained for a brief interval in prayer; then, throwing his cap vehemently upon the table, he shouted, "Let them fight! let them fight!"

The council shortly afterwards broke up, but before the king retired he desired Montluc to approach, and graciously laying his hand upon his arm, he said kindly; "On your return, Montluc, commend me to my cousin D'Enghien, and all my other captains; and tell them that if I have yielded to their wishes in opposition to the advice of my most trusty councillors, it has been because I have a firm confidence in their valour and discretion, and that I confidently anticipate a victory."

"I will repeat the message of your majesty, word by word," exclaimed the blunt soldier, "and those who may have wavered heretofore will become brave when they hear it."

As the Comte de Saint-Pol came into contact with Montluc, who remained stationary until all the members of the council had preceded him from the hall, he said bitterly: "Montluc, you are a madman, and you have this day caused either a great gain or a great loss to your country."

"Have patience, my good lord," said the Gascon, too much elated by his triumph to resent the uncourtliness of the address—"make yourself easy; and rely upon it, that the next intelligence which you receive from Piedmont will be that we have fricasseed the enemy, and have nothing left to do but to make a meal of them."

Montluc on the morrow took his formal leave of the king, and commenced his journey back to Italy, accompanied by a crowd of the young courtiers, who were anxious to join in a campaign which now promised them both excitement and renown, and among whom were scions of many of the most ancient and noble families of France. He was shortly afterwards followed by Du Bellay, whom Francis had promised to despatch with a strong reinforcement and the arrears of pay due to the troops. As usual, however, he only partially, and very inadequately, redeemed his pledge, for the sum thus sent amounted only to forty-eight thousand crowns, instead of the three hundred thousand requisite to release the prince from his obligations towards the army; and with such a mere handful of men that they barely sufficed to furnish him with a sufficient escort to protect him upon his way.

Disappointed as he was, M. d'Enghien would not suffer himself to be discouraged. Eager to meet Del Guasto upon equal terms, he borrowed a large sum of money from the young nobles who had joined his banner, and commenced paying his troops, who, immediately they were apprized that the king consented to their doing battle upon the enemy, became less eager to enforce their demands.

The imperialist general, who was as anxious as his adversary for an engagement which must decide the fortune of the campaign, no sooner learnt that the French were preparing for open hostilities than, declaring that he would soon rid Piedmont of their presence, he began his march, and halting before Sommeriva, which was garrisoned only by a very small body of troops, he summoned it to surrender. In reply, the commandant of the fortress merely desired him to survey the heights in the immediate neighbourhood, which were bristling with armed men; but the marquis, who from the previous reluctance of M. d'Enghien believed that he had little to fear, nevertheless commenced an assault, which was, however, soon silenced by the French artillery.

Had D'Enghien at that moment availed himself

of his advantage, and instead of resting satisfied with the preservation of Sommeriva followed the advice of his officers and immediately commenced the attack, he must have totally destroyed the body of troops by whom Del Guasto was accompanied, as it was subsequently ascertained that a large portion of his army were at a considerable distance in the rear, engaged in the extrication of the guns which had been swamped in a morass. Of this circumstance the French were not, however, aware, until it was too late; and the marquis, anxious to defer an engagement until he was joined by the whole of his troops, profited by their supineness to retire to Cerisola for the night.

Del Guasto had no sooner retreated than the prince was guilty of the serious error of abandoning the heights, which had hitherto rendered his position so advantageous, and in his turn retired to Carmagnola, leaving two hundred horsemen to observe the movements of the enemy.

It would appear that this duty was entrusted to a very inefficient officer, for it is certain that when, on the following day, the French were preparing to resume their ground, they discovered that it was already occupied by the imperialists, who had drawn up their army in readiness for the conflict, and who were at least one third stronger than themselves. The mortification of M. d'Enghien was intense, aware as he instantly became that his own imprudence had enabled Del Guasto to obtain this advantage. He had on the previous day refused to attack the imperialists owing to his apprehension that the exhaustion of his troops, from the sudden heat of the weather, would militate against their success; but he had confidently calculated upon resuming his position, which he now saw wrested from him. Under the circumstances he had, however, no longer an alternative, for he felt that should he fall back once more upon Carmagnola his army would become disheartened; and he consequently resolved to attack the marquis at Cerisola on the following day.

The brave De Boutières had meanwhile no sooner ascertained that the prince was authorized to engage the enemy than, forgetting his personal wrongs, he rejoined the army, and was put in command of the vanguard; the prince himself headed the main body; and Dampierre[1] was entrusted with the rear-guard; while Montluc, who always coveted a post of danger, was thrown forward with a body of three thousand harquebussiers, as a forlorn hope, to meet the first attack of the enemy.

As the sun rose the hostile armies faced each other, and the engagement commenced by a skirmish between the troops of the Gascon captain and a corresponding force of imperialists, which lasted from dawn until an hour before mid-day; Del Guasto being unwilling to abandon the heights,

---

[1] M. de Dampierre, Seigneur de Clermont-Tonnerre, was the representative of an illustrious family in Dauphiny, which traced its descent from the eleventh century, and the head of whose house had, until recently, borne the title of Comte de Clermont and Dauphin d'Auvergne.

and his enemy equally reluctant to attack him at such a disadvantage. It was the object of each leader to take the other in flank, but both were sufficiently on their guard to render this manœuvre impracticable. The gallantry displayed by Montluc and his little band was conspicuous; and although from their exposed position many among them fell, they nevertheless retained their ground, and fought bravely until the very close of the engagement.

At length the two main bodies came to a charge, and the battle became general. D'Enghien throughout the day proved himself worthy of the trust which had been reposed in him; and although, as Montluc had evidently foreseen, the Italians proved almost useless during the combat, and the Gryérians fairly turned and fled without striking a blow when they saw the enemy with Del Guasto approaching to charge them, he was nevertheless enabled through his own gallantry and that of the French gendarmerie to break through the imperial ranks, and to force them back upon the neighbouring forest in such disorder that they were cut to pieces on their retreat.

The Prince of Salerno had received express orders from the marquis not to quit the post assigned to him on the left wing of the imperialists, nor to suffer the division under his command to take any part in the conflict, until he received his permission to do so, however urgent circumstances might appear; and he obeyed these directions so implicitly that when the tide of battle had carried Del Guasto to such a distance that he was unable to revoke them, he remained perfectly passive, although he was aware that his co-operation must have enabled the main body to rally, and thus possibly have changed the fortunes of the day; nor did he even commence his retreat until he felt that further delay must involve his own safety and that of his troops, when he effected the manœuvre so skilfully that he escaped with very little loss.

Thus a victory was secured to D'Enghien for which he was in a great degree indebted to the injudicious measures of the enemy, but it was purchased by the sacrifice of many valuable lives, two of his own equerries and fifteen of his noble volunteers having perished during the charge—a casualty which was, however, counterbalanced by the fact that his total loss of rank and file amounted only to two hundred men.

The imperialists had, meanwhile, suffered much more severely. Del Guasto was himself struck in the knee by a musket-ball, and received a blow upon the head from a mace by which his helmet was crushed; and he found himself compelled from the anguish of his wounds to quit the field and make the best of his way to Ast, with a troop of four hundred horse, which were all that remained to him. The repose which he so greatly needed he was not, however, fated to find in what he had trusted would have been to him a city of refuge. On marching from Ast to encounter the French army he had arrogantly authorized the citizens to close their gates against him should he return otherwise than as a conqueror; and they no sooner saw him approaching, wounded and a fugitive, than they obeyed him to the very letter, and refused to admit him within their walls. He had, consequently, no alternative save to proceed to Milan, where, although shelter was conceded to him, he was bitterly taunted with his non-fulfilment of a promise which he had made to certain of the Milanese ladies, that he would bring the young French nobles who had joined the banner of M. d'Enghien as volunteers in chains to their feet—a vaunt which it appeared was intended to be less empty than those in which he usually indulged, as it is asserted by more than one historian that chains and padlocks were found in considerable numbers among the captured baggage. So enraged, moreover, were the population of Milan by a defeat for which they had been totally unprepared, that during his recovery he found it expedient to live in close retirement, as he was pursued through the streets, whenever he ventured to appear in public, by the jeers and execrations of the mob.

These indignities, which were as gall and wormwood to the arrogant spirit of the marquis, sufficed to fill up the measure of his mortification, for never was defeat more disastrous than his own at Cerisola. Ten thousand of his best troops had fallen during the battle; the whole of his artillery, ammunition, and baggage had become the prey of the enemy, as well as four thousand prisoners, among whom were several of his best officers. The costly armour, ponderous plate, and bulky treasure-chest by which he was always accompanied to the field, and which amounted in value to upwards of three hundred thousand crowns, shared the same fate; while the city of Carignano, and the whole marquisate of Montferrat, with the exception of Casal, were retaken by M. d'Enghien.

At this period, had the French king responded to the entreaties of the prince and furnished him with a sufficient reinforcement, the Milanese must inevitably have fallen into his power; but the league into which the emperor had entered with Henry VIII., and their meditated descent upon France, rendered him not only unable to do so, but compelled him moreover to withdraw a force of twelve thousand men from the victorious army for the defence of his own kingdom—a circumstance which decided the Comte d'Enghien to consent to a truce for three months, which was proposed by Del Guasto. This had no sooner been ratified by their respective sovereigns than the French prince reluctantly retired from Piedmont, and, after having strongly fortified all the fortresses of which he had possessed himself, marched his army back to France; while the imperialist general proceeded towards the frontiers of Picardy and Champagne to assist in the attack which Charles was about to make upon those provinces.

By the messenger whom he despatched to the

Court to request supplies, M. d'Enghien forwarded to his sister, the Duchesse de Nevers,[1] a superb watch which had been found in the tent of the marquis, with directions to present it to the king—a commission of which she gracefully acquitted herself in the presence of the assembled courtiers.

"Sire," she said, as bending upon one knee she tendered to him the costly trinket upon a small cushion of crimson velvet, "my brother D'Enghien having been unable to send you the Marquis del Guasto, thanks to the fleetness of his good horse, ventures to offer to you the watch of the fugitive imperialist, which, although perhaps in point of fact as valuable as its owner, did not chance to be so well mounted."

"I thank my good and brave cousin and lieutenant for the courtesy, madame," replied the king, as he accepted the jewel, and at the same time raised the duchess from her kneeling position, "and yourself no less. And I shall greatly value the offering, not only as a memorial of his valour, but also of your own wit and beauty."

Throughout the whole of that evening the *mot* of

---

[1] Marguerite de Bourbon, the sister of Antoine de Bourbon, Duc de Vendôme, afterwards King of Navarre, of François de Bourbon, Comte d'Enghien, and of Louis, Prince de Condé, was the wife of François de Cleves, Duc de Nevers, who, at the age of five years, succeeded his father in the sovereignty of the counties of Auxerre, Nevers, Eu, and Rhétel, which had belonged to his family since the commencement of the fourteenth century. In 1538 he had been created duke and peer of France by Francis I., and under the reign of his successor he was appointed Governor of Champagne, Brie, and Luxembourg. On his death in 1562 he left six children by his wife, Marguerite de Bourbon.

Madame de Nevers afforded more conversation than the manœuvres of her successful kinsman.

Nevertheless, the period was not one for idle jesting or empty frivolity. France was threatened to her very core. The emperor and the King of England had assembled a strong army upon the Rhine for the capture of Paris, which they had resolved to sack, and afterwards to lay the whole country waste to the banks of the Loire. The avowed object of the treaty into which they had entered was the entire conquest and subsequent partition of the kingdom between themselves, and they had even calculated with such security on success that Normandy and Guienne, with the title of King of France, were by the said treaty guaranteed to Henry, while Charles was to inherit the duchy of Burgundy and the northern provinces watered by the Somme.

The army with which Francis proposed to repel this threatened invasion was entrusted to the dauphin and D'Annebaut, but with the usual reservation that they should encamp on the banks of the Marne, and keeping that river between their own forces and those of the emperor, dispute the passage whenever it should be attempted, avoiding at all hazards a general engagement. Unfortunately for the king he could not at this juncture calculate upon the slightest assistance from without, his allies having indignantly abandoned him from the moment that the fleet of Barbarossa had anchored off the coast of Provence, while their indignation had been still further excited by the outrages committed by the Turkish admiral on his departure from Toulon, when, not content with devastating the surrounding country for the purpose of victualling his ships for their homeward voyage, he availed himself of the opportunity to carry off a number of the criminals from the arsenal to man his galleys, and some of the handsomest women of the province for his harem. Thus Francis could not venture to recall his Infidel allies even in the present perilous emergency, the hatred which they had engendered towards him, and the enormities of which they had been guilty even upon his own territories, having convinced him of the seriousness of his previous error.

The invading armies consisted of eighty thousand infantry and two thousand horse, and it had been agreed between the allied sovereigns that they should advance simultaneously upon Paris without lingering by the way to lay siege to any of the intervening cities. Had they pursued this course they must at once have made themselves masters of the capital, where a panic-terror and a great scarcity of troops would have rendered it impossible to offer any effectual resistance; but so great a jealousy still existed between the two allied potentates that, instead of honestly fulfilling the stipulations of their mutual contract, each determined to possess himself of the several fortresses which lay upon his route, and thus the unity of their action was destroyed.

Henry VIII. landed at Calais, accompanied by the Duke of Norfolk and an army of thirty thousand men, with the pomp of a conqueror rather than the prudence of an invading general; and he was joined upon his arrival in that port by a force of fifteen thousand imperialists under De Buren and De Rœux, who were to act in conjunction with his own troops. The emperor meanwhile pressed forward towards Champagne, whither Francis, who considered him the more formidable enemy of the two, had, as we have shown, despatched the main body of his army, taking no further precaution against the English king than that of fortifying Boulogne and the other important fortresses of Picardy.

Charles commenced his operations by the siege of Luxembourg, which, contrary to the anticipations of the king, capitulated almost immediately, the garrison having suffered from famine throughout the whole of the preceding winter, and being reduced to a state of exhaustion which rendered them unable to oppose his attack. He then continued his onward march, making himself master as he advanced of the citadels of Commerey on the Meuse, Ligny, and Brienne; after which, crossing the frontier of Champagne, he halted before St. Dizier, a place of great importance, inasmuch as it commanded the passage of the river.

Aware that its garrison was insignificant in number, its outworks very imperfectly fortified, and its position unfavourable for defence, Charles anticipated as easy a conquest of this city as that to which he had looked forward at Luxembourg. He was, however, fated to disappointment, the command having been confided to Louis de Beuil, Comte de Sancerre, the lieutenant of the Duc d'Orleans, and to M. de Lalande, who had so greatly distinguished himself during the preceding year at the defence of Landrecies, and who, upon receiving a summons from the emperor to surrender, replied by assuring him that there was not one traitor within the walls, and that if he coveted the place he must win it at the sword's point.

Irritated by this defiance, Charles V. at once sat down before the city, angry at an impediment which he considered gratuitous, and believing from day to day that the morrow must witness its reduction. Contrary, however, not only to his own expectations, but to those of Francis himself, the town resisted despite all its disadvantages for the space of six weeks, during which time the garrison not only thwarted the operations of the imperialists by continual sorties, but even sustained an assault which lasted for seven hours, and cost the emperor the lives of eight hundred of his best troops, while the remainder of his forces retreated in such disorder that they abandoned a great quantity of powder, which fell into the hands of the French. The loss on the side of the garrison did not amount to more than forty gendarmes and two hundred infantry; but the Comte de Sancerre was grievously wounded in the face by the fragments of his sword, which was shivered by a shot. On the following day the emperor sent a herald to Sancerre to offer him honourable terms if he would consent to capitulate; but the French general, who was aware of the importance of delaying the march of the enemy towards Paris, refused to admit the envoy within the walls, and declared his intention of still holding the city.

Convinced by this reply that he should obtain nothing from the fears of the count, and irritated by the loss of life which had already ensued, Charles resolved to starve out the garrison, which he was aware was already driven to great straits both for food and ammunition, and he consequently remained passively in his camp, awaiting the result of this determination. A few days subsequently a drummer was despatched from the beleaguered city to propose the exchange of some prisoners; and he had no sooner delivered his message and left the enemy's lines than a stranger, with an apparent amount of caution which disarmed suspicion, jostled him on his path, and at the same time thrust a sealed packet into his hand, which he hurriedly informed him he had received from the Duc de Guise, and was waiting an opportunity to convey to the Comte de Sancerre. A look of intelligence was then exchanged between the two men, and in a few moments the mysterious packet was delivered. The letter was written in the cypher adopted by the duke, of which M. de Sancerre had the key, and so much was he astonished at the nature of its contents that he at once called a council and read it aloud.

· In this missive Sancerre was enjoined to surrender the garrison upon the best terms he could make with the emperor, and that with all possible despatch, as it was found impossible to introduce either men or provisions into the city. Many of the officers entreated their commandant to disregard an order which had merely emanated from the governor, and not from the king himself, alleging that they could but surrender when their means of subsistence and defence were utterly exhausted, and that meanwhile they were doing their sovereign good service by checking the onward march of the enemy. The majority, however, had become disheartened by the privations and suffering which they had already endured, and strongly urged De Sancerre to immediate obedience. Yet, for a time, the count still hesitated, until his duty as a soldier at length overcame his pride as a man, and he consented to follow the directions of his superior officer. He therefore despatched in his turn a herald to the imperial camp, demanding to know upon what conditions he would be permitted to evacuate the fortress, should he consent to capitulate. These were immediately detailed, and were of the harshest description, the emperor declaring that M. de Sancerre had forfeited all claim to the lenity which he had previously determined to exert towards him by an obstinacy as weak as it was unavailing. He had, however, miscalculated the nature of the count, who at once peremptorily refused to accede to the terms proposed; and Charles at length reluctantly consented to permit the garrison to retain the fortress for the space of twelve days longer, when, if they did not receive succour from without, they were to be allowed to vacate the place at mid-day with all the honours of war, carrying with them the whole of their baggage and a portion of their artillery. The order which had been transmitted to him, and the death of M. de Lalande, who was killed during the assault, combined with the total exhaustion of his ammunition, determined Sancerre to comply with these conditions; and accordingly, on the appointed day, not having in the interval received the help on which he had still ventured to rely, he vacated the city, which was immediately garrisoned by the imperialists.

This protracted struggle had, however, very much exhausted the forces of the emperor; and it had also cost the life, among others, of Réné of Nassau, Prince of Orange, one of his favourite generals, who fell on the same day as M. de Lalande, to the regret of the whole army, to whom his courage and affability had greatly endeared him.

The intelligence of the surrender of St. Dizier affected Francis more deeply than any loss which he had previously sustained, it being the last formidable impediment to Charles's advance on Paris. At the moment when it reached him he was confined to his bed by indisposition, and the despatches were delivered to him in the presence of the Queen of Navarre, Madame d'Etampes, and other ladies of the Court who were assembled in his chamber for the purpose of beguiling his hours of enforced inaction. "Oh, my God!" he exclaimed when he had finished their perusal, "how dearly dost Thou make me pay for a kingdom which I had believed was freely given! Nevertheless, Thy will be done." Then turning to his sister he said sadly, "*Ma mignonne*, I entreat of you to attend *complines* at the cathedral, and to pray to God for me, that even should it be His will to support and favour the emperor more than myself, He may at least spare me the misery of seeing him encamped before the capital of my kingdom, and of having it placed on record that my rebellious vassal defied me to my beard, as his ancestor the Duc de Burgogne formerly defied Louis XI. Come what may, however, I am resolved to meet him and give him battle; and I pray God that I may die rather than be condemned to become a second time his prisoner."

Two days subsequently he appeared in public in the midst of the panic-stricken citizens, whom he endeavoured to reassure by the calm fearlessness of his own deportment. "Remember, my faithful burghers," he said, as they crowded about him with loud cries of terror and distress—"Remember, that although I may protect you from all harm, I cannot preserve you from fear, for God holds the hearts of men in His hand. You must strive, therefore, to do your duty, as I shall do mine."

These were brave words, and worthy the sovereign of a great nation, but unfortunately they were only lip-deep. The Court intrigues, to which frequent allusion has already been made, had at this period attained to such a height that plots and counterplots were perpetually circumventing the most prudent public measures. As Madame d'Etampes saw the king daily becoming more feeble she began to tremble at the consequences which his death must

inevitably entail upon herself; and although she cared little for the Duc d'Orleans personally, she determined to exert all her energies to induce Francis to accept the former proposition of the emperor, and to marry him to the Princess of Spain, in order that she might herself secure a safe asylum, either in the duchy of Milan or the Low Countries, after the demise of her royal lover.

This alliance would, moreover, as she was well aware, mortify the pride of Diane de Poitiers, by placing the younger prince in a position as advantageous as that of the dauphin; and accordingly, in pursuance of this resolution, she urged Francis to terminate the war by an alliance for which, as she assured him, the emperor was still anxious. The stipulation made by Charles, however, that the ceded territory should never be united to the French crown, induced the king to persist in his refusal, and she no sooner found that her influence was on the wane than she determined to effect her purpose by other and less unexceptionable means. We have already stated that Bossut, Comte de Longueval, was at once her lover and her slave; and, through his agency, she entered into a treasonable correspondence with Charles, to whom she communicated the most secret decisions of the council. The first-fruits of her infamous and selfish treachery were the loss of St. Dizier, the supposititious order of the Duc de Guise having been written by the imperial chancellor Granvella, to whom she had communicated the secret of his cypher.

From St. Dizier Charles wrote to apprize the English king that he was about to march forthwith upon Paris; but Henry, who had no sooner ascertained that his ally had taken Luxembourg than he determined to follow his example, drily replied by an assurance that he should not follow until he had possessed himself of Boulogne and Montreuil, the former of which places he had already invested in person with a force of twenty thousand men, while the Duke of Norfolk menaced the latter with the remainder of the English troops and the Flemish forces of De Buren and De Rœux.

The emperor, indignant at this selfish policy, which, although he had considered it legitimate on his own part, he condemned as a breach of faith upon that of his coadjutor, retorted by requesting that since such was the case, and as his army was seriously weakened by a delay which he had not foreseen, he might be permitted to save his honour by demanding a truce. To this request Henry, bent upon the conquests which he meditated, offered no opposition, declaring to those about him that he was quite strong enough to carry out his measures without extraneous aid; and thenceforward the two potentates ceased altogether to act in concert.

CHAPTER X

1544-45

Effects of the resistance of St. Dizier—Charles V. endeavours to effect a peace—The queen and Madame d'Etampes induce the king to enter into a negotiation with the emperor—The dauphin demands the recall of Montmorency—The Comte de Furstemberg is made prisoner by the French—Charles V. determines on a retreat to the Low Countries—Madame d'Etampes enables him to possess himself of Epernay and Château-Thierry—Alarm of the Parisians—Prudent measures of the dauphin—Henry VIII. takes Boulogne—Francis concludes a treaty with the emperor—The negotiation of marriage between the Duc d'Orleans and the daughter of the emperor is renewed—Discontent of the dauphin—He protests against the treaty—The French army marches into Picardy—The dauphin makes a night-attack upon Boulogne—The French are repulsed—Gallantry of Montluc—Termination of the campaign of 1544—The emperor resolves to suppress the league of Smalkalden—Charles V. determines to bestow the hand of his daughter upon the Duc d'Orleans—The emperor endeavours to conciliate the Pope—Persecution of the Flemish reformers—Massacre of the Vaudois—Imprudence of the dauphin—A Court banquet—Disgrace of the dauphin—Francis raises a naval armament against England—He sends succour to the dowager-queen of Scotland—An army is despatched to Picardy—The banquet on board the Carragnon—D'Annebaut sails with the French fleet—Operations on the English coast—The French land in Sussex—Destroy Brighton and Newhaven—And take possession of the Isle of Wight—The French fleet returns to Havre.

THE emperor meanwhile pursued the course of the Marne, and advanced so far into the province of Champagne that he found himself closely pressed by the troops of the dauphin, who cut off all his supplies and threatened his army with famine. The noble defence of St. Dizier had, notwithstanding the apprehensions of the king, proved the salvation of France by affording time on the one hand for the better organization of her army, and on the other by harassing and exhausting that of the enemy. But the most important of its results was the coolness and jealousy which it had produced between Charles and the English king, the refusal of Henry VIII. to march upon Paris, when he was apprized by the emperor of his own intention of proceeding thither, having convinced Charles that he must not calculate upon that blind deference to his wishes which he had led himself to expect from his equally arrogant ally; and, accordingly, while he resolved to advance unsupported, in order to impress upon Francis the peril to which he would expose himself by persisting in hostilities, he seconded the views of Madame d'Etampes by declaring to several French officers whom he had made prisoners that, so far from seeking to provoke a war, he was ready to effect a reconciliation with their sovereign; and at the same period a Spanish monk, of the order of St. Dominic, who was the confessor of Queen Eleonora, entered, by her commands, into a correspondence to this effect with Martin de Gusman,[1] who held a similar office about the emperor.

Granvella, his chancellor, strongly urged him to a reconciliation, and he was the more inclined to

[1] Martin de Gusman was a Dominican friar, to whom, upon an occasion when he had permitted himself to indulge in some disrespectful expressions regarding Francis I., M. de Neuilly, at that period the French ambassador in Spain, publicly gave a blow upon the mouth—a vehemence by which he deprived himself of the dignity of chancellor, which subsequently became vacant, and which was destined for him; the Cardinal de Tournon representing to the king that a man who could not control his temper was unfit to become either a magistrate or a judge.

such a measure, as the protracted resistance of St. Dizier, under the most unfavourable circumstances, had sufficed to convince him that his meditated campaign presented more difficulties than he was either prepared or enabled at that particular moment to surmount. On the other hand, both the queen and the favourite, although from very different motives, laboured to convince Francis of the impolicy of permitting the emperor to approach nearer to the capital, where the impossibility of effecting a safe retreat in the event of defeat would render the imperialist army desperate, and involve the whole country in bloodshed and ruin, while their success would equally prove the destruction of his kingdom.

At length a conference between the representatives of the two powers was opened at La Chaussée, a small village midway between Vitry and Châlons, but although it was admitted by all parties that the war must prove unprofitable to both potentates, and that a general peace was desirable for the welfare of Europe, they separated without having effected any definite arrangement.

During this negotiation, and, beyond all doubt, with the intention of alarming Francis into a compliance with the conditions upon which he had consented to forego all further hostilities, the emperor continued his onward march until he reached Châlons, where the Duc de Nevers, who held the city, immediately prepared for a siege. Charles V., however, who had received sure intelligence of the great strength of the garrison, continued his march without evincing any intention of attacking the fortress, to the extreme annoyance of the prince and his officers; and the disappointment so enraged several young nobles of the suite of the Duc de Nevers, who had thrown themselves into the place, that they made a sudden sortie, and commenced a skirmish with the rear-guard of the imperialists, by which imprudence they all sacrificed their lives—the German cavalry having a short time previously been armed with pistols, a fact of which their enemies were not aware.

The position of the dauphin became daily more difficult, as, in order to avoid an engagement, he was compelled to retreat as the emperor advanced, and, consequently, to fall back so closely upon the troops of Henry VIII. that a few forced marches would have enabled them to attack him in the rear. He had, moreover, lost all confidence in D'Annebaut, and urged the king, in this extremity, to permit the recall of Montmorency; but Francis was still too much exasperated against him to consent to such an arrangement—a fact of which Madame d'Etampes was well aware, and by which she so skilfully profited as to secure D'Annebaut in his post, and thus deliver herself from the peril to which she must have been exposed had she been compelled to exchange a fast friend for a watchful enemy during her secret negotiations with the emperor.

As the imperialists had ere long discovered that the dauphin, who they were aware was constitutionally brave, must be acting under stringent orders thus to suffer them to approach the capital unmolested, they resolved, if possible, to compel him to give them battle before the rapid exhaustion of their provisions forced them to an ignoble and dangerous retreat; and Comte Guillaume de Furstemberg, who had during his service in the French army made himself intimately acquainted with the surrounding country, volunteered to point out to his new master a ford a little below the town by which the troops might pass the river, and, turning the flank of the dauphin's forces, render an engagement inevitable. Anxious, however, not to fail in his promise, he resolved to attempt it himself during the night with a few followers—a purpose which he effected in safety, and he was about to return and report his success to the emperor when the advanced guard of the French suddenly surrounded his party, the whole of whom they either killed or made prisoners. The renegade count was among the captives, and so exasperated were those by whom he was taken that they assailed him with the most violent invectives, and he was forthwith conveyed under an escort to Paris, where he was committed to the Bastille.

This disappointment proved the more serious to Charles that his army was beginning to suffer seriously from want—the dauphin having laid waste the country on both banks of the Marne, after he had filled the storehouses of Epernay and Château-Thierry for the supply of his own troops; and, thus convinced of the failure of his enterprize, the emperor authorized Gusman secretly to pursue the negotiation which had been commenced at La Chaussée, after which, as a last resource, and still with the same view of compelling a peace, he resumed his march along the river, although uncertain how long his troops would be able to subsist.

He was not suffered, however, to remain in doubt upon this important point, for the Duchesse d'Etampes no sooner ascertained the jeopardy in which he was placed than, apprehending that the retreat of the emperor to the Low Countries must at once destroy all hope of the alliance which she was eager to forward, she desired De Longueval to tell him that she could give him information which would enable him to possess himself both of Epernay and Château-Thierry, and thus readily to victual his army. Charles at once accepted the offer, assuring the treacherous duchess that he would in requital of so signal a service pledge himself to second her own projects regarding the marriage of the Duc d'Orleans, upon which Jean de Bossut, by a heavy bribe, induced the captain who was entrusted with the destruction of the bridge of Epernay, by which the dauphin had designed to prevent the entrance of the enemy into the town, to delay the performance of his duty for so long a period that it afforded Charles sufficient time to attack the outpost, to force his way across, and to take possession of both places.

The consternation of the Parisians when they became assured that the imperialists were actually in Château-Thierry, and that they had even thrown their outposts forward to Meaux, exceeded all precedent; nor could the wise precautions taken by the dauphin serve to reassure them. Immediately upon the surprise of the two important posts, which had thus been wrested from him by treachery, he had despatched a force of nearly eight thousand men to occupy that city, while Charles, who was now at ease as regarded the subsistence of his army, did not again attempt to cross the Marne, but abandoning the course of the river, proceeded to Villars-Cotterets, and thence to the town of Soissons, which he delivered over to pillage for the space of three days.

The panic in the capital remained at its acme. The most opulent of the citizens fled to Rouen and Orleans for safety, carrying with them all the movable portion of their property, and the different roads were covered with waggons filled with household goods, women, and children, while equipages of every description threaded their way among the more cumbrous vehicles, and bands of robbers, to whom every public disorder affords a harvest, rifled the fugitives as they endeavoured to escape with the wreck of their fortunes.

In this season of individual peril all national pride and all sense of loyalty were alike forgotten. In vain did the king send the Duc de Guise to reassure the inhabitants, and subsequently attempt the same unprofitable errand himself—they were alike unheeded; and at that precise moment Francis received intelligence that Boulogne had capitulated, and that Henry VIII. was, in his turn, marching upon Paris. This information at once determined the measures of the king. D'Annebaut had already arrived with the conditions of the emperor, which he had previously resolved to reject; but fearing that Charles might become even more unreasonable in his demands should he learn the recent success of the English monarch, he hastened to conclude the treaty, and once more the maréchal was despatched to Brussels by express to procure the signature of Charles, whom he found on his arrival suffering severely from an attack of gout. Having received express injunctions not to return without having effected his mission, he however ventured to urge its immediate accomplishment, notwithstanding the undisguised reluctance of the emperor, when the latter said, with considerable irritation of manner, as he took the pen which had been prepared for him between his swollen fingers, "You are pressing, M. le Maréchal, but I pray you to observe from what you now see that I am not likely to forfeit the pledge which I have given, as he who cannot hold a pen in time of peace would be little able to wield a sword in the hour of battle."

"Sire," was the immediate and pertinent reply of D'Annebaut, accompanied, however, by a profound obeisance, "it is scarcely to be anticipated that your imperial majesty will be for ever afflicted with the gout."

The universal satisfaction evinced throughout France on the conclusion of the new treaty was, however, premature; for although wearied of a war which had impoverished their cities, devastated their provinces, and involved an enormous sacrifice of life, the unfortunate subjects of Francis I. had merely purchased a temporary tranquillity by a more threatening danger than even that from which they were thus delivered. The principal articles of the treaty set forth that "within the space of two years the emperor should bestow the hand of his daughter, or that of his niece, according to his own pleasure, upon the Duc d'Orleans, with either the Milanese or the Low Countries and the counties of Bourgogne and Charolois as her dowry, also at his own option. Should he decide upon thus ceding the Milanese, moreover, he was to retain the citadels of Milan and Cremorna until the princess should have male issue; while Francis was to resign his claim alike to the kingdom of Naples and the Milanese duchy, should he determine to endow the duke with the Low Countries, and moreover restore all the territories of the Duc de Savoie, although he was permitted to retain his fortresses until the emperor relinquished those of Milan and Cremorna, save such as had been taken since the truce of Nice, which were to be at once given up on both sides, as well as all those which had been taken in France and the Low Countries."

This treaty, however advantageous it was likely to prove to the Duc d'Orleans, was one by which France as a nation was at once weakened and endangered; and the dauphin accordingly protested strongly against its acceptance. It aggrandized his brother at his expense, and dismembered the kingdom which he regarded as his just inheritance. Rather, as he declared, would he still trust to the force of arms than consent to a concession by which he was humiliated, and which threatened to involve the nation in anarchy; but his representations were disregarded. The king, failing in health, with all his energies depressed, and surrounded by advisers who, from private interests or public policy, were anxious to secure a termination of the war, treated his arguments with a cold and resolute indifference which convinced him that further opposition would be useless; and, accordingly, he signed a solemn protest against it at Fontainebleau on the 12th of December, in the presence of the Duc de Vendôme, the Comte d'Enghien, and the Comte d'Aumale, afterwards Duc de Guise—a ceremony which, although common at the time, could be of little effect.

The treaty had no sooner been concluded by the two contracting parties at Crespy, on the 18th of September, than the emperor despatched an order to De Buren and De Rœux, who were assisting the English in the siege of Montreuil, to disband their troops and retire; while the Duc d'Orleans, the Cardinals of Lorraine and Meudon, and several nobles of high rank, proceeded to join Charles at Brussels, where they were to remain as hostages until the fortresses designated by the treaty were evacuated. The Maréchal d'Annebaut was also despatched to Brussels, and the dauphin marched to the relief of Montreuil, greatly to the chagrin of Henry VIII., who was vigorously besieging that city, but who, abandoned by his German allies, and unable to resist so powerful an army as that now brought against him, raised the siege, threw a strong garrison into Boulogne, and retreated with the remainder of his forces to Calais, where he at once embarked for England. He moreover retired in such haste that, although he had left a large body of troops to defend the city, he had not organized any plan by which that defence might be assured; the principal portion of his artillery was still planted outside the walls, and all his military stores remained in the lower town, which was rendered eminently unsafe by the numerous breaches that had induced the besieged to abandon it, and to retire into the upper portion of the place, where they were covered by the citadel.

The dauphin, apprized of this negligence, determined to hazard a night attack, for the double purpose of recovering the town and securing the stores which were housed in its magazines. Placing himself at the head of a few companies of infantry, the whole of whom by his orders wore their shirts over their uniforms, that they might be enabled to recognise each other in the darkness, he accordingly directed M. de Tais, his second in command, to march in profound silence towards the breaches in the walls of the lower town, which were defended only by a slender guard, while M. de Dampierre advanced upon the tower on the sea-shore with his corps of Grisons.

M. de Tais readily effected his entrance into the place by overpowering the few troops who were there stationed, but he was unfortunately so severely wounded during the attack that he was compelled to retire to the camp, upon which the French troops, although already in possession of the town, finding themselves without a leader, and being informed that the English were about to make a sortie and to repossess themselves of the breaches in order to intercept their retreat, became so terrified that they began to fly in the utmost confusion; nor could all the efforts of their other officers, among whom was the brave Montluc, succeed in inducing them to rally and hold their ground. Day was beginning to dawn when the place was abandoned, and Montluc was the last to pass the walls, with three arrows in his buckler and one in the sleeve of his coat-of-mail, declaring as he rejoined his friends that he bore about him all the booty that he had made at Boulogne. Immediately afterwards the fugitives were met by a strong force of lansquenets under D'Annebaut, who was advancing to their assistance. But it was already too late; and the dauphin having strengthened the garrison of Montreuil as a check upon its threatening neighbour, the campaign terminated for the winter.

The war which was thus closed, inglorious as it had proved to both sovereigns, had, nevertheless, been a source of immense suffering to the French people. The peasantry had been oppressed and outraged alternately by friends and enemies; their cattle had been slaughtered, their grain cut down before it ripened, their houses pillaged, their wives and daughters insulted, and the provinces of Champagne and Picardy, once so abundant in produce of every description, laid waste, and the cities abandoned; while even many of the nobles, who had hitherto lived in affluence, were compelled to quit their devastated estates, and to throw themselves upon the charity of those who had escaped a similar ruin.

The emperor, on quitting France, had disbanded a large portion of his army, but he had retained his most efficient force, and quartered all his Spanish troops in Lorraine. He had abandoned all further projects against the Infidels, and he was weary of making war against Francis, terminating, as it ever did, in new treaties, which each in turn disregarded when such a breach of faith suited his policy. Still he was unwilling to remain in inaction; and once more he resolved to humble the pretensions of the Protestant princes, whose partial independence he regarded as an affront to his own dignity.

Meanwhile his affection for the Duc d'Orleans increased daily; the lively, frank, and fearless disposition of the young prince amused his leisure and diverted his hours of suffering, while his undisguised ambition, and the jealousy which he evinced of his elder brother, only the more tended to increase his favour. Charles had already resolved to give him the hand of his daughter; but, at the suggestion of the duke himself, he addressed a letter to Francis, in which he affirmed his intention of marrying him to his niece, unless the king should consent to increase his appanage in France, which, by the treaty of Crespy, amounted only to a hundred thousand annual livres. Francis, as had ever been the fashion with both monarchs, made no definite reply to this demand, but deferred his decision until the period of the projected alliance should have arrived; and the emperor, absorbed by his newly-awakened hatred of the reformers, forbore on his side to urge him further upon the subject.

The emperor was eager to pursue his persecution of the Smalkalden league, and to compel the princes to submit once more to the dominion of the Roman Church, in order at the same time to secure his own supremacy and to conciliate the favour of the Pope, which he had forfeited by his alliance with Henry VIII. The pontiff had evinced his displeasure by convoking, without his concurrence, the Council of Trent, which reversed the *interim* granted by Charles to the Protestants; while at the same time he openly declared that Francis had conferred a greater benefit upon Christendom by his persecution of the heretics than injury by his momentary alliance with the Infidels. He had, moreover, addressed a caustic letter to the emperor, in which he advised him to refer to himself all the ecclesiastical questions in which he had hitherto permitted his imperial diets to intermeddle, declaring that he alone was competent to decide them, and threatening him with his vengeance should he disobey.

As this precise measure was at the moment that which appeared the best calculated to assist his own projects, Charles, instead of resenting the haughtiness of the pontiff, commanded all his subjects in the Low Countries to obey, on peril of their lives, the bull which had been issued, and immediately to discontinue the practices of their religion; but the Lutherans, although they dared no longer worship in public, as they had for some time been permitted to do, would not so lightly abandon the faith they had adopted; nor was it long ere Charles ascertained that the inhabitants of Tournay had summoned to their city a celebrated French preacher, called Pierre du Breuil, who was accustomed to perform the reformed service secretly, upon which he caused him to be arrested as he was returning from the ramparts, and burnt him by a slow fire in the great square on the 19th of February.

This fearful example aroused the jealousy of the French king, who, anxious not to be surpassed in zeal for the Church by a monarch who had already injured him in the opinion of all the Romanist princes by his crusades against the Infidels, determined, in his turn, to strike a decisive blow which should reinstate him in their esteem, by exceeding the efforts then making by his rival.

After the frightful religious persecution of the eleventh century, by which the Albigenses were exterminated, a few of the Vaudois, who had succeeded in effecting their escape, had concealed themselves in the narrowest and most secluded valleys of the Alps, where, by their exemplary industry and peaceful demeanour, they had so much ingratiated themselves with the surrounding nobles that they were permitted to pursue their agrarian avocations unmolested. Thus they had in time greatly increased in numbers, and while the rest of Europe was engaged in war they had quietly reared their crops, tended their herds, and made many a hitherto barren spot smile with vegetation. Their life was a purely pastoral one; and although occasionally disturbed by some passing persecution, they relied so implicitly upon the privilege accorded to them by Louis XII.—who, having compelled them to declare their submission to the Church of Rome, granted them free permission to remain unmolested in their mountain-fastnesses—that they had toiled and prospered, spreading themselves by degrees along the range of the Alps, and occupying some of the highest points above the marquisate of Saluzzo. Subsequently their agricultural skill became so greatly appreciated that they were, towards the close of the thirteenth century, put into possession of a confined and desert district to the north of the Durance; and there they had during nearly three centuries made their abode, converting the waste into a smiling garden, and peopling the adjacent heights with innumerable flocks and herds.

This prosperity, calm and patriarchal as it was, however, excited the envy and malevolence of their Romanist neighbours. Their territory, which extended from the foot of the Alps to the district of Venaissan, contained two towns, those of Mérindol and Cabrières, and about thirty villages; while midway between the towns stood the borough of Oppède, which belonged to the Baron Jean Meynier, president of the parliament of Provence, and was entirely inhabited by Roman Catholics, which faith he himself professed.

It unfortunately happened at the period to which we must now return (1545) that one of the vassals of De Meynier, having incurred a heavy debt to his rigorous master, which he was unable to liquidate, left his home stealthily, and fled for security to Cabrières—a fact which the baron no sooner ascertained than, determined to avail himself of so favourable an opportunity of persecuting his detested neighbours, he hastened to apprize the king that the whole district was in a state of revolt, and that it was apprehended the reformers had formed a plot to possess themselves of Marseilles.

Francis made no effort to assure himself of the truth of this statement, but at once authorized De Meynier to put in force the decree promulgated against the Vaudois in 1540, during his first persecution of the professors of the reformed religion—a decree which had consigned all the heads of families to the flames, their wives and children to slavery, their property to confiscation, and their habitations to demolition. This iniquitous sentence had, however, been remitted at the entreaty of Du Bellay-Langei, who, after having made a survey of the little colony, convinced the king of their usefulness and love of order; upon which, moved by his representation, and about to enter into a new war in which these border-allies might probably prove serviceable, Francis had consented to revoke the edict, and, by a declaration addressed to the parliament of Aix, pardoned the Vaudois all their past errors, and accorded to them a period of three months, at the termination of which they were called upon to recant them.

In reply to this summons the Vaudois forwarded to the king a written confession of their faith, humbly entreating that he would point out the errors which they were thus commanded to abjure; but, although no attention was vouchsafed to their appeal, they had since been suffered to remain unmolested.

Now, however, the cessation of hostilities and the mutual engagement of the emperor and the French king to exterminate all heresy throughout their respective dominions, had rendered his frontier-towns of comparatively small importance to Francis; and he resolved, although Charles had once more taken the initiative, and the pyres had been already lighted in Belgium, that he too would purchase his salvation by the same means. Unhappily for the victims whom he had resolved to immolate, he was again prostrated by a relapse of the malady to which he had long been a victim; and the Cardinal de Tournon, while entreating him to make his peace with God lest he should not survive the attack, assured him that he could not more effectually do so than by persisting in so pious an intention. The Archbishop of Arles, the Bishop of Aix, and sundry other ecclesiastics who were then assembled at Avignon, seconded the efforts of the cardinal, by conjuring him to revoke the amnesty which he had granted to the heretical Vaudois; and thus, even had he subsequently repented the barbarous order which he had caused to be transmitted to De Meynier, the hourly-increasing superstition of Francis, which always displayed itself under a fear of approaching death, hardened his heart against every thought of mercy; and the secret preparations of the vindictive baron were continued with a caution and celerity which blinded the wretched Lutherans to their danger, even when it had reached their very thresholds; nor was it until he issued an order that all individuals who were capable of bearing arms throughout the province should immediately assemble, well provided with food and weapons, for an expedition which was not explained, that they were awakened to a sense of their peril.

The fated victims of selfish bigotry immediately despatched messengers to inform the Lutheran princes and the Protestant cantons of Switzerland of the jeopardy in which they were placed, and to entreat their assistance; and their co-religionists lost no time in forwarding a deputation to the king, which was commissioned to implore his clemency for the poor mountaineers, and to petition that they might still be permitted to retain their liberty of conscience; offering, moreover, themselves to become sureties that, should he be prevailed upon to spare them, they would never in any way endeavour to disturb the tranquillity of the state.

Francis received the deputies, who were introduced into his sick-room, with great haughtiness; and the sole reply which he vouchsafed was to the effect that, as he never interfered with the national legislature of those whom they represented, he begged of them not to intermeddle in his own.

The levies which, by virtue of his office, De Meynier was authorized to make for the public service, joined to the local militia thus raised, formed a considerable force, which was augmented by a troop of horse under Iscalin, who had been recently created Baron de la Garde, and whose services in Italy had rendered both himself and his men callous to human suffering, and intolerant to all who rejected the Romish tenets. Nor had De Meynier failed to inform the popish legate, Antonio Trivulzio, of the proposed campaign, and from him he received a further reinforcement of a thousand foot-soldiers and several pieces of artillery.

The soul sickens at the record of the foul butcheries committed by this horde of legalized assassins. As they advanced towards the nearer villages the inhabitants fled in terror to the mountains, leaving their habitations to be burned and their flocks and herds to become the prey of the spoilers; those who, from bodily weakness, could not effect their escape were cut down, and soon the flames, which ascended to the sky on all sides, spread the alarm in the more distant parts of the district. In like manner the other hamlets were consecutively abandoned, pillaged, and finally burnt, as well as the cornstores and such trees as would ignite. No resistance was offered; the miserable victims, unprepared for such an attack, sought only to save themselves by flight; and on the following morning De Meynier divided his troops into two bodies, one of which pursued the mountain road, while the other followed the course of the river. The carnage that ensued was frightful; many of the fugitives were encumbered either by children of tender years or by aged parents, to whom they clung even in their despair, and all these perished miserably. Neither age nor sex proved a protection, and horrors were committed in the face of day which cried aloud to heaven for vengeance.

Thus was this army of extermination engaged until the 18th, when it reached Mirandola; but the once flourishing town, although it had so recently been warm with life, was totally abandoned save by a poor idiot, who, while wandering through the deserted streets, was seized, bound to an olive tree, and shot. At Cabrières, on the morrow, the royal army, which was to secure the salvation of its sovereign, found sixty men and half the number of women, who, still trusting that they might save themselves from the general slaughter, made a show of resistance, and then offered to capitulate. The proposal was accepted, and they were assured that their lives would be respected; but they had no sooner delivered up the town than they were informed that no terms could be kept with heretics, and they were one and all put to death.

Nor did those who had escaped from the city fail to become in their turn the prey of the still unsated barbarians. Eight hundred of the male inhabitants perished by the weapons of their remorseless enemies; while the women were, by the orders of De Meynier himself, shut up in a barn which was fired from without, and whenever a poor tortured wretch strove to save herself from the flames by leaping through the solitary window, she was immediately transfixed by a pike, and hurled back upon the reeking pile.

Suffice it, that before the work of death was finally accomplished, three thousand persons had shared the common fate, while a yet greater number were still wandering in the woods and among the fastnesses of the mountains; but the agents of murder were soon upon their track, and they also successively fell into the hands of De Meynier, who selected from among them six hundred and seventy of the younger and more vigorous, whom he consigned to the galleys, where they perished miserably within a few weeks. Upwards of two hundred and fifty others, after having been subjected to the mockery of a trial as heretics and traitors, were executed; and, finally, a proclamation was made that all individuals convicted of harbouring those who were still at large should suffer death—a threat which so terrified the few who might have possessed sufficient humanity to afford shelter to the miserable fugitives that they closed their hearts and their homes against them; and with the exception of a mere remnant, who succeeded in effecting their escape to Geneva and the Swiss territories, all ultimately died from famine. Twenty-two towns and villages were annihilated; such crops and timber as could not be destroyed by fire were torn up by the roots; and the flourishing district which had been for so long a period the garden of Provence was in a few short days converted into a desert and unpeopled waste.

With the exception of a few of the more bigoted of the priesthood, all Christendom concurred in regarding this wholesale and unprovoked butchery of an inoffensive population with undisguised and genuine horror; but Francis, whose increasing infirmities rendered him more, than ever anxious to conciliate the Church, and who weakly imagined that he was doing it good service by exterminating its enemies with a zeal even greater than that of the emperor himself, subsequently (on the 18th of August) registered his approval of the carnage, declaring that the Vaudois had only received a fitting chastisement for their obstinate heresy.

It was at this period that the dauphin committed an act of imprudence which strengthened the jealousy and dislike that the king had long evinced towards him. While his paternal ambition was flattered by the brilliant alliance about to be contracted by the younger prince (an alliance which promised to place him upon a throne little inferior to that of France), and his vanity was soothed by the conviction that the same qualities which in himself had excited the jealousy of the emperor in his youth had tended to attract him in his more mature years to the Duc d'Orleans, he gloomily remembered that the dauphin had neither aggrandized the dignity of the Crown by his espousals with Catherine de' Medici nor increased the glory of the nation by his arms. The open and ardent nature of the Prince Charles, moreover, which responded to that of his father, had led him to evince towards the king an affection and gratitude which were never exhibited by the dauphin, who, long habituated to consider himself as an object of suspicion and distrust, retorted the injustice by augmented reserve and indifference. The personal Court of the king was the chosen resort of the younger prince, and many of his closest friends were members of his father's household; whereas the dauphin formed a circle of his own, wherein figured all the friends and adherents of the exiled Montmorency.

It was when surrounded by these favourite nobles that he was betrayed into the imprudence to which allusion has been made. The banquet to which he had bidden them was nearly at its close, and the potent Hungary wine, which had been lavishly supplied to the guests, had heated more than one brain and quickened more than one pulse. The conversation of the party had turned upon the future, and the dauphin, believing himself to be surrounded by none but friends, began to explain his intentions so soon as he should have succeeded to the crown; and, finally, he declared to each the office which he had determined to confer upon him.

So interesting was the conversation to all parties that no one observed the presence of Briandas, a buffoon of the Court, who, however vacantly he affected to look around him, gathered up every sentence of this premature and ill-chosen discussion. Seated in the deep recess of a bay window, and perfectly motionless, he retained his station until a chorus of acknowledgments from the assembled guests convinced him that he had better retire as unobtrusively as he had entered. When convinced that he had heard all he accordingly withdrew, and at once proceeded to the apartments of the king.

"God help you, François de Valois!" he said abruptly, as he approached the divan upon which the monarch lay, and indulged in a shrill and sardonic laugh, which implied more of sarcasm than of merriment.

"How now, Briandas," exclaimed the king somewhat sharply; "who has taught you this lesson?"

"What matters it?" asked the buffoon in reply. "You are no longer king of France; I have just seen it proved; and you, M. de Thais, who believe yourself to be grand-master of the artillery, you are deceived—Brissac holds that rank; and you too, who stand so proudly beside the sick-couch, you are not as you suppose the first-chamberlain—Saint-André has the appointment." Thus, with a bitter chuckle, he transferred all the great offices of the Court; after which, once more addressing the astonished king, he added—"On the faith of a fool, Francis, you will soon see the Connétable de Montmorency back once more, who will rule you with a rod of iron, and teach you never again to play the madman. Fly while you can; I renounce you; you are dead."

"Inform me instantly of your meaning, sirrah, or I will wring it from you by the lash!" exclaimed the indignant monarch. "Are these seemly words to utter to your sovereign in the presence of his nobles?"

"I am but the echo of your own loyal and devoted son, M. de Valois," replied the unabashed buffoon. "Henry the dauphin, at his own board, has so declared it to his partizans."

"Say you so?" shouted Francis indignantly, as he sprang from the divan with an energy of which a moment previously he would have been incapable. "It is then indeed time that I should assert myself. Summon the captain of my Scottish guards."

This order was instantly obeyed; and, forgetting alike his suffering and his debility, the king placed himself at the head of the royal archers, and proceeded to the apartments of his offending son. The dauphin had, however, been already apprized that he was betrayed, and when the indignant monarch entered the banqueting-room he found it occupied only by a bevy of attendants, who were removing the remnants of the repast. Unable to suppress the rage by which he was at the moment wholly mastered, Francis commanded his escort to throw the whole contents of the saloon out of the windows, not only the plate, glass, and furniture, but also the officers themselves—an order which was so promptly put into execution that those members of the dauphin's household who could not effect their escape by other means were compelled to leap from the balcony in order to save themselves from the pikes of the guard. The whole suite of apartments was then emptied, and every article which could be wrenched from its place flung into the courtyard; after which, exhausted by so unwonted an exertion, Francis returned pallid and trembling to his sick-couch.

Nor was his indignation merely momentary; the very sense of his rapid decay only rendered him the more morbidly sensitive to all that touched his dignity or affected his authority; and so deeply was he wounded by the proceedings of the prince that it was only at the expiration of a month that he could be induced, by the entreaties of the whole Court, to permit the dauphin to appear once more in his presence; nor would he even then consent to receive him without enforcing the condition that no individual who had occupied a place at his board at the late ill-omened banquet should venture to accompany him.

The loss of Boulogne had deeply mortified the king, who felt that its capture had been a disgrace to the French arms, which it behoved him for the honour of his nation to efface; and, despite the fearfully exhausted state of the public finances, he resolved, if possible, to wrest it once more from the enemy. Aware, however, that so long as it was protected on its seaward side by the vessels of war which were stationed in the port, such an attempt must necessarily be attended by great uncertainty should he rely only on his land forces, he determined, while marching an army to its rescue, to avail himself at the same time of the services of a fleet which he had recently formed, and with which he proposed to attack the English on the high seas; or, failing in this attempt, to descend upon their coast in order to withdraw them from his own, and thus render the enterprize less hazardous.

In addition to this precaution he despatched a strong body of troops to Scotland under M. de Lorges,[1] to the support of the queen-mother, who was anxious to protect herself against the power of Henry VIII., and to prevent the marriage of the infant Princess Mary with his son. De Lorges had instructions to induce the Earl of Arran and the Cardinal-minister to invade the frontier of Northumberland—a mission in which he was so successful that he had no sooner communicated his errand than he was authorized to assume the command of the Scottish army, amounting to about fifteen thousand men, with which he at once marched upon the frontier.

Meanwhile, the French fleet had assembled in the port of Havre, and the command of the expedi-

---

[1] Jacques de Lorges, Earl of Montgomery, was the nephew of the Duc d'Aubigny, whom he succeeded, in 1543, in the command of the Scottish guard of Francis I. He was born in the duchy of Orleans, and was one of the ablest soldiers of the age. Two years previously he had come into possession of the earldom of Montgomery, which was his family inheritance. He it was who wounded the king with a burning log while he was engaged in the hazardous pastime of besieging the hotel of the Comte Saint-Pol at Paris—an incident which has been recorded in the body of this work. De Lorges, as he was constantly designated in France, died in 1559, in his eighty-first year.

tion was entrusted to D'Annebaut, who was shortly afterwards joined by the Baron de la Garde with the war-galleys of the king, which had previously been stationed at Marseilles, whither he had himself returned immediately after the massacre of the Vaudois. The armament, exclusive of the five and twenty galleys, consisted of a hundred and fifty ships of various sizes, most of them trading vessels, and of sixteen transports; several Genoese carracks had also been procured to strengthen the fleet, but they were, unfortunately, lost at the mouth of the Seine from the incapacity of their pilots.

The preparations on land were equally important. By raising strong levies of lansquenets and Gascons the army was augmented to a force of thirty-four thousand infantry, twelve hundred gensdarmes, and eight hundred light horsemen; and with this formidable body of troops Francis resolved, during the operations of his fleet, to attack Guines, lay waste the Terre d'Oye, and reduce the garrison of Boulogne by famine. The Terre d'Oye, whence the English drew their supplies, although inconsiderable in size, was extremely fertile, and abounded in pasture and cattle; it was, moreover, intersected by ditches which had enabled Lord Lisle, to whom the defence of the city had been entrusted, with the addition of a few redoubts, to defend it very efficiently; while the fortified town of Marcq, which was situated nearly in the centre of the district, and surrounded by marshy land, was strongly garrisoned; numerous outposts were stationed in the most exposed positions, and the arrangements of the English general had been so judiciously made that the whole force could be brought to bear simultaneously upon any given point in case of attack.

By the commencement of July the fleet was ready for sea; but before its departure the king resolved to visit Havre in order to inspect it, which he did in great state, attended by the whole of his Court. The novelty of the spectacle so delighted the royal and noble ladies by whom he was accompanied that Francis decided upon giving a banquet on board the Carraquon, a fine vessel of eight hundred tons burthen, carrying a hundred guns, and in every respect the most efficient ship of his navy. Preparations were accordingly made; the king's cooks and sewers were embarked two days previously; and on the appointed morning numerous barges lined with crimson damask and richly cushioned, manned by the most skilful sailors of the fleet, and bearing the national flag at their masthead, conveyed the invited guests to the admiral's ship. As the monarch had, in deference to the expressed wishes of the Court ladies, declined to embark under a salute, the heavy guns of the Carraquon, which had been prepared for this purpose, remained loaded, and the embarkation was effected amid no other demonstration than that of the amazed and delighted population of the town, who lustily cried "Noël" for their king, as they feasted their eyes upon the floating plumes, jewelled vestments, and brocaded draperies which passed before them, glittering in the sunlight like a fairy pageant.

A temporary canopy had been erected over the deck of the vessel, beneath which the tables were spread with the costly viands and delicate wines prepared for a repast which was not, however, destined to be eaten; the officers of the royal kitchen having disregarded the repeated expostulations of those about them, and persisted, in order to secure the perfection at which they aimed in their several departments, in kindling fires in places ill adapted for such a purpose—an imprudence which was fated to be productive of a frightful catastrophe.

The king had scarcely assumed his seat, having on his right hand the queen his consort, and on his left the Queen of Navarre, and the nobles and ladies of the royal train were in their turn respectively engaged in taking possession of the places assigned to them by the Court-usher, when flames were seen to issue from below, and in an instant all was horror and confusion. It fortunately chanced that several of the barges which had conveyed the monarch and his suite on board had remained in the immediate vicinity of the vessel, to be in readiness in the event of any of the august party requiring to be put on shore before the termination of the banquet; these were instantly brought alongside, and the king, the two queens, and all the ladies of their respective Courts, were rapidly conveyed from the vessel, together with the treasure-chest which had been destined for the supply of the fleet. While this hurried embarkation was taking place, the other vessels in the port, having first despatched their boats to the assistance of the sufferers, made all sail to escape from so dangerous a vicinity; but, as they had been unprepared for an event of this nature, several of them were unable to effect their object, and sustained great damage from the guns of the Carraquon, when she shortly afterwards blew up.

Once assured of the safety of the king, D'Annebaut hoisted his flag on board the Maitresse, now become the principal vessel of the fleet; re-embarked the treasure; and having repaired, in so far as was possible, the injuries sustained by his ships, at once put to sea. On the 18th of the month he arrived off the Isle of Wight, where he anchored in sight of the English fleet, and despatched the Baron de la Garde with four galleys to reconnoitre the enemy. By advancing to St. Helen's he was enabled to do this so effectually as to ascertain that it consisted of sixty large vessels of war fully manned and armed; and he had just finished his survey when he discovered that fourteen of the number were already making sail towards him; nor was it without considerable difficulty that he escaped.

A short time subsequently the whole fleet was in motion with a fair wind, bearing down upon the French ships, and several broadsides were fired in the hope of bringing them to a closer engagement; but though D'Annebaut returned the fire, he did not deem it prudent to advance, being unacquainted with the nature of the coast; and thus, although the cannonade was continued for a considerable time, little injury was sustained on either side. The mortification of the French admiral was, however, excessive when he discovered that the Maitresse, which had struck on leaving the port of Harfleur, was so seriously damaged that she leaked in several places, and was wholly unserviceable; once more, therefore, he was compelled to transfer his flag and the jeopardized treasure to a vessel of less calibre, while the disabled ship returned to Havre to be repaired.

On the following morning a dead calm enabled D'Annebaut to resume the engagement with his galleys, and throughout the space of an hour a brisk fire was maintained on both sides. Meanwhile his larger vessels, profiting by the tide, were enabled without entering the channel to approach sufficiently near to bring the enemy within range; and the English king, who had come in person to Portsmouth to watch the operations of the hostile fleets, had the mortification of seeing the Mary Rose, a noble ship carrying seven hundred men, sunk by the well-served guns of the French. This was, however, the last triumph they were destined to achieve, as the turn of the tide compelled the galleys to make a precipitate retreat, during which they were unable to return the fire of the enemy, by whom they were hotly pursued. They, however, succeeded in securing the safety of the main fleet by their skilful manœuvring; and D'Annebaut, convinced that it was impossible to renew the attack with any prospect of advantage while the English remained in their present position, resolved to make a descent on the coast of Sussex in order to induce them to abandon it. The stratagem proved unsuccessful, as the king, satisfied that they could not possess themselves of any important point of the coast, all of which were carefully defended, suffered them to land unmolested at Brighton and New Haven, where they destroyed the huts of the fishermen, and being unable to do any further mischief, re-embarked and returned to the Portsmouth roads.

Enraged by the immobility of the English fleet, which persisted in retaining its position, D'Annebaut next determined to effect a landing on the Isle of Wight, where he accomplished his purpose with equal facility, the English having prudently withdrawn from it all that could render its capture valuable. A few soldiers and about a hundred peasants alone opposed the disembarkation of the enemy, and they were, after a brief and useless struggle, overpowered; but once in possession of their conquest, the French were at a loss to decide upon the use to which it might be applied. A council was held, at which the expediency of retaining possession of the island was discussed, until it should be ransomed by the surrender of Boulogne; but this chimera was soon abandoned when it was remembered that the troops who must be left to protect it could not long contend against the force which would be brought against them, denuded as it was of every description of mural defence ; and this question was scarcely decided when D'Annebaut ascertained that a considerable reinforcement was expected by the English fleet—a piece of intelligence which determined him to return to France. He accordingly abandoned the conquered territory, and, regaining his ships, set sail for Boulogne, whither he was followed by the vessels of whose advent he had been apprized.

Once more the roar of cannon pealed over the waves ; but after a brisk and well-sustained fire of two hours, when the hostile fleets were at too great a distance to render it effectual, they eventually separated. D'Annebaut returned to the port of Havre, and the vessels of the English to their old anchorage, and so terminated the naval contest between the two countries, which, although it had been productive of no result to either, had nevertheless been the cause of an enormous outlay to both.

CHAPTER XI

1545-46

Military operations before Boulogne—The Comte d'Aumale is seriously wounded—The German levies of Henry VIII. arrive at Liege—Francis I. opposes their passage—Death of the Duc d'Orleans—Invasion of the Terre d'Oye—A treaty of peace is concluded between England and France—The emperor refuses to cede the duchy of Milan to the French Crown — Francis strengthens his frontiers — Death of Luther—The emperor makes war upon the Protestant princes—Horrible persecution of the Lutherans in France—Francis I. as a monarch and a man—Death of Henry VIII.—Last illness of Francis I.—Death of Francis I.—The chamber of the dauphiness—Accession of Henry II.

WHILE the French fleet had been engaged in its unsuccessful expedition, Francis resolved, in order to prevent the garrison of Boulogne from receiving supplies by sea, which would have rendered the devastation of the Terre d'Oye comparatively useless, to erect a fort that should command the harbour. This erection was entrusted to the Maréchal de Biez, who held the command in Picardy; but, through the ignorance of the engineer who selected the site, it proved a complete failure; and, to complete the annoyance of the king, as it was about to be roofed in the English garrison made a sudden sortie, and after a sharp skirmish, during which the maréchal, having had his horse shot under him, fought on foot at the head of his troops with a gallantry that for a time promised to prove successful, compelled the French troops to a retreat, which they did not effect before they had sustained considerable loss.

Shortly afterwards De Biez was informed that a convoy was about to pass from Calais to the besieged garrison, upon which he established his camp on the height of St. Lambert, in order to impede its arrival. Several skirmishes took place while he occupied this post, and during one of these the Comte d'Aumale was so seriously wounded that his recovery was considered almost a miracle. During the affray he received so vigorous a thrust from the pike of an English officer that the weapon, which struck him between the nose and the right eye, broke off short in the wound, leaving the iron and a portion of the wood firmly fastened in his head. Nevertheless, the young prince still retained his seat, and in the extremity of his agony dug his spurs into the flanks of his charger, which galloped furiously towards the French camp, where he was immediately lifted from the saddle and conveyed to his tent. The operation which ensued was a formidable one ; but the count, by his firm endurance of the consequent suffering, so ably seconded the skill of the surgeon that in a short time he was declared convalescent.

Meanwhile the troops whom Henry VIII. had levied in Germany had arrived at Fleurine, a village near Liege ; and Francis, in order to prevent their further progress, at once detached three divisions of his army to Guise, Champagne, and Messières, to cover his frontier. They then demanded a passage through the territories of the emperor, which was definitively refused; and thus, finding themselves impeded on all sides, after having been detained for three weeks at Fleurine, the Germans began to clamour for their pay; and their demands remaining unsatisfied, they disbanded themselves and returned home.

Anxious to expedite the capture of Boulogne, the king soon afterwards arrived in person at the Abbey of Toret-Moutiers, between Abbeville and Montreuil, accompanied by the two princes. Unhappily the plague was then raging in the environs, and the Duc d'Orleans, dissatisfied with the apartment which had been prepared for him in one of the houses of the village, selected another, of which he signified that he should take possession. The owner of the dwelling endeavoured to dissuade him from his purpose by informing him that it was rife with infection, the last three persons by whom it had been occupied having successively died there. With his usual recklessness, however, the duke adhered to his resolution, declaring that such a circumstance could not affect him, as there had never been an instance of a prince of the blood falling a victim to the pestilence. He accordingly passed the night in this fatal chamber; on the following morning unequivocal symptoms of the disease betrayed themselves; the skill of the physicians proved powerless; and in the course of a few days he ceased to breathe.[1]

[1] Other historians give a slightly different account of the cause of the duke's death:—"A contagious epidemic was raging amongst the

The grief of the king was excessive; his ambition as well as his affection had been bound up in his younger son, and the prince had no sooner expired than he left the village which had proved so fatal to his hopes, and established himself in a hamlet at the other extremity of the forest of Crecy.

Whilst Francis was still absorbed in the deep and bitter grief by which he had thus been so suddenly overwhelmed, the Maréchal de Biez announced his intention of attacking the fortifications erected by the English in the Terre d'Oye—an enterprize of so much danger that it was no sooner publicly known than crowds of the young nobles, anxious to share in the honour of so adventurous an attempt, hastened to the camp, and the Comte d'Enghien, newly risen from his sick-bed, the Duc d'Aumale, the Comte de Laval, the Duc de Nevers, and M. de la Trémouille, were among the foremost. The principal fort was attacked by the old French bands under M. de Tais, and taken by assault, when the victors made a cruel use of their success, for which they were indebted to their superior numbers, by putting the whole garrison to the sword. M. de Brissac, who commanded the

<small>soldiers, and the Duc d'Orleans, to show how little he feared the disease, said to be plague or typhus fever, entered a house with some of his companions where several persons had just died of it. The bedding they had used he turned over and over, cut open the beds with his sword, and taking feathers from them scattered them over himself and the young men with him. So vigorously did he exert himself at this strange occupation, laughingly exclaiming as he tossed each handful of feathers into the room, 'Never did a son of France die of the plague!' that he returned to his hotel tired and heated, and lay down on his couch to rest. From it he never arose. Fever supervened, and three days after he died."—Lady Jackson's *Court of France in the Sixteenth Century* vol. ii. pp. 174, 175.</small>

vanguard, consisting of several troops of gensdarmes, all the light cavalry, and a strong force of footsoldiers, marched meanwhile upon the town of Marcq; but he had not proceeded more than half a league when he encountered a body of two thousand English who were advancing to the relief of the beleaguered fort. After a desperate resistance these also were defeated, being unable long to cope with so unequal an enemy; and as no further impediment presented itself, the French troops continued to advance, pillaging and burning down all the villages, until they reached the gates of the town.

Here, however, they received a check. The bridges which had been prepared for the passage of the troops across the ditches had been forgotten; torrents of rain rendered the environs of Marcq one wide marsh, and they were reluctantly compelled to retire from before the walls of the threatened town in order to secure their own safety.

The fortress which De Biez had constructed was, meanwhile, finished; and the English garrison made continual sallies in the hope of taking it. Constant skirmishes occurred in consequence, which involved a serious loss on both sides, but no decisive result ensued; and both monarchs began to weary of a war which, while it exhausted their finances and weakened their armies, could not terminate favourably for either.

The energy of the French king was, moreover, shaken by the calamity which had befallen him; he saw the noble troops that it had cost him so much exertion to raise rapidly perishing alike under the weapons of the enemy and the attacks of the insidious disease which had reached his camp; he foresaw many difficulties in the completion of a new treaty with the emperor, now rendered necessary by the death of the Duc d'Orleans; and he became morbidly conscious of the failure of all his enterprises. Under such circumstances, therefore, he resolved rather to enter into a negotiation with the English king than to persist longer in so unavailing a contest.

Nor was Henry VIII. less anxious than himself to terminate the war. The immense outlay which it had occasioned could produce no remunerative return, while he moreover apprehended that the absence of so large a body of troops might occasion him much embarrassment should the Scotch army, as he had some reason to apprehend, profit by the opportunity to invade his frontiers. He was alarmed also by the attitude assumed at this period by Charles V., who had convoked his council, and was making preparations for a war against the Protestant princes of the League. Aware that he was personally as obnoxious to the Court of Rome as the German reformers, he began to apprehend that, should the emperor prove successful, the result might be fatal to himself; and thus, as a French courtier wittily remarked, a peace might be easily negotiated, one monarch being anxious to secure it, and the other compelled to do so.

Commissioners were accordingly appointed on both sides, who met midway between Ardres and

Guines; and on the 7th of June 1546 a treaty of peace was signed between France and England, in which Henry VIII., after some difficulty, consented that the Scotch should be included, provided they saw fit to avail themselves of it within the space of thirty days. By the conditions of this treaty Francis bound himself to pay off all the arrears of the pensions claimed by the English king, and to continue them during eight years; as well as to reimburse him for the expenses of the war, amounting to the sum of two millions of golden crowns, before the anniversary of St. Michael in 1554, at which period Henry VIII. was to deliver over to his officers the city of Boulogne.

The death of the Duc d'Orleans, as Francis had foreseen, afforded a new opportunity for the display of that selfish policy which formed so prominent a feature in the character of the emperor. At the close of the year 1545 he had despatched D'Annebaut and the Chancellor Olivier [1] to Charles to engage him in a new treaty, which might replace that of Crespy; but they were totally unsuccessful. He felt or affected a deep regret at the untimely death of the young prince who was so shortly to have been his son-in-law, but at once declared without hesitation that the event which he deplored had released him from all his engagements; that he never had and

[1] François Olivier de Lieuville, a talented and eloquent magistrate, was president of the parliament of Paris when Francis I. created him Chancellor of France in 1545. During the reign of Henry II. the influence of Diane de Poitiers deprived him of the seals; but he was recalled to Court by Francis II. He died in 1560.

never would acknowledge the claims of the French king to the duchy of Milan, which Francis had, moreover, personally renounced upon two separate occasions, and that he considered himself perfectly absolved from all the obligations to which the treaty of Crespy would, under other circumstances, have bound him; although he had no desire to enter into renewed hostilities with France, unless he should be compelled to do so.

With this ambiguous reply the baffled ambassadors returned to Court; and Francis, conscious that he was not at that period in a position to enforce his demands, and more anxious to repel aggression than to provoke a war which he was unable to sustain, suffered the declaration of his wily rival to remain without retort, and employed the remainder of the year in inspecting and strengthening his frontier-fortresses, which he did so effectually that he was enabled to await without apprehension the result of the new struggle in which Charles was about to engage.

The death of Luther,[1] at the commencement of this year, was a severe blow to the reformers, and an equally great source of rejoicing to the Pope, although it by no means disposed him to second the violent designs of the emperor against the new religion. He was well aware that the zeal which Charles affected for the Church had in every case been made subservient to his own interests; and he considered

[1] Luthur died at Eysleben, the place of his birth, on the 18th of February 1546, aged sixty-three years.

himself aggrieved, moreover, by the fact that after he had invested his son Pietro Luigi Farnese with the duchies of Parma and Placenza, the emperor had refused to recognize or to ratify his sovereignty; and consequently, even when he entered into a treaty with that monarch for the extirpation of the reformers, he could not divest himself of a distrust which rendered him less energetic in the cause than he might otherwise have been. Charles, with his usual subtle policy, had been anxious to keep his intentions secret until he could overwhelm his victims by some sudden *coup-de-main*—a desire which increased the suspicions of the pontiff, and accordingly he had no sooner pledged himself to assist in this religious war than he ordered public prayers to be put up in Rome for the success of the undertaking.

Had Francis at this period come to the succour of the Protestant princes whom he had formerly protected, there can be little doubt that he would have been enabled to ensure his kingdom thenceforward from all attempts at aggression on the part of the emperor. Many of those about him endeavoured to convince him of this fact, and of the magnanimity of assisting the oppressed, who were about to contend not only for their religious liberty, but also for that of their several states, by which alone the independence of all Europe could be secured against the insatiable ambition of Charles. They represented to him that he could do this without any breach of honour, as they were his allies, and had a right to look to him for help; that, moreover, his interference

in their behalf could not affect his conscience, inasmuch as the emperor had declared that he was not about to punish them for their schism, but for their rebellion against his authority; and that it well became a great monarch to uphold the cause of the weak against the strong.

These arguments, however, availed nothing; the languor of premature old age, a dread of increasing responsibility, and the persuasions of the Cardinal de Tournon, who was constantly about his person, rendered the king not only unwilling to reply to the appeal of the German princes, but even incited him to renew within the limits of his own kingdom the atrocious persecution of the reformers which had already affixed an indelible stigma upon his reign.

Once more the stake and the rack did their deadly office; inoffensive citizens, convicted of an adherence to Lutheranism, were seized in their houses, loaded with chains, put to the torture, and finally burned alive. A few were suspended by their armpits, in front of the pile on which their co-religionists were expiring under a slow fire, then publicly flogged, and finally flung into different monasteries, where the mind dare not follow them; four escaped with castigation and banishment; and others were imprisoned for life. As some of these victims of intolerance were on their way to Meaux, a weaver of their own persuasion followed the waggon in which they were performing their melancholy journey, and exhorted them to meet with faith and resignation all the sufferings which they might be called upon to endure, remembering that they would have a mighty and abiding reward in heaven. He did but add another martyr to the number. He was seized by the archers of the provost, bound with cords, and flung into the vehicle with those who were already condemned to death.

It is fearful to pursue so terrible a subject, but the faithful chronicler has no alternative. We will, therefore, record it in the very words of Theodore de Bèze, in his *Ecclesiastical History*, Book I. pp. 51-53.[1]

"Arrived at Meaux, they underwent the extraordinary question in all its cruelty, which they suffered with such resignation, that they never accused any of their brethren. On the 7th of September they were led to execution, the tongue of Étienne Mangin having been previously cut out, notwithstanding which he thrice exclaimed loudly and intelligibly, 'God's name be blessed!' He was then drawn upon a hurdle, as was also Guillaume le Clerc, the rest following in carts, to the market-place, where they were hoisted up and burnt upon fourteen gibbets, placed in a circle. Thus, face to face, they encouraged each other, and mingled their prayers and praises, which were, however, interrupted by the priests and the populace, who shouted aloud like madmen, *O salutaris hostia!* and *Salve Regina*. This accomplished, on the morrow, the 8th of the month, Picard (Doctor of the Sorbonne), in order to complete his triumph, went with a magnificent procession to the spot where the fire was still smoulder-

[1] Quoted from Sismondi.

ing, preaching under a canopy of cloth of gold; and said, among other things, after having displayed great violence, that it was essential to the salvation of all to believe that these fourteen condemned persons were damned in the bottomless pit of hell; and that should an angel from heaven come and declare the contrary, they must reject his evidence, as God would not be God if he did not damn them to eternity."

[As in the case of Cellini, Lady Jackson supplies us with further particulars of these persecutions, from which we take an interesting passage:—

" The most distinguished of the victims was the *littérateur* and printer, Étienne Dolet, the author of *Commentaires sur la Langue Latine*, and of many poems, and the translator of the *Dialogues of Plato*. In 1542 or 1543 he had been accused of heresy and atheism, by the Inquisitor-General of Lyons, who further charged him with the horrible crime of having eaten meat on days when it was prohibited by the Church. Dolet had then a friend at Court, the Bishop of Macon, the king's reader, who interceded for him as a young man of great ability, with the promise of a brilliant literary career before him. The 'Father of letters' could hardly decline to be merciful in such a case. The burning zeal of Cardinal de Tournon would willingly have sent the bishop to the flames from which he had snatched a victim. He was compelled to content himself with reproaching him for his daring act, as a Catholic bishop, of defending heretics and atheists. The bishop replied 'that in pleading for the unfortunate he had performed a bishop's duty, while the cardinal had taken upon him the functions of an executioner.'

"In 1544 Dolet was again denounced; this time on suspicion of having introduced prohibited books from Geneva into France. Aided by friends, he escaped to Piedmont, where he addressed some poetical epistles to the king and Madame d'Étampes. For the purpose of printing his *Dialogues* and other works, he secretly returned to Lyons, where he had left his family. He was shortly after arrested, and his writings seized. The Sorbonne found in the *Dialogues* a phrase which seemed opposed to the doctrine of the immortality of the soul, and at once condemned the translation.

"The Parliament, therefore, sentenced the translator to be tortured on the rack, then hanged, and afterwards burnt, together with his heretical books. 'Should he venture to utter any blasphemy or do aught to create scandal, his tongue was to be cut out, and he burned alive.'

"Dolet appears to have expected that the king would once more save him from the fate to which the wretched fanatics of the Sorbonne and the Parliament had condemned him. Vain expectation! Learning and the arts no longer interested Francis I. as formerly, and Dolet's sentence must be carried out to the end.

"He is said to have borne his sufferings with heroical firmness; so much so that the spectators—though one would scarcely credit those who were

willingly present at such a scene with the possession
of much feeling—sympathized deeply with him,
and were greatly affected. Perceiving this, as he
mounted, or—his limbs being dislocated and broken
on the rack—was borne to the scaffold, he said, extending his hand towards the people: 'Non dolet
ipse Dolet, sed pia turba dolet,' a clever *jeu de mots*,
more concisely expressed in Latin than in either
French or English. 'Dolet n'est point *dolent*, mais
ce peuple compatissant est *dolent* pour lui.' 'Dolet
is not *doleful*, but these compassionate people are
doleful for him.'

"Dolet was thirty-seven years of age. Many
epitaphs were written on this distinguished victim of
the Place Maubert. 'His friend Rabelais avenged
him in a different manner' (if he did not rather insult
him) 'by publishing at the foot, as it were, of his
funeral pile the second book of Pantagruel, "*avec
privilége du roi*"*!*' 'Rabelais,' says M. H. Martin
(who gives the greater part of these particulars),
'must have been as unprecedentedly clever as
audacious.' He must indeed; but with two cardinals for friends, one of whom had just obtained for
him the curacy of Meudon, what might not be
accomplished? Cardinal du Bellay, and afterwards
the powerful Cardinal Jean de Lorraine—persecutor
and sceptic—were the protectors of this coarse licentious writer."—*Court of France in the Sixteenth
Century*, vol. ii. pp. 179-182.]

We dare not venture to comment upon such a passage of history as this; but surely it offers a fearful

warning to after-ages. Moreover, the pyres which had been lighted and the racks which had been set in motion in the capital were emulated in the provinces; many other victims, and some of these men of exemplary lives and high literary attainments, fell victims to the atrocious persecution which disgraced the closing reign of the quasi-demigod of many an historian. The "chivalrous Francis I."—the "First Gentleman of France"—the monarch whose name has for three centuries been as a landmark of glory in the record of the French annals—to what conviction does a perfect knowledge of his real character lead? Surely but to this: that he was vain even to puerility in his youth, sensual even to profligacy in his manhood, and bigoted even to brutality in his decline. Conscious of his own enormities, he took refuge in a cruel superstition, and sought to win heaven by the tears and groans and agonies of his fellow-men. While he clung to his vices, feasted with his mistresses, laughed at the ribald jests of his obsequious courtiers, and wrung from his exhausted people the hard-earned produce of their industry, he strove to blind himself with the belief that all would be forgiven in his zeal for the Church, and that his own transgressions would be washed out in the blood of his sectarian victims.

It has been the fashion with modern authors to pass lightly over this frightful episode of the reign of Francis I. It destroys the illusion which attaches to his name; it renders him less attractive as a sovereign; and converts the splendid sensualist into a gloomy and heartless barbarian. But let the thinking mind fall back upon the whole chain of his previous career, and its close will scarcely prove matter of astonishment. The morals of the age were unhappily lax; the example of the most exalted of the priesthood venal, profligate, and degrading; religion, even by the several pontiffs, made subservient to expediency; the cardinals more celebrated in the annals of gallantry than in those of piety; the ambition of the great nobles confined to personal aggrandizement; and the bulk of the people buried in ignorance and superstition.

That there were glorious exceptions in all ranks is most true; but these have almost universally been overlooked,—many, too many of them, altogether forgotten. The pure gold sinks to the bottom of the stream, while the more worthless dross rises and sparkles upon the surface of the current. We admit, therefore, that the vices of Francis may find some extenuation in the character of the age and the nature of his education; but we repeat, that those who have recorded only the brilliant and attractive portions of his career, and have wilfully and advisedly buried his backslidings in oblivion, have not done their duty either to themselves or to those who may be influenced by their researches.

The flame and the wheel were still in full operation in France when, in January 1547, news arrived at St. Germain-en-Laye, where the Court was then sojourning, of the death of Henry VIII.—an event which produced the most fatal effect alike upon the moral and physical temperament of the French king. He had long indulged the hope that Henry, whose rupture with the emperor had rendered it necessary for him to strengthen his position, would be desirous of entering into a closer alliance with himself; while at the same time the similarity, not only of their ages, but also in many respects of their several characters, combined with a consciousness that the disease under which he was then suffering was daily becoming more virulent, filled him with alarm. He felt a conviction that his own end was approaching, and he became nervous and depressed. He commanded that a solemn funeral service should be performed at the cathedral of Notre Dame in honour of the deceased monarch—a ceremony which took place with great pomp; and then, in order to divert the melancholy that was rapidly gaining upon him, accompanied by a slow fever which robbed him of all rest, Francis, who could no longer brook a moment of inaction, removed to La Muette, a country-house which he had recently embellished, on the borders of the forest of St. Germain. There he sojourned for a whole week; but his mind was in so unsettled a state that he could not long remain upon one spot; and he accordingly proceeded to Villepreux, where an increase of his fever induced him to travel the following day to Dampierre, near Chevreuse; and thence he pursued his way in order to pass the period of Lent at Limours. Throughout the whole of this time he was accompanied by the Court, but even his favourites now sought in vain to arouse him from the lethargy into which he was rapidly falling. Nowhere could he find peace; and after having spent three days at Limours he once more removed to Rochefort, where he endeavoured to amuse himself by hunting. To this violent exercise, however, his strength was no longer equal; and every evening his fever increased to a degree which alarmed those about him so greatly that they urged his return to St. Germain-en-Laye.

After some difficulty the physicians succeeded in obtaining his consent to this measure by representing that he could travel slowly and indulge in his favourite pursuit by the way; and he accordingly left Rochefort for Rambouillet, where he had decided to remain only one night; but the game proved so plentiful and the sport so exciting that he was induced to change his resolution. Two or three days were consequently spent in field sports, in which once more Catherine de' Medici participated; but the fever of the king, which had hitherto been intermittent, became, by reason of this perpetual exertion, continuous, and his malady increased so rapidly that it was found impossible for him to proceed further.

Once apprized of his danger, Francis summoned the dauphin to his sick-bed, and conversed with him at intervals for several hours, giving him the most wholesome advice concerning the future government of the kingdom over which he must so soon be called upon to rule; and consequently, like many other monarchs, he, in this supreme moment, gainsaid, in almost every particular, the system which he had himself pursued. He recommended him to diminish the public taxes under which the nation was then groaning; to be guided in all things by the Cardinal de Tournon and the Admiral d'Annebaut; and, above all, to exclude from his confidence the Connétable de Montmorency and the family of the Duc de Guise. He then received the sacraments of the Church; and his persecutions of the Protestants had apparently convinced him so thoroughly of his own salvation that he expired peacefully, while the ashes of his victims were still floating between earth and heaven.

To say that he died unregretted would be to assert a fallacy. Too many interests were interwoven with his existence to render such an event possible. He had, moreover, during the later period of his life laboured to replenish the national treasury, in which attempt, despite the enormous outlay consequent upon the various wars that he had undertaken, and the expensive character of his Court, in which to the last he introduced no retrenchment, he had so far succeeded as to bequeath to his successor the sum of four hundred thousand crowns. But his death was not accompanied, like that of Louis XII., with the tears and regrets of his subjects. Three great events alone had signalized his reign—the victory of Marignano, the restoration of literature, and the struggle which he had sustained against Charles V.

And what had been the actual result even of these? The glory of Marignano had been quenched at Pavia, at which period his reign, as affected his own greatness, may well be said to have terminated; for his after-triumphs were all inconsequent and valueless. He never again hazarded his personal safety in an open engagement, although he was rigorous in his punishment of those through whose errors or want of courage he failed in the accomplishment of his designs; and it was therefore the nation which fought and bled and suffered, not its sovereign. He invited learned men to his Court; lured them thither by the brightest prospects and the most extravagant promises; and then, not content with disappointing the hopes that he had raised, not only ceased to encourage them when they no longer ministered to his own gratification and that of his favourites, but even persecuted them for their religious opinions, and abandoned them to the stake, to the rack, and to the anathemas of a bigoted priesthood.

That he manfully met and boldly opposed the usurpation of Charles V. is quite true; but to what abiding benefit had he turned this opposition? It had been throughout rather a personal struggle than a great question of national policy. Charles was the only sovereign of whose prowess he was jealous, and whose supremacy wounded his pride alike as a sovereign and as a soldier. He had expended millions, and sacrificed a fearful amount of human life, only to leave his kingdom to his son as he had received it from his predecessor. He had gained no territory, secured no advantage, realized no.

triumph. It is certain that he had driven the conqueror of Germany, Asia, Africa, and Turkey from his kingdom, but it must also be remembered that he had been unable to arrest his march even to the very neighbourhood of his capital.

While the king was in the last agony, the dauphin, who, whatever might be his failings, was endowed with a depth of feeling which caused him for the moment to forget all his real or imagined wrongs, cast himself in a fit of bitter grief upon the bed of his wife; while Catherine de' Medici herself, seated upon a low stool, remained with her face buried in her hands, like one utterly oppressed by sorrow, and did not reply to his lamentations by a single syllable. There were, however, other watchers in that spacious room, as anxious although less absorbed than either the future sovereign or his wife. The one was Diane de Poitiers, who, with flashing eyes and hurried step, traversed the floor, listening to every sound, and awaiting from moment to moment the announcement which was to make her a queen in all save the empty name; and the other was the Comte d'Aumale, the friend and favourite of the dauphin, who, in his impatience, repeatedly passed from the chamber of the dauphiness to the ante-room of the dying king, exclaiming, in an accent of undisguised triumph, from time to time, "The lady-killer is going!"

Francis expired on the 31st of March 1547, and was buried with a magnificence far surpassing anything which had yet been witnessed in

France; eleven cardinals assisted at his obsequies, and the ceremony extended over two and twenty days. The bodies of his two sons, the dauphin Francis and Charles Duc d'Orleans, were conveyed to St. Denis together with his own, and Henry II. succeeded to the vacant throne.[1]

Only a few months elapsed ere Montmorency was once more all-powerful at the Court; the unhappy queen under the protection of her imperial brother in Spain; and the Duchesse d'Etampes an exile on one of her estates. The *bâton* which had been broken over the coffin of Francis I. had involved more changes than that which placed the crown that he had worn so proudly upon the brow of his surviving son.

[1] " Henry decided on giving Francis I. the grandest funeral—that of Anne of Brittany perhaps excepted—that the French had ever witnessed, and proposed to erect a splendid tomb to his memory, surpassing, in the grandeur of its proportions and the richness of its sculptural decorations, all such monuments as had hitherto been erected in France. It took many years to complete the magnificent tomb, on which every French artist of note was employed."—Lady Jackson's *Court of France in the Sixteenth Century*, vol. ii. p. 200.

INDEX

ABBATE, Niccolo, dell', protected by Francis I., ii. 334

Abergavenny, Lord, his puerile alarm at the Field of the Cloth of Gold, i. 350

Adam, Villiers de l'Isle, his gallant defence of the Isle of Rhodes against the Turks, ii. 47-8

Adrian, Bishop of Tortosa, withdraws his troops from Navarre into the interior of Spain, i. 376; *see* note, *ib.*; elected Pope, ii. 23; his efforts to establish a peace alluded to, ii. 45; he endeavours to alienate the Venetian States from France, *ib.*; death of, alluded to, ii. 515

Agnadello, battle of, i. 62

Agrippa, Cornelius, a celebrated astrologer, ii. 268; enters the service of Louise de Savoie, *ib.*; his predictions offend the regent, and he is obliged to fly from France, ii. 269

Aigues Mortes, meeting of the emperor and Francis I. at, iii. 112

Aix, Archbishop of, summoned to Paris to devise means for the defence of the city, ii. 188

Alamanni Luigi, proscribed by the Emperor Charles V., finds a protector in Francis I., ii. 334; *see* note, *ib.*

Alcyat, André, a celebrated lawyer, *see* note, i. 269

Aléandro Jerômio, Chancellor of Liège, detects the treacherous conduct of Madame d'Angoulême towards his master the Prince-Bishop of Liège, i. 320

Alessandro Farnese. *See* Paul III.

Alva, Duke of, takes possession of Pampeluna, i. 83; takes up a position at St. Jean Pied-de-Port, i. 84; held in check by the Duc de Bourbon, *ib.*; besieged in Pampeluna, i. 85; drives the French beyond the Pyrenees, *ib.*; advises Charles V. to demand a ransom of Francis I. sufficient to recruit the exhausted finances of Spain and cripple France, ii. 200; *see* note, *ib.*

Amboise, Louise de Savoie exiled to, i. 18; arrival of the Court at, i. 20

Anne de Bretagne, *see* note, i. 5; passion of Louis XII. for, i. 6; affianced to the Archduke Maximilian of Austria, *ib.*; passion of the dauphin, afterwards Charles VIII., for, i. 7; proposals of marriage from Charles VIII. to, i. 12; her coronation at St. Denis, *ib.*; death of Charles VIII., i. 13; promises her hand to Louis XII. conditionally, i.

Anne de Bretagne—*continued*.
14; marries Louis XII., i. 15; quarrel with Louise de Savoie, mother of Francis I., i. 18; its consequences, *ib.*; her household, i. 21; her ostentation, i. 22; arrives at Amboise, *ib.*; her influence over the king, i. 24; opposes the marriage of her daughter with the young Comte d'Angoulême, i. 25; espouses the cause of the Pope, and remark of the king thereon, i. 26; forbids the attendance of the Bishops of Brittany at the Council at Pisa, *ib.*; her solicitude on hearing of the king's indisposition, i. 32; resolves to retire into Brittany on the demise of the king, *ib.*; her anger at the attempt of the Maréchal de Gié to detain her furniture and jewels, i. 34; influences the king against the maréchal, i. 35; her hatred to the maréchal, *ib.*; negotiates a marriage for her daughter, the Princesse Claude, with the Duc de Luxembourg, i. 37; offers no opposition to the will of the king disposing of the Princesse Claude to Francis, Comte d'Angoulême, i. 42; her motives explained, *ib.*; meets the king at Grenoble, i. 66; renewed hopes of, *ib.*; religious scruple of, respecting the wars of Louis XII. with the Pope, encourages Julius II. to resist the French, i. 80; influences Louis XII. to enter into a league with the Venetian States, i. 91; her second daughter, the Princesse Réneé, affianced to Prince Charles of Austria, *ib.*; stipulations of the emperor thereon, *ib.*; death of, i. 116; burial of, at St. Denis, i. 117

Anne de France entrusted with the guardianship of the dauphin, afterwards Charles VIII., i. 8; her love for the Duc d'Orleans, afterwards Louis XII., i. 9; imprisons the Duc d'Orleans, *ib.*; withdraws herself from government on the release of the Duc d'Orleans, i. 10; death of, alluded to, ii. 21

Anne de Pisseleu, *see* D'Heilly, Mademoiselle

Army, English, under the Earl of Surrey, destroys several towns on the coast of Normandy and Brittany, ii. 68; besieges Hesdin, ii. 71; compelled to retreat, ii. 72; commits wanton cruelties, *ib.*; advances within eleven leagues of Paris, ii. 94; driven back by the Duc de Vendôme, ii. 95; alarm of Francis at the advance of the, ii. 111; amount of, under the Duke of Norfolk, *ib.*; retreats to Calais, and sails for England, ii. 113

Army, French, amount and distribution of, previous to crossing the Alps to recover the Milanese, i. 168-9; the difficulty of the passage of the Alps overcome by a Piedmontese peasant, i. 170; vanguard of the, forces the Durance, i. 171; the passage of the Alps described, i. 171-2; perseverance of the troops, *ib.*; the vanguard enters Italy, i. 173; capture of Prosper Colonna, i. 175-6-7; taking of Villa Franca, i. 177; Alessandria and Tortona taken, i. 178; headquarters of the king at Marignano, i. 182; the junction of the Swiss and Spanish armies prevented by an accident, i. 183; General d'Alviano at Lodi, i. 185; the battle of Marignano, i. 185-95; loss of the French

INDEX

Army, French—*continued*.
at Marignano, i. 193-4; marches upon Milan, i. 198; the king disbands the, i. 210; the Emperor Maximilian compels the French to shut themselves up in Milan, i. 211; arrival of reinforcements, i. 212; refusal of the Swiss mercenaries to act with the French against their own countrymen, *ib.*; siege of Milan raised, i. 213; Brescia again taken, i. 214; Bayard defends the city of Mézières, i. 385-94; part of, disbanded, i. 398; exists by plunder in Italy, ii. 2; critical position of Maréchal Lautrec at Milan, ii. 6; the army retires to Milan, ii. 11; retreats to Como, ii. 12; takes up its winter quarters at Cremona, *ib.*; attacks Milan, but repulsed, ii. 26; takes Novara, but repulsed before Pavia, *ib.*; arrears of pay of, ii. 27; demands to be led against the enemy, *ib.*; attacks Colonna at Bicocca, ii. 28-31; retires to Cremona, ii. 32; invested at Cremona by Colonna, ii. 33; evacuates Lombardy, ii. 34; excesses of the troops for want of pay, ii. 43; relief of Fontarabia by, ii. 61; the Duc de Vendôme ordered to relieve Térouenne, ii. 71; assembles at Lyons previous to again invading Italy, ii. 72; command of the army against Italy given to Bonnivet, ii. 95; paralyzed by the defection of the Constable of France, ii. 110; the Duc de Guise repulses the Germans at Franche-Comté, ii. 111; the Spaniards are driven back upon Fontarabia by Maréchal Lautrec, *ib.*; Maréchals Tremouille and Vendôme compel the retreat of the Duke of Norfolk, ii. 113; Bonnivet

Army, French—*continued*.
commands the army in Italy, *ib.*; discontent of the troops at the appointment of Bonnivet, *ib.*; the French force in Italy, ii. 115; defence of Cremona by M. d'Herbouville, *ib.*; Bonnivet compels the imperialists to retreat to Milan, ii. 116; blockades Milan, ii. 117; raises the siege of Milan, ii. 119; Bonnivet detaches Lorenzo de Ceri to besiege Arona, ii. 121; repulsed, ii. 122; Bayard detached to Rebec, but attacked by Pescara with a superior force, and compelled to retreat, ii. 122-6; Bonnivet retreats to Novara, pursued by the Duc de Bourbon, ii. 127-9; Bonnivet wounded, ii. 129; Comte de Vandenesse and Bayard assume the command of, *ib.*; death of Vandenesse and Bayard, ii. 130-1; grief of the soldiers at the death of Bayard, ii. 131; the Duc de Lorraine and Richard de la Pole harass the imperial army under the Duc de Bourbon, ii. 139; Maréchal de Chabannes occupies Avignon, *ib.*; siege of Marseilles, ii. 138-42; Milan captured, ii. 147; encamps at Mirabello, assaults Pavia and is repulsed, ii. 149-50; position of the army before Pavia, ii. 152; Duc d'Aubigny commands nine thousand men against the Spaniards, ii. 153; thinned by sickness and desertions before Pavia, ii. 156; the Swiss and Italians desert from, before the battle of Pavia, ii. 157; castle of Chiavenna taken, *ib.*; four thousand Italians surprised by the imperialists and destroyed, *ib.*; Palavicino defeated by the imperialists, *ib.*; position of at Pavia, ii. 158;

Army, French—*continued*.
battle of Pavia fatal to, ii. 162-9; loss of the French at the battle of Pavia, ii. 176-7; evacuates Italy, ii. 177; the annihilation of, after the battle of Pavia alluded to, ii. 185; return of the remnant of the, from Italy, ii. 189; success of Maréchal de Lautrec in the Milanese, ii. 320; Pavia retaken, *ib.*; Naples besieged, *ib.*; the plague attacks the, *ib.*; death of Maréchal Lautrec, ii. 321; retires from Naples, and deaths of Novarra and Saluzzo, ii. 322; Italy again evacuated by, *ib.*; reorganized by Francis, iii. 17; defence of Fossano, iii. 55; manœuvres of, in Provence, iii. 64-6; reinforced by twenty thousand Swiss and six thousand Germans, iii. 68; Francis heads the army in person, iii. 70; pursues the imperialists, iii. 71; siege of Turin raised, iii. 75; at St. Rignier and Peronne, iii. 75-6; Hesdin taken by siege, iii. 90; St. Pol defended by, iii. 92; Annebaut relieves Térouenne, *ib.*; mutiny of, in Piedmont, iii. 95; the Pas-de-Suze forced by, iii. 99; commences a campaign in the Low Countries, iii. 184; disposition of, *ib.*; the Maréchal de Gueldres ravages the Low Countries, iii. 185; the Duc d'Orleans takes Luxembourg, iii. 187; defeats the imperialists at Sittard, iii. 202; besieges Binche, iii. 204; takes Luxembourg, iii. 210; the Comte d'Enghien defeats Marquis del Guasto, iii. 235; attacks Boulogne and repulsed, iii. 259-60; retrospect of the campaign of 1544, iii. 260-1; enters Picardy, iii. 277; invades the Terre d'Oye, *ib.*

Army, Imperialist: Prosper Colonna strengthens the army of the empire, ii. 2; threatens Parma, ii. 9; a quarrel between the generals neutralises the efforts of the, *ib.*; Prosper Colonna crosses the Po, ii. 10; drives the French out of Milan, ii. 12; retakes Como, *ib.*; repulses the French before Milan, ii. 26; surrenders Novara, *ib.*; Prosper Colonna defends Pavia, *ib.*; Prosper Colonna at Bicocca, ii. 27; defeats Maréchal Lautrec, and compels him to retreat to Cremona, ii. 28-31; Colonna invests Cremona, ii. 33; drives the French out of Lombardy, ii. 34; Genoa taken by treachery, and cruelty of the imperialist generals, ii. 35-6; advances within eleven leagues of Paris, ii. 94; defeated by the Duc de Vendôme, ii. 95; jealousy amongst the imperialist generals prevents a simultaneous attack upon France, ii. 110; the command of the papal troops entrusted to the Duke of Mantua, ii. 115; compelled to retreat to Milan before Bonnivet, ii. 116; Milan blockaded by the French, ii. 117; the French retire from Milan, ii. 119; death of Colonna, *ib.*; Marquis de Pescara attacks Bayard at Rebec, and compels him to retreat, ii. 126; the Duc de Bourbon compels Bonnivet to retreat, ii. 127-9; position of the Duc de Bourbon at the siege of Marseilles, ii. 139; retreats from Marseilles, ii. 142; surrenders Milan, ii. 147; repulses the French at the siege of Pavia, ii. 150; position of, at Pavia, ii. 152; mutinous state of the garrison of Pavia, ii. 153-4; joined by the Duc de Bour-

Army, Imperialist—*continued.*
bon at the head of a German force, ii. 155; the main body of the imperialists march upon Pavia, ii. 157; four thousand Italians surprised and destroyed by, *ib.*; Palavacino taken prisoner at Casal-Maggiore, *ib.*; battle of Pavia, ii. 160-3; loss of the imperialists at the battle of Pavia, ii. 177; exactions of the imperial soldiers in Italy, ii. 199; mutiny for pay, ii. 201; oppresses the Italian people, ii. 239; excesses of, at Milan alluded to, ii. 252; march against Rome, and sack the city, ii. 255-6; defence of Naples, ii. 320; the French again expelled from Italy by, ii. 322; Charles V. takes Tunis, and releases twenty thousand Christian slaves, iii. 17; invades Provence, iii. 56; pillages Aix, iii. 65; sufferings of, iii. 67; retreat of, iii. 68; slaughter of, iii. 71; quartered in the Milanese, iii. 73; enter Picardy, iii. 75; checked at St. Regnier, *ib.*; takes Guise, iii. 76; besieges Peronne, and repulsed, iii. 77; retreats from Provence, iii. 78; invests St. Pol, iii. 91; at Térouenne, iii. 92-4; takes Carmagnole, iii. 97; fortifies the Pas-de-Suze, iii. 98; raises the siege of Pignerol, and encamps at Moncalier, iii. 100; lands in Africa, under Charles V., iii. 182; dispersed by a tempest, *ib.*; returns to Spain, iii. 183; relieves Roussillon, iii. 187; defeated at Sittard, iii. 202; reorganized by the emperor, iii. 207; operations of the, in the duchy of Cleves, iii. 208; Landrecies, Guise, and Luxembourg besieged by, iii. 212; takes Cambray, iii. 214; defeated at

Army, Imperialist—*continued.*
Carmagnola, iii. 234-5; invades France, under Charles V. and Henry VIII., iii. 240; besieges St. Dizier, iii. 241; operations of, at Chalons, iii. 251; revictualled through the agency of Madame d'Etampes, iii. 254; advance of, on Paris, iii. 255; retrospect of the campaign of 1544, iii. 260-1
Arona, siege of, alluded to, i. 27
Asola, occupation of, by Marquis of Mantua, alluded to, i. 64
Ast, countyship of, ceded by the emperor to the Duke of Savoy, ii. 348; citizens of, refuse admittance to the imperialists, iii. 236
Astrologers, influence of the, upon the people, ii. 268
Augsburg, confession of, ii. 361
Autun, Bishop of, despatched by the Connétable de France, with his offers of allegiance to Francis I., ii. 92; seized by the king's troops near Lyons, *ib.*; imprisoned by the Parliament, but afterwards reinstated, ii. 97

BAGLIONI, Jean Paul, hereditary sovereign of Perousa, i. 51; attacked by Pope Julius II., *ib.*
Baillet, M., detects the gasconade of M. de Brion Chabot, ii. 112
Barbarossa, King of Algiers, defeated by Charles V. before Tunis, iii. 17; ordered by Solyman to co-operate with the French, iii. 202; anchors at Calabria, iii. 214; burns the city of Reggio, *ib.*; joined by Comte d'Enghien, attacks Nice, and repulsed, iii. 215-16; burns Nice, iii. 218; enormities perpetrated by, iii. 219
Barbesieux, Seigneur de, entrusted with the defence of Marseilles, iii. 51; *see* note, *ib.*

Baudemanche, Gilbert, his arrest and trial alluded to, ii. 94; acquitted by the Parliament of Paris, ii. 96

Bayard, Chevalier de, valour of, at the height of Belvidere, near Genoa, i. 55; see note, *ib.*; one of the leaders in Louis XII.'s army against Venice, i. 61; skilful movement of, at the battle of Agnadello, i. 62; joins the Marquis de la Palice against the Venetians, i. 66; wounded at Brescia, i. 71; reconnoitres the enemy's position at Ravenna, i. 74; at the battle of Ravenna, *ib.*; attacks Henry VIII.'s army, and carries off a gun, i. 101; taken prisoner by the English, and wins his ransom, i. 103-4-5-6-7-8; appointed Lieutenant-general of Dauphiny, i. 169; position of, in the army for the recovery of the Milanese, *ib.*; surprises and captures Prosper Colonna, i. 174-5-6-7; solicits permission from the king to attack the enemy, i. 182; bravery of, at the battle of Marignano, i. 189; nearly taken prisoner, i. 190; supplied with a third horse by the Duc de Lorraine, *ib.*; advises Francis not to pursue the Swiss after the battle of Marignano, i. 192; acknowledged the hero of Marignano, i. 196; confers knighthood on Francis I. on the field of battle, *ib.*; description of the ceremony, and the speech of, i. 197-8; requests permission from Francis I. to defend the town of Mézières, i. 385; compels the sheriff of the town to take an oath never to advise a surrender, i. 387; summoned to surrender by the imperial commanders, i. 388; his heroic reply, i. 389; by a *ruse*

Bayard—*continued.*
de guerre he causes a misunderstanding between the imperial generals, i. 390-1; makes a successful sortie, i. 393; the *ruse* of the bottle of wine, *ib.*; causes the Comte de Nassau to raise the siege of Mézières, i. 394; Francis I. confers the order of Philip Augustus upon, *ib.*; gratitude of the citizens of Mézières to, *ib.*; joins the French army in Italy, ii. 26; detached to Vigevano, ii. 118; detached to Rebec to intercept provisions to Milan, ii. 122; his interview with Bonnivet thereon, *ib.*; defends Rebec, ii. 124; demands reinforcements from Bonnivet, *ib.*; suspects Bonnivet of placing him in an ambush, *ib.*; his vigilance, ii. 125; attacked by Pescara with an overwhelming force, and compelled to fly, ii. 126; his gallantry, *ib.*; accuses Bonnivet of treachery, *ib.*; entrusted with the command of the troops by Bonnivet, ii. 129; wounded in the loins, ii. 130; his last moments, *ib.*; grief of the soldiers for, ii. 131; visited by the imperial general, ii. 132; homage of the imperialist general to, *ib.*; visited by the Duc de Bourbon, *ib.*; dying rebuke of, to Bourbon, *ib.*; death of, ii. 133; his funeral, *ib.*

Beaujeu, Madame de, *see* Anne de France

—— Sire de, entrusted by Louis XI. with the keeping of the dauphin, afterwards Charles VIII., i. 7; *see* note, *ib.*

Beaurain, Comte de, his visit to the Duc de Bourbon, ii. 40; induces the duke to revolt, ii. 41; visits England and negotiates with Henry VIII., ii. 42; joins

Beaurain—*continued*.
the English army under the Duke of Norfolk at Calais, ii. 111; bears the conditions of the emperor to Francis I., ii. 202; see note, *ib*.

Bédier, Noël, a celebrated syndic, his power over the minds of the Parisians alluded to, ii. 269

Bellay, Guillaume du, his family alluded to, ii. 336; see note, *ib*.; arranges a meeting between Henry VIII. and Francis I., ii. 363

—— Jean du, Bishop of Bayonne, ambassador of Francis I. at the Court of England, ii. 310; Bishop of Paris, delivers a Latin oration to the Pope, ii. 388; provisions Paris, iii. 78-9

—— Martin du, intercedes for the Duke of Wurtemberg with Francis I., ii. 383; taken prisoner, iii. 92; appointed counsellor to the Duc d'Orleans, iii. 98; Lieutenant-general in Piedmont, iii. 175; accuses the Marquis del Guasto of murdering two French ambassadors, iii. 177; superseded by d'Annebaut in Piedmont, iii. 188; death of, *ib*.; see note, *ib*.; exclamation of Charles V. on hearing of his death, iii. 189

Bentivoglio, Jean, attacked by Pope Julius II., retires from Bologna to Milan, i. 52-3

Berguin, Louis de, his re-arrest and trial alluded to, ii. 342; see note, *ib*.; burnt for heresy, ii. 343

Biagrasso, evacuated by Bonnivet, ii. 128; besieged and taken by Sforza, *ib*.

Bibbiena, Cardinal de, letter from the Pope, Leo X., to, alluded to, i. 301

Bicocca, battle of, ii. 27-8-9

Bier, Sire du, his gallant resistance to the Earl of Surrey at the siege of Hesdin alluded to, ii. 71

Biez, Maréchal de, his operations against Boulogne, iii. 284; invades the Terre d'Oye, iii. 287

Binche, siege of, iii. 204

Black Bands, forces of the Duc de Gueldres; see note, i. 187; at the battle of Pavia, ii. 164

Bohemia, King of, votes for Charles V. at the diet of Frankfort, i. 331

Boissy, Adrian de, receives a cardinal's hat, i. 209

—— de M., one of the witnesses to the secret protest of the king when a prisoner, ii. 229

—— Gouffier de, appointed Grand Master, i. 144; attached to the embassy of Admiral de Bonnivet to the English Court, i. 288; death of, i. 326; his death a serious loss to Francis I., i. 327; his influence over Francis I. alluded to, i. 336-7

Boleyn, Anne, one of the maids of honour to the Princess Mary of England at her marriage with Louis XII. at Abbeville, i. 126; her thirst for admiration alluded to, *ib*.; attracts the attention of the Princesse Claude, *ib*.

—— Sir Thomas, one of the witnesses to the betrothal of the dauphin to the Princess Mary of England, i. 294; officiates as proxy for Henry VIII. at the baptism of the second son of Francis I., i. 333

Boncar, M. de, volunteers with the Chevalier Bayard to defend the city of Mézières, i. 386

Bonnivet, Admiral, *see* Gouffier Guillaume

Bontems, Pierre, his works in the palace of Chambord alluded to, ii. 264

Bossut, Nicholas de, Sire de Longueval, position of, in Brabant, iii. 184; instigated by the Duchesse d'Etampes, betrays the designs of Francis to the emperor, iii. 186

Boulogne, taken by Henry VIII., iii. 255; attack upon, by the dauphin, iii. 259-60; military operations before, iii. 284

Bourbon, Antoine de, Duc de Vendôme, his marriage with Jeanne de Navarre alluded to, iii. 211; see Vendôme, Duc de

—— Duc de, see Montpensier, Charles de

—— François de, killed at the battle of Marignano, i. 193

—— Suzanne de, one of the suite of Anne de Bretagne, i. 22

Bourg, Antoine du, president of the Parliament of Paris, appointed to the chancellorship, iii. 26; death of, iii. 105

Boutières, M. de, assumes the command of the army at Turin, iii. 189; see note, *ib.*; superseded in his command in Piedmont by the Comte d'Enghien, iii. 220; joins the army under the Comte d'Enghien, iii. 233

Boyer, Bishop of Bourges, created a cardinal, i. 320

Brancas, Madame de, Comptroller of the Household of Louise de Savoie, ii. 44-5

Brandenburg, Albert of, Archbishop of Mayence, one of the Electors of Germany, i. 299; see note, *ib.*; his speech at the Electoral Diet at Frankfort in favour of Charles V., i. 328

—— Joachim, Marquis de, one of the Electors of Germany, i. 299; votes for Charles V. at the Diet of Frankfort, i. 331

Brantôme, quoted as the panegyrist of Marguerite de Valois, i. 40;

Brantôme—*continued*.
his remarks upon the position of the Princesse Claude and Mary of England alluded to, i. 129-30; his heinous slander on Queen Mary alluded to, i. 135; his description of the Court circle of Queen Claude, i. 148; observations of, respecting the intrigue of Admiral de Bonnivet and the Comtesse de Châteaubriand, i. 259

Brescia, taken by Louis XII., i. 63; taken by the French under Gaston de Foix, i. 70; given up to pillage, i. 71; siege of, raised by the Emperor Maximilian, i. 211; again captured by the French, i. 214

Bretons, the discontent of, at the cession of Brittany to Francis I., i. 134-5

Breuil, Pierre du, a Protestant preacher, burnt by order of Charles V., iii. 263

Brézé, Louis de, Seneschal of Normandy, informs Francis of the treason of the Duc de Bourbon, ii. 73; marries Diane de Poitiers, ii. 98; his jealousy, *ib.*; his pedigree, ii. 100; endeavours to persuade his wife not to attempt to save the life of her father, ii. 101; his reason for not accompanying his wife to Court, ii. 102

—— Madame de; see Diane de Poitiers

Briandas, a Court jester, betrays the private conversation of the dauphin to the king, iii. 272-4

Bricot, Thomas, a canon of Notre Dame, speech of, at the assembly of the States-General, i. 45

Brindici, cession of, to the King of Spain alluded to, i. 64

Brion, Bertrand, his arrest and trial alluded to, ii. 94; de-

INDEX

Brion—*continued.*
spatched by Francis I. to Paris as attendant to the dauphin, ii. 228; one of the witnesses to the secret protest of the king when a prisoner, ii. 229

Brittany, efforts of Francis to annex the duchy of, to the crown of France, ii. 353; the Bretons resist the claim, ii. 354; Louis des Desserts undertakes to secure their consent, ii. 355; the duchy united to the French throne, ii. 356

Brosse, Comte Jean de, his impoverished condition alluded to, ii. 285; marries Mademoiselle de Heilly, and is created Duc d'Etampes, ii. 286

Bruto, a Florentine historian, protected by Francis I., ii. 334

Bucet, Charles de, Comte de Sancerre, his death alluded to, iii. 90

Budée, Guillaume, sent by Francis I. as ambassador to Rome, i. 158; *see* note, *ib.*; advises Francis I. to invite Erasmus to France, i. 270

Buren, Comte de, joins the Earl of Surrey upon the French frontier, ii. 68; invests Saint-Pol, and carries it by assault, iii. 90-1; *see* note, *ib.*; destroys Saint-Pol, iii. 92; marches upon Térouenne, *ib.*; at the siege of Térouenne, iii. 92-3

Burgundy revolts against Louis XII., i. 110; States of, refuse allegiance to the Emperor Charles V., ii. 236

—— herald to the Emperor Charles V., detained by Francis I. in Fontarabia, ii. 316; pretexts of the King of France to evade an interview with, ii. 317; follows Francis to Paris, *ib.*; refuses to remove his coat of

Burgundy, herald—*continued.*
mail, *ib.*; Francis grants him an audience, but refuses to let him deliver the hostile message of the emperor, ii. 318; leaves France, *ib.*

Burie, M. de, *see* note, iii. 79; taken prisoner at Casal, iii. 80

CADAMOSTO, Carolo, taken prisoner at Villa Franca, i. 177

Cæsar Borgia delivers to Louis XII. the Pope's Bull dissolving his marriage with Jeanne de France, i. 14

Calais, conference at, between the ministers of France and Germany, i. 382; second conference at, between the ministers of Charles and Francis, ii. 12

Calvimont, M. de, his withholding the message of Charles V. to Francis I. alluded to, ii. 311; his explanation, *ib.*

Calvin, tenets of, promulgated through France, iii. 18

Cambray, treaty of, alluded to, i. 60; ii. 323-6

Camilla, Julio, an Italian impostor, i. 270; attempts to teach Francis I. Latin and Greek in one month, *ib.*

Caravaggio taken by assault by Louis XII., i. 62

Cardona, Raymond de, avoids giving battle to Gaston de Foix, i. 72; description of, by Pope Julius II., *see* note, *ib.*; flight of, from the battle of Ravenna, i. 74; stigmatized by Colonna as the "Miscreant Moor," i. 75; position of, in the neighbourhood of Verona, i. 178; refuses to pass the Po, and by his delays prevents the co-operation of the Swiss, i. 183

Carignano, battle of, iii. 233-5

Carmagnole besieged and taken by the Marquis del Guasto, iii. 96-7

Carraquon, burning of the, iii. 279

Castelnau, M. de, death of, in a street brawl, iii. 29

Castiglione, Balthasar, applied to by the Emperor Charles V. to become his second in his anticipated duel with Francis I., ii. 315; insulted by one of the lacqueys of Maraviglio, ii. 377; his death, ii. 379

Castille, Constable of, at the ratification of the treaty of Cambray, and exchange of the French princes, ii. 326

Catherine de' Medici, her reception by the Queen of France, ii. 386; preliminaries of her marriage with the Duc d'Orleans alluded to, ii. 389; remark of Philippe Strozzi respecting her dower, ii. 390; the emperor endeavours to prevent her marriage, *ib.*; her marriage described, ii. 391-2; her position at the Court of Francis, iii. 1; state of the French Court on her marriage, iii. 4; her personal appearance, *ib.*; character of, alluded to, iii. 5; becomes the friend of Diane de Poitiers, iii. 6; her Court ladies, iii. 8; suspected of poisoning the dauphin, iii. 63-4; her dissimulation alluded to, iii. 85; her policy towards Diane de Poitiers, iii. 191; her Court described, iii. 192; her power over Francis, iii. 193; her extraordinary self-command alluded to, *ib.*

Cellini, Benvenuto, his career in France, iii. 161-70

Céri, Lorenzo de, besieges Arona, but is repulsed, ii. 121-2; impedes the mining operations of the imperialists at the siege of Marseilles, ii. 141

Cervia, capture of, alluded to, i. 63

Chabannes, Maréchal de, at Calais, i. 382; joins the French army in Italy with supplies, ii. 26; takes possession of Avignon, ii. 139; attacks the rear of the imperialists on their retreat from France, ii. 142

Chabot, Philippe, Sire de Brion, affection of Francis I. for, alluded to, i. 144; *see* note, i. 145; his exaggeration of the criminal intentions of the Bourbon conspiracy alluded to, ii. 95; his gasconade on being sent to assure the citizens of Paris that Maréchal Vendôme was marching to their aid, ii. 112; despatched by the king to assure the Marseillaise of relief, ii. 137; created an admiral, ii. 244; invested with the Order of the Garter by Henry VIII., ii. 364; overruns the duchy of Savoy, iii. 24; fortifies the frontier of France, iii. 50; arrest of, iii. 144; condemned to death, iii. 145; pardoned by the king, iii. 146; his death, iii. 147

Challon, Claudine de, her marriage with Comte Henry de Nassau alluded to, i. 151

Chalnau, hunting seat of, alluded to, ii. 357

Chalon, Philibert de, *see* Orange, Prince of

Chambord, palace of, description of, ii. 263

Chambre Ardente, members of the, their duties described, ii. 269

Champdivers, Odette de, introduces cards to amuse Charles VI., i. 237

Champion, M. Clermont, betrays the intended flight of the French king to Charles V., ii. 224

Charles V. sends ambassadors to congratulate Francis on his ac-

Charles V.—*continued.*
cession, i. 149; is promised the hand of the Princesse Rénée, *ib.*; accession of, to the throne of Spain, i. 217; his early application to state affairs, i. 218; his prospects, i. 219; forms an alliance with Francis, i. 221; conditions of the peace of Noyon, i. 222; promises to espouse the infant daughter of Francis I., *ib.*; induces the Emperor Maximilian to accede to the treaty of Noyon, i. 223; his increasing power induces Francis to form an alliance with England, i. 285; aspires to be Emperor of Germany, i. 298-9-300; his diplomatic talents alluded to, i. 303; his pretensions to the empire contrasted with those of Francis I., i. 306; personal appearance of, i. 307; his position at the death of Cardinal Ximènés, i. 308; unostentatiously strengthens his party, i. 310; secures the votes of the Marquis of Brandenburg and the Bishop of Mayence, i. 312; Robert de la Mark and the Prince-Bishop of Liège join the cause of, i. 321; Seckingen takes part with the king, i. 323; attacks and disperses some Turkish galleys, i. 325; proclaimed Emperor of Germany, i. 331; invited to proceed to his new dominions, *ib.*; fails to fulfil his engagement relative to the kingdom of Navarre, i. 339; misunderstanding between the Courts of France and Spain, i. 340; the critical position of Spain alluded to, *ib.*; visits England, i. 343; his interview with Henry VIII., i. 344; embarks for Flanders, *ib.*; secures the interest of Cardinal Wolsey, i. 345; appoints Wolsey Bishop

Charles V.—*continued.*
of Badajoz and Valencia, i. 365; his meeting with Henry VIII. at Gravelines, *ib.*; accompanies Henry VIII. to Calais, i. 366; departs for Aix-la-Chapelle, where he is crowned King of the Romans and Emperor of Germany, i. 367; convokes a diet of the empire at Worms to suppress the doctrines of Luther, i. 369; his bad faith with Francis I. alluded to, i. 371; quarrels with Robert de la Mark, *ib.*; defied by him, *ib.*; enters into a league with the Pope to drive the French out of Italy, i. 374; his Spanish subjects revolt, i. 375; accuses Francis I. of sheltering his enemies, *ib.*; despatches the Comte de Nassau to ravage the territories of Robert de la Mark, i. 379; his appeal to the English king to mediate between him and Francis I. alluded to, i. 380; his duplicity, i. 381-2; disregards the treaty of Noyon, i. 383; betrothed to the Princess Mary of England, i. 384; joins his retreating army near Valenciennes, i. 396; his formidable power alluded to, ii. 24; visits England and induces Henry VIII. to ratify the betrothal of the Princess Mary, and to land 40,000 men in France, ii. 25; induces the Duc de Bourbon to rebel against Francis I., ii. 41; promises the duke the hand of his sister, the widowed Queen of Portugal, *ib.*; averse to act in concert with Francis I. against the Turks, ii. 48; lands at Dover, his reception by Henry VIII., ii. 63; invested by Henry VIII. with the Order of the Garter, *ib.*; his politic conduct

Charles V.—*continued*.
with Cardinal Wolsey, ii. 64; his bad faith to the Duc de Bourbon, ii. 110; causes the defeat of Cardinal Wolsey for the popedom, ii. 120; illness of, alluded to, ii. 153; refuses to restore the ecclesiastical ornaments taken from the churches of Pavia to pay his troops, ii. 155; his hypocrisy on receiving the intelligence of the capture of Francis I., ii. 181; his crafty policy with Henry VIII., ii. 198; concludes a truce with France, ii. 199; the ransom of the French king discussed in the council of, ii. 200; Louise de Savoie endeavours to ingratiate herself by betraying her allies to the emperor, ii. 201; terms imposed by Charles upon Francis I. for his release from captivity, ii. 203; exultation of Charles on hearing that the French king was in a Spanish fortress, ii. 206; rewards the Viceroy of Naples for bringing Francis I. to Spain, *ib.*; visits the sickbed of the French king, ii. 210; warned of the secret league against him, ii. 212; a sobriquet, ii. 213; his evasive reply to Louise de Savoie on receiving her warning of the secret league against him, *ib.*; receives Marguerite de Valois at the gates of Madrid, ii. 215; his bad faith alluded to, ii. 217; removes the Dowager-Queen of Portugal to Guadaloupe to avoid her meeting with Marguerite de Valois, *ib.*; grants an audience to Marguerite de Valois, ii. 217-22; receives intelligence of the intended flight of Francis I., ii. 224; meditates the arrest of Marguerite de Valois, ii. 225;

Charles V.—*continued*.
demands of the emperor for the release of the French king, ii. 229-31; indignation of, on hearing of the breach of faith of Francis I., ii. 238; summons Francis to return to Madrid as his prisoner, *ib.*; his army oppresses the Italian people, ii. 239; his position in Italy, ii. 253; disclaims the responsibility of the sack of Rome, ii. 278; the remonstrances of his council prevent the removal of the Pope to Spain, *ib.*; his power in Italy threatened by the armies of England and France, ii. 279; the Kings of France and England declare war against, ii. 310; his reply to the heralds of France and England, *ib.*; accuses Francis I. of basely violating his pledge given at Madrid, ii. 312; defies the French king, *ib.*; his letter to Francis I. challenging him to single combat, ii. 315; applies to Balthasar Castiglione to become his second, *ib.*; Francis I. refuses to allow Burgundy, the herald, to deliver his challenge, ii. 317-18; the exhausted state of his treasury alluded to, ii. 322; ratifies a treaty of peace with the Pope, ii. 323; concessions of, at *La Paix des Dames*, ii. 324; advised to invest Francisco Sforza with the duchy of Milan, ii. 345; meeting between the Pope and the Emperor, ii. 346; concludes a treaty with the Pope, *ib.*; coronation of, at Bologna, ii. 347; restores the Milanese to Sforza, *ib.*; indifference of the emperor to the claims of the French Crown, ii. 348; appoints the Queen-Dowager of Hungary Gouvernante of the Low Countries, ii. 359; pro-

Charles V.—*continued.*
ceeds to Flanders, *ib.*; persuades the Pope to refuse to sanction the divorce of Henry VIII. and Katherine of Aragon, *ib.*; convenes a diet at Spires, and enforces the observance of church ceremonies, ii. 360; his contempt for the German Protestants, ii. 361; his diet at Augsburg, *ib.*; summons Francis to send an army against the Turks, ii. 367; takes the field against Solyman and compels him to retreat, *ib.*; his advice to the Pope respecting the marriage of his niece, Catherine de' Medici, with the Duc d'Orleans, ii. 368; meets the Pope at Bologna, ii. 369; the dismissal of Maraviglia from the Court of Milan demanded by, ii. 376; bestows the hand of his niece Christina on the Duke of Milan, ii. 382; endeavours to prevent the marriage of Catherine de' Medici with the Duc d'Orleans, ii. 390; makes propositions of friendship and alliance to Francis, iii. 15; takes Tunis, and releases twenty thousand Christian slaves, iii. 17; popularity of the emperor, *ib.*; applied to by the Duke of Savoy for protection against France, iii. 24; restores Alessandro de' Medici to the sovereignty of Florence, iii. 26; offers to concede the duchy of Milan to the Duc d'Angoulême, iii. 39; requests the Duc d'Orleans to accompany him to Algiers, iii. 40; secures the fealty of Alessandro de' Medici by marriage, *ib.*; renews his alliance with the Venetians, *ib.*; renews his negotiations with Francis respecting the Milanese, iii. 41; makes overtures to the Pope and Henry

Charles V.—*continued.*
VIII., *ib.*; proceeds to Rome, and accuses Francis before the Conclave, iii. 42; he temporizes with the French ambassadors, iii. 43; repents of his accusation against Francis, iii. 44; his address to the Conclave is garbled and despatched to France, iii. 46; interview of, with the Cardinal de Lorraine on the affair of the Milanese, iii. 47; his superstition, iii. 48; excites the German Protestants against Francis, iii. 49; declares himself Suzerain of Provence, iii. 51; despatches Da Leyva to besiege Turin, iii. 53; determines to invade Provence, iii. 55; surprises a French force at Tourbes, iii. 56; accused of promoting the death of the dauphin by poison, iii. 63; indignation of, *ib.*; enters Aix and destroys the town, iii. 65; sufferings of his troops and death of his general, Antonio da Leyva, iii. 68; abandons the siege of Arles, *ib.*; death of his general, De la Vega, iii. 72; embarks at Genoa for Spain, iii. 73; is overtaken by a violent storm, *ib.*; his failure alluded to, *ib.*; the invasion of France by, causes the Italian princes to form a league, iii. 75; cited by Francis I. to appear before the French tribunals, iii. 89; disregards the summons, iii. 90; truce between France, Picardy, and the Low Countries proposed by, iii. 94-5; endeavours to effect a general peace throughout Europe, iii. 103; offers the hand of his niece to the Duc d'Orleans, *ib.*; the Pope arranges an interview between Francis and the emperor, iii. 107; the Pope mediates be-

Charles V.—*continued.*
tween the two potentates, iii. 110; concludes a truce for ten years with Francis, iii. 111; returns to Barcelona, *ib.*; the emperor invites Francis to a personal interview, iii. 112; meets Francis at Aigues Mortes, *ib.*; his admiration of the beauties of the French Court, iii. 113; the city of Ghent revolts against the emperor, iii. 119; requests permission to traverse France, iii. 121; arrives at Bayonne and refuses to receive hostages for his safety while in France, iii. 131; meets Francis I. at Châtellerault, *ib.*; triumphant reception of, at Poitiers, iii. 132; distrust of the emperor at the hospitality of the French king, iii. 133; accident to, iii. 134; unfortunate coincidences, iii. 135; his retinue, *ib.*; Francis informs the emperor of the advice of the Duchesse d'Etampes, iii. 136; reply of, iii. 137; his politic conduct to the duchess, *ib.*; his entry into Paris, iii. 138; proceeds to Valenciennes, iii. 140; refuses to ratify the cession of the Milanese, *ib.*; tergiversation of, *ib.*; proposes an alliance between his son Philip and the Princess of Navarre, iii. 149; offers the hand of the Princess of Spain to the Duc d'Orleans, *ib.*; disappointment of the emperor at the refusal of Francis, iii. 150; invests his son, Dom Philippe, with the duchy of Milan, iii. 173; alarm of, at the treaty between the Venetians and the Turks, *ib.*; his reply to Francis on being summoned to make reparation for the murder of two French ambassadors, iii. 179; desires to become the

Charles V.—*continued.*
champion of Christendom, *ib.*; his interview with the Pope at Lucca previous to his campaign against the Turks, iii. 180; enters into a truce with the Protestant princes, iii. 181; conducts an expedition against the Algerines, *ib.*; dispersion of his fleet, iii. 182; returns to Spain, iii. 183; effects a rupture between England and France, iii. 206; reorganizes his army, iii. 207; ravages the duchy of Cleves, iii. 208; pardons the Duke of Cleves on condition of his renouncing the Reformed religion and his allegiance to France, iii. 209; his army, reinforced by the English, besieges Landrecies, Guise, and Luxembourg, iii. 212; takes Cambray, iii. 214; position of, in 1544, iii. 222; invades France in conjunction with Henry VIII., iii. 240; takes Luxembourg, *ib.*; besieges St. Dizier, *ib.*; takes St. Dizier, iii. 245; his distrust of Henry VIII. prevents co-operation of the allied forces, iii. 248; endeavours to conclude a peace with Francis, iii. 251; marches on Chalons, *ib.*; revictuals his army through the treachery of Madame d'Etampes, iii. 254; advance of the emperor, iii. 255; concludes a treaty with Francis, iii. 256; conditions of the treaty, iii. 257; withdraws his troops from the English army, iii. 258; resolves to bestow the hand of his daughter upon the Duc d'Orleans, iii. 261; determines to subjugate the league of Smalkalden, iii. 262; endeavours to conciliate the Pope, *ib.*; persecutes the Flemish reformers,

Charles V.—*continued.*
iii. 263; refuses to cede the duchy of Milan to Francis, iii. 291; makes war upon the Protestant princes, iii. 292

Charles VIII. betrothed to Margaret of Austria, i. 6; his hand declined by the Princesse Marie and Elizabeth of England, *ib.*; educated in seclusion by Louis XI., i. 7; his romantic passion for Anne de Bretagne, i. 8; releases the Duc d'Orleans from prison, i. 10; influenced by Anne de France, *ib.*; refuses to marry Margaret of Austria, i. 11; reconducts her to Flanders with great honour, *ib.*; marries Anne de Bretagne, i. 12; his death, i. 13

Châteaubriand, Comte de, marries Françoise de Foix, i. 228; fears to trust his beautiful countess at the Court of Francis, i. 229; his stratagem to detain her in Brittany defeated, i. 232; accuses his countess of dissimulation, i. 233-4; story of the ring contradicted, *see* note, i. 235; annoyed at the attentions of Francis to his wife, i. 237; anxiety of, to attach his wife to the circle of Queen Claude, i. 238; his mistaken violence, i. 239; departs from Court on finding himself dishonoured, i. 241; his vengeance on his wife on her return from Court, ii. 195; his alleged treatment of his wife on her return from Court, ii. 297

—— Comtesse de, her birth and childhood, i. 228; her marriage, *ib.*; the story of the three rings, i. 229-30; summoned to Court and her meeting with Francis I., i. 231-6; welcomed to the Court of Louise

Châteaubriand—*continued.*
de Savoie, i. 239; her *liaison* with the king, i. 240; her increasing power over the king alarms Louise de Savoie, i. 250; the intrigues of her brothers alluded to, i. 251; induces Francis to recall the Connétable de France from Milan, i. 252-6; her conduct towards the Duc de Bourbon, i. 258; her profligacy, i. 259; her intrigue with Admiral de Bonnivet, *ib.*; her unbounded favour with the king, i. 276; maintains her influence over the king notwithstanding her *liaison* with Bonnivet, i. 277; obtains for her second brother the *bâton* of maréchal, i. 284; increasing favour of the king for, ii. 3; the enamelled gems, *ib.*; advises her brother not to return to Milan without supplies, ii. 6; her influence insufficient to induce the king to grant an audience to her brother, Maréchal de Lautrec, ii. 49; applies to the Duc de Bourbon for assistance, ii. 50; the king reconciled to her brother, ii. 57; her faction, of whom composed, ii. 58; her misunderstanding with Francis, ii. 83; the Duchesse d'Alençon attempts a reconciliation, ii. 86; banished from Court, ii. 193; her reception by her husband, *ib.*; confined by the count in a chamber hung with black, ii. 195; her reflections, ii. 196; on hearing of the return of Francis I. makes her escape and joins the Court at Bayonne, ii. 233; the increased affection of the king for, ii. 240; scheme of Louise de Savoie to supplant the countess in the affection of the king, ii. 241; her person

Châteaubriand—*continued.*
described, ii. 242 ; her alarm at the king's admiration of Mademoiselle de Heilly, ii. 247 ; waning influence of, ii. 265 ; her remonstrance to Francis, ii. 281 ; her last interview with Francis, ii. 294-6; retires from Court to her husband in Brittany, ii. 297; the king demands the return of her jewels, ii. 299; her rebuke to the king and its consequences, ii. 300 ; reconciled to her husband, ii. 356 ; the king presents her with two valuable estates, *ib.*

Châteaufort, Seigneur de, charged with despatches from the Connétable de France to Cardinal Wolsey, ii. 42.

Châtellerault, Duc de, serves in the vanguard of the army for the recovery of the Milanese, i. 168

Châtillon, Duc de, indignation of, at the stipulations of the Earl of Worcester on the surrender of Tournay, i. 294-5 ; death of, on his march to Fontarabia, ii. 60-1

—— Odet de, created a cardinal in his thirteenth year, ii. 392

Chaumont, M. de, Lieutenant-general, marches on Bologna, i. 52 ; *see* note, *ib.* ; commands first division of Louis XII.'s army against Venice, i. 61 ; death of, at the battle of Pavia, ii. 176

Cheyne, Sir Thomas, desired by Henry VIII. to remonstrate with Francis I. on his interference in Scotland, ii. 65 ; dignified reply of the French king to, ii. 66-7

Chiavenna, castle of, taken by Gian Giacomo de' Medici, ii. 157

Chièvres, M. de, instigates the Archduke Charles to preserve a peace with France, i. 149 ; his reply to the French ambassador on the early application of Charles of Spain to business, i. 218 ; induces Charles to form an alliance with Francis, i. 219 ; his jealousy of the power of the Cardinal Ximénés, i. 220 ; his death alluded to, i. 383

Christina, Princess, her marriage with Lorenzo Sforza, ii. 382, *see* note, *ib.*

Claude, afterwards queen of Francis I., daughter of Louis XII. and Anne of Bretagne, betrothed to the Duc de Valois, i. 46 ; marriage of, with the Duc de Valois, afterwards Francis I., i. 117 ; evil omen at her nuptials, i. 118; peculiar position of, at the Court of Louis XII., i. 129; becomes Queen of France and cedes her estates to Francis I., her husband, i. 133 ; the purity of her Court contrasted with that of Madame d'Angoulême, i. 147 ; her Court described by Brantôme, i. 148 ; gives birth to a princess, *ib.* ; her farewell reception of the nobles on their departure to recover the Milanese under Francis I., i. 160-1 ; her Court, i. 226; her interview with Madame de Châteaubriand, i. 237 ; gives birth to a dauphin, i. 243 ; meekness and resignation of, i. 244 ; her forbearance alluded to, i. 250 ; gives birth to a third daughter, i. 277 ; gives birth to a second son, i. 333; her interview with the Queen of England at the Field of the Cloth of Gold, i. 358-9 ; her position at Court during the rival factions, ii. 58 ; urges the marriage of the Princesse Rénée

Claude—*continued.*
with Bourbon, ii. 59; her death, ii. 144; heartlessness of the king, *ib.*; her amiable character, *ib.*

Clement VII., his election to the popedom alluded to, ii. 120; secretly favours the League, and is desirous for the expulsion of the French from Italy, *ib.*; undertakes to furnish Francis I. with supplies for carrying on the war in Italy, ii. 148; declares his neutrality, ii. 150; endeavours to establish a truce between France and Spain for five years, *ib.*; enters into a secret treaty with Francis I., ii. 151; warns the emperor of the secret league against him, ii. 213; enters into a treaty with France, known as the Holy League, ii. 237; enters into a league with Pompeio Colonna, ii. 250; disbands his forces in Romagna, *ib.*; attacked by Cardinal Colonna, takes refuge in the castle of St. Angelo, *ib.*; taken prisoner by the Prince of Orange, ii. 256; his captivity causes a general indignation throughout Europe, ii. 272-3; makes terms with the emperor, ii. 320; meeting between the Pope and the Emperor Charles V., ii. 346; concludes a treaty with Charles V., *ib.*; refuses to sanction the divorce of Henry VIII. and Katherine of Aragon, ii. 359; indignation of Henry VIII. against, ii. 365; incredulity of the Pope at the offer of the hand of the Duc d'Orleans to Catherine de' Medici, ii. 368; consults Charles V. thereon, *ib.*; meets the emperor at Bologna, *ib.*; two French bishops are sent by the Kings of France

Clement VII.—*continued.*
and England to threaten, *ib.*; anxious to secure the friendship of Francis I., ii. 371; his ruling passion, ii. 372; a meeting is arranged between the Pope and Francis, ii. 373; proceeds to Marseilles to meet the French king, ii. 383; his reception, ii. 385; homage of Francis I. to, ii. 386; the emperor endeavours to prevent the marriage of his niece with the Duc d'Orleans, ii. 390; his exultation on the marriage of his niece, ii. 391; creates four new French cardinals, ii. 392; leaves France and returns to Italy, *ib.*; excommunicates Henry VIII., iii. 15; death of, *ib.*

Clerc, Guillaume le, burnt alive at Meaux for heresy, iii. 294

——— Jean le, burnt alive at Meaux for heresy, ii. 340

Clermont, Comte de, destroys the bridges in his way through Piedmont, after the battle of Pavia, ii. 177

Cleves, Duc de, his marriage with the Princess of Navarre, iii. 151-3; *see* note, *ib.*; leaves France, iii. 154; his marriage annulled, *ib.*; declared the enemy of the empire, iii. 181; his territory ravaged by the Emperor Charles V., iii. 208; throws himself on the mercy of the emperor, iii. 209; degrading concessions of, *ib.*

Coligny, Gaspard de, at the siege of Binche, iii. 204

College, Royal, efforts of Francis I. to establish a, ii. 336; Francis dissuaded from founding the, by the insinuations of the Chancellor Duprat, *ib.*

Colonna, Fabrizio, commands in the combined army of the Pope

Colonna, Fabrizio—*continued.* and Ferdinand of Spain at the battle of Ravenna, i. 72; *see* note, *ib.*; his bravery at the battle of Ravenna, i. 75; taken prisoner, *ib.*
—— Marco-Antonio, his military abilities at Verona, i. 214; *see* note, *ib.*
—— Pompeio, Cardinal, enters into a league with Clement VII., ii. 250; *see* note, *ib.*; marches on Rome and compels the Pope to take refuge in the castle of St. Angelo, *ib.*
—— Prosper, entrusted with the passes of the Alps against Francis I., i. 173; *see* note, *ib.*; his arrogance, i. 174-5-6; captured and surrenders to Bayard, i. 177; profits by the discontent in the French army, ii. 2; quarrel with the Marquis of Pescara about precedence, ii. 9; its consequences, *ib.*; crosses the Po unimpeded, ii. 10; takes up his quarters at Bicocca, ii. 27; defeats the French under Maréchal Lautrec, and compels them to retreat to Cremona, ii. 29-32; invests Cremona, and compels M. de Lescun to capitulate, ii. 33-4; appointed general of the Italian League, ii. 72; defends the Milanese, ii. 116; his able defence of Milan, ii. 117-18; his death, ii. 119
Commines, Philippe de la Clite, Sire de, *see* note, i. 11
Concordat, the, *see* Pragmatic Sanction, i. 208; signed, i. 209; recognition of, urged forward by Francis, i. 261; *see* Parliament
Coni, fortress of, iii. 53
Connétable de France, *see* Montpensier, Charles de, and Montmorency, Anne de; office of, alluded to, i. 142-3

Cop, Guillaume, an eminent physician, i. 268; *see* note, *ib.*
Cousin, Jean, his works in the palace of Chambord alluded to, ii. 264; *see* note, *ib.*
Crema, taken by Louis XII., i. 63
Cremona, citadel of, surrendered to Louis XII., i. 63; gallant defence of, by M. d'Herbouville, ii. 115
Créqui, Antoine de, defends Térouenne against the Earl of Shrewsbury and Lord Talbot, i. 99
Crote, Seigneur la, one of the captains in Louis XII.'s army at the battle of Agnadello, i. 61
Croy, Guillaume de, a letter from Louis XII. seeking to excuse his treaty with the Austrian Court on the subject of his daughter's marriage, alluded to, i. 47; *see* note, *ib.*

D'ABILA, Diégo, assists at the capture of Francis I. at Pavia, ii. 170
D'Aerschott, Duc, scheme to entrap the, ii. 69-70
Daillon, Jacques de, Seigneur de Lude, his defence of Fontarabia, ii. 59; *see* note, *ib.*; arrives at Court, ii. 62
D'Alarçon, M., Francis I. consigned to the custody of, after the battle of Pavia, ii. 179; succeeds to the command of the Spanish infantry on the death of Prosper Colonna, *ib.*; his alarm at the anger of Francis I. on his reading the terms proposed by Charles for his release from captivity, ii. 202; ordered by Charles V. to attend Francis I. during his captivity, ii. 207

INDEX

D'Albret, Jean, throws himself into Pampeluna, i. 83; forced to retire beyond the Pyrenees, *ib.*
—— Henry, King of Navarre, his claims upon Navarre alluded to at the treaty of Noyon, i. 221; invited by the Navarrese to claim his crown, i. 376; supplied with troops by Francis I., i. 377; taken prisoner at the battle of Pavia, ii. 176; effects his escape, *ib.*; marries Marguerite de Valois, ii. 300; his character alluded to, ii. 301; his issue, ii. 302; improves the condition of his people, *ib.*; his Court of Bearn, *ib.*; suspects the fidelity of his queen, ii. 306; the king is partially converted to Lutheranism, *ib.*; his interests abandoned by France at the treaty of Cambray, ii. 325; entrusted with the defence of Guienne, iii. 51; appointed governor of Guienne and Languedoc, iii. 98; disappointment of, at the refusal of Francis to accept the hand of Philip of Spain for the Princess of Navarre, iii. 150

D'Alençon, Duc, one of the suite of Louis XII., i. 22; his marriage with the sister of Francis I. alluded to, i. 23; description of, i. 39; observations on his union with Marguerite de Valois, *ib.*; commands the rear-guard of the army for the recovery of the Milanese, i. 169; successfully resists a charge of the Swiss at the battle of Marignano, i. 192; at the baptism of the second son of Francis I., i. 333; appointed to the government of Champagne, i. 381; approaches within three leagues of Mézières, i. 393; retakes Mouzon, i. 395; commands the vanguard of the

D'Alençon, Duc—*continued.*
French army, i. 396; at the battle of Pavia, ii. 163; his cowardice, ii. 167; his claims as a candidate for the throne alluded to, ii. 186; his interview with the duchess, *ib.*; vindication of, *see* note, *ib.*; his death alluded to, *ib.*
—— Duchesse, *see* Marguerite de Valois

D'Alviano, General, insolence of, to Louis XII., i. 4; defeated by Louis XII. at the battle of Agnadello, i. 62; restored to liberty by Louis XII. and placed at the head of the Venetian army, i. 91; at Lodi, i. 183; at the battle of Marignano, i. 185; pursues the Swiss after the battle, i. 192; his death, i. 193

D'Amboise, Cardinal, Louis XII. instigated by, to make a will directing the Princesse Claude to marry Francis, Comte d'Angoulême, i. 41; *see* note, *ib.*; his death, i. 69
—— Bussy, nephew of the cardinal, killed at Marignano, i. 193
—— slain at the battle of Pavia, ii. 168
—— Clermont, death of, at the battle of Pavia, ii. 164

Dammartin, Comte de, death of, at Peronne, iii. 77

Dampièrre, M. de, commands the rear-guard at Carmagnola, iii. 233; *see* note, *ib.*

D'Andelot, Chevalier, unhorsed by Francis I. at the battle of Pavia, ii. 169

Danés, Pierre, *see* note, i. 268

D'Angoulême, Mademoiselle, *see* Marguerite de Valois
—— Duc Charles, son of Francis I., distinguishes himself at a tournament, iii. 27; his resem-

D'Angoulême, Duc Chas.—*contd.* blance to his father alluded to, iii. 28; engaged in a street brawl, iii. 29; his grief at the death of M. de Castelnau, iii. 30; his open and ardent nature alluded to, iii. 191; death of, iii. 286; *see* note, *ib.*

Daniel, Le Père, extract from, describing the burning of six reformers by order of Francis I., iii. 19

D'Annebaut, Admiral, his defence of Turin alluded to, iii. 79; *see* note, *ib.*; relieves Térouenne, iii. 92; taken prisoner, iii. 93; increasing power of, iii. 172; commands an army in Piedmont, iii. 185; his errors at the siege of Roussillon alluded to, iii. 187; supersedes Du Bellay-Langei, iii. 188; appointed Admiral of France, iii. 190; military operations of, at Landrecies, iii. 203; advises the king not to allow the Comte d'Enghien to engage the imperialists, iii. 227; despatched to Brussels by Francis I. to conclude a treaty of peace with the emperor, iii. 256; sails with the French fleet, iii. 277; engages the English fleet at St. Helens, iii. 280-1; sinks the Mary Rose, iii. 281; lands at Brighton and the Isle of Wight, iii. 282; returns to Havre, iii. 283.

D'Ars, Sire Louis, at the battle of Ravenna, i. 74

D'Aubigny, Duc, jealousy of Henry VIII. alluded to, i. 153; *see* note, *ib.*; at the capture of Prosper Colonna, i. 175; his presence in Scotland made a pretext by Henry VIII. to declare war against France, ii. 64; his attempt to create a war between England and Scotland

D'Aubigny, Duc—*continued.* alluded to, ii. 65; commands nine thousand men against the Spaniards, ii. 153; escorts Catherine de' Medici to Marseilles, ii. 384

D'Augsbourg, Longman, captain of the lansquenets at the battle of Pavia, death of, ii. 168

D'Aumale, Comte, seriously wounded at Boulogne, iii. 285

Dauphin, the birth of, i. 243; the Pope invited to become sponsor to, *ib.*; baptism of, i. 245-6; betrothed to the Princess Mary of England, i. 293, *note*; sent as a hostage to Spain, by Francis I., as a guarantee for the fulfilment of a treaty with Charles V., ii. 232; removed to Old Castile, ii. 238; restored to France, ii. 326; proclaimed Duke of Brittany under the title of François III., ii. 356; his death, iii. 57; the Comte de Montecucullisuspected of poisoning the, iii. 59; Catherine de' Medici suspected of poisoning the, iii. 63

De Heilly, Mademoiselle, her personal appearance, ii. 241; introduced by Louise de Savoie to the notice of the king, ii. 246; effects of her appearance, ii. 247; her increasing power over the king, ii. 282; takes up her abode at the palace of the Tournelles, *ib.*; description of her apartments, ii. 283; Francis proposes to marry her to a noble of his Court, ii. 284-5; marries Duc d'Etampes, ii. 286; her arrogance, ii. 287; her jealousy of Diane de Poitiers, ii. 288; receives a set of jewels from the king, ii. 298; her interview with Francis thereon, *ib.*; instigates Francis to demand the return of

De Heilly, Mdlle.—*continued.* the jewels he had presented to the Comtesse de Châteaubriand, *ib.*; her disappointment, ii. 299; her presentation to Queen Eleanora, ii. 329; her arrogance and rapacity, *ib.*; provides for her family, ii. 330; protects men of letters, ii. 331; her profligacy, iii. 2; dangerous position of the royal favourite, iii. 3; her ostentation alluded to, *ib.*; her jealousy of Diane de Poitiers, iii. 36; demands the dismissal of Diane from Court, and is refused by Francis, iii. 37-8; feud between, and Diane de Poitiers, iii. 84-5; virulence of, iii. 86; the king's infatuation for, *ib.*; her apprehensions at the king's declining health, iii. 87; her passion for Montmorency alluded to, iii. 88; plots the ruin of Montmorency, iii. 122; advises Francis to arrest Charles V. on his progress through France, iii. 124; Charles V. presents her with a diamond ring, iii. 137; her stolen interview with Christian de Nancy, iii. 155-8; surprised by the king, iii. 159; clever stratagem of, *ib.*; offended by Benvenuto Cellini, iii. 167; betrays the designs of Francis I. to the emperor, iii. 186; her hatred for Diane de Poitiers alluded to, iii. 191; her selfish treachery causes the loss of St. Dizier, iii. 247; induces the king to enter into negotiations with the emperor, iii. 251; enables the emperor to revictual his army, iii. 254; her exile alluded to, iii. 305

D'Enghien, Comte, takes command of the war galleys at Marseilles, iii. 215; surprised by Andrea Doria, iii. 216; humiliating posi-

D'Enghien, Comte—*continued.* tion of, iii. 217; joins the king at Landrecies, iii. 218; appointed to the command of Piedmont, iii. 224; blockades Carignano, *ib.*; requests the king to allow him to give battle to the enemy, iii. 226; attacks Del Guasto, iii. 233; defeats Del Guasto, iii. 235; concludes a truce for three months, and retires from Piedmont, iii. 237

Derby, Earl, attends in the retinue of Cardinal Wolsey, during his mission to France, ii. 274

D'Esse, Sire, one of the governors of the citadel of Luxembourg, iii. 212; *see* note, *ib.*

Desserts, Louis des, undertakes to obtain the consent of the Bretons to annex their duchy to the throne of France, ii. 355-6

D'Este, Alphonso, takes Fabrizio Colonna prisoner at the battle of Ravenna, i. 75; *see* note, *ib.*

D'Estourmel, M., his devotion at the defence of Peronne, iii. 76

D'Etampes, Duc, *see* Brosse, Comte Jean de

—— Duchesse, *see* De Heilly, Mademoiselle

D'Herbouville, M., his gallant defence of Cremona alluded to, ii. 115

D'Humières, M., entrusted with the defence of Dauphiny, iii. 51; appointed to the command of the French army in Italy, iii. 95

Diane de Poitiers, *see* Poitiers

Diesbach, Jean de, a leader of the Swiss mercenaries, i. 179

Dijon, treaty signed at, between M. de Tremouille and the Swiss, i. 113-14-15

D'Imbercourt, Marquis, joins the French army at Blangy, i. 99; *see* note, *ib.*; slain at the battle of Marignano, i. 193

D'O, Comte, taken prisoner at Térouenne, ii. 93; see note, *ib.*
Dolet, Etienne, his sentence and execution, iii. 296-7
Doria, Andrea, his attack on the imperial flotilla at the siege of Marseilles alluded to, ii. 140; conveys the remnants of the French army from Civita Vecchia to Marseilles, ii. 189; see note, *ib.*; enters the service of the Emperor Charles V., ii. 320; revictuals Naples, *ib.*; escorts the Pope from Marseilles to Civita Vecchia, ii. 393; Toulon taken by, iii. 64; supplies the emperor's camp with provisions, iii. 70; rescues the emperor from his position on the coast of Africa, after the destruction of his fleet by tempest, iii. 182; surprises the galleys of the Comte D'Enghien, iii. 216
D'Orleans, Duc, sent as a hostage to Spain by Francis I. for the fulfilment of a treaty with Charles V., ii. 232; removed to Old Castile, ii. 238; return of, to France, ii. 326; his marriage with Catherine de' Medici described, ii. 391-2; efforts of Diane de Poitiers to attract his notice, iii. 35-7; becomes dauphin, iii. 66; joins the camp in Provence, *ib.*; marches to Lyons, iii. 97; appointed the king's Lieutenant-general, *ib.*; forces the imperial general to retreat and takes the city of Moncalier, iii. 101; position of, in Luxembourg, iii. 184; takes Luxembourg, iii. 187; his personal appearance, iii. 191; suppresses the revolt at La Rochelle, iii. 196; harasses the troops of the emperor, iii. 249; critical position of, iii. 252; advises the

D'Orleans, Duc—*continued.*
recall of Montmorency, *ib.*; prudent measures of, iii. 253; protests against the treaty between Francis and the emperor, *ib.*; forces Henry VIII. to raise the siege of Montreuil and retire to England, iii. 258; makes a midnight attack upon Boulogne, iii. 259; imprudently appoints his officers of state previous to the king's death, iii. 272; anger of the king, iii. 274-5; succeeds to the throne as Henry II., iii. 305
D'Orleans, Duchesse, *see* Catherine de' Medici
Dorset, Marquis of, lands in Spain with fifty thousand men, i. 82; disgusted with the perfidy of Ferdinand, withdraws his troops, *ib.*; present at the meeting on the Field of the Cloth of Gold, i. 350
D'Orval, Albret, despatched by Francis I. to Frankfort, to secure the votes of the electors, i. 302
Du Châtel, Pierre, *see* note, i. 268; observations of Francis I. respecting, i. 269
Duelling, observations on, ii. 319
Duerne, city of, attacked and destroyed by Charles V., iii. 208
Dunois, Comte de, warns the Duc d'Orleans against the blandishments of Anne de France, i. 9
Duprat, Antoine, created Chancellor of France by Francis I., i. 144; observations on his appointment, *ib.*; prompts Francis to issue several edicts, which are unpalatable to his subjects, i. 216; encourages the libertine propensities of Francis, i. 277; present at the interview between Francis and Henry VIII., i. 349; at the conference at Calais between the ministers of Francis I. and

Duprat, Antoine—*continued*.
Charles V., i. 382; assists Louise de Savoie in persecuting the Connétable de France, ii. 37; Parliament refuses to ratify the decision of the judge against the connétable, ii. 39; enters into holy orders, takes possession of the abbey of St. Benoit, ii. 257; assists Louise de Savoie in ruining M. de Semblançay, ii. 259; endeavours to defraud the Emperor Charles V. in giving false weight and value to the specie for the ransom of the French princes, ii. 326; dissuades Francis from founding the Royal College, ii. 336; persecutes the reformers, ii. 344; secures the confidence of Louis des Desserts, and annexes Brittany to the throne of France, ii. 354-6; death of, iii. 26

D'Urbiéta, Juan, assists at the capture of Francis I. at the battle of Pavia, ii. 170

D'Urbino, Duc, marches against Romagna, and takes Rimini, Ravenna, and Cervia, i. 63; *see* note, *ib.*; Francis I. stipulates, during his conference with the Pope, for the restoration of the domains of the duke, i. 207; Francis I. is induced to withdraw his protection from the duke on the marriage of Lorenzo de' Medici with Madelaine de la Tour-d'Auvergne, i. 247; refuses to attack the Spanish army without the aid of the Swiss, ii. 249, 254

D'Usez, Duchesse, her position at the Court of Louise de Savoie, ii. 244; her wit alluded to, ii. 261-2

ELEANORA of Austria, her hand offered by Ferdinand of Spain to

Eleanora of Austria—*continued*.
Louis XII., i. 119; *see* note, *ib.*; her marriage with Francis I. described, ii. 327; her melancholy position at Court, ii. 328; her reception of Anne of Pisseleu, the king's mistress, ii. 329; attachment of the young princes for, ii. 331; her dignified retirement, ii. 332; alarmed at the prospect of a war between Francis and the emperor, endeavours to effect a meeting between the two sovereigns, ii. 349; her reception of Catherine de' Medici at Marseilles, ii. 386; neglect of by Francis I., iii. 3; her resignation attracts the notice of the Maréchal de Montmorency, iii. 9; the maréchal declares his love for the queen, and is repulsed, iii. 11; her compact with the maréchal, iii. 12; accident to, at Villa Franca, iii. 110; her joy at the reconciliation of the emperor and Francis, iii. 113; presents M. de Montmorency with an enamelled chain, iii. 126-8; induces Francis to enter into negotiations with the emperor, iii. 251; returns to Spain on the death of Francis, iii. 305

Electoral Diet convened at Frankfort, i. 326; proceedings opened by the Archbishop of Mayence, i. 328; speech of the Archbishop of Treves, i. 330; electors offer the throne to Frederick, Duke of Saxony, i. 331; elect Charles V. as emperor, *ib.*

Ely, Bishop of, one of the witnesses to the betrothal of the dauphin to the Princess Mary of England, i. 294

Erasmus, the Prince of Wales, afterwards Henry VIII., edu-

Erasmus—*continued.*
cated by, i. 271; efforts of the Pope to retain him in Florence, *ib.*; his declaration that England was the most honourable and advantageous sojourn for men of genius alluded to, *ib.*; created an honorary counsellor by the Princess Regent Marguerite, *ib.*; invited by Francis I. to become a president of the Royal College of France, *ib.*; declines the offers of the French king, i. 272; urged by Henry VIII. to establish his abode in England, *ib.*; inconsistency of his conduct respecting the Romish Church alluded to, ii. 340

Este, capture of, alluded to, i. 64

Europe, state of literature and science in, ii. 335

FABRI, Jacques, saved from the inquisitors by Marguerite de Valois, ii. 192

Farel, Guillaume, saved from the inquisitors by Marguerite de Valois, ii. 192

Farnese, Pietro Luigi, meets Charles V. at Genoa, iii. 207; *see* note, *ib.*

Ferdinand the Catholic, of Spain, the hand of Germaine de Foix demanded by, i. 43; terms of the marriage treaty, *ib.*; obtains by cession Brindici and Otranto, i. 64; undertakes the siege of Trani, *ib.*; enters into a league with the Pope after the treaty of Cambray, i. 68; designs of, upon Navarre, i. 82; disgusts the Marquis of Dorset by his perfidy, *ib.*; demands a guarantee from the Navarrese sovereigns not to assist the French king against the Holy League, *ib.*; joins the cause of the Pope against France, i. 94;

Ferdinand the Catholic—*contd.*
offers the hand of Eleanora of Austria to Louis XII., i. 119; endeavours to alarm the Pope and the Emperor Maximilian on Francis marching his troops towards Burgundy, i. 156; efforts of, to excite the jealousy of Henry VIII. against France, i. 210; death of, i. 214; he bequeaths his kingdom to the Archduke Charles, i. 215

Ferdinand of Austria, brother of Charles V., elected King of the Romans, ii. 360-1; his quarrel with the Duke of Wurtemberg alluded to, ii. 382; enters into a treaty with the league of Smalkalden, ii. 383

Feronnière, La Belle, intrigue of Francis I. with, iii. 114-17

Ferrara, Duke of, captures Polésina de Rovigo, Este, Montagnana, and Monselica, i. 64; joins the army of Gaston de Foix, near Bologna, and commands the vanguard in conjunction with the Marquis de la Palice, i. 72; at the battle of Ravenna, i. 74; his forfeiture of the territories of Modena and Reggio alluded to, i. 207

Field of the Cloth of Gold, description of, i. 345; the arrangements for the reception of the Queens of France and England, i. 347; meeting of the two Kings of England and France, 348-52; the banquet, i. 352-3; the tournay, i. 355; the King of France throws the King of England in a wrestling match, i. 359; good feeling of the French and English at the, i. 360; inutility of the business transacted at the, i. 363; exhausts the treasury of both nations, i. 364

Fiennes, Marquis de, ordered to make a demonstration before Térouenne, ii. 70; extricates himself from the forces of the Duc de Vendôme, ii. 71

Fleuranges, Marquis de, by reconnoitring the enemy, brings on the battle of Marignano, i. 185; knighted by Francis I., i. 198; despatched by Francis I. to secure the votes of the electors, i. 302; his services alluded to, i. 314; besieges Vireton, i. 373; engaged in the scheme to entrap the Duc d'Aerschott, ii. 70; repulses the imperialists at Peronne, iii. 77; death of, iii. 78

Foix, Adet de, Sire de Lautrec, gallant efforts of, to save the life of Gaston de Foix, i. 76; appointed Governor of Guienne, i. 143; see note, *ib.*; compelled to raise the siege of Brescia and retire to Milan, i. 211; appointed Governor of Milan, i. 256; disgusts the Milanese by his extortions, i. 280; his treatment of the Maréchal de Trivulzio, i. 280-2; suspects the sincerity of the Pope, and advises Francis I. to delay the ratification of the league, i. 375; arrives in France to negotiate a marriage with the daughter of Comte d'Orvál, ii. 1; demands supplies, ii. 2; returns to Milan, ii. 7; his tyranny, *ib.*; the Swiss troops desert, ii. 9; his critical position alluded to, *ib.*; imprudently refuses to attack the imperialist army, and permits Prosper Colonna to cross the Pô unimpeded, ii. 10; disgusts his troops by his inactivity, ii. 11; driven out of Milan, ii. 12; takes up his winter quarters at Cremona, *ib.*; despatches his brother to France,

Foix, Adet de—*continued.*
ib.; receives supplies from France, and attacks Milan, ii. 26; joined by Navarro and Bayard, *ib.*; his critical position alluded to, ii. 27; compelled by the Swiss mercenaries to give battle, is defeated, and retreats to Cremona, ii. 27-9; departs for Paris, ii. 32; arrives at Court, ii. 48; refused an audience, ii. 49; his interview with Francis leads to the discovery of the appropriation of the public money by the king's mother, ii. 50-6; reconciled to the king, ii. 57; forwards proofs to the king of the treason of the Duc de Bourbon, ii. 91; compels the Spaniards to fall back upon Fontarabia, ii. 111; appointed to the command of the confederated army of England and France in Italy, ii. 279; his success in the Milanese alluded to, ii. 319; besieges Naples, ii. 320; his death, ii. 321

Foix, Françoise de, *see* Châteaubriand, Comtesse de

—— Gaston de, one of the captains in Louis XII.'s army against the Venetians, i. 61; appointed general of the forces in his twenty-third year, i. 70; saves Bologna, *ib.*; takes Brescia from the Venetians, and puts the population to the sword, i. 71; advances upon Ravenna, *ib.*; joined by the Duke of Ferrara at Bologna, i. 72; meets the combined armies of the Pope and the King of Spain at Castel St. Piero, *ib.*; sends the Chevalier Bayard to reconnoitre the enemy's position at Ravenna, i. 74; death of, i. 76-7; burial of, i. 78

Foix, Germaine de, one of the suite of Anne de Bretagne, i. 22; her marriage with Ferdinand of Castile described, i. 43-4; her hauteur to the French nobility at Savona, i. 58; after the death of Ferdinand applies for permission to return to France, i. 310; her marriage with the Marquis de Brandebourg secures to Charles V. the suffrages of the Elector Joachim and the Bishop of Mayence, i. 312

—— Maréchal de, *see* Lescun, M. de

Follembray, pavilion of, alluded to, ii. 357

Fontainebleau, palace of, alluded to, ii. 357

Fontarabia, relieved by M. de Palice, ii. 61; sufferings of the garrison of, ii. 62

Fontrailles, Sire Imbaud de, joins the French army at Blangy with his Albanian light-horse, i. 100; *see* note, *ib.*; gallantry of, at the siege of Térouenne, i. 102

Forbins, Louis de, despatched by Francis I. to open negotiations with the Helvetic body, i. 224

Fossano, fortress of, betrayed to the imperialists by the Marquis de Saluzzo, iii. 54, 55

France, critical position of, after the battle of Pavia, ii. 183; discontent of the people, ii. 185

Francis I., King of France, his extreme beauty alluded to, i. 2; misgivings of Louis XII. respecting, *ib.*; born at Coignac, i. 16; *see* note, *ib.*; loses his father in his second year, i. 17; becomes the ward of the Duc d'Orleans, *ib.*; Maréchal de Gié appointed governor to, i. 18; rapid improvement of the prince under

Francis I.—*continued.*
his tuition, i. 19; his taste for martial exercises alluded to, *ib.*; his affection for his sister Marguerite, i. 28; challenges M. de Montpensier to single combat, i. 29; his matrimonial prospects with the Princesse Claude referred to, i. 37; at the assembly of the States-General, when the subject of his marriage with the Princesse Claude is alluded to, i. 45; betrothed to the Princesse Claude, i. 46; meets Louis XII. at Grenoble, i. 66; invested with the command of the army of the Milanese, i. 84; sends a challenge to the Spanish general, *ib.*; gives earnest of his future prowess, i. 85; his *liaison* with the advocate's wife, i. 86-90; again entrusted with the command of the army, i. 109; marries the Princesse Claude, i. 117; invested with the administration of the Duchy of Brittany, i. 118; receives the Princess Mary of England at Abbeville, i. 125; attracts the attention of the Princess Mary, i. 128; declares his passion to the queen, i. 129; warned by M. de Grignaud against the consequences of an intimacy with the queen, i. 130; at the death of Louis XII., i. 132; proclaimed King of France as Francis I., i. 133; the estates of the queen in Brittany, Nantes, Blois, Etampes, and Montfort ceded to him, *ib.*; discontent of the Bretons thereat, i. 134; enthusiasm of the French nation at his accession to the throne, i. 135; crowned at Rheims by the Archbishop of Paris, *ib.*; his interview with the widow of Louis XII., *ib.*; his caution to

INDEX

Francis I.—*continued.*
the Duke of Suffolk, i. 136; his anger with Suffolk for privately marrying the Dowager-Queen Mary of France, i. 137; the marriage of the queen and Suffolk supposed not to be unwelcome to, *ib.*; makes his public entry into Paris, i. 138; his profusion exhausts the treasury, i. 139; his taste for chivalrous romances,*ib.*; attaches an undue value to personal prowess, i. 140; ambitious to become a *preux chevalier*, i. 141; redeeming qualities of, *ib.*; bestows the title of duchess upon his mother, i. 142; bestows the office of Constable of France upon Charles de Montpensier, *ib.*; forms his government, i. 143-4; retires to Amboise to celebrate the marriage of Mademoiselle de Bourbon with the Duc de Lorraine, i. 145; his combat with the wild boar, i. 146; his licentious tastes at the Court of his mother alluded to, i. 147; endeavours to replenish his treasury by arbitrary and impolitic measures, i. 149; resolves to recover Milan, *ib.*; the Archduke Charles sends an embassy to, *ib.*; promises the hand of the Princesse Rénée to the archduke, *ib.*; state of Europe in 1515, i. 151; his frankness wins the goodwill of Henry VIII., i. 152; the Pope and the Swiss his only formidable enemies, *ib.*; treaty between England and France, i. 153; the Swiss threaten to invade France, i. 156; organizes his army and marches towards Burgundy, *ib.*; secretly induces the Doge of Genoa to put himself under the protection of France, i. 157; amount of his forces concentrated

Francis I.—*continued.*
in Dauphiny, *ib.*; sends an embassy to Rome, i. 158; replenishes his treasury by the sale of judicial offices, i. 165; appoints the Duchesse d'Angoulême regent during his absence in the wars in Italy, i. 166; the Pope, alarmed at the success of the French arms, sends a messenger to Francis to assure him of his neutrality, i. 178; endeavours to conciliate the Swiss, but fails through the agency of the Cardinal of Sion, i. 179-80; leaves Lyons for Turin, i. 182; joined by the Duc de Gueldres with six thousand lansquenets, *ib.*; establishes his headquarters at Marignano, *ib.*; the junction of the Swiss and Spanish armies prevented by an accident, i. 183; the king is anxious to attack the Swiss, *ib.*; at the battle of Marignano, i. 185; advances to the attack at the head of "The Black Bands," i. 187; furious charge of, i. 188; nearly taken prisoner, *ib.*; the king sleeps on a gun-carriage, i. 190; the action renewed in the morning and the Swiss defeated, i. 191-2; his letter to his mother after the battle, *ib.*; receives knighthood from the Chevalier Bayard on the field of battle, i. 196; marches upon Milan, i. 198; his generosity to Maximilian Sforza, i. 200; enters Milan and receives the oath of allegiance from the authorities, i. 201; the Pope enters into a treaty with the king at Viterbo, i. 203; the king proceeds to Bologna to meet the Pope, i. 204; fascinated by the sophistry of Leo X., i. 205; enters into a league with the Pope, i. 206; its conditions,

Francis I.—*continued.*
ib.; the Pope induces the king to abandon his designs upon Naples, i. 207; the question of the Pragmatic Sanction is discussed by commissioners, i. 208; his treaty with the Pope gives offence to the University of Paris, *ib.*; the Pope endeavours to persuade the king to undertake a crusade against the Turks, i. 209; disbands his army and arrives in France, i. 210; exultation of the French people at the success of the king, *ib.*; the death of Ferdinand and the accession of the Archduke Charles favourable to the views of the king, i. 215; prompted by the chancellor, the king issues several ordinances unpalatable to his subjects, i. 216; his parliament refuses to register his ordinance purporting to protect his forest rights, i. 217; enters into an alliance with Charles V. of Spain, i. 221; the hand of his infant daughter promised to the King of Spain, *ib.*; the peace of Noyon secures no real advantages to the French, i. 222; the king concludes a treaty of amity with Switzerland, i. 224; the Swiss recognize the claim of the king to the Milanese, *ib.*; domestic life of the king, i. 226; resolves to form a Court of his own, i. 227; fails to attract the Comtesse de Châteaubriand to his Court, i. 228; his meeting with the countess, i. 236; his *liaison* with the countess, i. 240; forms projects for the embellishment of France and the encouragement of literature, i. 243; invites the Pope to become sponsor to the dauphin, *ib.*; his

Francis I.—*continued.*
cruelty to the queen, i. 244; festivities of the king and his Court on the marriage of Lorenzo de' Medici and Madelaine de la Tour-d'Auvergne, i. 248-9; his interview with the Comtesse de Châteaubriand in the forest, i. 252-6; instigated by the Comtesse de Châteaubriand, the king recalls the Duc de Bourbon from Milan, i. 256; appoints the Maréchal de Lautrec, brother to the countess, governor of Milan, *ib.*; jealousy of Francis, i. 258; his increasing dislike for the connétable alluded to, *ib.*; the connétable's affection for his sister known to Francis, i. 259; efforts of the king to effect the recognition of the *Concordat*, i. 261; his interview with the president of parliament thereon, *ib.*; threatens to throw the two delegates from parliament into the castle moat, i. 265; compels the parliament to register the *Concordat*, *ib.*; unpopularity of, i. 266; invites Leonardo da Vinci to his Court, i. 267; encourages talent, *ib.*; devotes a portion of his time to the society of learned men, i. 269; his interview with Julio Camilla, an Italian impostor, i. 270; invites Erasmus to France, i. 271; efforts of the king to found the Royal College, *ib.*; the unbounded influence of Madame de Châteaubriand over the king, i. 276; permits his mother to take an active part in his government, i. 277; arrogance of, i. 278; his ingratitude to the Maréchal de Trivulce, i. 280; bestows the *bâton* of maréchal upon M. de Lescun, i. 284; the increasing popularity

Francis I.—*continued.*
of Charles V. of Spain induces the king to form an alliance with Henry VIII., i. 285; sends Bonnivet on a mission to England, i. 286; offers the hand of the dauphin to the Princess Mary of England, *ib.*; his anxiety to secure the goodwill of Henry VIII., i. 295; fortifies Tournay, Térouenne, and Havre, i. 296; endeavours to conciliate Charles of Castile, *ib.*; offers to undertake a crusade against the Turks, i. 298; his jealousy of Charles V. alluded to, i. 299; his advice to the Pope on the Emperor Maximilian demanding the crown of Rome, i. 301; despatches Bonnivet to Frankfort to purchase the votes of the electors, i. 302; distributes four hundred thousand crowns among the electoral princes, i. 305; his pretensions to the empire contrasted with those of Charles V., i. 306-9; wily policy of the Pope to, during his contest for the empire, *ib.*; duplicity of Henry VIII. to, i. 310; discourages the return of the Queen-Dowager of Spain to his Court, and loses the votes of two electors, i. 310-12; offends the Flemings by his impolitic conduct towards the citizens of Tournay, i. 312; offends Robert de la Mark, i. 313; his interview with Seckingen at Amboise, i. 316; offends Seckingen by concealing from him that he aspired to the empire, i. 317; accused by Robert de la Mark of a breach of good faith, i. 320; loses the services of Robert de la Mark and the Prince-Bishop of Liege, i. 321; bold reply of

Francis I.—*continued.*
Seckingen to, i. 322; loses the services of Seckingen, i. 323; neglects to attack some Turkish corsairs, which influences the votes of the electors against the king, i. 325; death of M. de Boissy a serious loss to, i. 327; Leonardo da Vinci dies in the arms of, i. 328; mortification of Francis I. at the elevation of Charles V. to the imperial throne, i. 332-3; instructs Sir Richard Wingfield to solicit Henry VIII. to stand sponsor for his second son, i. 333; purchases the Tuileries for his mother, i. 335; resolves to rebuild the Louvre, *ib.*; Bonnivet incites the king to commence a new war, i. 337; endeavours to secure the friendship of Henry VIII. of England, i. 338; bribes Wolsey, i. 339; the Navarrese question is revived between the king and the Emperor Charles, i. 339; the preparations for the interview between the king and Henry VIII., i. 341; the visit of Charles V. to the King of England at Dover excites the apprehensions of, i. 345; ceremony of the meeting of the king with Henry VIII. at the Field of the Cloth of Gold, i. 348; his appearance at the meeting with the English king, i. 349-51; his courteous bearing to Henry VIII. described, i. 352; the tourney at the Field of the Cloth of Gold, i. 355; Francis, annoyed at the restraints upon the free intercourse between the two Courts, visits the English king unattended, i. 356; mutual pledge of friendship, i. 357; exchange of visits between the two kings, i. 358; the King of

Francis I.—*continued.*
France throws Henry VIII. in a wrestling match, i. 359; gives a grand banquet to the English king, i. 360; at the parting mass, i. 361; returns to France, i. 362; serious accident to, i. 367; his generosity, i. 368; reluctance of Francis to commence the war against the emperor, i. 369; his attachment to Madame de Châteaubriand, i. 370; receives the allegiance of Robert de la Mark, i. 372; enters into a treaty with the Pope to expel the Spaniards from Naples, i. 375; supplies Henri d'Albret with troops to recover his territories from Charles V., i. 377; his appeal to the English king to mediate between him and the Emperor Charles alluded to, i. 380; agrees to a conference at Calais, *ib.*; fortifies his frontiers and prepares for war with the emperor, i. 381; sends Bonnivet with an army into Navarre, *ib.*; his indignation at the bad faith of Henry VIII., i. 384; his self-reliance, *ib.*; confides the defence of the city of Mézières to Bayard, i. 385; overtakes the army of the Comte de Nassau, but neglects to fight, i. 387; his grief at his error, *ib.*; departs for Flanders, *ib.*; confers the order of Philip Augustus upon Bayard, i. 394; his letter to his mother on the relief of the city of Mézières, i. 395; influenced by the Maréchal de Châtillon, the king neglects to attack Charles V., i. 396; confers the command of the vanguard on the Duc d'Alençon, and offends the Connétable de Bourbon, *ib.*; disbands a portion of his army, i. 398; the exhausted

Francis I.—*continued.*
state of his treasury, ii. 2; his increasing affection for the Comtesse de Châteaubriand, ii. 3; presents her with costly ornaments, *ib.*; the Pope declares war against France, ii. 9; becomes convinced of the bad faith of Henry VIII. and Wolsey, ii. 13; his indignation on hearing of the reverses of the French army in Milan, *ib.*; his remark to the Duc de Bourbon, on the magnificence of Bonnivet, ii. 20; the hand of the Princesse Rénée demanded by the Duc de Bourbon, ii. 22; resolves to reconquer the Milanese, ii. 24; anticipates a war with England, *ib.*; levies a tax on the states of Languedoc, ii. 25; forwards supplies to Maréchal Lautrec in Italy, ii. 26; insulted in his palace of the Tournelles, ii. 44; neglects to defend the frontiers at Champagne and Picardy, *ib.*; the Venetian states enter the League against France, ii. 46; averse to act in concert with Charles V. against the Turks, ii. 48; irritation of Francis on the arrival of Maréchal Lautrec at Court, ii. 49; at the request of the Duc de Bourbon, grants an interview to Lautrec, ii. 50; his interview with the maréchal leads to the discovery of the appropriation of the public monies by Louise de Savoie, ii. 51-6; reconciled with Maréchal Lautrec, ii. 57; orders troops to the relief of Fontarabia, ii. 60; writes to Henry VIII. respecting the Duc d'Aubigny's presence in Scotland, ii. 64; his dignified reply to Sir Thomas Cheyne, the English ambassador, previous to the declaration of war, ii. 66-8;

Francis I.—*continued.*
returns to Lyons, ii. 68; coins a silver screen, erected by Louis XI. round the tomb of St. Martin, to pay his troops, ii. 69; by his vanity prevents the capture of the Duc d'Aerschott, ii. 70; prevents the Duc de Vendôme from attacking the Marquis de Fiennes, ii. 71; pursues his measures for reconquering Milan, ii. 72; informed of the treason of the Connétable de France, ii. 73; accuses the connétable, but suffers him to escape, ii. 74; his suspicions against the connétable increase, ii. 77; visits the connétable at his palace at Moulins, ii. 78; the dissimulation of the connétable removes the king's suspicions, ii. 79; takes the precaution of sending M. de Wartz to watch the connétable, ii. 80; gives a hunting-party in the forest of Bussy, ii. 81; misunderstanding between the king and Madame de Châteaubriand, ii. 82; the king orders the arrest of the Comte St. Vallier, a partizan of the Duc de Bourbon, ii. 91; indignation of the king at the treason of the Duc de Bourbon, *ib.*; sends an expedition against the Duc, ii. 92; gives the command of the army against Italy to Bonnivet, ii. 95; confiscates the estates of the Duc de Bourbon, *ib.*; his anger at the leniency of the Parliament of Paris to the Bourbon conspirators, ii. 97; his interview with Diane de Poitiers, who arrives at Court to intercede for the life of her father, ii. 103-4; Francis commutes the sentence of Jean de Poitiers, ii. 105; makes overtures to the Duc de Bourbon to

Francis I.—*continued.*
return to his allegiance, ii. 108; recalls the Duc de Vendôme to the defence of Paris, ii. 112; reaps no benefit from the elevation of Clement VII. to the popedom, ii. 120; assured of the immediate safety of his kingdom, gives himself up to pleasure, ii. 121; his observation on hearing of the death of Bayard, ii. 134; Milan lost to France, ii. 136; despatches Brion Chabot to assure the Marseillaise of relief, ii. 137; endeavours to regain the affections of his people, *ib.*; regulates the taxes, ii. 138; rouses himself from his selfish indulgences, and levies a force to oppose the advance of the Duc de Bourbon, *ib.*; resolves to make another attempt to regain the Milanese, ii. 143; persists in heading the army in person, *ib.*; his heartlessness on hearing of the death of Queen Claude, ii. 144; the king and Mademoiselle de Voland, ii. 145; takes Milan, ii. 147; imprudently suffers the imperialists to concentrate their forces, ii. 148; enters into a treaty with the Pope, *ib.*; hangs the garrison of a fort, *ib.*; encamps at Mirabello, assaults Pavia, and is repulsed, ii. 149; refuses the Pope's mediation to establish a truce with Spain for five years, ii. 151; enters into a secret treaty with the Pope, *ib.*; position of his army before Pavia, ii. 152; gives the command of nine thousand men to the Duc d'Aubigny, ii. 153; his army is reduced by sickness and desertion before Pavia, ii. 156; the imperial generals endeavour to bring the king to a general

VOL. III 72

Francis I.—*continued.*
engagement, ii. 158; his charge before Pavia, ii. 159; evil influence of Bonnivet on the councils of the king, ii. 160-61; advised by his ablest generals to raise his camp, but overruled by Bonnivet, ii. 161; at the battle of Pavia, ii. 162-8; kills the Marquis de St. Angelo, ii. 169; unhorses the Chevalier d'Andelot, *ib.*; his horse shot under him, *ib.*; endeavours to escape from the field of battle, ii. 170; taken prisoner, *ib.*; is saved from violence by M. de Pompérant, the friend of the Duc de Bourbon, ii. 171; refuses to surrender his sword to the Duc de Bourbon, *ib.*; extract from his poetical epistles, ii. 172; claims the hospitality of the Marquis del Guasto, ii. 173; his wounds are dressed, *ib.*; delivers his sword to Lannoy, the Viceroy of Naples, ii. 174; refuses the homage of the Duc de Bourbon, *ib.*; summoned by Pescara to set forth for Pavia, ii. 175; his celebrated letter to his mother alluded to, *ib.*; his capture causes a powerful sensation in the imperialist camp, ii. 177-8; imprisoned in the citadel of Pizzighittona, ii. 178; his interview with Bourbon, *ib.*; discusses the battle of Pavia with Pescara, *ib.*; pardons M. de Pompérant, ii. 179; accepts the services of M. de Montpezat, ii. 181; ransoms M. de Montpezat, *ib.*; writes to the Emperor Charles V. to decide upon his future destiny, *ib.*; a double guard upon the king's person, ii. 201; indignation of the king on receiving the conditions of the emperor for his release, ii. 202;

Francis I.—*continued.*
rejects the emperor's conditions, ii. 203; is persuaded by the Viceroy of Naples to trust to the clemency of the emperor, and proceed to Madrid, *ib.*; lands in Spain, ii. 205; mutiny in the royal guards of Spain suppressed by the king, ii. 206; Francis is kept a close prisoner, ii. 207; indignities offered to the royal captive, *ib.*; illness of, alarms the emperor, who visits Francis, ii. 209; the interview between the two monarchs, ii. 210; visited by Marguerite de Valois in prison, ii. 216; his act of abdication alluded to, ii. 221; the king attempts to escape from his prison, but fails in consequence of the treachery of a servant, ii. 223-4; recalls his act of abdication, ii. 228; his vanity alluded to, *ib.*; signs a secret protest, declaring his intention not to fulfil the conditions imposed upon him by the Emperor Charles V., ii. 229; concessions imposed upon France by the emperor, ii. 229-30; betrothed to Eleanora, Dowager-Queen of Portugal, ii. 231; departs for France, ii. 232; his meeting with his two sons, *ib.*; meets the Court at Bayonne, *ib.*; his delight on meeting the Comtesse de Châteaubriand, ii. 234; illness of the king, *ib.*; his evasive reply to the envoys of the emperor, who urge the ratification of the treaty of Madrid, *ib.*; writes to Henry VIII., *ib.*; receives the ambassadors from the Pope and the Venetian states, and complains of the harsh measures of the emperor, ii. 235; replaces the generals who fell at Pavia,

Francis I.—*continued*.
ib.; receives a fall while hunting, which endangers his life, *ib.*; convokes an assembly of the princes of the kingdom and the Burgundian deputies, ii. 236; the assembly declares allegiance to France, in defiance of the treaty extorted from the king when a prisoner to Charles V., *ib.*; signs a treaty with the Pope, Henry VIII., Francisco Sforza, and the Venetians, *ib.*; its object, ii. 237; his breach of faith with the emperor, ii. 238; neglects to assist his allies, *ib.*; endeavours to negotiate with the emperor, offers an equivalent in specie for the duchy of Burgundy, ii. 239; his triumphant reception in the south of France alluded to, *ib.*; his increased affection for Madame de Châteaubriand, ii. 240; Mademoiselle de Heilly introduced to, ii. 246; effects of her appearance upon the king, ii. 247; suspected by the Italian states, ii. 250; accepts the services of Pietro da Navarro, ii. 252; his consternation on hearing of the fall of Rome, ii. 256; visits Paris, ii. 257; forbids the Parliament to interfere in matters of state or ecclesiastical preferment, ii. 259; his injustice to M. de Semblançay, *ib.*; notices the Duchesse d'Usez, ii. 261; builds the Palace of Chambord, ii. 262-3; retires to Chambord, ii. 265; the Court beauties alluded to, *ib.*; his inattention to business alluded to, ii. 266; his prolonged absence from the capital renders the citizens disorderly, *ib.*; his inactivity alluded to, ii. 271; sends envoys to Spain to negotiate for the liberation of Cle-

Francis I.—*continued*.
ment VII., ii. 272; enters into a treaty with Henry VIII. against Spain, *ib.*; his interview with Cardinal Wolsey respecting the captivity of Clement VII., ii. 273; refuses the hand of Marguerite de Valois to Henry VIII., ii. 275; refuses to bestow the hand of his sister-in-law on the English king, ii. 277; Francis and Henry VIII. send a combined army against Italy, ii. 279; rivalry between the two favourites, the Comtesse de Châteaubriand and Anne de Pisseleu, at the Court of, ii. 280; his interview with the countess, ii. 281; selects a husband for Mademoiselle de Heilly, ii. 284-5; his last interview with the Comtesse de Châteaubriand, ii. 294-6; presents Anne de Pisseleu with a set of jewels, ii. 298; demands the jewels he had presented to the Comtesse de Châteaubriand to be returned to him, ii. 299; cites his sister to Paris on her being accused of seceding from the Romish Church, ii. 307; sends Anne de Montmorency as ambassador to England, ii. 309; accused by the Emperor Charles V. of breaking his pledge, ii. 310; anger of Francis I., ii. 312; arrests Perenot de Grandeville, the imperial ambassador, *ib.*; his intemperate reply to the challenge of the Emperor Charles V., ii. 313; evades the imperial herald, ii. 315-16; grants an audience to the imperial herald, but refuses to let him deliver his message, ii. 317-18; the king forfeits his claim to be the most chivalrous monarch in Christendom, *ib.*; bad example

Francis I.—*continued.*
of duelling upon the French nobility, ii. 319; the exhausted state of his treasury alluded to, ii. 322; negotiates with Charles V. for the release of his sons, ii. 323; undignified concessions of, at *La Paix des Dames*, ii. 324; consents to marry Eleanora, Queen of Portugal, *ib.*; he abandons his allies at the treaty of Cambráy, ii. 325; his interview with Eleanora, ii. 326; his infatuation for Madame d'Etampes, ii. 329-31; his efforts to establish a royal college alluded to, ii. 333; protects Luigi Alamanni, *see* note, *ib.*; encourages learned and scientific men to settle in France, *ib.*; is dissuaded by Duprat from founding the college, ii. 336; the jealousy of the king is excited by the progress of the Reformation, ii. 337; abandons the cause of the reformers, more from policy than religious scruples, ii. 341; his superstition, *ib.*; he persecutes the Lutherans, *ib.*; cruelty of the king to the reformers, ii. 343; indignation of Francis at the treaties entered into by the emperor with the Pope, ii. 347-9; is anxious to avoid hostilities with Spain, *ib.*; death of his mother, *ib.*; liberates the Low Countries with the treasures left by Louise de Savoie, ii. 351; the king endeavours to annex Brittany to the crown of France, ii. 353; visits the Comte de Châteaubriand, ii. 356; erects new palaces, ii. 357; erects the Château of Madrid, ii. 357-8; concludes a treaty of mutual defence with Henry VIII., ii. 359; advises Henry VIII. to marry Anne Boleyn in defiance

Francis I.—*continued.*
of the Church, ii. 360; reply of, to the Protestant princes of Germany, ii. 361; the King of Hungary sends ambassadors to the French Court, ii. 362; policy of Francis, *ib.*; proceeds to Boulogne to meet Henry VIII., ii. 363; his interview with Henry VIII., *ib.*; invests the Dukes of Norfolk and Suffolk with the collar of St. Michael, ii. 364; concludes a treaty with Henry VIII. against the Turks, ii. 365; complains to Henry VIII. of the exactions of the prothonotaries of Rome, ii. 366; summoned by Charles V. to send an army against the Turks, ii. 367; his refusal, *ib.*; his bad faith to Henry VIII. alluded to, ii. 368; offers the hand of the Duc d'Orleans to Catherine de' Medici, *ib.*; sends two French bishops to threaten the Pope, ii. 369; a meeting is arranged between the Pope and Francis, ii. 373; indignation of Francis at the execution of his agent at Milan, ii. 379; dismisses the envoy of the Duke of Milan with ignominy, ii. 381; aids the Duke of Wurtemburg, ii. 383; meets the Pope at Marseilles, ii. 385; homage of Francis to the Pope, ii. 386; advises the Pope to sanction the divorce of Henry VIII., ii. 388; invests four papal dignitaries with the order of St. Michael, ii. 392; the Court returns to Amboise, ii. 393; his female Court described, iii. 1-4; his household, how composed, iii. 6, 7; his profligacy, iii. 8; reorganizes his army, iii. 17; Francis is accused of sympathising with the Turks, *ib.*; his barbarity towards the reformers, iii. 18;

Francis I.—*continued.*
burns six reformers, iii. 19; abolishes printing throughout France, iii. 22; the league of Smalkalden declares against Francis, iii. 23; invites Melancthon to France, *ib.*; declares war against Savoy, iii. 24; his interview with Diane de Poitiers respecting the melancholy of the Duc d'Angoulême, iii. 30-3; refuses to banish Diane de Poitiers from Court, iii. 38; Charles offers the Duchy of Milan to the Duc d'Angoulême, iii. 39; the king demands Milan for the Duc d'Orleans, iii. 40; the negotiations with the emperor respecting the Milanese renewed, iii. 41; accused by the emperor before the Conclave at Rome, iii. 42; moderation of Francis at the accusations of the emperor, iii. 46; directs the Cardinal de Lorraine to demand the duchy of Milan of Charles, iii. 47; accused by the emperor of cruelty towards the German Protestants, iii. 49; sends Guillaume du Bellay to Germany to explain to the Germans the fallacy of the accusation, *ib.*; disarms the army of Savoy, iii. 50; fortifies his frontier, iii. 51; proceeds to Lyons to resist the attempt of the emperor to invade Provence, *ib.*; prepares for an invasion, iii. 53; entrusts Fossano to the Marquis de Saluzzo, *ib.*; his grief at the death of the dauphin, iii. 57; orders his Court to be present at the execution of the murderer of the dauphin, iii. 62; accuses the imperial generals of instigating the murder, iii. 63; his instructions to the Duc d'Orleans on joining the camp of Montmorency, iii. 66; deter-

Francis I.—*continued.*
mines to head the army in person, iii. 70; joins the camp at Avignon, *ib.*; seconds the efforts of the Italian princes to form a league against Charles V., iii. 75; proceeds to Marseilles and strengthens Provence, iii. 80; meets James V. of Scotland at Lyons, iii. 81; gives James V. his daughter in marriage, *ib.*; rival factions at the Court of, iii. 84-5; disunion in the royal family, iii. 86; lays claim to Flanders, Artois, and Charlerois, iii. 88; convokes a parliament thereon, and cites the emperor to appear before the French tribunal, iii. 89; marches troops into Artois, and takes Hesdin, iii. 90; a truce is effected between France, Picardy, and the Low Countries, iii. 94-5; avows his alliance with the Sultan, *ib.*; appoints M. d'Humières to the command in Italy, iii. 96; proceeds to Lyons, after providing for the safety of France during his absence, iii. 98; commences the campaign by forcing the Pas-de-Suze, iii. 99; the king resolves to take the field in person, iii. 101; jealous of the success of his son, *ib.*; terminates the war by negotiation, *ib.*; disbands his army, *ib.*; objects to the terms proposed by the emperor for a general peace, iii. 104; the Pope arranges an interview between Francis and the emperor, iii. 106; the Pope mediates between the two potentates, iii. 110; concludes a truce for ten years with the emperor, iii. 111; returns to Avignon, *ib.*; meeting of the French king and the emperor at Aigues Mortes, iii. 112; confidence of, *ib.*; re-

Francis I.—*continued.*
turns to Paris, and plunges into dissipation, iii. 114; his intrigue with La Belle Feronniere, iii. 115-17; illness of, iii. 117; refuses the allegiance of the Ghentese, iii. 119; gives permission to Charles V. to traverse France on his visit to the Low Countries, iii. 121; his interview with the Duchesse d'Etampes thereon, iii. 122-3; advised by the Duchesse to arrest Charles V., iii. 124; his magnanimity, iii. 126; his adventure with the enamelled gold chain intended for the Connétable de Montmorency, iii. 127-8; his hatred of the connétable, iii. 129; meets the emperor at Châtellerault, iii. 131; hospitality of, towards Charles V., iii. 133; his anger at the Court perfumer, iii. 135; the king informs the emperor of the advice of Madame d'Etampes, iii. 136; becomes suspicious of his counsellors, iii. 141; arrests Chabot, iii. 144; pardons Chabot, iii. 145-6; refuses the hand of Philip of Spain for the Princess of Navarre, and of the Princess of Spain for the Duc d'Orleans, iii. 150; offers the hand of the Princess of Navarre to the Duke of Cleves, iii. 152; orders the connétable to leave Court, iii. 153; his indulgence to Benvenuto Cellini, iii. 168; changed aspect of his Court alluded to, iii. 172; his anger at the treaty between the Venetians and the Turks, iii. 174; summons the emperor to make reparation for the murder of his two ambassadors, iii. 178; arrests the Archbishop of Valence, the natural son of the emperor, iii. 179; resolves to declare

Francis I.—*continued.*
war against the emperor, iii. 183; his army attacks the Low Countries, iii. 184; his dislike to the Connétable de Montmorency, iii. 190; his illness increased by the growing enmity of his two sons, *ib.*; influence of Catherine de' Medici over the king, iii. 191-3; increases the salt tax, iii. 195; revolt of the inhabitants of La Rochelle, *ib.*; visits Rochelle, suppresses the insurrection, and pardons the citizens, iii. 196-8; persecutes the Lutherans, iii. 199-200; sends an ambassador to the Sultan, iii. 201; marches his army northward, and opens the campaign of 1543, iii. 202; retires to Rheims, iii. 204; war with England alluded to, iii. 206; his inactivity permits the emperor to reorganize his army, iii. 207; takes Luxembourg, iii. 210; fortifies Luxembourg, iii. 211; orders the Comte d'Enghien to take command of the war galleys at Marseilles, iii. 215; degrading concessions of the king to Barbarossa, iii. 218-19; indignation of the princes of Europe at his alliance with the Turks, iii. 221; exhausted state of his treasury, iii. 223; replenishes his treasury by the sale of judicial offices, *ib.*; raises a new army for the Comte d'Enghien, iii. 224; permits the Comte d'Enghien to give battle to the imperialists, iii. 229; receives the jewelled watch of the Marquis del Guasto, iii. 238; France invaded by Charles V. and Henry VIII., iii. 240; his regret at the capitulation of St. Dizier, iii. 245-6; calms the fears of the citizens of Paris,

Francis I.—*continued.*
iii. 246; his declining health alluded to, *ib.*; endeavours to appease the alarm of the citizens on the approach of the imperialists, iii. 255; concludes a treaty with the emperor, iii. 256; conditions of the treaty, iii. 257; massacre of the Vaudois, iii. 265-71; his anger at the imprudence of the dauphin, iii. 274-75; raises a fleet, and sends reinforcements to the Dowager-Queen of Scotland, iii. 276; visits his fleet, iii. 278; burning of the Caraquon, iii. 279; arrives in the vicinity of Boulogne, iii. 286; his grief at the death of the Duc d'Orleans, iii. 287; concludes a treaty of peace with England, iii. 289-90; strengthens his frontiers, iii. 291; refuses to assist the Protestant princes in their war with the emperor, iii. 292-3; persecutes the Lutherans, iii. 293; observations on his character, iii. 298; the death of Henry VIII. produces a fatal effect upon Francis, iii. 300; summons the dauphin to his deathbed, iii. 301; concluding remarks upon his reign, iii. 302-3; death of, iii. 304; his burial, iii. 305; *see* note, *ib.*

Franget, Captain, appointed to the command of Fontarabia, ii. 61; *see* note, *ib.*; his surrender of Fontarabia alluded to, ii. 111

Frankfort, electors assemble at, i. 308; opinions of the electors of the conduct of Francis I. and Charles V., *ib.*; electoral diet convened at, i. 326; deliberations opened at by the Archbishop of Mayence, i. 328; speech of the Archbishop of Treves, i. 330; Charles V. proclaimed Emperor of Germany at, i. 331

Frederic, Duke of Saxony, one of the electors of Germany, *see* note, i. 299; refuses the imperial crown of Germany and recommends the electors to elevate to the throne Charles V., i. 331; protects Luther, i. 334, 370

Fregosa, Cæsar, an ambassador from Francis I. to the Porte, iii. 174; murdered by order of the Marquis del Guasto, iii. 176-7

—— Ottavio, promises Francis I. to abdicate the throne of Genoa, and put himself under the protection of France, i. 157

Frundsberg joins the army of the Duc de Bourbon, ii. 254; his death by apoplexy alluded to, ii. 255

Furstemberg, Comte Guillaume de, defeated at Fontarabia by the Marquis de la Palice, ii. 61; ordered by Francis I. to levy troops in Germany to invade the Milanese, iii. 24; taken prisoner by the French, iii. 253

GAILLART, Louis, deprived of the bishopric of Tournay by Cardinal Wolsey, i. 287

Gattinara, Mercurio, endeavours to dissuade Charles V. from visiting the French king in prison, ii. 72

Genoa, revolt of, alluded to, i. 53; wanton cruelties of the Genoese, i. 54; attacked by Louis XII., *ib.*; surrenders to Louis XII., i. 55; terms of the surrender of, i. 56; the revolt of the citizens of, and the election of one of the Fregosi as Doge alluded to, i. 81; attacked and pillaged by the Marquis de Pescara, ii. 35-6

Genouilhac, Jacques Gaillot de, commands the French artillery at Pavia, ii. 158

Germany, critical position of, under the rule of Maximilian, i. 303; Protestant princes of, protest against the authority of Charles V., ii. 360; their remonstrances treated with contempt, ii. 361; apply to France and England for support, *ib.*; reply of Francis I., *ib.*
—— electors of, their views of the conduct of Charles V. and Francis I., i. 328
Ghent, militia of, desert the Marquis de Fiennes and retreat beyond the Lys, ii. 71; revolt of the citizens of, iii. 119
Ghiberti, Juan Matteo, despatched by Clement VII. to Francis to endeavour to establish a truce between France and Spain for five years, ii. 150
Gié, de, Maréchal, appointed governor of Francis I., i. 18; *see* note, *ib.*; rapid improvement of the prince under his tuition, i. 19; his attachment to Louise de Savoie and its consequences, i. 20; the king visits him at Amboise, *ib.*; interferes between Francis and Comte de Montpensier, i. 30; detects M. de Vandenesse in an intrigue with Louise de Savoie, i. 31; his anger on hearing that the queen had despatched her jewels and furniture to Nantes, in anticipation of the king's death, i. 33; endeavours to detain them *in transitu*, i. 34; cited before the king for *lèse majesté*, i. 35; his observation to Louise de Savoie on her appearing against him, *ib.*; deprived of his titles, i. 36; his dignified retirement, *ib.*
Giustiniani, Demetrius, a Genoese general, execution of, in Corsica, i. 56

Gonsalvo di Cordova, admiration of Louis XII. for, i. 58
Gonzaga, Ferdinand, accused of promoting the death of the dauphin by poison, iii. 61; *see* note, *ib.*; denies the accusation, iii. 63
Gouffier, Boisy, Artus de, tutor of Francis I., i. 17
—— Guillaume, Seigneur de Bonnivet, one of the suite of Louis XII., i. 23; *see* note, *ib.*; one of the companions of Francis at the Court of Amboise, i. 27; instigates Francis to quarrel with the Comte de Montpensier, i. 29; created Admiral of the Fleet to Francis I., i. 144; his jealousy on witnessing the emotion of Marguerite de Valois on beholding the Connétable de Bourbon, i. 162; his observation to the Comte de St. Vallier thereon, i. 163; his intrigue with the Comtesse de Châteaubriand, i. 258; sent on a mission to England, i. 286; the embassy arrives at Greenwich, i. 288; his reception by Henry VIII. *ib.*; his success with Wolsey, i. 289-93; returns to France, i. 293; despatched to Frankfort to secure the votes of the electors of the empire for Francis I., i. 302; arrives in France with the state chest from the diet of Frankfort, i. 332; excites the king to commence a war, i. 337; marches into Navarre to revenge the defeat of Marshal Lesparre, i. 381; his successes in Biscay at Fontarabia, i. 396; his intrigue with Marguerite de Valois alluded to, i. 419; dislike of the Connétable de Bourbon for, *ib.*; ordered to establish himself at Suza with six thousand men, ii. 72; demands the sword of Jean

Gouffier, Guillaume—*continued.*
de Poitiers, suspected of treason, ii. 91; entrusted with the command of the army of Italy, ii. 95; his inefficiency, ii. 113; amount of his army, ii. 115; compels the imperialists to retreat to Milan, ii. 116; neglects to pursue his advantage, *ib.*; blockades Milan, ii. 117; takes Monza, Lodi, and Cremona, *ib.*; his error in detaching the Chevalier Bayard to Vigevano, ii. 118; raises the siege of Milan, and takes up winter quarters near Biagrasso, ii. 119; applies for reinforcements, ii. 121; besieges Arona, but is repulsed, *ib.*; detaches Bayard to Rebec to intercept supplies for Milan, ii. 122; his interview with Bayard thereon, *ib.*; his jealousy of Bayard alluded to, ii. 124; accused of attempting to sacrifice Bayard, ii. 126; attempts to provoke the Duc de Bourbon to an engagement, ii. 127; determines to retreat to Novara, *ib.*; pursued by the Duc de Bourbon and wounded, ii. 129; enters France in confusion, ii. 136; assures Francis that his presence will ensure the subjugation of Milan, ii. 143; evil influence of his council upon the king, ii. 160-61; advises the king to fight the imperialists at Pavia, ii. 162; death of, at battle of Pavia, ii. 166

Goujon, Jean, a famous sculptor, ii. 264; *see* note, *ib.*

Grammont, Cardinal de, apprizes Francis I. of the Pope's desire for a personal interview, ii. 365; despatched by the kings of France and England to threaten the Pope, ii. 369

Grandvelle, Perenot de, ambassa-

Grandvelle, Perenot de—*contd.*
dor from the Emperor Charles V., retires from France, ii. 313; his interview with Francis, *ib.*

Gravelines, interview between the Emperor Charles V. and Henry VIII. at, i. 365-7

Greiffenklau, Richard de, Archbishop of Treves, one of the Electors of Germany; *see* note, i. 299; his speech at the electoral diet in favour of Francis I., i. 330

Grignaud, M. de, the Duc de Valois warned by, against the consequences of an intimacy with the queen, i. 129

Gritti, Andreo, retires within the Venetian territory, ii. 34

Gros, Jean, of Picardy, sends to Bayard for a bottle of wine, i. 393; its results, i. 394

Gruget, Claude, at the Court of Bearn, ii. 303

Guasto, Marquis del, his stratagem before Pavia, ii. 159; *see* note, *ib.*; at the battle of Pavia, ii. 162-3; Francis requests his hospitality on being taken prisoner at the battle of Pavia, ii. 173; retreats with the imperial troops into the Milanese, iii. 73; successfully pursues the war in Piedmont, iii. 95; besieges Carmagnole, iii. 96; his cruelty, iii. 97; fortifies the Pas-de-Suze, iii. 98; raises the siege at Pignerol, and encamps at Moncalier, iii. 100; endeavours to prevent the Venetians from forming an alliance with Solyman, iii. 174; murders two French ambassadors, iii. 177; accused by Du Bellay, *ib.*; relieves Nice, iii. 218; besieges Montdovi, iii. 219; his treachery, iii. 220; takes Carignano, *ib.*; endeavours to throw supplies into

Guasto, Marquis del—*continued.*
Carignano, iii. 225; military manœuvres of, at Sommeriva, iii. 231-2; defeat of, at Carignano, iii. 235; wounded, *ib.*; refused admittance to Ast, iii. 236; taunted by the Milanese, *ib.*

Gueldres, Maréchal de, position of, in Brabant, iii. 184; *see* note, *ib.*; ravages the Low Countries, iii. 185

—— Duc de, *see* Mark, Robert de la

Guinegatte, flight of gensdarmes from the heights of, i. 102; designated "the Battle of the Spurs," i. 103

Guise, Claude, Duc de, joins the army for the recovery of the Milanese, i. 169; repulses the Germans from Franche-Comté, ii. 111; disperses the insurrection of the German reformers, ii. 190; at the interview between Henry VIII. and Francis I., ii. 363; reinforces Peronne, iii. 77; appointed Lieutenant-general of Burgundy and Champagne during the absence of Francis I., iii. 98; commands a division of the French army at Luxembourg, iii. 184; *see* note, *ib.*; retakes Montmedy, iii. 187

Gusman, Martin de, negotiates between the emperor and Francis, iii. 250; *see* note, *ib.*

HALLWIN, Louis de, Lieutenant-general in Picardy, i. 99; restrains the impetuosity of the Chevalier Bayard, i. 101; his misunderstanding with the Duc de Longueville alluded to, i. 109; taken prisoner at Térouenne, iii. 93; *see* note, *ib.*

Hampton Court, description of, ii. 309

Haye, Jean de la, President of the Parliament, deputed to present a remonstrance to Francis on the forced presence of the Bastard of Savoy during the sitting of Parliament, i. 261; at the Court of Bearn, ii. 303

Henry VII. of England refused the hand of Marguerite de Valois by the Grand Council, i. 38

—— VIII. of England, league made by him with the Pope and Ferdinand of Spain alluded to, i. 70; joins the cause of the Pope against France, i. 94; invades France and besieges Térouenne, i. 99-101; his army attacked by Bayard, who captures a gun, i. 101; joined by the Emperor Maximilian at Térouenne, *ib.*; his interview with the Chevalier Bayard, i. 107; demolishes Térouenne and besieges Tournay, i. 110; embarks for England, i. 116; enters into a treaty with Francis I., i. 153-4; furnishes the Emperor Maximilian with money to recover the Milanese, i. 211; his efforts to induce Erasmus to reside in England alluded to, i. 272; persuaded by Wolsey, enters into a closer alliance with Francis I., i. 292-3; enters into a treaty of marriage for the Princess Mary of England and the dauphin, i. 293; withdraws from the contest for the empire of Germany, i. 302-4; regrets declining the possession of Milan, offered to him by Maximilian, i. 305; his duplicity to Francis I. during his contest for the imperial crown, i. 310; becomes sponsor to the second son of Francis I., i. 333; Francis I. endeavours to secure his alliance on commencing hostili-

Henry VIII.—*continued.*
ties against Charles V., i. 339; consents to an interview with the French king, i. 341; the preparations for the king's interview with Francis, i. 343; visited by the Emperor Charles V. at Dover, *ib.*; the emperor weakens the interest of Francis I. with Henry, i. 344; preparations for the king's reception at Guisnes, i. 346; ceremony of the meeting of the king and Francis I. at the Field of the Cloth of Gold, i. 349; his appearance at the meeting with the French king, i. 351-2; his courteous bearing to Francis described, i. 353-4; visited by Francis I. without attendants, i. 356; mutual pledge of friendship, i. 357; exchange of visits between the two kings, i. 358; distances all competitors at archery at the Field of the Cloth of Gold, i. 359; the King of England thrown by the King of France in a wrestling match, *ib.*; gives a grand banquet to the French king, i. 360; departs for Gravelines, i. 362; his interview with the Emperor Charles V. at Gravelines, i. 365; violates the pledges given to Francis I., *ib.*; the emperor accompanies the king to Calais, i. 366; returns to England, i. 367; appealed to by Francis I. and Charles V. to mediate between them, i. 380; his bad faith to Francis I. alluded to, i. 384; visited by Charles V. and ratifies the betrothal of the Princess Mary, and promises to land forty thousand men in France, ii. 25; enters into a compact with the Connétable de France to invade Normandy, ii. 42; his

Henry VIII.—*continued.*
interview with Charles V. at Dover, ii. 63; invests his imperial guest with the Order of the Garter, *ib.*; his pretext for declaring war against France, ii. 64; his letter to Francis I. alluded to, ii. 65; Charles V. confers the protectorate of the Low Countries upon, ii. 67; declares war against France, ii. 68; his policy in reference to France before the battle of Pavia referred to, ii. 197; coolness of, towards Charles V., *ib.*; his demands upon the emperor respecting the French monarch, ii. 198; signs a new treaty with France, *ib.*; enters into a treaty known as the Holy League, ii. 237; prepares to send an envoy to Spain to negotiate for the liberation of Clement VII., ii. 272; his treaty with Francis I. against Spain explained, *ib.*; concludes a treaty of mutual defence with Francis I., ii. 359; called Defender of the Faith, *ib.*; his unpopularity alluded to, ii. 360; proceeds to Calais to meet Francis I., ii. 363; his interview with Francis, *ib.*; concludes a treaty with Francis against the Turks, ii. 365; his indignation against the Pope, *ib.*; endeavours to persuade Francis I. not to submit to the degradation of kissing the Pope's toe, *ib.*; in conjunction with Francis I. he despatches two French bishops to threaten the Pope, ii. 369; returns to England, ii. 370; despatches Bishop Bonner to the Pope, to announce that the king had appealed from the decision of his holiness to that of a general council, ii. 388; his marriage with Anne Boleyn

Henry VIII.—*continued.*
alluded to, iii. 14; he is excommunicated by the Pope, *ib.*; avows himself the head of the reformers, *ib.*; persecution of the Romanists by, iii. 15; his jealousy at the marriage of James V. of Scotland with the Princesse Marguerite, iii. 82; furnishes Charles V. with ten thousand men, iii. 207; invades France in conjunction with Charles V., iii. 240; his jealousy of Charles, *ib.*; his distrust of Charles V. prevents the co-operation of the allied forces, iii. 248; Boulogne taken by, iii. 255; abandoned by Charles V., retreats to Calais and embarks for England, iii. 258-9; arrives at Portsmouth and witnesses the loss of the Mary Rose, iii. 281; his German levies refused a passage through the territories of the emperor, iii. 286; concludes a treaty of peace with France, iii. 289-90; death of, iii. 299; its effect upon Francis I., iii. 300

Hesdin, city of, taken by siege, iii. 90

Hesse, Landgrave of, compelled to pay tribute to François de Seckingen, i. 315; *see* note, *ib.*

Holy League signed by Francis I., the Pope, Henry VIII., Francisco Sforza, and the Venetians, ii. 237

Hungary, King of, *see* Zapolski, John de

ISABELLA of Spain, her death alluded to, i. 43

Iscalin, Paulin, ambassador from Francis to the Sultan, iii. 200; *see* note, *ib.*; induces Solyman to co-operate with Francis, iii. 202

Italy, exhausted state of, during the wars between Charles V. and Francis I. alluded to, ii. 322; literature and art in, ii. 335

JAMES IV. of Scotland, his death alluded to, at Flodden Field, i. 115

—— V. of Scotland meets Francis I. at Lyons, iii. 81; marries the Princesse Marguerite, *ib.*; his knight errantry, iii. 83; death of the Princesse Marguerite, *ib.*; marries Marie de Guise, iii. 84; his death alluded to, iii. 206

Jamets, Seigneur de, son of Robert de la Mark, his services alluded to, i. 314

Jeanne de France, queen of Louis XII., i. 5; personal appearance of, *ib.*; intercedes with Charles VIII. for the release of her husband when Duc d'Orleans, i. 10; her marriage with the king declared null and void by the Pope, i. 15; founds the convent of the Annunciation, *ib.*; death of, *ib.*

—— de Navarre, her marriage with the Duc de Cleves annulled, iii. 211; marries the Duc de Bourbon, *ib.*

—— la Folle, widow of the Archduke Philip, her miserable condition, i. 48; her jealousy of her dead husband, i. 49; helpless condition of her children, *ib.*

Julius II. determines on war, i. 50; character of, *ib.*; his chagrin on finding that the treaty between himself and Louis XII. for the invasion of Venice had been annulled, *ib.*; resolves to attack Bologna, i. 51-2; establishes republics at Perousa and Bologna, i. 53; avoids an inter-

Julius II.—*continued.*
  view with Louis XII., i. 58;
  endeavours to subjugate Venice,
  i. 59; despatches an army into
  Romagna under the command
  of the Duc d'Urbino, i. 63; hostility
  of, to France, i. 67; attacks
  Mirandola, i. 69; returns
  to Ravenna, *ib.*; enters into a
  league with Ferdinand and
  Henry VIII., i. 70; alarm of,
  at the success of the French in
  Italy, i. 79; persuaded by Giulio
  de' Medici not to offer terms to
  Louis XII., i. 80; instructs the
  Cardinal of Sion to raise troops
  against the Milanese, *ib.*; the
  vaunt of the Pope accomplished,
  i. 81; efforts of, to undermine
  the interests of France, i. 92;
  death of, *ib.*

KATHERINE of Aragon, her interview
  with the Queen of France
  at the Field of the Cloth of Gold,
  i. 358-9; her death alluded to,
  iii. 15
King of Navarre, *see* D'Albret,
  Henri

LAFAYETTE, Admiral, his attack
  upon the imperial flotilla at the
  siege of Marseilles alluded to, ii.
  140; conveys the remnant of
  the French army from Civita
  Vecchia to Marseilles, ii. 189
Lalande, M. de, Governor of the
  citadel of Luxembourg, iii. 212;
  see note, *ib.*; death of, iii. 245
Lambesc, François de, death of, at
  the battle of Pavia, ii. 168
La Muette, chateau of, alluded to,
  ii. 357
Landrecies taken by Annebaut, iii.
  203; fortified by Francis, *ib.*
Languedoc, Francis I. levies a tax
  on the states of, for the purpose
  of repairing the fortifications of

Languedoc—*continued.*
  Narbonne and the fortresses of
  the Pyrenees, ii. 24-5
Lannoy, Charles de, Viceroy of
  Naples, position of, on the commencement
  of the campaign of
  the French to recover the Milanese,
  ii. 116; enters Milan, ii.
  119; engages to assist at the
  siege of Marseilles, ii. 137; his
  delay alluded to, ii. 140; surrenders
  Milan, ii. 147; refuses
  the Pope's mediation to establish
  a truce for five years between
  Spain and France, ii.
  151; leaves Naples defenceless
  in order to strengthen his army
  in the Milanese, ii. 153; introduces
  supplies into Pavia by
  stratagem, ii. 154; at the battle
  of Pavia, ii. 159; Francis I. surrenders
  his sword to, on being
  taken prisoner, ii. 174; forbids
  the imperialist soldiers to approach
  the camp of Francis I.,
  ii. 178; transfers the king to
  the citadel of Pizzighettona, *ib.*;
  persuades Francis I. to place
  confidence in Charles V. and
  remove to Madrid, ii. 202-4;
  conducts the king to Spain, ii.
  205; makes his escape from the
  mutineers of the royal guard, ii.
  206; Charles V. rewards him
  for his treachery, *ib.*; accused
  by the Duc de Bourbon
  and the Marquis de Pescara of
  perfidy and cowardice, ii. 210;
  introduced to the assembly convoked
  by Francis to decide between
  the emperor and himself,
  ii. 236; indignation of, at the
  non-fulfilment of the treaty on
  the part of Francis I. with
  Charles V., ii. 237; returns to
  Spain, ii. 238
Lansquenets, the, mercenary troops
  in the pay of France, i. 184; they

Lansquenets—*continued.*
give way before the attack of the Swiss at Marignano, i. 185
La Paix des Dames, conditions of, ii. 324
Lascaris, John, his services in oriental learning alluded to, i. 268
Lauffen, Wittemberg de, death of, at the battle of Pavia, ii. 168
Lautrec, Maréchal de, *see* Foix, Adet de
Lenoncourt, Robert de, Archbishop of Paris, crowns Francis I. at Rheims, i. 135
Leo X., *see* Medici, de, Cardinal
Lescun, M. de, created a Maréchal of France, i. 284 ; receives temporary command of the army in Italy, ii. 1 ; his interview with Francis, on the loss of Milan, ii. 12 ; at Bicocca, ii. 30 ; left in command in Italy during the absence of Maréchal Lautrec, ii. 32 ; invested in Cremona by Colonna, ii. 33 ; undertakes to surrender, unless supplies arrive from France, ii. 34 ; evacuates Lombardy, *ib.* ; his advice to the king previous to the battle of Pavia, ii. 161 ; seeks for the body of Bonnivet, ii. 175 ; death of, *ib.*
Lesparre, Marquis de, appointed to the command of the army in Navarre to recover the territories of Henri d'Albret, i. 377 ; takes Pampeluna, i. 378 ; his imprudence, i. 379 ; defeated and taken prisoner, *ib.*
Leyva, Antonio da, General, defends Pavia against the French, ii. 149 ; *see* note, *ib.* ; introduces supplies into Pavia by stratagem, ii. 154 ; robs the churches to pay his troops, ii. 155 ; his evasion with the priests, *ib.* ; harasses the French troops, ii. 158 ; at the battle of

Leyva, Antonio da—*continued.*
Pavia, ii. 163-8 ; overhears his meditated assassination by Morone, ii. 213 ; arrests Morone, ii. 214 ; governor of Milan, ii. 382 ; attacks Fossano, iii. 54 ; besieges Turin, iii. 55 ; accused of promoting the death of the dauphin by poison, iii. 61 ; denies the accusation, iii. 63 ; death of, iii. 68
Lisle, Lord, his government of Boulogne alluded to, iii. 277
Literature, progress of, i. 267-72
Livry, hermit of, a Lutheran, burnt by order of Louise de Savoie, in front of Nôtre Dame, ii. 191
Logrogno, siege of, alluded to, i. 378
London, Bishop of, attends upon Cardinal Wolsey on his mission to France, ii. 274
Longueville, Francis, Duc de, commands the rear-guard of Louis XII.'s army against the Venetians, i. 61 ; his quarrel with the Duc de Bourbon alluded to, i. 83 ; *see* note, *ib.* ; gallant attempt of, to throw provisions into the town of Térouenne, i. 101 ; a prisoner to the English, i. 103 ; his quarrel with M. de Piennes alluded to, i. 109 ; wins fifty thousand crowns from Henry VIII. at tennis, with which he purchases his liberty, i. 121 ; negotiates for the hand of the Princess Mary of England, *ib.* ; represents the King of France at the marriage of the Princess Mary, i. 125
Lorges, Jacques de, Earl of Montgomery, despatched by Francis I. with troops to support the Dowager-Queen of Scotland, iii. 276 ; *see* note, *ib.*

INDEX

Lorraine, Duc de, his marriage with Mademoiselle de Bourbon alluded to, i. 145 ; one of the sponsors at the baptism of the dauphin, i. 244 ; compelled to pay tribute to François de Seckingen, i. 315 ; ordered by Francis to harass the imperialists, ii. 139 ; death of, at the battle of Pavia, ii. 176
—— Cardinal de, his profligacy alluded to, iii. 8 ; *see* note, *ib.* ; directed by Francis I. to remind the Emperor Charles V. of his promise of ceding the duchy of Milan to the French prince, iii. 47 ; informs the king that the dauphin died from poison, iii. 60 ; exile of, iii. 170
Louis XI., his crafty policy towards the dauphin, afterwards Charles VIII., alluded to, i. 7
—— XII., his misgivings respecting the ambition of his successor, Francis I., i. 2 ; called the father of his people, *ib.* ; his prudence, *ib.* ; encourages learning, i. 3 ; discourages extravagance in his nobility, *ib.*; his courage alluded to, i. 4 ; his magnanimous reply to his courtiers on dismissing General d'Alvino, *ib.* ; observations on his marriage with Jeanne de France, i. 5 ; his romantic passion for Anne de Bretagne, *ib.* ; the love of Anne de France for, when Duc d'Orleans, alluded to, i. 9 ; warned by the Comte de Dunois against the blandishments of Anne de France, *ib.* ; claims the right of governing the kingdom during the minority of Charles, *ib.* ; confined in the tower of Bourges, *ib.* ; released by order of the king, i. 10 ; consoles Anne de Bretagne on the death of her husband, Charles VIII., i. 14 ; marries Anne de

Louis XII.—*continued.*
Bretagne, widow of Charles VIII., i. 15 ; calls Louise de Savoie to Court, i. 17 ; its consequences, *ib.* ; indisposition of the king at Amboise, i. 23 ; influenced by the queen, i. 24 ; remark of the king on Anne of Bretagne espousing the cause of Pope Julius II., i. 26 ; departs from Amboise, *ib.* ; increasing illness of, i. 32 ; anxiety of the queen, *ib.*; determination of the king to bestow the hand of Marguerite de Valois upon Charles III., Duc d'Alençon, i. 38 ; his motives, i. 39 ; the king suffers a relapse, and at the instigation of Cardinal d'Amboise executes a will directing the Princesse Claude to marry Francis, Comte d'Angoulême, i. 41-2 ; recovery of the king, *ib.*; marriage of his niece Germaine de Foix with Ferdinand of Castile, i. 43-4 ; applies himself to the internal economy of his kingdom, *ib.* ; assembles the States-General, and stratagem of the king to procure a marriage between the Duc de Valois and the Princesse Claude, i. 45-6 ; his bad faith in violating a treaty of his daughter's marriage alluded to, i. 47 ; his liberality towards the sons of the Archduke Philip, i. 49 ; orders M. de Chaumont to march upon Bologna, i. 52 ; instigated by Cardinal d'Amboise, refuses assistance to Prince Bentivoglio, i. 53 ; enraged at the cruelties of the Genoese, marches an army against Genoa, i. 54-5 ; entry of the king into Genoa, *ib.* ; hangs seventy-nine Genoese, i. 56 ; condemns Genoa to pay a fine of three hundred thousand florins, disbands his

INDEX

Louis XII.—*continued.*
army, and proceeds to Milan, *ib.*; entertained by the Marquis de Vigevano, i. 57; proceeds to Savona, *ib*; his respect for Gonsalvo de Cordova, i. 58; his desire for an interview with Pope Julius II. defeated, *ib.*; the king re-enters Italy with a large army, i. 60; compelled to retreat before the Count Pitigliano, i. 61; wins the battle of Agnadello, i. 62; success of the king's arms in Italy, *ib.*; puts the citizens of Peschiera to death, *ib.*; Brescia, Crema, Pizzighettona, and Cremona taken by, i. 63; returns to France, i. 66; resides at Blois, i. 67; hostility of the Pope towards France, *ib.*; the Swiss troops desert the king, i. 68; the instability of the Emperor Maximilian prevents him taking the field against the Pope, *ib.*; calls a council of his own prelates at Tours, *ib.*; the council of prelates authorizes the king to resist the Pope, *ib.*; preparations of the king to resist the league of the Pope, Ferdinand of Spain, and Henry VIII. of England, i. 70; advises Gaston de Foix to bring the enemy to a speedy engagement, i. 72; his reply when congratulated upon the conquest of Ravenna, i. 78; the religious scruples of the queen encourage Julius II. not to offer terms to, after the battle of Ravenna, i. 80-1; resolves to assist the King of Navarre, i. 83; invests the Duc de Valois with the command of his army, i. 84; enters into a league with the Venetian States, i. 90; efforts of to conciliate Leo X. ineffectual, i. 93; concludes a treaty

Louis XII.—*continued.*
of peace for twelve months with Spain and the Venetian States, *ib.*; the Swiss take up arms against him, i. 94; again invades the Milanese, *ib.*; captures their principal cities, i. 95; battle of Vivegano, i. 95-6; his troops driven out of Italy, i. 97; mortgages part of his crown land, i. 98; conveyed to Amiens in a litter to oppose the advance of the English under Henry VIII., i. 99; profiting by the supineness of Henry VIII. and Maximilian, withdraws his army into Picardy, i. 108; the divisions amongst his generals induce the king to appoint the Duc de Valois to the command of the army, i. 109; Burgundy revolts against the king, i. 110; refuses to ratify the treaty signed at Dijon between M. de Tremouille and the Swiss generals, i. 114; endeavours to conciliate the Swiss, *ib.*; treaty of Orleans, granting a truce for twelve months, i. 116; the king accedes to all the demands of the Pope, *ib.*; death of the queen, and grief of the king, *ib.*; urged to take a third wife, i. 118; Ferdinand of Spain offers the king the hand of Eleanora of Austria, i. 119; negotiates with Henry VIII. for the hand of the Princess Mary of England, i. 120; conditions of the marriage treaty, i. 122; impatience of the king to see his bride, the Princess Mary, i. 125; fascinated with her beauty, i. 126; gorgeous ceremony of his nuptials at Abbeville, i. 127; symptoms of his approaching death appear before the festivities of his marriage terminate, i. 131; summons

Louis XII.—*continued*.
his successor, Francis, to his bedside, and expires, *ib.*; his death, i. 132
—— Count Palatine of the Rhine, one of the electors of Germany, i. 299; *see* note; protects Luther, i. 334
—— King of Bohemia, one of the electors of Germany, i. 299; *see* note
Louise de Savoie, *see* Savoie
Louvre, the, commencement of, alluded to, ii. 357
"Loyal Servant," the, his description of the armies of Pope Julius II. and Ferdinand of Spain, previous to the battle of Ravenna, i. 72-3; description of the death of Gaston de Foix, i. 76-7; extracts from, on the capture of Villa Franca, i. 177; extract from, respecting the godmother of the dauphin, i. 244; *see* note, *ib.*
Loyola, Ignatius, gallantry of, at Pampeluna, i. 377; wounded, i. 378
Lunato, occupation of, by Marquis of Mantua alluded to, i. 64
Luther, Martin, the extortions of Leo X. exposed by, i. 273-6; increase of his party, i. 334; protected by the Duke of Saxony and the Elector Palatine, *ib.*; excommunicated by Pope Leo X., i. 369; invited to the Diet at Worms by the Emperor Charles V., *ib*; protected by the Elector of Saxony, i. 370; his death alluded to, iii. 291; *see* note, *ib.*
Lutherans, persecution of the, ii. 340; burning of Jean le Clerc, *ib.*; of Louis de Berguin, ii. 343; the Inquisition at Toulouse and Lyons, *ib.*; persecution of, by Francis I., iii. 199; massacre

Lutherans—*continued*.
of, iii. 265-71; persecution of, in France, iii. 293
Luxembourg, capture of, by the Duc d'Orleans, iii. 187; besieged by the imperialists, *ib.*
—— Duc de, intended marriage of, with the Princesse Claude alluded to, i. 25-37

MADRID, Château of, in the Bois de Boulogne, ii. 357-8
Mailli, Antoine de, his death, iii. 90
Mantua, Marquis of, occupies Asola and Lunato, i. 64; the Papal army commanded by, ii. 115
Maraviglia, his position at Milan, ii. 375; agent for Francis I., *ib.*; his vanity alluded to, *ib.*; the emperor demands his dismissal from the Court of Milan, ii. 376; quarrel of one of his lacqueys with the Count Castiglione, ii. 377; trial of, and death, ii. 379
Margaret of Austria betrothed to Charles VIII. of France, i. 6; *see* note; refusal of the king to perform the contract, i. 11; persuades Robert de la Mark and the Prince-Bishop of Liège to join the cause of her nephew, Charles V., i. 321; accompanies Charles V. to Gravelines to meet Henry VIII., i. 365-6; her regret at the rupture between Charles V. and Robert de la Mark, i. 372; meets Louise de Savoie at Cambray, to arrange the conditions for the release of the French princes, ii. 323; concludes a peace known as *La Paix des Dames*, ii. 324; protects the allies of the emperor, ii. 325; her death alluded to, ii. 352

Marguerite de Valois, *see* Valois, Marguerite de
—— Princesse, her marriage with James V. of Scotland, iii. 81-2; her death, iii. 83
Marignano, battle of, i. 185-95
Mark, Evrard de la, Bishop of Liège, his government alluded to, i. 313; treacherous conduct of Madame d'Angoulême to, i. 320; joins the cause of Charles V., i. 321
—— Robert de la, Duc de Gueldres, one of the leaders in the army of Louis XII. against Venice, i. 61; desperate bravery of, at the battle of Vivegano, i. 96-7; *see* note, *ib.*; joins the army for the recovery of the Milanese, i. 169; withdraws from the army in Italy, to check the aggressions of the Brabanters, i. 180; joins Francis at Turin, with six thousand lansquenets, i. 182; his services to Francis I. alluded to, i. 314; his intimacy with François de Seckingen. *ib.*; recommends François de Seckingen to Francis I., i. 315-17; disgraced by Francis, at the instigation of his mother, i. 319; his indignation on detecting the treachery of Madame d'Angoulême, i. 320; deserts the cause of Francis I., and joins Charles V., i. 321; ingratitude of the emperor to, i. 371; quarrels with the emperor, and returns his allegiance to Francis, i. 372; defies the emperor at the Diet at Worms, i. 373; besieges Vireton, *ib.*; his territories ravaged by order of the emperor, Charles V., i. 380-1; his interests abandoned by France, at the treaty of Cambray, ii. 325
Marot, Clement, the French poet,

Marot, Clement—*continued.*
see note, i. 336; *valet-de-chambre* to Marguerite de Valois, ii. 192; committed to prison for eating meat during Lent, and released by Marguerite de Valois, *ib.*; inconsistency of his conduct during the progress of the Reformation, ii. 339-40
Marseilles, siege of, ii. 137; relieved by Lorenzo de Céri, *ib.*; noble defence of the citizens of, ii. 139; the ladies' trench, *ib.*; disappointment of the Duc de Bourbon at the protracted defence of, ii. 140-1; the imperialists retire from, ii. 142
Mary, Princess, of England, sister of Henry VIII. (queen of Louis XII.), negotiations for her marriage with Louis XII., i. 120-1; conditions of the marriage treaty, i. 122; disparity of their ages, i. 123; her love for Brandon, Duke of Suffolk, *ib.*; her declaration previous to the ratification of her marriage, i. 124; married by proxy at Greenwich, i. 125; her reception in France by the king, *ib.*; Anne Boleyn one of her maids of honour, i. 126; her extreme beauty, i. 127; gorgeous ceremony of her second marriage at Abbeville, *ib.*; crowned at St. Denis, *ib.*; festivities on her entering Paris, i. 128; her love for Francis, Duc de Valois, i. 129-30; imprudence of, during her short reign as Queen of France alluded to, i. 131; interview with Francis I. previous to his coronation, i. 135; her marriage with the Duke of Suffolk, i. 137-8; returns to England, *ib.*
—— Princess, of England, daughter of Henry VIII., betrothed to the dauphin, i. 293, note; performs

Mary, Princess—*continued.*
in several comedies for the amusement of the French courtiers, ii. 309
—— Queen of Scots, alluded to, iii. 206
Maximilian, Emperor, indignation of, on the refusal of Charles VIII. to marry his daughter, the Princess Margaret, i. 11; the treaty between Louis XII. and, alluded to, i. 50; the revolt of Genoa attributed to the machinations of, i. 54; attacks Trevisa, i. 64; his weakness induces the Venetians to retake Padua, i. 66; applies to Louis XII. for assistance, *ib.*; flight of, *ib.*; desertion of his Swiss troops, *ib.*; treacherous conduct towards Louis XII., i. 81; withdraws his forces from the French army, i. 83; consents to the marriage of the Princesse Rénée with the Prince Charles of Austria, provided the princess is educated at his Court, i. 91; Leo X. obtains his co-operation against France, i. 94; joins the army of Henry VIII. at Térouenne, i. 101; his interview with the Chevalier Bayard, i. 107; induces Henry VIII. to demolish Térouenne, i. 110; his bad faith alluded to, i. 152; his confederacy with Leo X. and the Swiss against Francis I. alluded to, i. 166; raises a powerful army, and compels the French to shut themselves up in Milan, i. 211; threatens to raze Milan, i. 212; his Swiss mercenaries refuse to act, i. 213; leaves his army, and flies to Germany, *ib.*; his endeavours to extort money from Henry VIII. and Francis I. alluded to, i. 298; his anxiety to secure the empire

Maximilian, Emperor—*contd.*
of Germany for his grandson, i. 299; demands the crown of Rome, *ib.*; his imbecile rule alluded to, i. 303; death of, *ib.*; its effect upon the affairs of Europe, i. 304
Mayence, Archbishop of, *see* Brandenbourg, Albert de
Medici, family of the, ii. 372
—— Alessandro de', reinstated in government of Florence, ii. 346; restored to the sovereignty of Florence by Charles V., iii. 26; *see* note, *ib.*
—— Cardinal de', position of, in the army of Italy and Spain previous to the battle of Ravenna, i. 72; taken prisoner at the battle of Ravenna, i. 75; ascends the Papal throne as Leo X., i. 92; efforts of Louis XII. to conclude a peace with, i. 93; Ferdinand of Spain and Henry VIII. of England join his cause, i. 94; joy of, at the battle of Vivegano, and expulsion of the French from Italy, i. 98; disregards the caution of Ferdinand respecting the attitude assumed by Francis I. in Burgundy, i. 156-7; the King of France sends an embassy to, i. 159; his confederacy with Maximilian and the Swiss against Francis I. alluded to, i. 166; alarm of, at the success of the French in Italy, i. 178; enters into a treaty with Francis at Viterbo, i. 203; suspects Francis has designs upon Naples, *ib.*; meets the French king at Bologna, i. 204; his policy alluded to, i. 205; enters into a league with Francis I., i. 206; induces Francis to abandon his designs upon Naples, i. 207; the question of the Pragmatic Sanction discussed by com-

Medici, Cardinal de'—*continued.* missioners, i. 208; endeavours to induce Francis I. to undertake a crusade against the Turks, i. 209; sends Lorenzo de' Medici as his proxy at the baptism of the dauphin, i. 243; his munificence to the Queen of France on the marriage of Lorenzo de' Medici with Madelaine de la Tour-d'Auvergne, i. 248; his efforts to retain Erasmus in Florence alluded to, i. 271; recruits his treasury by the sale of indulgences, i. 272; his order to the mendicant monks of St. Dominic, *ib.*; Martin Luther exposes the extortions of the Pope, i. 273; his intrigues with Francis I. and Charles V. and the Emperor Maximilian respecting the empire, i. 300-1; endeavours to dissuade Francis from advancing his claim to the empire,*ib.*; endeavours to undermine the interest of Francis I. and Charles V., and to secure the imperial crown to some less powerful prince, i. 310; excommunicates Luther, i. 369; his crafty policy with Francis I. and the Emperor Charles V., i. 374-5; his bad faith to Francis alluded to, i. 382; declares war against France, ii. 9; his anxiety undermines his health, ii. 14; death of, supposed by poison, *ib.*; his death a loss to the confederated sovereigns, ii. 23
—— Gian Giacomo de', takes the castle of Chiavenna, ii. 157; its consequences, *ib.*
—— Giovanni de', threatens the Maréchal de Foix to open the gates of Cremona to the enemy unless his troops are paid their arrears, ii. 33; movements of, at the Ticino, ii. 128

Medici, Giulio de', persuades Pope Julius II. not to offer terms to Louis XII., i. 80
—— Lorenzo de': the Pope, alarmed at the success of the French, orders him to halt his army within the frontiers of Modena, i. 178; attends at the baptism of the dauphin as proxy for the Pope, i. 243; his marriage with Madelaine de la Tour-d'Auvergne, i. 246-9; his death, i. 250
Melancthon, employed by the reformers in writing the profession of their faith, ii. 361; invited to France by Francis I., iii. 23
Melfi, Prince de, appointed to the command of the city of Luxembourg, iii. 211; *see* note, *ib.*
Metz, citizens of, tribute paid by, to François de Seckingen, i. 315
Meynier, Baron Jean, his efforts to cause the destruction of the Lutherans, iii. 265-70
Mézières, defended by the Chevalier Bayard, i. 385-95
Milan, revenues of, increased by Louis XII., i. 63; return of the French army to, with the body of Gaston de Foix, i. 78; entered by Francis I. after the battle of Marignano, i. 201; authorities of, take the oath of allegiance to Francis, *ib.*; fauxbourgs of, destroyed by the Duc de Bourbon, i. 211; threat of the Emperor Maximilian to raze the city and strew its site with salt, i. 212; siege of, by the Emperor Maximilian, raised, i. 213; despair of the Milanese citizens at the devastation of the French soldiers, ii. 2; able defence of the city of, by Prosper Colonna, ii. 117-18; Bonnivet retires from, ii. 119; again taken by the French, ii.

Milan—*continued.*
147; its impoverished condition alluded to, *ib.*; despair of the Milanese at the persecution of the emperor's troops, ii. 252; duchy of, offered to the Duc d'Angoulême by the emperor, iii. 39-44

Mirandola attacked by Pope Julius II. in person, i. 69

Molart, Seigneur de, one of the captains at the battle of Agnadello, i. 61

Monçada, Ugo de, Viceroy of Sicily, attacks and disperses some Turkish galleys, i. 325; *see* note, *ib.*; supplies the imperialist army at the siege of Marseilles with provisions, ii. 137

Monselica, capture of, alluded to, i. 64

Montagnana, capture of, alluded to, i. 64

Montdovi, inhabitants of, put to the sword by the Marquis del Guasto, iii. 220

Montecuculli, Conte Sebastian de, suspected of poisoning the dauphin, iii. 59; admits his guilt, iii. 61; execution of, iii. 62-3

Montejan, M. de, surprised and taken prisoner at Tourbes, iii. 56; *see* note, *ib.*; appointed Lieutenant-general of Piedmont, iii. 103; made a marshal of France, iii. 105

Montluc, Blaise de, sent by Comte d'Enghien to Francis I. to request permission to give battle to the imperialists, iii. 226; *see* note, *ib.*; his eloquence persuades the king to give battle, iii. 228-30; his gallantry, iii. 233-4; bravery of, at Boulogne, iii. 260

Montmoreau, Seigneur de, surrenders Mouzon, i. 382; *see*

Montmoreau—*continued.*
note, *ib.*; volunteers with the Chevalier Bayard to defend the city of Mézières, i. 386

Montmorency, Anne Seigneur de, affection of Francis I. for, alluded to, i. 144; *see* note, *ib.*; at the capture of Prosper Colonna, i. 173; one of the hostages delivered to Henry VIII., to secure the payment of six hundred thousand golden crowns, i. 293; joins the army in Italy with supplies, ii. 26; wounded, ii. 29; commissioned by Francis to raise twelve thousand men in Switzerland, ii. 72; enthusiastic counsel of, misleads the king, ii. 160; at the battle of Pavia, ii. 163; takes command of Paris, ii. 188; despatched by Francis I. to Paris, as attendant upon the dauphin, ii. 228; one of the witnesses to the secret protest of the king when a prisoner, ii. 229; appointed Grand-Master and Governor of Languedoc, ii. 244; sent as ambassador to Henry VIII., ii. 308; entertained at Hampton Court by Cardinal Wolsey, ii. 309; sent to the Spanish frontier to ransom the French princes, ii. 326; invested with the Order of the Garter by Henry VIII., ii. 364; conceives a passion for the Queen of France, iii. 9; declares it, and is repulsed, iii. 11; his singular compact with the queen, iii. 12; his devotion to the queen, iii. 13; fortifies the frontier of France against invasion, iii. 50; position of, in Provence, iii. 66; advises the king not to join the main army, iii. 68; marches to Lyons, iii. 97; forces the Pas-de-Suze, *ib.*; commanded by Francis to suspend operations until his arrival

Montmorency—*continued*.
at headquarters, iii. 101; created connétable, iii. 105; offers protection to the Duke of Savoy, iii. 108; his offer to the Duke of Savoy refused, iii. 109; his increasing power during the illness of the king, iii. 117; persuades Francis to permit the emperor to traverse France unconditionally, iii. 121; Madame d'Etampes plots his ruin, iii. 122; an enamelled chain sent by the Queen Eleanora to, iii. 126-8; entertains Charles V. at Chantilly, iii. 140; accompanies the emperor to Valenciennes, *ib.*; returns to France, iii. 141; exile of, iii. 153; cause of his disgrace, *ib.*; restored to Court by Henry II., iii. 305

Montpensier, Charles de, Duc de Bourbon, one of the suite of Louis XII., i. 23; *see* note, *ib.*; one of the companions of Francis at the Court of Amboise, i. 27; his attachment to Mademoiselle d'Angoulême discovered by Gouffier, i. 29; challenged by. Francis to single combat, *ib.*; retires from Amboise, i. 30; position of, in the army of Louis XII. against the Venetians, i. 61; his quarrel with the Duc de Longueville alluded to, i. 83; holds the Duke of Alva in check at St. Jean Pied-de-port, i. 84; made Connétable de France by Francis I., i. 142; his marriage alluded to, *ib.*; his magnificent appearance, i. 161; appointed to the chief command of the army of Milan, *ib.*; his stateliness offends Francis, i. 162; at the battle of Marignano, i. 185; charges the Swiss column, i. 189; appointed Lieutenant-general of the Milanese, i. 210; dis-

Montpensier—*continued*.
bands the Swiss troops, i. 212; his recall from Milan occasioned by the intrigues of the Comtesse de Châteaubriand, i. 251-6; his affection for Marguerite de Valois alluded to, i. 257; becomes enthralled with the Comtesse de Châteaubriand, i. 258; distaste of the king for, *ib.*; his attachment to Marguerite de Valois known to the king, i. 259; at the interview of Francis and Henry VIII. at the Field of the Cloth of Gold, i. 349; at the banquet given by the king at Guisnes, i. 360; his indignation on being deprived of the command of the vanguard of the army, i. 396-7; retires to Paris, ii. 15; unexpectedly summoned to the presence of Louise de Savoie, ii. 16; rejects the hand of Louise de Savoie, ii. 18; his hatred to Louise de Savoie, how caused, *ib.*; his dislike of Bonnivet, ii. 19; his magnificence at Moulins, ii. 20; his lawsuits alluded to, ii. 21; demands the hand of the Princesse Rénée, the sister of Queen Claude, ii. 22; exposes the offer of Louise de Savoie to his friends, *ib.*; Louise de Savoie urges her claims against, ii. 37-8; parliament refuses to ratify the decision of the judges against, ii. 39; his estates are put under sequestration, *ib.*; his violence against Louise de Savoie, ii. 40; induced by the overtures of Charles V. to rebel against Francis I., ii. 41; negotiates with Wolsey for an invasion of France by England, ii. 42; induces Francis I. to grant an interview with Maréchal Lautrec, ii. 51; his union with the Princesse Rénée

Montpensier—*continued*.
alluded to, ii. 59; the king is informed of his treason, ii. 73; surprised by Francis in the apartments of Queen Claude, and accused of treason, *ib*.; suffered by the king to escape, ii. 74; expostulates with his friends on his wrongs, ii. 75; visited by Francis at Moulins, ii. 78; feigns illness and partially removes the suspicions of Francis, ii. 79; watched by M. de Wartz by order of Francis, ii. 80; deceives M. de Wartz, who returns to Court, *ib*.; escapes to his fortress of Chantelle, ii. 81; offers to return to his allegiance, ii. 92; flies from Chantelle on the approach of the royal troops, ii. 93; ultimately escapes to Mantua, ii. 94; his estates confiscated, ii. 95; fate of his adherents, *ib*.; hatred of Louise de Savoie against the connétable causes a bias in the parliament in favour of his followers, *ib*.; Francis makes overtures to him to return to his allegiance, ii. 108; rejects the overtures of the king, ii. 109; declared guilty of *lèse majesté*,' *ib*.; bad faith of Charles V. to, ii. 110; his ability as a general contrasted with Bonnivet, ii. 114; joins the imperialists with six thousand men, ii. 119; weakens the army of Bonnivet by skirmishes, but declines a general action, ii. 127; compels Bonnivet to retreat, ii. 128; at the death of Bayard, ii. 132; the good knight's dying rebuke to, *ib*.; pursues the French army, ii. 136; proposes to Pescara to march into France, *ib*.; besieges Marseilles, ii. 137; critical position of, ii. 139; his disappointment at the protracted defence

Montpensier—*continued*.
of Marseilles, ii. 140; taunted by the Marquis de Pescara, ii. 141; retreats from Marseilles, ii. 142; joins the imperial army in Italy at the head of a German force, ii. 155; suggests an immediate attack upon the French before Pavia, ii. 156; at the battle of Pavia, ii. 163-9; Francis I. refuses to surrender his sword to, ii. 171; the king refuses to receive the homage of, ii. 174; his observation over the dead body of Bonnivet on the battle-field of Pavia, ii. 176; tenders his services to Francis at dinner, ii. 178; his overtures to Henry VIII. alluded to, ii. 185; deceived by the viceroy of Naples, consents to the departure of Francis I. to Genoa, ii. 205; his exasperation on discovering the treachery of the viceroy, ii. 210; departs for Madrid, and accuses the viceroy of perfidy and cowardice, *ib*.; contempt of the Castilian nobility for, ii. 211; reply of the Marquis de Villana respecting, *ib*.; treated with indifference by the emperor and contempt by Francis, *ib*.; reveals to Marguerite de Valois the designs of the emperor towards Francis I., ii. 219; warns Marguerite de Valois that the emperor meditates her arrest, ii. 225; appointed by the emperor to command in Italy, ii. 238; marches to Milan with the main body of the imperial army, ii. 252; expostulations of the Milanese to, on the excesses of the emperor's troops, *ib*.; his vow to the citizens, ii. 253; joined by Frundsberg, marches upon Rome, ii. 254-5; attacks the city, and is killed, *ib*.

Montpezat, M. de, one of the hostages delivered to Henry VIII. by Francis I. to secure the payment of six hundred thousand crowns, i. 293; offers his services to Francis I. when a prisoner in the citadel of Pizzighettona, ii. 180; ransomed by the king, ii. 181; appointed ambassador at the English Court, ii. 370; exiled by order of the king for the loss of Perpignan, iii. 190
More, Sir Thomas, attends upon Cardinal Wolsey during his mission in France, ii. 274
Moreto, Conte de, a Piedmontese peasant, in the service of the Count, conducts the army of Francis by a comparatively unknown path across the Alps, i. 170-1; at the capture of Prosper Colonna, i. 174
Morgante, Piero, taken prisoner at Villa Franca, i. 177
Morone, Jerômio, plans a secret league against Charles V., ii. 212; betrayed by Pescara to the emperor, *ib.*; treachery of Pescara at a private interview, ii. 213; arrest of, ii. 214
Mottino ———, death of, i. 98
Moulin, Antoine du, at the Court of Bearn, ii. 303
Mouy, Charles de, one of the hostages delivered to Henry VIII. by Francis I. to secure the payment of six hundred thousand crowns, i. 293

NANÇAY, Christian de, his stolen interview with the Duchesse d'Etampes, iii. 155-8; surprised by the king, iii. 159; clever stratagem of, *ib.*
Naples, besieged by Lautrec, ii. 320; plague at, *ib.*

Napoli, Cesare du, entrusted to guard the Pas-de-Suze, iii. 98
Narbonne, Cardinal, joins in the *Bransle* at the feast given by the Marquis de Vigevano to Louis XII., i. 57
Nassau, Count Henry of, arrival of, in Paris on a mission from the Archduke Charles, i. 150; *see* note, *ib.*; marries Claudine de Challon, i. 151; ordered by the Emperor Charles V. to ravage the territories of the Duc de Gueldres, i. 379; takes Mouzon, i. 382; escapes from Francis I. between Cambray and Valenciennes, i. 387; summons Bayard to surrender the town of Mézières, i. 388; his quarrel with Seckingen, i. 390-2; disorganization of his army, *ib.*; raises the siege of Mézières, i. 394; his visit to the Court of Francis, iii. 15; entrusted by the emperor with proposals of friendship to Francis, *ib.*; enters Picardy, attacks St. Regnier and Peronne, iii. 75-7; retreat of, iii. 78
Navarre, King of, *see* D'Albret, Henri
——— Princess of, her marriage with the Duke of Cleves, iii. 152; banquets in honour of her marriage, iii. 154; her marriage annulled, *ib.*; marries the Duc de Vendôme, *ib.*
——— right of Henry II. to, alluded to, i. 340
Navarro, Conte Pietro da, Captain-general of the infantry in the combined armies of Pope Julius II. and Ferdinand of Spain at the battle of Ravenna, i. 73; *see* note, *ib.*; taken prisoner at Ravenna, i. 75; commands six thousand men under Francis I., i. 157; his skill in overcoming the diffi-

Navarro—*continued*.
culties in conducting the army of Francis I. over the Alps alluded to, i. 171; joins the French army in Italy, ii. 26; reinforces Genoa with two hundred men, ii. 35; enters the service of Francis I. and joins the combined fleets of the Pope and the Venetians, ii. 251; death of, ii. 322

Nemours, Duchesse de, at the baptism of the second son of Francis I., i. 333

Neuville, Nicolas de, Seigneur de Villeray, exchanges the site of the Tuileries for Chanteloupe, near Montlhéry, i. 335

Nevers, Duc de, commands at Chalons, iii. 251

—— Duchesse de, presents the jewelled watch of the Marquis del Guasto to the king, iii. 238; *see* note, *ib.*

Nice, citizens of, refuse admission to the Pope, iii. 109; burned and pillaged by Barbarossa, iii. 218

Norfolk, Duke of, commands an English army, which advances upon Paris, ii. 111; joined by the Comte de Beaurein, *ib.*; fearful of being enclosed between the armies of Tremouille and Vendôme, retires to Calais and sails for England, ii. 113; at the interview between Henry VIII. and Francis I., ii. 363; receives the collar of St. Michael from Francis I., ii. 364

Novi, Paul de, elected Doge of Genoa, i. 54; evacuates Genoa when attacked by Louis XII., i. 55; execution of, in Corsica, i. 56

Noyon, conditions of the peace of, i. 221-2

Nuremberg, peace of, alluded to, ii. 383

ODET, captain in the army of Louis XII. at the battle of Agnadello, i. 61

Olivier, François, despatched by Francis I. to the emperor to engage him in a treaty in lieu of Crespy, iii. 290; *see* note, *ib.*

Orange, Prince of, offended at his cold reception by Francis, offers his services to Charles V., i. 245; assumes the command of the imperial army on the death of the Duc de Bourbon, ii. 255; takes the Pope and thirteen cardinals prisoners in the castle of St. Angelo, ii. 256; defeated by Martin Von Rossem, iii. 186; retires to Antwerp, *ib.*; commands the emperor's army in the duchy of Cleves, iii. 208; his death alluded to, iii. 245

Orleans, treaty signed at, its objects, i. 116

Osma, Bishop of, his conditions for restoring Francis I. to liberty not accepted by Charles V., ii. 199; *see* note, *ib.*

Otranto, cession of, to the King of Spain alluded to, i. 64

PADUA, keys of, transferred to the Emperor Maximilian, i. 64; retaken and fortified by the Conte di Pitigliano, i. 65

Palice, Marquis de la, *see* note, i. 23; one of the leaders in Louis XII.'s army against the Venetians, i. 61; ordered by Louis XII. to assist the Emperor Maximilian, i. 65; induces Bayard to accompany him against the Venetians, i. 66; elected general of the army after the death of Gaston de Foix, i. 78; powerless position of, on the Emperor Maximilian withdrawing his forces from the French army, i. 81; seizes the pass of the valley

Palice, Marquis de la—*continued.* of Roncal, and conducts a division of the French army within two leagues of Pampeluna, i. 84; compelled to retreat beyond the Pyrenees, i. 85; taken prisoner by the English, i. 103; made Maréchal of France, i. 144; at the capture of Prosper Colonna, i. 176; relieves Fontarabia, ii. 61; his advice to the king before the battle of Pavia overruled by Bonnivet, ii. 160; at the battle of Pavia, ii. 163; melancholy death of, at the battle of Pavia, ii. 164-5

Palissis, Bernard, *see* note, ii. 358

Pallavicini, Signor Cristoforo, condemned to death by Maréchal Lautrec, ii. 8

Paluda, Marquis de la, taken prisoner at Ravenna, i. 75

Paris, university of, refuses to recognize the right of Francis I. to enter into a treaty, called the *Concordat*, with the Pope, i. 208; orders solemn services to be performed on the parliament registering the *Concordat*, i. 265; the plague in, ii. 43; excitement of the citizens of, on hearing of the captivity of Francis I., ii. 188; disorderly state of, in 1527, ii. 266; influence of the alchymists and astrologers upon the citizens of, ii. 267; turbulence of the students alluded to, ii. 270; an effigy of the Virgin is desecrated in, ii. 340; alarm in, at the siege of Peronne, iii. 78; provisioned by Cardinal du Bellay, iii. 79; alarm of citizens of, at the capture of St. Dizier, and the march of Charles V. towards the capital, iii. 246; alarm of the citizens of, at the capture of Château Thierry by the imperialists, iii. 254

Parliament of France refuses to sanction the acts of Francis I. to raise money, i. 166; refusal of, to register the ordinance of Francis to protect his forest rights, i. 217; the presentation of the *Concordat* openly opposed by M. de Sièvre, i. 261; the Bastard of Savoy, the king's uncle, requested to retire from, *ib.*; the president of, remonstrates with Francis on the illegality of the presence of M. de Savoy, *ib.*; decides not to register the *Concordat*, and convenes a national council, i. 263; Messrs. de Soyen and Verjus deputed by, to wait upon the king on the subject of the *Concordat*, *ib.*; the deputies of, ordered to leave Amboise, i. 265; the king compels the, to register the *Concordat* under a protest, *ib.*; refuses to ratify the decision of the judges against the estates and honours of the Duc de Bourbon, Connétable de France, ii. 39; proceeds to the trial of the Bourbon conspirators, ii. 95; sentence of, against the conspirators, ii. 96; anger of the king at the leniency of the judges, ii. 97; requisition of, respecting the Lutherans, ii. 191; forbids the sale of Calvinistic works, iii. 200

Paul III., accession of, iii. 15; endeavours to pacify the French ambassadors at the negotiations between Charles V. and Francis, respecting the duchy of Milan, iii. 45; reply of the French envoys to, *ib.*; determines to preserve a strict neutrality between the emperor and Francis, iii. 46, 48; attempts the reconciliation of the emperor and Francis I., iii. 106; refused ad-

Paul III.—*continued.*
mission into Nice, iii. 109; mediates between Francis and the emperor, and concludes a truce between them for ten years, iii. 110, 111; expostulates with the emperor on his intended campaign against Solyman, iii. 180; his suspicions of the intentions of the emperor, iii. 292

Pavanes, Jacques, a Lutheran, burnt by order of Louise de Savoie, in the Place de Grève, ii. 191

Pavia, defence of, by General da Leyva, ii. 149; mutiny of the garrison, ii. 152; supplies introduced into the garrison of, by stratagem, ii. 154; battle of, ii. 162-9; loss of the French at the battle of, ii. 177; retaken by the Comte de St. Pol, ii. 320

Pechy, Sir John, one of the witnesses to the betrothal of the dauphin to the Princess Mary of England, i. 293

Periers, Bonaventure des, at the Court of Bearn, ii. 303; *see* note, *ib.*

Peronne, attacked by the imperialists, iii. 76; defence of, *ib.*

Perpignan, loss of, alluded to, iii. 190

Pescara, Marquis de, one of the commanders in the combined army of the Pope Julius II. and Ferdinand of Spain, at the battle of Ravenna, i. 72; taken prisoner at Ravenna, i. 75; quarrels with Prosper Colonna about the command of the imperial army, ii. 9; pursues Maréchal Lautrec, ii. 12; pillages Genoa, ii. 36; his jealousy of the Duc de Bourbon alluded to, ii. 110; departs for Valladolid, ii. 116; enters Milan, ii. 119; his dislike to the Duc

Pescara, Marquis de—*continued.*
de Bourbon, ii. 120; attacks Bayard at Rebec with a superior force, ii. 125; visits the deathcouch of Bayard, ii. 132; pursues the French army, ii. 136; objects to the proposal of Bourbon to march into France, *ib.*; besieges Marseilles, ii. 137; taunts the Duc de Bourbon on a priest being killed at the altar by the shot from Marseilles, ii. 141; retreats from Marseilles, ii. 142; refuses to hazard an engagement with the French in Italy, ii. 153; attempts to effect an entrance into Mirabello, and to relieve the garrison of Pavia, ii. 158; his efforts to bring on a general engagement at the battle of Pavia, ii. 162; wounded, ii. 168; escorts Francis to Pavia, ii. 175; the king discusses the details of the battle of Pavia with the, ii. 179; assures the French king of the clemency of Charles V., *ib.*; deceived by the Viceroy of Naples, consents to the departure of Francis I. to Madrid, ii. 205; his exasperation on discovering the treachery of the viceroy, ii. 210; treated with indifference by Charles V., ii. 212; betrays Morone to the emperor, *ib.*; his treachery and death, ii. 214-15

Peschiera, citizens of, put to the sword by Louis XII., i. 62

Philip, Archduke, the, death of, i. 48; madness and jealousy of his widow, *Jeanne la Folle*, *ib.*

—— Dom, son of Charles V., appointed Duke of Milan, iii. 173

Pico, Comtesse Francesca, her defence of Mirandola alluded to, i. 69

Piennes, Seigneur de, *see* Hallwin, Louis de

Pierre, Albert de la, one of the leaders of the Swiss mercenaries, i. 179; joins the French army at Milan, i. 212; death of, ii. 29

Pitigliano, Conte di, compels Louis XII. to retreat, i. 61; opposes d'Alviano's wish to give battle to the French king, *ib.*; fortifies Padua, i. 65; slain at the battle of Marignano, i. 193

Pizzighettona, fortress of, taken by Louis XII., i. 63

Plague, the, in Paris, ii. 43

Plessis, Charles du, despatched by Francis I. to open negotiations with the Helvetic body, i. 224

Poitiers, Diane de, her marriage, ii. 98; her home, *ib.*; her birth, ii. 99; her extreme beauty alluded to, ii. 100; hears of her father's sentence and determines to save him, ii. 101; arrives at Court, ii. 102; her audience of Francis, ii. 103-4; saves the life of her father, ii. 105; her biographers alluded to, *ib.*; banished from Court, ii. 193; received by her husband with a warm welcome, *ib.*; her power at the Court of Francis alluded to, ii. 288-9; her characteristics, ii. 290; her return to Court alluded to, iii. 5; becomes the friend of Catherine de' Medici, iii. 6; her interview with the king on the melancholy of the Duc d'Angoulême, iii. 30-3; her appearance in her thirty-first year described, iii. 33-4; she resolves to attempt the conquest of the Duc d'Orleans, iii. 35; extract from a poem by, iii. 36; excites the jealousy of the Duchesse d'Etampes, *ib.*; the king refuses to banish her from Court to appease the jealousy of the Duchesse d'Etampes, iii. 38;

Poitiers, Diane de—*continued.*
feud between, and the Duchesse d'Etampes, iii. 84-5; gives birth to a daughter, iii. 86; her hatred of the Duchesse d'Etampes alluded to, iii. 191; position of, at the death of Francis I., iii. 304

—— Jean de, Comte de St. Vallier, observations of Bonnivet to, respecting the passion of Madame d'Angoulême and the Duchesse d'Alençon for Charles de Bourbon, i. 163; endeavours to persuade the Connétable de France to return to his allegiance, ii. 74; *see* note, *ib.*; his brief interview with M. de Pompérant, ii. 86; his interview with the Duchesse d'Alençon in the forest, ii. 89; arrest of, ii. 91; condemned to death, ii. 96; reprieved upon the scaffold, ii. 105

Pole, Richard de la, banished to Metz in obedience to the wishes of Henry VIII., at the treaty for the marriage of the Princess Mary of England with Louis XII., i. 122; *see* note, *ib.*; engaged in the scheme to entrap the Duc d'Aerschott, ii. 70; ordered by Francis I. to harass the imperial army under the Duc de Bourbon, ii. 139; death of, at the battle of Pavia, ii. 163

Polésina de Rovigo, capture of, alluded to, i. 64

Policastro, Conte de, taken prisoner at Villa Franca, i. 177

Pommeroye, M. de, arranges a meeting between Henry VIII. and Francis I., ii. 363; the ambassador sent by Francis I. to announce to Henry VIII. the marriage of James V. of Scotland to the Princess Marguerite, iii. 82

Pompérant, M. de, reply of, to the Connétable de Bourbon, i. 397; his interview with the king at Amboise, ii. 87; flies from Amboise to Chantelle, and joins the Connétable de France in his revolt against the king, ii. 88; protects Francis I. from violence after his capture at the battle of Pavia, ii. 171-2; pardoned by Francis I. for his services at the battle of Pavia, ii. 179

Pontbriant, M. de, chamberlain to the Comte d'Angoulême, i. 34

Pontdormy, M. de, resolute charge of, at Bicocca, ii. 31; *see* note, *ib.*

Pope, the, *see* Leo X., Julius II., Adrian IV., Clement VII., and Paul III.

Poucher, Etienne, Archbishop of Sens, *see* note, i. 268

Poyer, President, his ignorance of Latin alluded to, ii. 387

Poyet, Guillaume, appointed chancellor, iii. 105; dislodges a billet of wood upon the head of Charles V., iii. 134; his cruel policy towards Maréchal Chabot, iii. 144; arrest of, iii. 147; deprived of his dignity of chancellor, iii. 149; death of, *ib.*

Pragmatic Sanction, the question discussed by commissioners, i. 208; the treaty receives the name of *Concordat*, *ib.*; the treaty gives offence to the university of Paris, *ib.*; *see* Concordat and Parliament

Prelates, council of, convened at Tours by Louis XII. in opposition to Pope Julius II., i. 68

Prie, Aimar de, joins the French army at Blangy, i. 100; enters Genoa, and takes Alessandria and Tortona, i. 178; his arrest and trial alluded to, ii. 94

Primaticcio, Francisco, his works alluded to, ii. 262; *see* note, *ib.*; summoned to France to complete the construction of the palace of Chambord, ii. 263

Protestant princes, conditions of the truce between the, and Charles V., iii. 181

Protestants, persecution of, iii. 20-3

Puy, Bishop of, his arrest and trial alluded to, ii. 94; acquitted by the parliament of Paris, ii. 96

QUEEN-DOWAGER of Hungary appeals to Francis I. and the Duke of Cleves on the Duc de Gueldres ravaging the Low Countries, iii. 185

RABELAIS, François, his position during the progress of the Reformation alluded to, ii. 339; *see* note, *ib.*; *see* note, iii. 188

Ramassot, Captain, mentioned as a leader of two thousand foot at the battle of Ravenna, i. 73

Rangon, Conte Guy de, appointed general of the forces of the Italian league, iii. 75

Ravenna, capture of, alluded to, i. 63; battle of, i. 74-6; city of, pillaged, i. 78

Ravenstein, Sire de, despatched by Charles of Spain to France to terminate hostilities, i. 220

Reformation, the, progress of, alluded to, ii. 337-42

Renée, Princesse, Francis I. refuses to bestow her hand on the English king, ii. 277

Rhodes, Isle of, attacked by Solyman, ii. 47; gallant defence of, by Villiers de' l'Isle Adam, the Grand-Master of the Knights of St. John, *ib.*

Richemont, Seigneur de, one of the captains in Louis XII.'s army at the battle of Agnadello, i. 61

Richmond, Earl of, at the interview between Henry VIII. and Francis I., ii. 363

Rimini taken by the Duc d'Urbino, i. 63

Rincon, Antoine, murdered by order of the Marquis del Guasto, iii. 176-7

Rochelle, revolt of the inhabitants of, in consequence of the increase of the salt tax, iii. 195-8

Rochfort, Gui de, his reply to the States' deputies on the subject of the marriage of the Duc de Valois with the Princesse Claude, i. 46; *see* note, *ib.*

Rohan, Pierre de, *see* Gié, Maréchal de

Rome attacked by the Duc de Bourbon, ii. 255; sack of, ii. 256

Rossem, Martin van, *see* Gueldres, Maréchal de

Rosso, Rosso del, executes the paintings and statues for the palace of Fontainebleau, ii. 334; *see* note, *ib.*

Roussillon, Comte de, at the battle of Agnadello, i. 61

—— siege of, raised, in consequence of the treachery of the Duchesse d'Etampes, iii. 186

Rovera, Francesco-Maria de la, *see* d'Urbino, Duc

St. ANGELO, Marquis de, killed by Francis I. at the battle of Pavia, ii. 169

St. Bonnet, Comte de, his arrest and trial alluded to, ii. 94; acquitted by the parliament of Paris, ii. 96

St. Dizier, siege of, described, iii. 241-5

St. Dominic, a mendicant order of monks, alluded to, i. 272

St. Germain, palace of, alluded to, ii. 357

St. John, Lord, one of the witnesses to the betrothal of the dauphin to the Princess Mary of England, i. 293

—— of Jerusalem, Knights of, defend Rhodes against the Turks, ii. 47; retire to Viterbo, ii. 48; finally settle at Malta, *ib.*

Saint Mesme, M. de, despatched by Francis I. to invite the Pope to become sponsor to the dauphin, i. 243

St. Pol, Comte de, Louis de Luxembourg, his treason alluded to, i. 142; *see* note, *ib.*

—— accident to the French king occurs at the hotel of the, i. 367; appointed governor of Dauphiny, ii. 244; wounded at the battle of Pavia, ii. 176; his singular escape, *ib.*; retakes Pavia, ii. 320; his army totally routed in the Milanese, ii. 322; at the interview between Francis I. and Henry VIII., ii. 363; advises the king not to permit the Comte d'Enghien to engage the imperialists, iii. 227

—— invested by the imperialists, iii. 91; capture of, *ib.*; fired by the imperial general, iii. 92

St. Regnier, heroism of the women of, iii. 76

St. Severin, Cardinal, joins in the *Bransle* at the feast given by the Marquis de Vigevano to Louis XII., i. 57

St. Séverino, Galeaz de, devotion of, to Francis I., and death at the battle of Pavia, ii. 167

Salerno, the Prince of, immobility of, at the battle of Carignano, iii. 235

INDEX

Salt-tax increased by Francis I., iii. 195; revolt of the inhabitants of La Rochelle, *ib.*

Saluzzo, Marquis de, his lands harried and laid waste by the forces of Prosper Colonna, i. 172; four thousand Italians raised by, cut to pieces by the imperialists while crossing the Alessandrino, ii. 157; attempts to relieve Milan, ii. 252; his treachery alluded to, iii. 48; his treachery to Francis I., iii. 54; is appointed the emperor's lieutenant beyond the Alps, iii. 55; assists at the siege of Carmagnole, and is killed, iii. 96

Sancerre, Comte de, gallant defence of St. Dizier by, iii. 241-5

Sanga, Juan Baptista, despatched by the Italian states to ascertain the cause of the indifference of Francis I. to their interests, ii. 251

Sanguin, Antoine, uncle of Mademoiselle de Heilly, mistress to Francis I., made an abbot, a bishop, and a cardinal, ii. 230

Sansac, Baron de, taken prisoner, iii. 93; *see* note, *ib.*

Savoie, Louise de, mother of Francis I., i. 16; remarkable extract from her journal, *ib.*; *see* note; summoned to Court, her quarrel with the queen of Louis XII., i. 17; exultation of, on the death of the infant sons of the queen, i. 18; ordered by the king to reside at Amboise, *ib.*; her conduct to M. de Gié, i. 20; her request to Louis XII. on his departure from Amboise, i. 26; her passion for M. de Vandenesse, i. 30; detected in an intrigue with M. de Vandenesse, and revenge of Maréchal de Gié, i. 31; the matrimonial prospects of her son and the Princesse Claude alluded to, i.

Savoie, Louise de—*continued.*
37; her triumph on her son's betrothal to the daughter of Louis XII., i. 46; her conduct to her daughter-in-law, the Princesse Claude, i. 129; warned by M. de Grignaud of the possible consequences of her son's intimacy with the Queen of France, i. 130; flatters the vanity of her son, Francis I., i. 140; created a duchess, and the palace of Amboise given to her by Francis I., i. 142; profligacy of her Court at Amboise, i. 146-7; her love for the Connétable de Bourbon described, i. 163; appointed Regent of France during the absence of Francis in Italy, i. 166; her talents for government considered, i. 167; her Court, i. 227; welcomes the Comtesse de Châteaubriand to her Court, i. 239; her alarm at the increasing power of the countess over the king, i. 250; her indignation at the recall of the Connétable de France from Milan, i. 257; takes an active share in the government, i. 277; her anxiety to secure the goodwill of Henry VIII., i. 295; opposes the return of Germaine de Foix, the Dowager-Queen of Spain, to the Court of Francis I., i. 311; her courtesy to François de Seckingen alluded to, i. 316; her dislike to the Duc de Gueldres, i. 318; persuades Francis I. to disgrace the duke, i. 319; her treacherous conduct to the Bishop of Liège, *ib.*; i. 322; induces Francis I. to purchase the Tuileries, i. 335; the differences between England and Scotland submitted to the arbitration of Cardinal Wolsey and, i. 364; effects a re-

Savoie, Louise de—*continued.*
conciliation between the Duc de Gueldres and Francis I., i. 372; undertakes to recruit the exhausted treasury of Francis, ii. 4; her interview with M. de Semblançay, the finance-minister, ii. 4-6; importunes the king to order Lautrec to Milan, ii. 7; her lawsuit against the Connétable de France alluded to, ii. 16; summons the connétable to her presence, *ib.*; offers him her hand and is rejected, ii. 18; her hatred to the connétable alluded to, *ib.*; her offer to the connétable exposed, ii. 22; vows his ruin, *ib.*; urges her lawsuit against the connétable, ii. 37; detected in appropriating four hundred thousand crowns intended for the army in Italy, ii. 53-6; her faction described, ii. 57; endeavours to ruin the finance-minister, *ib.*; her hatred to the Connétable de France alluded to during the trial of the Bourbon conspirators, ii. 97; the command of the army in Italy given to Bonnivet at the request of, ii. 114; expostulates with the king on his renewed attempt to reconquer the Milanese, ii. 144; appointed Regent of France, *ib.*; her persecution of M. de Semblançay, ii. 145; anguish of, on hearing of the battle of Pavia, ii. 184; her vengeance against M. de Semblançay, *ib.*; her unpopularity, ii. 185; endeavours to regain the confidence of the citizens, ii. 188; denounced from the pulpit, ii. 189; secures the fidelity of the soldiers, *ib.*; persecutes the Lutherans, ii. 191; burns Jacques Pavanes and the Hermit of Livry to appease the

Savoie, Louise de—*continued.*
parliament, *ib.*; banishes from Court the Comtesse de Châteaubriand and Diane de Poitiers, ii. 193; endeavours to conciliate the European powers, ii. 196; enters into a new treaty with Henry VIII. of England, ii. 198; concludes a truce for six months with Spain, ii. 199; betrays her allies to Charles V. to ingratiate herself with the emperor, ii. 201; evasive reply of the emperor to, ii. 213; departs for Bayonne, accompanied by her grandsons as hostages to Charles V., ii. 231; meets the king at Bayonne, ii. 232; indignation of, on the arrival of Madame de Châteaubriand at Court, ii. 233; resolves to supplant Madame de Châteaubriand, ii. 240; her instructions to her maid of honour, ii. 241; presents her to the king, ii. 246; urges the king to consent to the trial of M. de Semblançay, ii. 259; anger of, at the wit of the Duchesse d'Usez, ii. 261; her tyrannical government alluded to, ii. 266; takes the celebrated Cornelius Agrippa into her service as physician and astrologer, ii. 268; entertains Cardinal Wolsey, ii. 275; meets Margaret of Austria at Cambray to arrange the conditions for the release of the French princes, ii. 323; concludes a peace known as *La Paix des Dames*, ii. 324; abandons her allies, ii. 325; persecutes the reformers, ii. 344; her failing health, and death, ii. 349-50; her burial, ii. 351; her avarice, *ib.*

—— Philiberte de, her hand promised to Giuliano de' Medici, i. 209

Savoy, Bastard of, departure of, from Amboise to join the army against Milan, i. 64; *see* note, *ib.*; concludes a treaty of amity between the Swiss and the French, i. 224; his presence in the Parliament of Paris made the subject of a remonstrance to Francis, i. 261; joins the French army in Italy with supplies, ii. 26; death of, alluded to, ii. 176
—— Duke of, refuses Francis I. a passage through Savoy for his army, iii. 24; his territories overrun by the French, applies to the emperor for aid, *ib.*; instigates the emperor to destroy Aix, iii. 65; returns to Nice, the victim of the emperor and Francis, iii. 102; alarm of, at the proposed meeting of Charles and Francis at Nice, iii. 108; applies to the emperor for advice, *ib.*; mistrusts the promises of his allies, and induces the citizens of Nice to refuse admission of the Pope, iii. 109; his destitution, iii. 111, 112
Saxony, Duke of, *see* Frederic
Scheiner, Matthew, persuades the Swiss troops to desert the cause of France, i. 67
Schomberg, Theodoric de, death of, at the battle of Pavia, ii. 168
Seckingen, François de, his intimacy with Robert de la Mark, i. 314; his energy and manners render him popular with many of the petty princes of Germany, *ib.*; compels the Duc de Lorraine, the citizens of Metz, and the Landgrave of Hesse to pay him tribute, i. 315; recommended by Robert de la Mark to Francis I., *ib.*; his interview with the French king at Amboise, i. 316; Francis I. gives

Seckingen—*continued.*
offence to, by his want of confidence, i. 317-18; bold reply of, to Francis I., i. 322; joins Robert de la Mark and Charles V. against the interest of Francis, i. 323; his attempt to seize Bonnivet with the state chest alluded to, i. 332; at the siege of Mézières, i. 388; his quarrel with the Comte de Nassau, i. 390-1; devastates Picardy, i. 392
Sedan, Sire de, commands ten thousand lansquenets, i. 157
Selim, Sultan, equips a naval force, i. 297; his views respecting Italy alluded to, *ib.*; his death, i. 298
Semblançay, M. de, his interview with Louise de Savoie on raising the supplies for the war against the Milanese, ii. 4-6; exposes the treachery of Louise de Savoie, ii. 53-6; insists that commissioners be appointed to examine the public accounts, ii. 56; enmity of Louise de Savoie against, *ib.*; enmity of the Chancellor Duprat alluded to, ii. 57; persecuted by Louise de Savoie, ii. 145; refuses to advance a loan to the king, and is dismissed from Court, ii. 146-7; his protracted imprisonment alluded to, ii. 184; his trial, ii. 259; condemned and executed, ii. 260-1
Sénéchale, Le Grande, *see* Poitiers, Diane de
Sforza, Francisco Maria, brother of Maximilian, Duke of Milan, referred to by Pope Leo X. in his treaty with the Emperor Charles V. as the future Duke of Milan, i. 374; *see* note, *ib.*; enters into a treaty known as the Holy League, ii. 237; besieged in

Sforza, Francisco Maria—*contd.*
Milan, ii. 239; breach of faith of the French king to, *ib.*; the Milanese restored to, by the Emperor Charles V., ii. 347; his marriage with the emperor's niece alluded to, *ib.*; death of, iii. 25
—— Lorenzo, his position at Milan alluded to, ii. 374; his hatred to Da Leyva, *ib.*; courts the friendship of Francis I., *ib.*; the emperor demands the dismissal of Maraviglia from the Court of, ii. 376; his duplicity to Francis respecting the murder of Maraviglia, ii. 379-80; his envoy is dismissed from the Court of France, ii. 381; his marriage with Christina, the niece of the Emperor Charles V., alluded to, ii. 382; death of, *ib.*
—— Ludovic Maria, *see* note, i. 80-1
—— Maximilian, enters Milan without opposition, i. 81; surrenders himself to Francis I. and receives a pension of thirty thousand crowns, i. 200; death of, in Paris, i. 201
Shrewsbury, Earl of, Térouenne besieged by, i. 99; anger of, at the timidity of the Earl of Abergavenny at the Field of the Cloth of Gold, i. 350
Sièvre, M. de, Advocate-General, opposes the registration of the *Concordat*, i. 261
Sion, Cardinal de, his relentless animosity to France alluded to, i. 155; animates the Swiss against the French, i. 180-1; harangues the Swiss, and exhorts them to engage the French, i. 184; revolt of the Swiss against the cardinal after the battle of Marignano, i. 199; flight of, with Francesco Sforza, *ib.*; per-

Sion, Cardinal de—*continued.*
suades another body of Swiss mercenaries not to fight against their own countrymen, i. 212; his undying hatred to the French alluded to, i. 224; again induces the Swiss mercenaries to desert the cause of Francis I., ii. 11; his efforts to induce the Swiss to desert France alluded to, ii. 31
Sismondi, his description of the burning of the reformers by order of Francis I., iii. 20
Smalkalden, League of, alluded to, ii. 361; declare against Francis I., iii. 23; the emperor resolves to subjugate the league of, iii. 262
Solyman, Sultan of Turkey, attacks the Isle of Rhodes, ii. 47; alliance of Francis I. with, alluded to, iii. 95; enters Albania, *ib.*; his power alluded to, iii. 102; menacing position of, alarms the Pope, iii. 106; power of, after the destruction of the fleet and army of the Emperor Charles V., iii. 183; orders his admiral to co-operate with the French fleet, iii. 202; takes Strigonia and Alba, iii. 214; sends a fleet under Barbarossa to the assistance of Francis, *ib.*
Sorbonne, College of, description of, ii. 269; the spies of, alluded to, *ib.*; its privileges, ii. 271
Souliers, Charles de, one of the hostages delivered to Henry VIII. by Francis I. to secure the payment of six hundred thousand crowns, i. 293
Soyon, M. de, ordered by parliament to present a document to Francis I. respecting the registration of the *Concordat*, i. 263-4; the king threatens to throw him into the moat, i. 265

Savoy, Bastard of, departure of, from Amboise to join the army against Milan, i. 64; *see* note, *ib.*; concludes a treaty of amity between the Swiss and the French, i. 224; his presence in the Parliament of Paris made the subject of a remonstrance to Francis, i. 261; joins the French army in Italy with supplies, ii. 26; death of, alluded to, ii. 176
—— Duke of, refuses Francis I. a passage through Savoy for his army, iii. 24; his territories overrun by the French, applies to the emperor for aid, *ib.*; instigates the emperor to destroy Aix, iii. 65; returns to Nice, the victim of the emperor and Francis, iii. 102; alarm of, at the proposed meeting of Charles and Francis at Nice, iii. 108; applies to the emperor for advice, *ib.*; mistrusts the promises of his allies, and induces the citizens of Nice to refuse admission of the Pope, iii. 109; his destitution, iii. 111, 112

Saxony, Duke of, *see* Frederic

Scheiner, Matthew, persuades the Swiss troops to desert the cause of France, i. 67

Schomberg, Theodoric de, death of, at the battle of Pavia, ii. 168

Seckingen, François de, his intimacy with Robert de la Mark, i. 314; his energy and manners render him popular with many of the petty princes of Germany, *ib.*; compels the Duc de Lorraine, the citizens of Metz, and the Landgrave of Hesse to pay him tribute, i. 315; recommended by Robert de la Mark to Francis I., *ib.*; his interview with the French king at Amboise, i. 316; Francis I. gives

Seckingen—*continued.*
offence to, by his want of confidence, i. 317-18; bold reply of, to Francis I., i. 322; joins Robert de la Mark and Charles V. against the interest of Francis, i. 323; his attempt to seize Bonnivet with the state chest alluded to, i. 332; at the siege of Mézières, i. 388; his quarrel with the Comte de Nassau, i. 390-1; devastates Picardy, i. 392

Sedan, Sire de, commands ten thousand lansquenets, i. 157

Selim, Sultan, equips a naval force, i. 297; his views respecting Italy alluded to, *ib.*; his death, i. 298

Semblançay, M. de, his interview with Louise de Savoie on raising the supplies for the war against the Milanese, ii. 4-6; exposes the treachery of Louise de Savoie, ii. 53-6; insists that commissioners be appointed to examine the public accounts, ii. 56; enmity of Louise de Savoie against, *ib.*; enmity of the Chancellor Duprat alluded to, ii. 57; persecuted by Louise de Savoie, ii. 145; refuses to advance a loan to the king, and is dismissed from Court, ii. 146-7; his protracted imprisonment alluded to, ii. 184; his trial, ii. 259; condemned and executed, ii. 260-1

Sénéchale, Le Grande, *see* Poitiers, Diane de

Sforza, Francisco Maria, brother of Maximilian, Duke of Milan, referred to by Pope Leo X. in his treaty with the Emperor Charles V. as the future Duke of Milan, i. 374; *see* note, *ib.*; enters into a treaty known as the Holy League, ii. 237; besieged in

VOL. III

Sforza, Francisco Maria—*contd.* Milan, ii. 239; breach of faith of the French king to, *ib.*; the Milanese restored to, by the Emperor Charles V., ii. 347; his marriage with the emperor's niece alluded to, *ib.*; death of, iii. 25
—— Lorenzo, his position at Milan alluded to, ii. 374; his hatred to Da Leyva, *ib.*; courts the friendship of Francis I., *ib.*; the emperor demands the dismissal of Maraviglia from the Court of, ii. 376; his duplicity to Francis respecting the murder of Maraviglia, ii. 379-80; his envoy is dismissed from the Court of France, ii. 381; his marriage with Christina, the niece of the Emperor Charles V., alluded to, ii. 382; death of, *ib.*
—— Ludovic Maria, *see* note, i. 80-1
—— Maximilian, enters Milan without opposition, i. 81; surrenders himself to Francis I. and receives a pension of thirty thousand crowns, i. 200; death of, in Paris, i. 201
Shrewsbury, Earl of, Térouenne besieged by, i. 99; anger of, at the timidity of the Earl of Abergavenny at the Field of the Cloth of Gold, i. 350
Sièvre, M. de, Advocate-General, opposes the registration of the *Concordat*, i. 261
Sion, Cardinal de, his relentless animosity to France alluded to, i. 155; animates the Swiss against the French, i. 180-1; harangues the Swiss, and exhorts them to engage the French, i. 184; revolt of the Swiss against the cardinal after the battle of Marignano, i. 199; flight of, with Francesco Sforza, *ib.*; per-

Sion, Cardinal de—*continued.* suades another body of Swiss mercenaries not to fight against their own countrymen, i. 212; his undying hatred to the French alluded to, i. 224; again induces the Swiss mercenaries to desert the cause of Francis I., ii. 11; his efforts to induce the Swiss to desert France alluded to, ii. 31
Sismondi, his description of the burning of the reformers by order of Francis I., iii. 20
Smalkalden, League of, alluded to, ii. 361; declare against Francis I., iii. 23; the emperor resolves to subjugate the league of, iii. 262
Solyman, Sultan of Turkey, attacks the Isle of Rhodes, ii. 47; alliance of Francis I. with, alluded to, iii. 95; enters Albania, *ib.*; his power alluded to, iii. 102; menacing position of, alarms the Pope, iii. 106; power of, after the destruction of the fleet and army of the Emperor Charles V., iii. 183; orders his admiral to co-operate with the French fleet, iii. 202; takes Strigonia and Alba, iii. 214; sends a fleet under Barbarossa to the assistance of Francis, *ib.*
Sorbonne, College of, description of, ii. 269; the spies of, alluded to, *ib.*; its privileges, ii. 271
Souliers, Charles de, one of the hostages delivered to Henry VIII. by Francis I. to secure the payment of six hundred thousand crowns, i. 293
Soyon, M. de, ordered by parliament to present a document to Francis I. respecting the registration of the *Concordat*, i. 263-4; the king threatens to throw him into the moat, i. 265

Spain, Queen-Dowager of, *see* Foix, Germaine de

Spires, Charles V. convenes a diet at, and enforces the observance of mass and other church ceremonies, ii. 360

Spurs, battle of, why so called, i. 103

Squiros, battle of, alluded to, i. 379

Suffolk, Brandon, Duke of, espouses the cause of Louis XII. against Henry VIII., i. 100; love of the Princess Mary of England for, alluded to, 123-4; foster-brother to Henry VIII., *ib.*; ambassador at the Court of France, i. 128; warned by Francis I. not to peril his friendship with the King of England by marrying the Dowager-Queen of France, i. 136; marries the dowager-queen, i. 137; reconciled to the king, i. 138; returns to England, *ib.*; command under Francis I., i. 157; his command in the French army alluded to, ii. 72; his advice to the king before the battle of Pavia, ii. 160; death of, at the battle of Pavia, ii. 176

Suffolk, Duke of, at the interview between Henry VIII. and Francis I., ii. 363; receives the collar of St. Michael from Francis I., ii. 364

Surrey, Earl of, a commission of Spanish admiral given to the earl by the Emperor Charles V., ii. 63; destroys several towns on the coasts of Normandy and Brittany, ii. 68; joined by the Comte de Buren, the Lieutenant-general of the Emperor Charles V. in the Low Countries, *ib.*; besieges Hesdin, ii. 71; compelled to retreat, ii. 72; his wanton cruelties alluded to, *ib.*

Swiss, the, determine to invade France, i. 111; enter into a treaty with the French general at Dijon, i. 112; Louis XII. endeavours to conciliate the, i. 114; contribute during the reigns of Louis XI. and Charles VIII. to the success of the French armies, i. 154; excite the indignation of Louis XII., who declines their services, *ib.*; threaten Francis I. to invade Burgundy and Dauphiny, i. 156; the confederacy of Leo X. and the Emperor Maximilian against Francis I. alluded to, i. 166; anger of the Swiss troops on the non-arrival of their pay, i. 179; they rob the chest of the papal commissary and retire to Verceil, *ib.*; Francis endeavours to conciliate them, but fails through the agency of the Cardinal of Sion, i. 180; attempt to seize the public chest at Buffaloro, i. 181; inflamed by the eloquence of the Cardinal of Sion, they march upon Marignano to attack the French, i. 185; gallantry of, at the battle of Marignano, i. 186-92; they retreat and enter Milan, i. 192; retire to their mountains, pursued by D'Alviano, *ib.*; enormous loss of, *ib.*; they revolt against the Cardinal Sion after the battle of Marignano, i. 199; the payment of their claims alluded to, i. 210; refuse to act under Maximilian, i. 212; receive an order from the Diet to return home, i. 213; treaty of amity between Switzerland and France, i. 224; recognise the claim of Francis to the Milanese, *ib.*; desert Maréchal Lautrec in Milan, ii. 9; weary of the war in Italy under Maréchal Lautrec, demand to be led against

Swiss—*continued.*
the enemy, ii. 27; disorderly charge of, ii. 29; great slaughter of, *ib.*; desert Maréchal Lautrec and escape to their mountains, ii. 31; once more desert Francis in his hour of need, ii. 157

TAGLIACARNO, Bishop of Grasse, ii. 334
Talbot, Lord, besieges Térouenne, i. 99
Talmont, Prince de, bravery of, at the battle of Marignano, i. 189; death of, i. 193
Tarbes, Bishop of, one of the witnesses to the treaty between Henry VIII. and Francis I. against Spain, ii. 292; obtains permission from Francis for the emperor to traverse the French territories, iii. 121
Tauzannes, Montagnac, dresses himself in the clothes of the Duc de Bourbon to aid the duke's escape, ii. 93
Tavannes, Maréchal de, suppresses the revolt at La Rochelle, iii. 196
Taverna, Francisco, envoy from Sforza, Duke of Milan, to Francis I., ii. 379; is dismissed from the French Court, ii. 381
Tay, Bastard du, skirmish of, leads to the death of Gaston de Foix, i. 76
Té, castle of, ii. 263; *see* note, *ib.*
Téligny, François de, Sénéchal de Rovergné, defends Térouenne against the Earl of Shrewsbury and Lord Talbot, i. 99
Tende, Comte de, pursues the retreating army of Charles V., iii. 71; *see* note, *ib.*
Térouenne, siege of, alluded to, i. 99; famine in the city of, i. 101; gallantly relieved by the Alba-

Térouenne—*continued.*
nian light-horse, i. 102; capitulates to Henry VIII., i. 112
Tonnerre, Comte de, death of, at the battle of Pavia, ii. 168
Tortosa, Cardinal of, *see* Adrian, Bishop of Tortosa
Tour-d'Auvergne, Madelaine de la, her marriage with Lorenzo de' Medici, i. 246-9; *see* note, i. 247; her death, i. 250
Tournay, besieged by the Emperor Maximilian and Henry VIII. of England, i. 115; taken by the English king, *ib.*; its possession by the English alluded to, i. 287; impolitic measures of Francis I. to the citizens of, i. 312-13
Tournon, Cardinal, despatched by the Kings of France and England to threaten the Pope, ii. 369; advises the king to increase the salt-tax, iii. 195; *see* note, *ib.*
Treaty of the 20th April 1527, between Henry VIII. and Francis I., conditions of, ii. 272; modification of, ii. 273
Tremouille, M. de la, *see* note, i. 8; appointed to the command of the French armies in Italy, i. 91; captures the principal cities of the Milanese, i. 95; defeat of, at Vivegano, i. 96-7; wounded, *ib.*; enters into a treaty with the Swiss army at Dijon, i. 112-13; indignation of Louis XII. against, i. 114; reply of, to the letter of the king, *ib.*; bravery of, at the battle of Marignano, i. 189; presents himself to the Chamber, and commands the members to register the *Concordat*, i. 265; in concert with the Duc de Vendôme, defeats the imperialists near Paris, ii. 94; advises

Tremouille, M. de la—*contd.*
the king to raise his camp and meet the imperialists in the plain, ii. 161; death of, at the battle of Pavia, ii. 168
Treves, Archbishop of, *see* Greiffenklau, Richard de
Trevisa, attack on, by the Emperor Maximilian, alluded to, i. 64
Triboulet, jester to Francis, present at the interview between the king and Madame d'Etampes respecting the safe conduct of Charles through France, iii. 125-6
Trivulce, Jean Jacques, Marquis de Vigevano, entertains Louis XII., i. 56; *see* note, *ib.*; commands first division of the army of Louis XII. at Venice, i. 61; excites the animosity of Maréchal de Lautrec, and is declared a traitor, i. 281-2; demands an audience of the king, i. 282; the king refuses, and he dies broken-hearted, i. 283
Trivulzio, Maréchal de, *see* Trivulce, Jean Jacques
Tuileries, origin of the palace of the, i. 335
Turenne, Viscount de, one of the witnesses to the treaty between Henry VIII. and Francis I., ii. 272
Turin, siege of, raised, iii. 75; exhausted state of the garrison of, alluded to, iii. 100

VALAISAN, George de Supersax, one of the leaders of the Swiss mercenaries, i. 179
Valois, Duc de, *see* D'Angoulême, Francis, Comte
—— Marguerite de, her birth and education, i. 27; her accomplishments, *ib.*; her affection for her brother, Francis I., *ib.*; her attachment for Comte

Valois, Marguerite de—*contd.*
Charles de Montpensier, i. 29; her hand demanded in marriage by Henry VII. of England, i. 38; her attachment to Charles de Montpensier alluded to, i. 40; originates a singular custom between friends of opposite sexes, *ib.*; invested with the dignity of *Madame* by Francis I., i. 142; her creation of Duchesse de Berri alluded to, *ib.*; her emotion on seeing the Connétable de Bourbon enter the courtyard at Amboise armed for war, i. 161; her love for the Connétable de Bourbon described, i. 164; her intrigue with Bonnivet alluded to, ii. 19; attempts to reconcile Francis I. and the Comtesse de Châteaubriand, ii. 86; her interview with Jean de Poitiers in the forest of Bussy, ii. 89; her affection for the Duc de Bourbon, ii. 90; indignation of, at the cowardice of her husband, ii. 184; reproaches her husband, ii. 186; exerts herself in behalf of the persecuted Lutherans, ii. 192; obtains the release of Clement Marot, her *valet-de-chambre*, *ib.*; protects Guillaume Farel and Jacques Fabri from the inquisitors, *ib.*; isolation of, at the Court of her mother, the Regent of France, ii. 193; her attachment to the Comtesse de Châteaubriand alluded to, *ib.*; her anguish during the captivity of the king, ii. 208; resolves to visit the king in prison, *ib.*; departs for Spain, ii. 209; lands at Barcelona, and proceeds to Madrid, ii. 215; her interview with Francis, ii. 216; her efforts to obtain the release of the king, ii. 217;

Valois, Marguerite de—*contd.*
her love for the King of France alluded to, *ib.*; her audience with the emperor, *ib.*; her spirited remonstrances to Charles, ii. 219-21; fails in effecting the release of the king, ii. 222; plans his escape, *ib.*; her plan betrayed to the emperor, ii. 224; expostulates with Charles V. on the increased hardships inflicted on her brother, ii. 225; warned by Bourbon that Charles V. meditated her arrest, *ib.*; escapes to France, ii. 226; her meeting with the king at Bayonne, ii. 232; her person described, ii. 243; refuses the hand of Henry VIII., ii. 276; marries the King of Navarre, ii. 300; her dislike to the marriage, ii. 301; their issue, ii. 302; improves the condition of her people, *ib.*; her saloon the resort of talent, *ib.*; protects the reformers, ii. 304; causes the Latin prayers of the Church to be translated into French, and is persecuted by the Sorbonne, *ib.*; her fidelity is suspected by the king, ii. 306; partially converts the king to Lutheranism, *ib.*; she is cited to Paris, at the instigation of Cardinals Armagnac and Grammont, on her secession from the Romish Church, ii. 307; her false position, *ib.*; her efforts to save the persecuted Lutherans alluded to, ii. 343; her influence on Francis misapplied, iii. 2; her Court ladies, iii. 8; arrives at Amboise, iii. 27; tournament in honour of her visit, *ib.*; disappointed at the refusal of Francis I. to accept the hand of Philip of Spain for her daughter, the Princess of Navarre, iii. 150

Vandenesse, Comte de, one of the suite of Louis XII., i. 23; *see* note, *ib.*; one of the companions of Francis at the Court of Amboise, i. 26; attracts the attention of Louise de Savoie, *ib.*; detected by the Maréchal de Gié in an intrigue with the mother of Francis, and ordered to quit Amboise, i. 31; takes General d'Alviano prisoner at the battle of Agnadello, i. 62; assumes the command of the French artillery, ii. 129; death of, ii. 130

Vatican, plundered by Cardinal Colonna, ii. 250

Vaudois, massacre of, iii. 265-71

Vauguyon, M. de, condemned to "*the question*," ii. 96; ultimately banished to Orleans, ii. 97

Vega, de la, Garcilasso, death of, iii. 72; *see* note, *ib.*

Velly, Sire de, despatched by Francis to congratulate Charles V. on his victories in Africa, iii. 39; demands an audience of Charles V. on the affront offered by the emperor to Francis, iii. 43; the Pope endeavours to pacify the envoy, iii. 45; reply of, to the Pope, *ib.*

Vendôme, Duc de, receives the Princess Mary of England on her landing at Boulogne, i. 125; appointed governor of the Isle of France by Francis I., i. 144; appointed to the government of Picardy, i. 381; enters Artois and Hainault, i. 394; entrusted with command of the seat of war, ii. 69; marches to relieve Térouenne, ii. 71; beats the imperialists near Paris, ii. 94; called to the defence of Paris, ii. 111-12; compels the Duke of Norfolk to retreat from Paris, ii. 113; his claims upon the

Vendôme, Duc de—*continued*. throne supported by the people, ii. 187; appointed president of the Council, *ib.*; at the interview between Francis I. and Henry VIII., ii. 363; entrusted with the protection of the Flemish frontiers, iii. 184; his death alluded to, iii. 202

Venice, efforts of Pope Julius II. to subjugate, i. 59; the Venetians attempt to propitiate Germany and Spain, i. 60; despair of the citizens of, at the conquests of Louis XII., i. 63-4; the weakness of the Emperor Maximilian gives them hope, *ib.*; the Venetians retake Padua, i. 65; partial success of the Venetians against the French, i. 66; state of the territories of, after the peace of Noyon, i. 223-4; states of, decline to enter into a treaty with France, ii. 34; the Venetian states enter into the European league against France, ii. 46; states of, send ambassadors to Henry VIII. on the necessity of preserving the balance of power in Europe, ii. 199; the Pope joins in the league, *ib.*; states of, enter into a treaty known as the Holy League, ii. 237; new league entered into by the states of, with Charles V., alluded to, iii. 40; states of, conclude a treaty of peace with Solyman, iii. 174; condemn the assassins of Fregosa and Rincon, iii. 178

Verjus, M. de, ordered by parliament to present a document to Francis I. respecting the registration of the *Concordat*, i. 263-4; the king threatens to throw him into the castle moat, i. 265

Verona, keys of, transferred to the Emperor Maximilian, i. 64; siege of, alluded to, i. 214

Vicenza, keys of, transferred to the Emperor Maximilian, i. 64

Vied, or Wied, Hermand, Comte de, Archbishop of Cologne, one of the Electors of Germany, *see* note, i. 299

Villa Franca, capture of, i. 177

Villalva, Col., alluded to, at St. Jean Pied-de-Port, i. 84

Villana, Marquis de, reply of, to Charles V. respecting the Duc de Bourbon, ii. 211

Villars, Coteret, alluded to, ii. 357

—— Marquis de, taken prisoner, iii. 94; *see* note, *ib.*

Villebon, Seigneur de, defends St. Pol against the imperialists, iii. 91; *see* note, *ib.*; taken prisoner, iii. 92

Vinci, Leonardo da, invited by Francis I. to Court, i. 267; dies in the arms of Francis I., i. 328; his works in the palace of Chambord alluded to, ii. 264

Visconti, Anchiso, compels Renzo de Céri to raise the siege of Arona, ii. 122

Vivegano, battle of, described, i. 95-8

Viverots, Sire de, death of, i. 77

Voland, Mademoiselle, throws sulphuric acid on her face to avoid the licentious advances of Francis I., ii. 145

WARTZ, Seigneur de, ordered by Francis to keep watch upon the actions of the Duc de Bourbon, ii. 80; deceived by the Duke, ii. 81

Watteville, Jacques de, heads eighteen thousand Swiss, and invades France, i. 111

Wingfield, Sir Richard, instructed by Francis I. to solicit Henry VIII. to stand sponsor to his second son, i. 333; entertains

Wingfield, Sir Richard—*contd.*
Cardinal Wolsey on his route to France, ii. 274

Wolsey, Cardinal, his negotiations respecting the marriage of the Princess Mary of England with Louis XII. alluded to, i. 122; his power alluded to by Francis I. in his instructions to his ambassador, Bonnivet, i. 286; causes himself to be appointed Bishop of Tournay, i. 287; accepts an annual pension of twelve thousand livres in lieu of the bishopric of Tournay, i. 291; enters into a correspondence with Francis I., and advises Henry VIII. to accept the hand of the dauphin for the Princess Mary, i. 292; his policy respecting Francis I. and Charles V., i. 339; his preparations for the Field of the Cloth of Gold, i. 342; seduced by the promises of Charles V., undertakes to negative the attempts of Francis to secure an alliance with Henry VIII., i. 345; his ostentation, i. 348; suspicions of, at the meeting of the Kings of England and France at the Field of the Cloth of Gold, i. 349; arranges mutual visits between the two Courts, i. 354; at the banquets given by the kings at Guisnes, i. 360; performs a solemn mass before the Kings of France and England, i. 361; the differences between England and Scotland submitted to the arbitration of the Cardinal and Louise de Savoie, i. 365; the Cardinal appointed to the bishoprics of Bajadoz and Valencia by Charles V., *ib.*; the Cardinal arranges another interview with Henry and the Emperor of Germany, *ib.*; induces Henry VIII.

Wolsey, Cardinal—*continued.*
to violate the pledges given to Francis I., *ib.*; visits the Pope at Bruges during the conference at Calais, i. 382-3; gives a secret pledge to assist the Emperor Charles with forty thousand men, *ib.*; presides at a second conference at Calais, ii. 12; its consequences, ii. 13; his crooked policy to secure the Popedom defeated, ii. 23; his changed feelings towards Charles V. alluded to, ii. 62; receives an assurance from the emperor of his support on the death of the Pope, ii. 64; receives a life pension from the emperor of nine thousand golden crowns, *ib.*; defeated in his efforts for the Popedom, ii. 120; loses faith in the promises of Charles V., ii. 197; his progress from Hampton Court to France described, ii. 273-4; entertained by the king and Louise de Savoie, ii. 275; demands the hand of Marguerite de Valois for Henry VIII., *ib.*; meets with a refusal, ii. 276; demands the hand of the Princesse Réné for Henry VIII. and is refused, ii. 277; leaves France for England, *ib.*; entertains Anne de Montmorency, ambassador from France, ii. 309; his arrest alluded to, ii. 359

Worcester, Earl of, despatched by Henry VIII. to witness the ceremony of the betrothal of the dauphin to the Princess Mary of England, and to surrender up the city of Tournay, i. 293-4; his reluctance to deliver up the city of Tournay, i. 294-5; festivities at Paris in honour of, *ib.*

Worms, Diet at, convoked by the Emperor Charles V. to suppress the doctrines of Luther, i. 369

Wurtemberg, Duke Christopher of, solicits the aid of Francis against the aggressions of the emperor, ii. 382 ; establishes the reformed religion in his duchy, ii. 383
—— Duke Ulric of, invades France at the head of a Swiss army, i. 111

XIMÉNES, Cardinal, Archbishop of Toledo, *see* note, i. 219 ; ap-

Ximénes, Cardinal—*continued*.
pointed Regent of Spain, i. 220; jealousy of M. de Chièvres of the power of, *ib.*; his able government alluded to, i. 307 ; his death, i. 308

ZAPOLSKY, John de, ambassadors sent by, to Francis I., ii. 362 ; policy of Francis respecting, alluded to, *ib.*

The stamped Design used on the cover of this work is copied from a cut in Dibdin's *Bibliographical Decameron*, where it is given as a specimen of the skill in this kind of ornament possessed by the celebrated Diane de Poitiers,—"in which she has contrived to interweave her initials with those of her royal lover, as well as to introduce the *insignia* of the heathen goddess whose name she bore."

THE END

www.ingramcontent.com/pod-product-compliance
Lightning Source LLC
Chambersburg PA
CBHW020106010526

44115CB00008B/711